Essential
Client/Server
Survival Guide

Essential Client/Server Survival Guide

Robert Orfali • Dan Harkey • Jeri Edwards

JOHN WILEY & SONS, INC.

New York   Chichester   Brisbane   Toronto   Singapore

Publisher: Katherine Schowalter
Editor: Theresa Hudson
Managing Editor: Frank Grazioli
Text Design & Composition: Robert Orfali, Dan Harkey, and Jeri Edwards

This text is printed on acid-free paper.

This publication is designed to provide accurate and authoritative information in regard to the subject matter covered. It is sold with the understanding that the publisher is not engaged in rendering legal, accounting, or other professional service. If legal advice or other expert assistance is required, the services of a competent professional person should be sought.

Library of Congress Cataloging-in-Publication Data:

Orfali, Robert.
        Essential client/server survival guide / Robert Orfali, Dan Harkey, Jeri Edwards
            p.   cm.
        Includes index.
        ISBN 0-471-13119-9
        1. Client/server computing.   I. Harkey, Dan. II. Edwards, Jeri. III. Title.
QA76.9.C55076   1994
004'.36--dc20   94-20084
                                                                                    CIP

Printed in the United States of America
10 9 8 7 6 5

Dedication

This book is dedicated to my wife and daughter, Michiko and Tomomi, and to my parents, Howard and Barbara. Their support and encouragement were invaluable.

— Dan Harkey

This book is dedicated with love to my wife Jeri and my mother Mimi.

— Robert Orfali

This book is dedicated with all my love to husband, Robert (we have the good fortune to experience love as a two-way street), and to my mother, Mary.

— Jeri Edwards

Other Books By the Authors

Client/Server Programming with OS/2 2.1, Third Edition
by Robert Orfali and Dan Harkey (VNR, 1993)

Client/Server Survival Guide with OS/2
by Robert Orfali and Dan Harkey (VNR, 1994)

Foreword

Captain Zog

by Zog the Martian

Greetings, Earthlings! I'm Zog, the captain of the Martian team that visited earth to understand what client/server computing is all about and what it can do for us today. We found the **Essential Client/Server Survival Guide** to be as advertised: absolutely essential on our mission to explore this new technology.

So what did I like about this book? It felt like it was talking directly to me and to my crew in a friendly voice. We were initially apprehensive about visiting a foreign planet, but the book made it painless and fun. We covered a lot of territory—including OSs, NOSs, middleware, database, TP monitors, groupware, distributed objects, and system management. It was a comprehensive tour; we got our money's worth many times over. Martians plan to make a big investment in client/server technology. We now have a good feeling for the lay of the land and where the good opportunities are.

In summary, this Survival Guide helped me understand client/server technology and how to use it in practical Martian situations. The personal touch was great; it felt like we had our own private tour guides. The artwork and cartoons were wonderful. The Soapboxes are a lot of fun to read. We like to hear *real* earthling debates—not just the sterilized material we read in most books. I can't recommend this book enough to my fellow Martians. Through this foreword, I highly recommend this book to earthlings. If I can understand it, so can you.

Zog

Preface

We Live in Uncertain Times

For better or for worse, our industry is going through a deep paradigmatic shift. The old paradigm—centralized mainframe computing—is being replaced by a new paradigm—open client/server computing. A paradigm shift is akin to a revolution: Dominant structures crumble, vacuums are created, and the world is in turmoil. The transition period is marked by confusion, deep uncertainty, and exhilaration. Confusion is the result of seeing familiar bedrock structures disappear. Uncertainty comes from not knowing what the next day will bring. And the exhilaration comes from realizing the new possibilities that are being created by the new paradigm. The **Essential Client/Server Survival Guide** is our attempt to understand this revolution. The new client/server paradigm is fielding a lineup of competing technologies, each vying to become the new emperor. We hope the new emperor will have clothes.

And We Can't Turn Back the Clock

Before we tell you all about this book, let's answer some questions that we've been wrestling with: Is client/server just a passing fad? Can mainframes make a comeback? Can things go back to the way they were? We're the first to admit that client/server has become the industry's most overhyped and overloaded term; but it's not a passing fad. This is because the world is populated with more than 120 million PCs that need to be served in the style they expect. The *client is the heart of the application*; servers are just an extension of the client's universe. Client/server computing is unabashedly client-centric, and there's no turning back of the clock to mainframe-centric computing. This is not to say that mainframes will disappear—there's room for them to thrive as long as they can transform themselves into humble servants of the client. It's an open world where only the most competitive servers can survive. However, the deployment of intergalactic client/server technology will not be a picnic either. So mainframes will survive until they can be replaced by a technology that's got the same built-in robustness. The revolutionary chaos of the open systems world may make many MIS managers yearn for the good old days, but the time machine only marches forward.

What the Survival Guide Covers

This Survival Guide explores client/server computing from the ground up. It consists of nine parts, each one can almost be read independently. (One of our reviewers even read the book backwards and found that it made sense.) We'll give you a short description of what the parts cover. If you find the terminology too foreign, then by all means read the book to find out what it all means.

- **Part 1** starts with an overview of what client/server is and what the fuss is all about. We develop a client/server model that will serve as a map for the rest of the book. We go over the state of the client/server infrastructure to get a feel for how much of it is already here and what remains to be built.

- **Part 2** examines the client/server capabilities of our current crop of operating systems—including Windows 3.X, OS/2, Windows NT, Unix, and NetWare. We feel like war correspondents covering the battlefield of the operating system wars.

- **Part 3** explores the NOS and transport middleware substrate. We take a look at communication stacks such as TCP/IP, SNA, IPX/SPX, and NetBIOS. Then we look at the distributed computing environments created by NetWare, LAN Server, and DCE. We also look at messaging middleware.

- **Part 4** explores the very popular database server model of client/server. We cover SQL-92, SQL3, ODBC, IDAPI, SAG, DRDA, RDA, stored procedures, and triggers. We spend some time looking at new database opportunities such as information warehouses and middleware for federated databases.

- **Part 5** explores the TP Monitor model of client/server. We cover the different transaction types—including flat transactions, sagas, nested transactions, chained transactions, and long-lived transactions. We bring you up-to-date on what's happening with the X/Open Distributed Transaction standard. Then we dive into the great debate that's pitting the *TP Lite* model offered by the database servers against the *TP Heavy* model offered by TP Monitors. We explain why TP Monitors are needed in a world dominated by database servers.

- **Part 6** explores the groupware model of client/server. We look at the world of Lotus Notes, workflow, and interpersonal applications. Groupware shows us what client/server can really do—its paradigm goes much further than just recreating mainframe-like applications on PCs.

- **Part 7** explores the distributed object model of client/server. We look at DOMs, CORBA, Object Databases, OpenDoc, OLE-2, and Taligent frameworks. We explore how object technology can be used to create a new generation of client/server information systems. The product chapter covers SOM and DSOM.

- **Part 8** is about how to manage client/server applications. The biggest obstacle to the deployment of client/sever technology is the lack of integrated system management platforms. Fortunately, the situation is changing. We will look at some exciting technologies that will semi-automate the management of client/server systems. We also cover system management standards—including SNMP2, RMON, CMIP, DMI, UI-Atlas, and DME.

- **Part 9** is about how to design, build, and deploy client/server applications. We look at what tools can and cannot do for you. This part ends the survival journey and ties all the pieces together.

How to Read This Book

The best way to read this book is to ask your boss for a one-week, paid sabbatical to go sit on a beach and read it. Tell him or her that it's the cheapest way to revitalize yourself technically and find out where this industry is going. Once you sink into that comfortable chair overlooking the ocean, we think you'll find the book a lot of fun—maybe even downright relaxing. You won't get bored; but if you do, simply jump to the next part until you find something you like. You can jump to any part of the book and start reading it. We recommend, however, that you carefully go over the cartoons so that you have something to tell the boss back at the office.

What do you do after you finish the book and find yourself wishing there was a sequel? You can read our expanded version of this book, the **Client/Server Survival Guide with OS/2**. It's 1000 pages and weighs a ton, but the length gave us the luxury of being able to cover almost 100 products and delve into some of the issues we had to leave out of this book.

What the Boxes Are For

We use shaded boxes as a way to introduce concurrent threads in the presentation material. It's the bookform version of multitasking. The *Soapboxes* introduce strong opinions or biases on some of the more controversial topics of client/server computing. Because the discipline is so new and fuzzy, there's lots of room for interpretation and debate—so you'll get lots of Soapboxes that are just another opinion (ours). The *briefing* boxes give you background or tutorial type information. You can safely skip over them if you're already familiar with a topic. The *detail* boxes cover some esoteric area of technology that may not be of interest to the general readership. Typically the same readers that skip over the briefings will find the details interesting (so you'll still get your money's worth). Lastly, we use *warning* boxes to let you know where danger lies—this is, after all, a Survival Guide.

Who Is This Book For?

The answer is—we hope—anybody who's associated with the computer industry and needs to understand where it's heading. We know we enjoyed reading it over three times (but we're biased). We're relying on word-of-mouth to let people know about the book, so if you enjoy it please spread the word. It was a big effort with long hours of "labor of love" on our part; we hope you'll find it valuable and helpful. So who should know about this book? Here's our short list:

■ The person sitting on that beach chair next to you. She or he may have run out of reading material.

■ The people you work with. Use this book to get the people around you to join the postmodern bandwagon. We found that people are easier to work with if they share a common mindset.

■ Anybody involved with computers—including system analysts, programmers, managers, pundits, marketing and sales people, instructors, computer science students, and those of us that are between jobs, contemplating a career change, or working on resumes.

We hope you enjoy the reading, the cartoons, and the Soapboxes. Drop us a line if you have something you want to "flame" about. We'll take compliments too. We also want to thank you, as well as our Martian friends, for trusting us to be your guides.

Acknowledgments

- To our reviewers: Lisa Haut, Claus Mikkelsen, Lynda Hansen, Bobby Sujishi, and Theo Mandel. They helped us catch all the first pass of "nasty errors" and gave us some valuable feedback. If you're lucky, they left some errors for you to discover.

- To Dave Coffman and David Pacheco. They lent us a hand when we really needed it.

- To our tireless copy editor, Larry Mackin, for keeping us honest and consistent. It's a tough job, and we're glad Larry's willing to do it.

- To Dianne Littwin, Executive Editor at Van Nostrand Reinhold. She is always a pleasure to work with. We also thank the members of Dianne's staff.

- To Gary Bolen, Susan Rutherford, and John Gomez of Backup Incorporated, who did our fantastic cover. They worked with us late into the night as we agonized over the revisions.

Contents at a Glance

Contents

Part 4. SQL Database Servers 161

Part 1
The Big Picture

An Introduction to Part 1

Welcome to our client/server planet. We hope you will like it here, because there's no going back. You've long passed the point of no return. Don't panic: You're in good hands. We'll somehow find our way through the swamps, deserts, and roaring waters. We will show you how to avoid the dangerous paths infested with rattlesnakes and scorpions. Our adventure will be challenging—and exciting. In the course of the journey, we may even help you find the fabled land of client/server "milk and honey."

Part 1 of any good Survival Guide always starts with mapping the treacherous terrain. This is where you get the birds-eye view of things—continents, oceans, forests, and Manhattan traffic jams. We create such a map for the world of client/server.

We start with an overview of what client/server is and what the fuss is all about. We explain what client/server computing can do, as well as what makes a product client/server. Then we develop a game using client/server building blocks that will help you navigate through the treacherous terrain. Finally, we go over the state of the client/server infrastructure—the equivalent of roads, bridges, and airports for client/server.

Chapter 1

Your Guide
to the
New World

---

*D*on't stand in the doorway
Don't block the hall
For he that gets hurt
Will be he who has stalled...
  For the times they are
  a-changin

— Bob Dylan, 1963

THE GOOD OLD DAYS

Back in the days when mainframes roamed the earth, life was simple. The big choice of the day was how to pick the "right" computer vendor. And there were only a few to choose from. Once that choice was behind you, everything else fell into place. A staff of superbly trained analysts supervised the powering up of a great big box with a matching operating system. Data communications specialists could fine-tune, in a matter of hours, the octopus-like front-end network that brought hundreds of remote terminals into the fold. They were followed by storage specialists who would hookup "farms" of disk and tape drives. Maintenance and system management were built into every component. If anything went wrong, you knew exactly who to call—your on-site systems engineer.

If you had to write applications, your vendor would provide the "right" set of top-down methodologies, case tools, and run-time subsystems. There were, of course, five-year plans and grand architectures to help you design your future growth and budget for it. Most importantly, there was job security, a career path, and a bright future for everybody in the computer industry. And revenues were good for mainstream computer vendors and for the niche players that marketed within their orbits. These were the good old days before the client/server and "open" systems revolution.

LIFE AFTER THE REVOLUTION

Life is not as simple in the new world of client/server and open systems. Client/server computing is the ultimate "open platform." Client/server gives you the freedom to mix-and-match components at almost any level. You can put together an incredible variety of networked client and server combinations. Everything in the client/server world is sold *a la carte*.

At every turn, you will be presented with a Chinese restaurant menu of choices: Which server platform? Which client platform? Which network protocols? Which distributed computing infrastructure? Which database server? Which set of middleware? Which system management base? If you get past the first set of choices, you will face even tougher new choices in the area of client/server application development and tools. There are at least four major technologies that can be used to create client/server applications: Database Servers, TP Monitors, Groupware, and Distributed Object Managers. Which one is best?

You're the one who makes the tough decisions in this new world order. To succeed, you'll need to pick the right client/server platform, tools, vendors, and architecture base. You must identify and ride the *right* client/server technology wave. If the winning wave is distributed objects, it doesn't make sense to invest time and energy in database servers. But if you pick the object wave too soon, it may shipwreck your business. So it's important that you know exactly what the technology can do for you at a given point in time. To figure this out, you must be able to sort your way through the marketing slogans and architectural promises. Most importantly, you need to know exactly what existing products can do for you *today*.

The good news in all of this is that client/server technology is liberating, low-cost, and allows you to do the great things we will describe later in this book. The bad news is that you're on your own. The vendors will sell you their products at near-commodity prices, but you'll have to figure out how to make the pieces work together. If they don't work, it's your problem. No promises were made when the

goods were sold. Yes, system integrators can help, but they don't come cheap. So what happened to the good old days? They're gone. Vendors now sell piecemeal components. Everything is unbundled. Even service is priced separately. In this new *a la carte* world, you are the system integrator.

THE SURVIVAL PLAN

We, the authors, have been roaming in the wilderness for quite some time, and the result is this Client/Server Survival Guide. It will help you survive, but it won't be easy. Nobody, unfortunately, has that magic map with all the correct paths. We will share with you our insights which, when combined with yours, may help you take the least treacherous path. A Survival Guide is more than just a map. It contains instructions for how to find food, build shelter, navigate in strange terrain, and protect yourself from snakes and scorpions. We'll provide all of this.

We will first go over the client and server sides of the equation. We will then work on the slash (/) in client/server—that's the glue that ties the client with the server. We will go over the four leading technologies for developing client/server applications: database servers, TP Monitors, groupware, and distributed objects. We will conclude by covering system management platforms and tools.

Chapter 2

Welcome to Client/Server Computing

Downsizing and client/server computing have become the hottest topics in the computer industry...IS managers need to learn how to retool IS to take advantage of this new technology.

— James Martin (1993) [1]

I'm not sure if I'm downsizing, upsizing, rightsizing, or capsizing.

— Anonymous

At times, it seems as if everyone associated with computing has something to say about the client/server relationship. In this chapter, you get one more "definitive" viewpoint of what this all means. We will first look at the market forces that are driving the client/server industry today. We then peek through our crystal ball at the computer industry in the advanced stages of the client/server era. After coming this far, we feel we can handle even more danger in our lives, so we tackle the big

---

[1] This is from the foreword by James Martin to Dawna Dewire's excellent book, **Client/Server Computing** (McGraw-Hill, 1993).

issue of trying to answer the question: *Just what is client/server anyway?* We end this chapter with a lively diatribe on fat clients versus fat servers.

THE MARKET FORCES DRIVING CLIENT/SERVER

Client/Server computing is an irresistible movement that is reshaping the way computers are being used. Although this computing movement is relatively young, it is already in full force and is not leaving any facet of the computer industry untouched. Big transformations in the computer industry are usually driven by a combination of new technologies and needs. The technologies and needs pushing client/server computing come from three directions: *downsizing, upsizing,* and *rightsizing* (Figure 2-1).

Downsizing

Downsizing is the downward migration of business applications from superminis and mainframes to PCs, PS/2s, Macintoshes, and Unix workstations. The downsizing process breaks up large supermini and mainframe-type applications into program modules that run on one or more network servers. User-interface functions move to the client workstations and replace the "green screen uglies" with state-of-the-art graphical user interfaces. The centralized processors with time-shared terminals are replaced by networked client/server machines.

Client/Server software solutions on low-cost standard hardware are the driving force behind downsizing. Today's low-cost desktop machines are as powerful as last decade's top-of-the-line mainframes. Client/Server software solutions allow us to create coherent environments out of these autonomous desktop machines. By doing this, client/server computing combines the best of two worlds: the cost-effective and almost addictive power of desktop computers with multiuser access to shared resources and data.

Upsizing

Upsizing is the bottom-up trend of networking standalone PCs at the departmental or workgroup level. The majority of PCs are no longer living in isolation. The early PCs were originally attached to LANs to share expensive peripheral devices such as laser printers and scanners. The LANs are now used primarily for electronic mail and for sharing databases and files (including repositories of images and documents). In addition, a new generation of client/server groupware software promises to introduce finely tuned levels of interaction in the workgroup.

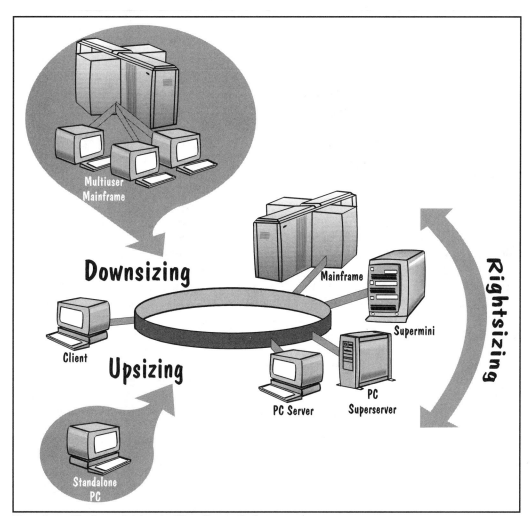

Figure 2-1. The Forces Driving the Client/Server Market.

PC LAN connections are growing equally among all types of environments. Growth is particularly strong in small (PC only) business environments: "the forgotten one million." Intel-based PCs account for over 95% of all servers. According to Forrester, roughly 411,000 Intel-based servers shipped in 1992, representing a 20-22% growth over 1991.

Rightsizing

Rightsizing moves applications to the most appropriate server platform. Clients request services over the network and the server best suited for the job provides it. In this "open" model, a server can be a PC, a supermini, or a mainframe. Servers from different vendors can happily coexist: *the network is the system*. This is especially important for large companies, where this *enterprise network* articulates the business. Rightsizing moves information and server power to the points of impact. It matches the job to the server without having to resort to "islands of automation."

Personal computers and LANs are now equipped with the technology to support enterprise networking. Mainframes and superminis are learning how to compete on the enterprise network. Open standards for enterprise client/server interoperability are now in place that define exactly what it takes to become "just another server." Computer system vendors—such as IBM, DEC, HP, and Tandem—are embracing client/server open standards as the strategic platform that ties together their disparate product lines (workstations, superminis, and mainframes). For their customers, client/server standards finally enable cost-effective, multivendor integration at the enterprise level.

According to the Gartner Group, the *Enterprise Server Platform (ESP)* will allow large corporations to leverage the benefits of personal, workgroup, and mainframe resources. Instead of centralized enterprise megaservers, Gartner envisions "a collection of services, which will typically be distributed across a variety of computers for price/performance, high availability, and platform specialization advantages." The critical services provided will include mail routing, file and print sharing, OLTP and decision support, network and systems management, resource brokering, software distribution and license management, security, and inter-enterprise gateways.

THE CLIENT/SERVER COMPUTING ERA

What will the brave new world of client/server computing look like? What effect will it have on MIS shops? What does it mean to compete in an open client/server computing market? What new opportunities does it create for software developers? Let's try to answer these questions now.

Which Client/Server Vision?

Client/Server computing has the unique distinction of having strong champions across the entire spectrum of the computer industry. For the "PC can do it all" crowd, client/server computing means scrapping every mainframe that can't fit on the desktop and the demise of host-centric computing. For mainframe diehards, client/server computing means unleashing a new breed of "born-again" networked mainframes that will bring every PC in the enterprise back to the fold. For the middle of the roaders, client/server is "computer glasnost," which really means a new era of coexistence and openness in which all can play.

There is some truth in all these visions. Client/Server computing provides an open and flexible environment where mix and match is the rule. The client applications will run predominantly on PCs and other desktop machines that are at home on LANs. The successful servers will also feel at home on LANs and know exactly how to communicate with their PC clients. Beefy PCs make natural superservers. For mainframes to succeed as servers, however, they will have to learn how to meet PCs as equals on the LAN. In this world of equals, mainframe servers cannot treat PCs as dumb terminals. They need to support peer-to-peer protocols, interpret PC messages, service their PC clients' files in their native formats, and provide data and services to PCs in the most direct manner. Ultimately, the server platform with the best cost/performance and services wins.

Client/Server and the "New MIS"

Client/Server application development requires hybrid skills that include transaction processing, database design, communications experience, and graphical user interface savvy. The more advanced applications require a knowledge of distributed objects and object DBMSs. Mastering these skills will require renaissance programmers who can combine the best of "big-iron" reliability-driven thinking with the PC LAN traditions. Where will these renaissance programmers come from? Will MIS shops be able to provide solutions and services in this new computing environment? Or will that service be provided by consultants and system integrators who have taken the time to learn these new skills?

Most client/server solutions today are PC LAN implementations that are personalized for the group that uses them. Everything from LAN directories to security requirements must be properly configured, often by the users themselves. MIS departments have the skills to not only manage and deploy large networks but also to provide interoperability standards. They also know how to fine-tune applications, distribute fixes, and ensure data integrity. MIS traditionally caters to the large data centers—not to the line departments that own the PCs and LANs. The key is for them to do what they do well in a distributed client/server environment where they share the power, responsibility, computing know-how, and financial budgets with the line business managers (the end users). Consequently, distributing the MIS function is essential.

Client/Server computing may be best served by two-tiered MIS organizations: a line MIS for managing and deploying departmental systems, and an enterprise MIS for managing the internet and setting interoperability standards. This type of organization will not only preserve departmental autonomy but also allow the local LANs to be part of the multiserver, multivendor enterprise internet.

Competition in the Client/Server Market

Client/Server, the *great equalizer* of the computer business, encourages openness and provides a level playing field in which a wide variety of client and server platforms can participate. The open client/server environment serves as the catalyst for "commoditizing" hardware and system software. The PC is a good example of a computer commodity; it can be obtained from multiple suppliers and is sold in very price-competitive market situations. LAN adapters, LAN protocol stacks, network routers, and bridges are also becoming commodities. On the software side, workstation operating systems, SQL Database Management Systems (DBMSs), and imaging software are approaching commodity status. The Distributed Computing Environment (DCE) will make instant commodities out of remote procedures, network directory software, security services, and system management. These trends are good news for computer users.

But, where are the *great differentiators* that will set vendors apart in this highly competitive commodity environment? What will happen to the computer vendors when commodity-priced client/server computing power satisfies the needs for computerization as we know it today?

Computer vendors will in the short run differentiate themselves by the power of the superservers they provide. This will last until commodity operating systems start to routinely support multiprocessor hardware platforms. We anticipate that the most sustained differentiation will be in the area of new client/server software and not hardware platforms. Low-cost, easy to deploy client/server solutions will unleash a massive new wave of computerization. For example, image and multimedia enhanced client/server solutions have ravenous appetites for storage, network bandwidth, and processing power. These solutions will easily consume the new supply of low-cost client/server systems as long as software providers can create enough applications.

We foresee a brave new era of ubiquitous client/server computing. Clients will be everywhere. They will come in all shapes and forms—including desktops, palmtops, pen tablets, intelligent appliances, mobile personal communicators, electronic clipboards, TV sets, intelligent books, robots, automobile dashboards, and myriads of yet-to-be-invented information hungry devices. These clients, wherever they are, will be able to obtain the services of millions of other servers. This bullish view of the industry puts us in the camp of those who believe that *the supply of low-cost MIPs creates its own demand.*[2]

WHAT IS CLIENT/SERVER?

Even though client/server is the leading industry buzzword, there is no agreed upon definition of what that term means. So, we have a fine opportunity to create our own definition. As the name implies, clients and servers are separate logical entities that work together over a network to accomplish a task. So what makes client/server different from other forms of distributed software? We propose that all client/server systems have the following distinguishing characteristics:

- *Service:* Client/Server is primarily a relationship between processes running on separate machines. The server process is a provider of services. The client is a consumer of services. In essence, client/server provides a clean separation of function based on the idea of service.

- *Shared resources:* A server can service many clients at the same time and regulate their access to shared resources.

- *Asymmetrical protocols:* There is a many-to-one relationship between clients and server. Clients always *initiate* the dialog by requesting a service. Servers are passively waiting on requests from the clients.

---

[2] The Forrester report, **The Third Act** (January 27, 1993), is in the same bullish camp. Forrester predicts that the next phase of client/server is social computing, "a type of computing that will be embedded in the way people work, live, and play by permeating, but not intruding on, all facets of human interaction and life."

- **Transparency of location:** The server is a process which can reside on the same machine as the client or on a different machine across a network. Client/Server software usually masks the location of the server from the clients by redirecting the service calls when needed. A program can be a client, a server, or both.

- **Mix and match:** The ideal client/server software is independent of hardware or operating system software platforms. You should be able to mix and match client and server platforms.

- **Message-based exchanges:** Clients and servers are loosely coupled systems which interact through a message-passing mechanism. The message is the delivery mechanism for the service requests and replies.

- **Encapsulation of services:** The server is a "specialist." A message tells a server what service is requested; it is then up to the server to determine how to get the job done. Servers can be upgraded without affecting the clients as long as the published message interface is not changed.

- **Scalability:** Client/Server systems can be scaled horizontally or vertically. Horizontal scaling means adding or removing client workstations with only a slight performance impact. Vertical scaling means migrating to a larger and faster server machine or multiservers.

- **Integrity:** The server code and server data is centrally maintained, which results in cheaper maintenance and the guarding of shared data integrity. At the same time, the clients remain personal and independent.

The client/server characteristics described here allow intelligence to be easily distributed across a network. These features also provide a framework for the design of loosely coupled network-based applications.

WILL THE REAL CLIENT/SERVER PLEASE STAND UP?

Many systems with very different architectures have been called "client/server." System vendors often use client/server as if the term can only be applied to their specific packages. For example, file server vendors swear they first invented the term, and database server vendors are known in some circles solely as *the* client/server vendors. To add to the confusion, this book adds distributed objects, TP Monitors, and Groupware to the list of client/server technologies. So who is right? Which of these technologies is the real client/server? The answer is all of the above.

The idea of splitting an application along client/server lines has been used over the last ten years to create various forms of Local Area Network software solutions.

Typically these solutions sell as shrink-wrapped software packages, and many are sold by more than one vendor. Each of these solutions, however, is distinguished by the nature of the service it provides to its clients, as shown in the following sections.

File Servers

With a file server, the client (typically a PC) passes requests for file records over a network to the file server (Figure 2-2). This is a very primitive form of data service that necessitates many message exchanges over the network to find the requested data. File servers are useful for sharing files across a network. They are indispensable for creating shared repositories of documents, images, engineering drawings, and other large data objects.

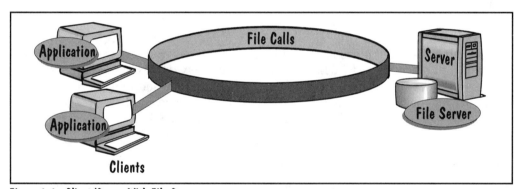

Figure 2-2. Client/Server With File Servers.

Database Servers

With a database server, the client passes SQL requests as messages to the database server (Figure 2-3). The results of each SQL command are returned over the network. The code that processes the SQL request and the data reside on the same machine. The server uses its own processing power to find the requested data instead of passing all the records back to a client and let it find its own data as was the case for the file server. The result is a much more efficient use of distributed processing power. With this approach, the server code is shrink-wrapped by the vendor. But you often need to write code for the client application (or you can buy shrink-wrapped clients like Enfin/3, Quest, or Paradox). Database servers provide the foundation for decision-support systems that require ad hoc queries and flexible reports.

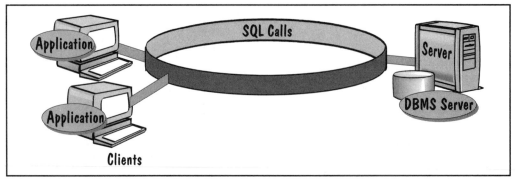

Figure 2-3. Client/Server With Database Servers.

Transaction Servers

With a transaction server, the client invokes *remote procedures* that reside on the server with an SQL database engine (Figure 2-4). These remote procedures on the server execute a group of SQL statements. The network exchange consists of a single request/reply message (as opposed to the database server's approach of one request/reply message for each SQL statement in a transaction). The SQL statements either all succeed or fail as a unit. These grouped SQL statements are called *transactions*.

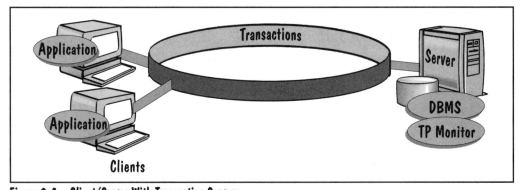

Figure 2-4. Client/Server With Transaction Servers.

With a transaction server, you create the client/server application by writing the code for both the client and server components. The client component usually includes a Graphical User Interface (GUI). The server component usually consists of SQL transactions against a database. These applications have a name: "Online Transaction Processing," or *OLTP.* They tend to be mission-critical applications that require a 1-3 second response time 100% of the time. OLTP applications also require tight controls over the security and integrity of the database. Two forms of

OLTP will be discussed in this book: *TP Lite*—based on the stored procedures provided by database vendors, and *TP Heavy*—based on the TP Monitors provided by OLTP vendors.

Groupware Servers

A new class of systems is emerging today to address the management of semi-structured information such as text, image, mail, bulletin-boards, and the flow of work. These new client/server systems place people in direct contact with other people. Lotus Notes is the leading example of such a system, although a number of other applications—including document management, imaging, multiparty applications, and workflow—are addressing some of the same needs. Specialized groupware software can be built on top of a vendor's canned set of client/server APIs. In most cases, applications are created using a scripting language and form-based interfaces provided by the vendor. The communication middleware between the client and the server is vendor-specific (Figure 2-5).

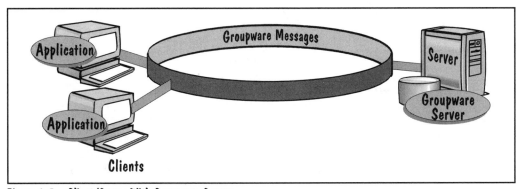

Figure 2-5.   Client/Server With Groupware Servers.

Object Servers

With an object server, the client/server application is written as a set of communicating objects (Figure 2-6). Client objects communicate with server objects using an *Object Request Broker (ORB)*. The client invokes a method supported by an object server class. The ORB locates an instance of that object server class, invokes the requested method, and returns the results to the client object. Server objects must provide support for concurrency and sharing. The ORB brings it all together. After years of incubation, some "real life" commercial ORBs have shipped. Examples include **DSOM** from IBM, **DOMS** from HyperDesk, **DOMF** from HP, and **DOE** from Sun.

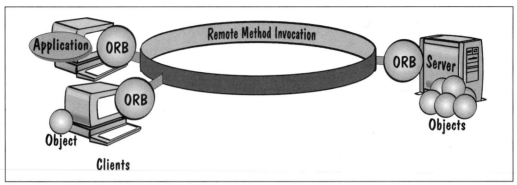

Figure 2-6.   Client/Server With Distributed Objects.

So What is "Middleware"?

Briefing

Mid.dle.ware: 1) A hodgepodge of software technologies; 2) a buzzword; 3) a key to developing client/server applications.

— *Information Week (November 1, 1993)*

Middleware is a vague term that covers all the distributed software needed to support interactions between clients and servers. Think of it as the software that's in the middle of the client/server system. In this Survival Guide we refer to middleware as the slash (/) component of client/server. It's the glue that lets a client obtain a service from a server. Where does the middleware start and where does it end? It starts with the API set on the client side that is used to invoke a service, and it covers the transmission of the request over the network and the resulting response. Middleware does not include the software that provides the actual service—that's in the server's domain. Nor does it include the user interface or the application's logic—that's in the client's domain.

We divide middleware into two broad classes:

■ **General Middleware** is the substrate for most client/server interactions. It includes the communication stacks, distributed directories, authentication services, network time, remote procedure calls, and queuing services. This category also includes the network operating system extensions such as distributed file and print services. Products that fall into the general middleware category include OSF's DCE, NetWare, Named Pipes, LAN Server, LAN Manager, Vines, TCP/IP, APPC, and NetBIOS. We also include the Message-Oriented Middleware (also known as MOM) products from Peerlogic, Covia, Message Express, and System Strategies.

■ ***Service-specific Middleware*** is needed to accomplish a particular client/server type of service. This includes:

◆ Database-specific middleware such as ODBC, IDAPI, DRDA, EDA/SQL, SAG/CLI, and Oracle Glue.

◆ OLTP-specific middleware such as Tuxedo's ATMI and /WS, Encina's Transactional RPC, and X/Open's TxRPC and XATMI.

◆ Groupware-specific middleware such as MAPI, VIM, VIC, and Lotus Notes calls.

◆ Object-specific middleware such as OMG's ORB and Object Services and ODMG-93.

◆ System Management-specific middleware such as SNMP, CMIP, and ORBs.

You can probably tell by now that middleware was created by people who love acronyms. To the best of our knowledge, few technologies have as many buzzwords and acronyms as client/server middleware. We will cover, in gruesome detail, the middleware standards that apply to the different client/server application types. By the time you finish reading this Survival Guide, you'll know exactly what all these middleware acronyms mean. In the meantime, please bear with us as we gradually pull together the pieces of this story. ❏

FAT SERVERS OR FAT CLIENTS?

So far, we've shown you that client/server models can be distinguished by the service they provide. Client/Server applications can also be differentiated by how the distributed application is split between the client and the server (see Figure 2-7). The *fat server model* places more function on the server. The *fat client model* does the reverse. Groupware, transaction, and object servers are examples of fat servers; database and file servers are examples of fat clients.

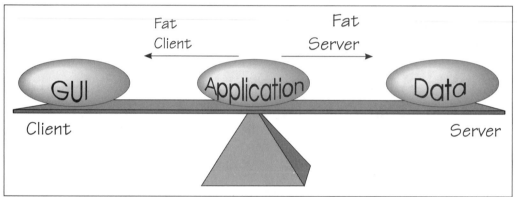

Figure 2-7. Fat Clients or Fat Servers?

Fat clients are the more traditional form of client/server. The bulk of the application runs on the client side of the equation. In both the file server and database server models, the clients know how the data is organized and stored on the server side. Fat clients are used for decision support and personal software. They provide flexibility and opportunities for creating front-end tools that let end users create their own applications.

Fat server applications are easier to manage and deploy on the network because most of the code runs on the servers. Fat servers try to minimize network interchanges by creating more abstract levels of service. Transaction and object servers, for example, encapsulate the database. Instead of exporting raw data, they export the procedures (or methods in object-oriented terminology) that operate on that data. The client in the fat server model provides the GUI and interacts with the server through remote procedure calls (or method invocations).

Each client/server model has its uses. In many cases, the models complement each other, and it is not unusual to have them coexist in one application. For example, a groupware imaging application could require an "all-in-one" server that combines file, database, transaction, and object services. Fat servers, used for mission-critical applications, represent the new growth area for PC-based client/server computing.

Chapter 3

Client/Server Building Blocks

---

*W*hat are you able to build with your blocks? Castles and palaces, temples and docks.

— *Robert L. Stevenson,*
A Child's Garden of Verses

We are all familiar with the concept of *architecture* as applied in the construction of buildings. Architectures help us identify structural elements that may be used as building blocks in the construction of ever more complex systems. Just like we buy homes, not plans, users in the computer industry buy solutions to business problems, not grand client/server architectures. But architecture determines the structure of the houses, high rises, office buildings, and cities where we live and work. In the computer analogy, architecture helps us determine the structure and shape of the client/server systems we can build to meet various needs.

The "million dollar" architectural questions we will cover here are: How is the application split between the client and the server? What function goes in the client and what function goes in the server? Can the client/server model accommodate businesses of all sizes? How are the new tribes of nomadic laptop users brought into the client/server fold? Can client/server play in the home? Where do peer networks fit in this picture? Will client/server disappear in a post-scarcity computing world?

We start this chapter with a quick discussion of how business demographics are changing. We then present a model of client/server topologies that can accommodate the new demographic patterns. We end this chapter with a discussion of peer networks. In future chapters, we will go over the extensive software, middleware, and communications infrastructure that is needed to transform these topologies into real systems.

NEW AGE BUSINESS DEMOGRAPHICS

A few years ago, we came across an IDC study of business demographics that changed our perspective of the client/server market (to put it mildly—we were never the same after that). Table 3-1 is a top-level summary of this report. Please take a minute to digest the implications. Yes, there are an overwhelming number of small establishments. They are called the *forgotten one million*. They're forgotten in the sense that the major computer vendors don't cater to their needs—they are too busy selling to the Fortune 500.

Table 3-1. IDC US Business Demographics (1991).

Business Sector	Small Businesses	Medium Business	Large Business
Retail	1,055,000 (under $50M)	773	236
Discrete Manufacturing	256,000 (under $100M)	930	345
Process Manufacturing	26,500 (under $100M)	230	170
Travel	25,000 (under $10M)	900	100
Wholesale	324,000 (under $50M)	1,900	286
Insurance	30,000 (under $100M)	1,600	400
Banking	12,000 small banks	2,200	600
Higher Education	2,250 (under 2,500 students)	850	362

Big Business, Nomads, and the Forgotten Millions

A huge transformation of the workforce has taken place since IDC published its 1991 report. Large companies are going through a massive restructuring that includes scaling back staff, outsourcing work, and using more outside contractors.

The parts of the business establishment that survived the restructuring are becoming more decentralized, autonomous, and loosely coupled. This restructuring is also creating millions of new one-person "establishments" in homes—in 1992, more than 23 million people in the US worked out of their home. The drop in prices of basic office equipment such as computers, printers, modems, and fax machines is making it possible to operate almost any type of enterprise from the home. Client/server technology allows home offices to connect to the world-at-large as either clients, servers, or both.

For many of us, the office of the future will increasingly mean *no office at all*, especially in occupations with high levels of customer contact: sales positions, telemarketers, insurance adjusters, and so on. These folks will likely be given a laptop, a cellular telephone, and a way to hook into the client/server network from the road—we call this the *portable office*. By the end of the century, more than 13 million PCs may be using wireless networks, which will result in a new $4 billion market. Nomadic users hardly existed when IDC published its demographic findings.

Home and portable offices have made the number of small establishments larger than ever before. They should now, more appropriately, be called the *forgotten multiple millions*.

So What Do the Numbers Say?

Over 80% of LAN-based client/server solutions are deployed on PC LANs. They run in departmental-sized establishments consisting of twenty (or fewer) clients talking to a single PC server that provides database, file, and mail services. The other 20% run on mixed LANs, involve one or more servers (PCs, workstations, superminis, and mainframes), support thirty or more clients, and are more likely to be attached to an enterprise backbone. There is also a growing population of mobile users that are part of "nomadic" client/server establishments. Finally, we're seeing many more home users that run businesses from the home—these are really one-person establishments.

CLIENT/SERVER: A ONE SIZE FITS ALL MODEL

Can a single client/server model accommodate all these types of users? We think we have such a model. It is deceptively simple, and it works well with today's technologies. It is ideally suited for dealing with the needs of a *post-scarcity computing* world, where client/server becomes the ultimate medium for sharing and collaborating.

The model we present in this section is really a game of putting together things with building blocks. We will show you how we can meet a wide spectrum of client/server needs—from the tiny to the intergalactic—with just three basic building blocks: a client, a server, and the slash (/) that ties the client to the server (see Figure 3-1). Kids of all ages will love this game. It should help you identify some durable structures in the design of client/server systems.

Figure 3-1. The Three Basic Building Blocks of Client/Server.

The Building Blocks of Client/Server

We make the claim that the three basic building blocks can be used to create client/server configurations that range from the tiny to the intergalactic. To prove it, after a few days of deep thinking and heavy meditation, we created four basic Client/Server *arrangements*. We propose that these four arrangements can handle all of today's (and tomorrow's) client/server needs. Yes, you read that right. We claim these four arrangements cover the entire spectrum: from the nomadic user to the largest corporate establishments. Yes, they're also ideal for introducing new post-scarcity software technologies. Yes, they can take care of the needs of the new one-person establishments that are sprouting from homes everywhere. Yes, they make the world look simple, and things will never be the same after that. Have we got your attention?

In the next few sections, we explain (and illustrate) how the four building-block arrangements are used to do all these wonderful things. But it will help if we first give them some meaningful names:

■ *Client/Server for tiny shops and nomadic tribes* is a building block implementation that runs the client, the middleware software, and most of the business services on the same machine. It is the suggested implementation for the one-person shops, home offices, and mobile users with well-endowed laptops. This is a new opportunity area for client/server technology.

■ *Client/Server for small shops and departments* is the classic client/single-server building block implementation. It is used in small shops, departments, and branch offices. This is the predominant form of client/server today.

■ *Client/Server for intergalactic enterprises* is the multiserver building block implementation of client/server. The servers present a single system image to the client. They can be spread out throughout the enterprise, but they can be made to look like they're part of the local desktop. We will be discussing two variations of this model: one that we like and one that we don't like.

■ *Client/Server for a post-scarcity world* transforms every machine in the world into both a client and a server. Personal agents on every machine will handle all the negotiations with their peer agents anywhere in the universe. This dream is almost within reach.

You will discover many similarities in the four arrangements. This is because they all use the same type of software, middleware, and communications infrastructure. Different arrangements handle the different topologies, business sizes, and budget sizes. You pick the level of service and complexity that satisfy your business needs. It's your choice.

Client/Server for Tiny Shops and Nomadic Tribes

The nice thing about client/server is that it's infinitely malleable. It is easy to run the client and server portion of an application on the same machine. Vendors can easily package single-user versions of a client/server application (Figure 3-2). For example, a client/server application for a dentist office can be sold in a single user package for offices consisting of a single dentist and in a multiuser package for offices with many dentists. The same client/server application covers both cases. The only caveat is that you need to use an operating system that is robust enough to run both the client and server sides of the application.

Figure 3-2.   Client/Server for Tiny Shops and Nomadic Users.

The example of the tiny dentist office also works for the tiny in-home business office and the mobile user on the road. In all cases, the business-critical client/server application runs on one machine and does some occasional communications with outside servers to exchange data, refresh a database, and send or receive mail and faxes. For example, the one-person dentist office may need to communicate with outside servers such as insurance company billing computers.

Can that one person computer also act as a server for the outside world? Yes, but it's not very easy to do today. In order for this to become a reality, we need ubiquitous ISDN-like digital telephones in every home and office; we need higher-bandwidth (lower-cost) cellular networks that integrate the nomadic road warriors. In other words, we're waiting for the portions of the information highway—the pieces promised by the Clinton/Gore administration—to materialize! We'll have more to say about that in the post-scarcity section.

So, we've used a client, server, and middleware (/) block to create a very workable client/server environment for tiny offices and people on the road. Let's move on and see what other magic can be performed with these three blocks.

Client/Server for Small Shops and Departments

The client/server architecture is particularly well-suited for the LAN-based single server establishments. So, it's no wonder that they account for around 80% of today's client/server installations. This is the "archetypical" model of client/server. It consists of multiple clients talking to a single "local" server (Figure 3-3). This is the model used in small businesses—for example, a multiuser dentist office—and by the departments of large corporations—for example, the branch offices of a bank.

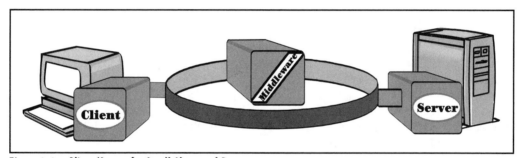

Figure 3-3. Client/Server for Small Shops and Departments.

The single-server nature of the model tends to keep the middleware simple. The client only needs to look into a configuration file to find its server's name. Security is implemented at the machine level and kept quite simple. The network is usually relatively easy to administer; it's a part-time job for a member of the group. There are no complex interactions between servers, so it is easy to identify failures—they're either on the client or on the local server.

Braver souls may be using their server to interact in a very loosely-coupled way with some enterprise server. For example, data (such as a price list) may be downloaded once a day to refresh the local server. Or inventory data may be uploaded to an enterprise server. Fax and mail can be sent or received any time through the mail server gateway. Typically, the software that interacts with remote servers will reside on the departmental server.

Departmental servers will continue to be popular, especially in large enterprises, because they provide a tremendous amount of user autonomy and controls. Users feel that it is *their* server and they can do anything they want with it. A departmental server's applications typically address the specific needs of the local clients first, which make users very happy. With fiber optic and high-speed ATM connections, it will be hard to detect a performance difference between a "local" departmental server and an enterprise server a continent away. However, the psychology (and politics) of "ownership" will always provide a powerful motivator for holding on to that "local" server.

In summary, this implementation of client/server uses our three building blocks to create the "classical" single-server model of client/server that is so predominant. This model works very well in small businesses and departments that depend on single servers or on very loosely-coupled server arrangements. In its marketing literature, Oracle calls this model the "first generation" of client/server. This implies that there is already a "second generation" of client/server, which is the topic of our next section.

Client/Server for Intergalactic Enterprises

The client/server intergalactic model addresses the needs of establishments with a mix of heterogeneous servers (about 20% of the current client/server market). This is an area that's getting a lot of industry attention as solutions move from a few large computers to LAN-based servers. Multiple servers are used in environments that require more processing power than that provided by a single server (see Figure 3-4). One of the great things about the client/server model is that it is upwardly scalable. When more processing power is needed for various intergalactic functions, more servers can be added (thus creating a pool of servers), or the existing server machine can be traded up for the latest generation of superserver machine.

We can partition servers based on the function they provide, the resource they control, or the database they own. In addition, we may choose to replicate servers for fault tolerance or to boost an application's performance. There can be as many server combinations as your budget will tolerate. Multiserver capability, when properly used, can provide an awesome amount of compute power and flexibility, in many cases rivaling that of mainframes.

To exploit the full power of multiservers, we need low-cost, high-speed bandwidth and an awesome amount of middleware features—including network directory services, network security, remote procedure calls, and network time services (see next Soapbox). Middleware creates a common view of all the services on the network called a "single system image."

Good software architecture for intergalactic enterprise client/server implementations is all about creating system "ensembles" out of modular building blocks. With some practice, you may develop creative skills akin to those of a symphony composer in the articulation of servers. You will need to find creative ways to

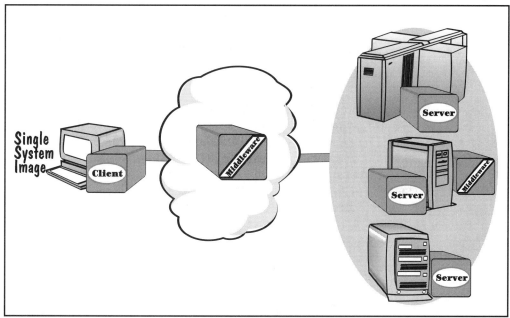

Figure 3-4.   Client/Server for Intergalactic Enterprises.

partition work among the servers. For example, you may partition the work using the concept of object managers. An object manager accepts message-based requests to perform actions against the objects it controls.

You will also need to design your servers so that they can delegate work to their fellow servers. A complex request may involve a task force of servers working together on the request. Preferably, the client should not be made aware of this behind-the-scenes collaboration. The server that the client first contacted should be in charge of orchestrating the task force and returning its findings to the client.

Intergalactic client/server is the driving force behind middleware standards and distributed objects. We're all looking for that magic bullet that will make the distributed multivendor world as integrated as single-vendor mainframes. Tools for creating, deploying, and managing scalable client/server applications are getting a lot of attention. There are fortunes to be made in intergalactic client/server because nobody has yet put all of the pieces back together.

Middleware Servers to the Rescue?

Soapbox

Middleware is an exploding area. Vendors keep adding layer upon layer of software, promising that the last layer is the ultimate "glue" that will finally tie all clients to all servers. We don't believe the ultimate glue will materialize in our lifetimes. In the meantime, it's important to create a "single system image" of all the services a client workstation can use. This is really a Houdini-sized illusion that makes all servers of the world—we're talking about a multiserver, multiservice, multivendor, and multinetwork world—appear to the client as one big happy family. So the "million dollar" question is: What middleware software (or "glue") should reside on each *client* machine to create such an illusion?

There are two evolving approaches for solving this problem:

■ The ***brute force*** approach adds new middleware software on each client machine as fast as vendors roll-out the new pieces. The problem with this approach is that your client machines and applications are always in a state of flux, playing catch-up with all the new and exciting middleware that's constantly being introduced. The clients will grow very fat over time. The complexity of the client environment greatly increases with each new added piece of middleware. Who works out the coexistence issues? How is the mixed environment managed? Nobody knows.

■ The ***middleware gateway*** approach introduces a middleware service that handles all communications with the servers of the universe on behalf of its clients. The gateway server is just a piece of software that typically runs on the "local" server. The client only needs to run the minimum amount of middleware (a "skinny" layer) that allows it to communicate with the server where the middleware gateway software resides. This approach buffers the client from the middleware flux and makes it easier to introduce new server functions without involving every client machine. Of course, if you can afford the fat, you can always run the middleware gateway server on every client machine. This is precisely how the tiny shop and post-scarcity world arrangements are packaged.

We obviously prefer the gateway approach. It provides maximum flexibility using the client/server model. Because the gateway software is itself a server package, it can be moved to any machine on the network to fit your needs. If you run the gateway software on every client machine, you're back to the first option. We like this flexibility. ❑

Client/Server for a Post-Scarcity World

In this section, we up the ante. We will investigate what new systems can be created on a client/server platform when memory and hardware become *incredibly affordable*. Every machine is both a client and a full-function server (see Figure 3-5). We call this plentiful environment *the post-scarcity world*. We imagine the typical post-scarcity machine as a $1000 cellular notebook powered by a 200 MHz Pentium and loaded with a gigabyte of nonvolatile RAM and 100 GBytes or more of disk space. And, of course, this machine runs all the middleware that vendors will be able to dream of over the next few years.

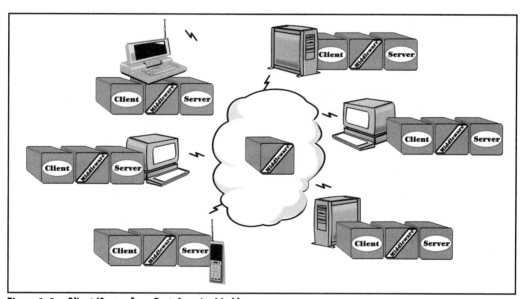

Figure 3-5. Client/Server for a Post-Scarcity World.

What do we do with all this power other than run middleware? What happens when every machine in the world becomes a universal server and client? Because every machine is a full-function server, we should assume it will run, at a minimum, a file server, database server, mail server, TP Monitor, and Distributed Object Manager (DOM). This is in addition to all the client software and middleware.

What we're saying is that in the next few years, a hundred million machines or more may be running *almost all* the forms of client/server software described in this book. This should be good news to TP Monitor, DOM, groupware, and database vendors—it's a huge opportunity. Are they thinking about it? Do they have the proper packaging and marketing channels to go after it? After you read this book, you'll have a better appreciation for how complex, powerful, and essential this software is.

So who will manage and run all that software on behalf of the user? *Personal agents*, of course. The best way to understand the capabilities of agent technology is to read the next Briefing box that describes an agent-controlled automated travel agency.

The Automated Travel Agent is an example of a new type of cooperative application that makes full use of the advanced software features of PCs. From an architectural viewpoint, we've gone past the concept of client/server where every event is generated by the client. We've augmented this architectural paradigm with the concept of *autonomous agents* that reside in the network machines and perform background tasks. The agents can analyze data and perform actions based on a set of rules. And the agents are always on *fact-finding* missions on the network working on your behalf.

It is easy to imagine that the next step is to have a personal version of the Automated Agent run on your own PC. You will have your own personal agent to take care of your vacations. Your agent knows your vacation schedule and preferences. It has also kept a history of your previous vacations in the database and has learned your likes and dislikes from it. Your personal agent knows you like to take your vacations in March, so it started a search sometime in December to find you the best bargains. Your agent is of course always negotiating with other agents all over the world, always "wheeling and dealing" on your behalf. Your agent and you communicate using multimedia, continuous speech recognition facilities, and e-mail. It communicates with the world at large using the intergalactic services of an Object Request Broker (ORB). The best part is that you do not have to babysit your agent while it's out there doing all this work on your behalf. Wouldn't you love to have one of those agents? The post-scarcity age of client/server computing is sure to be amazing, at least to those of us who are trying to make today's technology work.

How far in the future is this post-scarcity vision? In November 1993 at Comdex, IBM demonstrated an intelligent rules-based agent technology that allows an OS/2 or Windows user to delegate all kinds of everyday work to an agent. The agent can intercept input from many devices—including phones, fax machines, e-mail, and server applications—make decisions based on inputs, and act on the decisions. The agents can be programmed using instruction "rule books" created with a graphical instruction editor. The agent-managed objects can be expanded to include IBM and customer objects.

In January 1994, General Magic unveiled Telescript, a communication language that will provide the foundation of AT&T's Personal Link on-line service, scheduled to begin later this year. With Telescript, a computer user has no idea of "connecting" to a remote service at all. Instead, an agent travels from the user's computer through the network, looking for information or even making purchases based on commands given by the user.

A View of Post-Scarcity Paradise

Briefing

You walk into the *Paradise Travel Agency* to discuss your vacation plans. Its name is definitely enticing. You are greeted by the Automated Travel Agent, a PC with an Object-Oriented User Interface (OOUI). You start a friendly conversation with the Automated Agent. A few interactions later (this machine does advanced continuous speech recognition), the Automated Agent knows that you have ten days of vacation coming in March, you want to spend them on a nice beach, and you have at most $2000 to spend on your vacation.

The Automated Agent searches its local database for a vacation strategy that fits your needs and offers you a set of alternative choices in the form of iconic objects placed on a map. The best choices for this time of the year are Tahiti, Hawaii, Cancun, and other "paradises." You pick Tahiti, and the Automated Travel Agent displays a set of resort choices that include the Club Meds at Bora Bora and Morea. You choose to explore the Club Med alternative, and then ask for more information about the Club Med Villages in Tahiti. You are now placed in a Hypermedia-like environment that allows you to explore the sports offered, the beaches, the room accommodations, and so on. Embedded in the Hypermedia displays are *links* that allow you to view and zoom in on pictures and videos of beaches, lagoons, huts on the water, and romantic restaurants with views of the sunset. After spending a delightful 30 minutes or so browsing through screens of dreamland and imagining what your vacation will be like, you decide to book your vacation now!

The Automated Agent presents you with more choices, and by the time you are finished you've decided you want to spend six days in Bora Bora and four in Morea. You want a hut on the lagoon, of course, with a double bed, and you opt for low-cholesterol dinners. You may even decide to make table reservations for your first night in the romantic restaurant with the view of the sunset.

The Automated Agent now has all the information it needs from you to carry out the transaction, so it starts a background process that places a call to Club Med's computer using its Object Request Broker (ORB). It also starts another background ORB process that deals with your credit card company's computer. While all this activity is happening, the Automated Agent keeps you occupied by listing information in a window that may be relevant to your trip, like what kind of clothes to bring, passport requirements, and so on. It can even sell you the clothes while you're waiting!

A few seconds elapse. Now all the parties are ready to carry out the transaction. We have established an inter-ORB rendezvous between the Club Med computer, the credit card company's computer, and the Automated Agent who is your broker. The transaction is electronically prepared. You have your reservation, Club Med has your money, the Automated Agent has the commission, and you are set for a wonderful vacation. You are asked one last time if you want to confirm the transaction. Click OK, and you will be in Tahiti next March. Life is sweet! ❑

Sharing Data in the Post-Scarcity Age

Each machine on the network contains an *information agent* that runs in the background and performs useful tasks, such as dealing with requests for remote information, both outgoing and incoming. Your machine's information agent—think of it as a specialized personal agent—is always operating on your behalf in the background, accumulating and sorting information on topics that interest you. It does this by conducting constant transactions with fellow information agents on remote machines. The information agents communicate with one another using the client/server remote procedure call (RPC) exchanges. More sophisticated agents may incorporate a TP Monitor that can handle X/Open's transactional RPC (TxRPC) and participate in a two-phase commit. The most sophisticated agents will implement the OMG's ORB 2 with object-oriented transactional services. We're creating a brave new world of *agents* that are programmed to have a ravenous appetite for

information on a list of topics, and they know how to cooperate with other agents on the network to get their work done.

ARE PEER SERVICES A VIABLE ALTERNATIVE?

If you're coming from the low-end of the networking business, you may already be familiar with products such as Artisoft's LANtastic, Novell's NetWare Lite, IBM's LAN Server 3.0 Peer Services, AppleTalk, and Microsoft's Windows for Workgroups and Windows NT. These products provide file and print sharing and some kind of electronic mail without requiring a dedicated server. Everybody is equal on the peer network. Each computer on the network is both a client and a server. Further, each computer is responsible for controlling access to its own resources and has equal access to resources that are on any other computer.

Peer services usually sell for a fraction of the cost of equivalent client/server software. So is it time to toss away the local server? Has post-scarcity client/server already arrived? No! No! (See the following Soapbox.) Peer servers are usually very limited in function, and typically they will let only one client connect at a time to access a shared resource. So peer networks support multiuser sharing as long as only one user gets in at a time. Is that a problem? Not if you have a small office environment.

But how do peer networks handle distributed security, audit trails, fault tolerance, and all the good things you expect to get on a shared server? Peer services are too limited to give you all that function. And don't even think about running a shared database server, TP Monitor, or Distributed Object Manager in that environment.

Remember, in the post-scarcity model of client/server, every machine is a client and a *full-function* server. Without these features you're liable to get into a lot of trouble. Peer services are *not* full-function servers, and they're notoriously hard to manage and control. You need the sophisticated agent software we described in the previous section to create *true* peer services. Without this function you have a network of crippled peers.

To Peer or Not To Peer?

Soapbox

Peer-to-peer networks are still not ready for prime time for many reasons. A single peer can kill an entire network by limiting access to a key shared file (for example, if the owner of that machine calls in sick). Everybody must keep their shared machines powered up over the weekend to let workaholics access the information they need at all hours. In addition, a single peer can break the security of the entire network by providing shared access to sensitive files. And, with today's peer technology, it is almost impossible for an administrator to fully control every machine on a peer network: When are resources backed up? When can a system shut down safely? Who gets to run *Popeye* on their machines (or any other program that chews up system resources)?

But let's face it: Peer services are very attractive because they're an embryonic microcosm of our final destination—post-scarcity client/server computing. Should you deploy peer services today? Yes, as long as you have at least one machine that's a full-function server on the network. This is the machine with the redundant disk drives, uninterruptable power supply (UPS), full-function server software, and network security. It's the machine that always stays up— after hours and on weekends. In other words, it's a *super peer* also known as the local server. So much for equality and freedom for all! ❑

Chapter 4

The State of the Client/Server Infrastructure

If something inert is set in motion, it will gradually come to life.

— *Lao Tzu*

We hope to have convinced you, by now, that our planet will soon be covered with ubiquitous client/server webs. Using these webs, we will be able to communicate more effectively with other humans—customers, suppliers, the boss, coworkers, family, and friends—and with the everyday machines that serve us—cars, gas pumps, TV sets, and even intelligent homes.

This chapter provides an overview of the extensive infrastructure that supports these client/server webs. An *infrastructure* provides the components that make it easy to create, deliver, and manage client/server applications. We will identify the components of this infrastructure and use them to create the roadmap that ties together the pieces of the puzzle. We will briefly explain the different components and where they fit. But our emphasis will be on the lower level middleware and base components of the infrastructure—the bedrock elements on top of which everything else is built. We've got to start somewhere.

WHAT'S AN INFRASTRUCTURE?

Every epoch-making technology requires an infrastructure. For example, where would airplanes be today without the vast commercial airway infrastructure that provides airports, traffic controllers, air corridors, flights, booking agents, customs, security gates, ground transport, and luggage handling systems? This infrastructure has grown over the years and now has the bandwidth to comfortably move hundreds of millions of passengers across the globe (except around Christmas, it seems). Entire industries were created around this infrastructure—car rental agencies, air cargo, shuttle services, travel agents, mass tourism, long-term parking, hotels, and airport shops and restaurants.

Client/server has its own infrastructure. The industry has recently delivered many of the key software technologies needed to create ubiquitous client/server webs. But the technology to help deliver, deploy, and manage the client/server applications that reside on the web is still in its infancy. To use the airway analogy, the client/server infrastructure is at the stage that the airline industry found itself right after World War II. We have many airplane builders, some great battle-tested airplanes (from the OS wars), a few semi-isolated airports, and great radar technology. But we still haven't found the Howard Hughes of client/server (young Howard created TWA and started the modern airline industry).

The horizontal diversification and commoditization of the computer industry may have come a tad too early for the client/server mass market. Nothing is better than horizontal competition within an established vertical infrastructure. Unfortunately, the vertical infrastructure that will create the client/server playing field still needs to be deployed. The next Soapbox speculates on who may pull the pieces together for the client/server industry to take off big time.

The telephone and cable companies are doing a phenomenal job renewing the physical infrastructure and paving the country with 1) high bandwidth transport media—the fiber backbones already strung across the US by AT&T, MCI, and Sprint; 2) the coax connections installed in millions of homes by cable TV companies; and 3) the twisted pair connections brought to nearly every home by local telephone companies. In addition, they are developing the new generation of switching systems that will transfer voice, video, and data around the network using several technologies, including ATM, FDDI, and Frame Relay.

The challenge for the computer industry is how to add on top of this physical infrastructure the client/server structures that bring all the pieces together. We must provide:

■ The transport protocols that support networked exchanges and allow information to be moved reliably.

- The network operating systems that guarantee security and privacy and help users and programs find the services they need on the internet.
- The databases for storing, retrieving, and organizing massive amounts of multimedia information.
- The groupware systems that enable networked person-to-person exchanges and group conferencing.
- The intelligent agents that help humans organize their activities in cyberspace.
- The distributed system management platforms that keep the whole thing running on a day-to-day basis.

So what's the state of our infrastructure?

Who Can Bring the Pieces Together?

Soapbox

If it succeeds as envisioned, the data highway could help businesses find information more easily, open up new modes of research and education, and give consumers a wide choice of services.

— Andy Reinhardt, Byte Magazine
(March, 1994)

Everywhere you turn these days, someone is talking about the "digital highway." For now, the network providers are the big spenders in the digital highway convergence. The spate of alliances involving cable TV, Telcos, and entertainment companies are creating physical transmission backbones that are faster, cheaper, more widespread, and have more capacity than anything the phone companies could have created on their own. The merger of the US West Telco with Time Warner's fiber optic networks can result in the offering of transparent LAN services on a nationwide basis. AT&T spent $12.6 billion to acquire McCaw Cellular Communications to consolidate its end-to-end offerings.

These companies are renewing the existing voice network and augmenting it with the bandwidth to support highly interactive multimedia transmissions. But the infrastructure they're creating is not being neatly planned and then built. Instead, a large "multifaceted communications web" is being spun that is already expanding in fits and starts, across the globe.

In the midst of this chaotic growth, who in the computer industry will provide the *client/server nervous system* that articulates this physical infrastructure?

Our short list of potential candidates includes Bill Clinton, Bill Gates, system integrators (like Arthur Anderson or EDS), a "born-again" client/server IBM, a Novell/Oracle alliance, and a super-consortium that includes everyone but Microsoft. Here's how each of them might do it:

■ ***Bill Clinton*** wants an information highway that will bring together the worlds of CATV and data networks. His *National Information Infrastructure (NII)* will use existing transports and concentrate on smoothing the path for developing the "on-ramps" and "off-ramps" to this highway. The "NII Testbed" is also helping explore several switching technologies, including ATM, FDDI, and Frame Relay. Could the airline infrastructure have succeeded without government intervention? It's doubtful. Bill Clinton proposes to build the client/server equivalents of airports.

■ ***Bill Gates*** is cooking up his *At Work* and *At Home* strategies based on "Windows everywhere." His *Windows Open Systems Architecture (WOSA)* is an ambitious plan to bring every gadget, appliance, workstation, and server into the Windows fold. Windows APIs are being proposed for every known activity. WOSA may succeed on the client, but it will go nowhere without the server side of the equation. This is where Windows NT comes into the picture. Microsoft now spends more than $100 million a year and employs more than 200 people to research and develop software for interactive TV and other technologies to connect homes to the data highway. Microsoft, like everybody else in the industry, is going after the strategic "set-top box" that sits on the TV—it's working on MIMOSA, an operating system for interactive TV. Bill Gates is also a partner in the $9 Billion Teledesic venture with McCaw.

■ ***The System Integrators***—like Arthur Andersen and EDS—are some of the main beneficiaries of the fragmentation of the computer industry. They're getting paid to bring the pieces back together using "vendor-neutral solutions." Can they pull enough of the pieces together to create a vendor-neutral cohesive infrastructure?

■ ***The new IBM*** is leapfrogging the competition by combining client/server and distributed object technologies. Its goal is to create a client/server infrastructure around a "sea of objects." This time IBM is leading the push for "open" standards based on objects and the OSF DCE technology. DSOM and Taligent object frameworks are making IBM the technology leader in distributed objects. In spite of all the layoffs, IBM still has the industry's largest channel for distributing, deploying, and supporting client/server applications. Finally, IBM has a lot of in-house experience in the area of mission-critical distributed systems. As Jim Cannavino puts it, "IBM has had a decade of experience making heterogeneous systems work together—mostly our own."

- **The Novell/Oracle alliance** created around *OracleWare*. The packaging of the Oracle DBMS with NetWare brings together two very potent technologies and, even more importantly, two major distribution channels. Novell wants to embed NetWare, or some mutation of it, everywhere—including in our refrigerators and toasters. And Oracle is working with US West to build a worldwide digital network to be managed by massively parallel versions of the Oracle7 database. This network is also intended to support interactive wireless and cable services. What we're seeing here is a marriage of LANs, WANs, and massively parallel database technology—all the pieces needed to move, distribute, and store massive numbers of multimedia objects.

- **The "Everybody but Microsoft" alliance**, called COSE, is intended to shake the balance in the industry and accelerate the introduction of de facto standards. The stability of the COSE alliance is directly proportional to how well Microsoft does with Windows NT and Cairo. If they falter, so will the COSE alliance. Can a consortium built for defensive purposes create the infrastructure that brings the industry together?

Finally, there are those who dream that the invisible hand of the market coupled with open standards will create this infrastructure from the bottom up—no divine intervention required.

Which are you betting on? ☐

CLIENT/SERVER INFRASTRUCTURE: THE COMPONENTS

Last chapter we introduced the three *building blocks* of client/server: the client, the server, and the middleware slash (/) that ties them together. Figure 4-1 peels the next layer off the onion and provides more detail about what goes into each of the building blocks. What you see in this figure is, in a nutshell, the entire client/server software infrastructure. Let's go over the pieces:

- **The client building block** runs the client side of the application. It runs on an operating system (OS) that provides a graphical user interface (GUI) or an Object Oriented User Interface (OOUI) and that can access distributed services, wherever they may be. The operating system most often passes the buck to the middleware building block and lets it handle the non-local services. The client also runs a component of the *Distributed System Management (DSM)* element. This could be anything from a simple agent on a managed PC to the entire front-end of the DSM application on a managing station.

- **The server building block** runs the server side of the application. The server application typically runs on top of some shrink-wrapped server software package. The four contending server platforms for creating applications are SQL Database Servers, TP Monitors, Groupware Servers, and Object Servers. The server side depends on the operating system to interface with the middleware building block that brings in the requests for service. The server also runs a DSM component. This could be anything from a simple agent on a managed PC to the entire back-end of the DSM application (for example it could provide a shared object database for storing system management information).

■ *The middleware building block* runs on both the client and server sides of an application. We broke this building block into three categories: transport stacks, network operating systems (NOSs), and service-specific middleware. Middleware is the nervous system of the client/server infrastructure. We will explain the division in the middleware building block in the next section. Like the other two building blocks, the middleware also has DSM software components.

The Distributed System Management application runs on every node in a client/server network. A *managing* workstation collects information from all its *agents* on the network and displays it graphically. The managing workstation can also instruct its agents to perform actions on its behalf. Think of management as running an autonomous "network within a network." It is the "Big Brother" of the client/server world, but life is impossible without it.

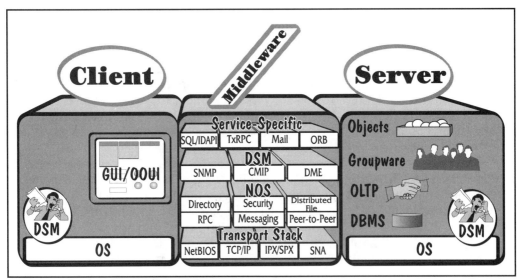

Figure 4-1. The Client/Server Software Infrastructure.

THE MIDDLEWARE BUILDING BLOCK: A CLOSER LOOK

Middleware is a very convenient term, which, unfortunately, also creates lots of confusion. This is not surprising because middleware refers to the software that's in the *middle* of the client/server system. We're using middleware as a general "catch-all" term that refers to three layers of glue: the transport stacks, the network operating system (NOS), and service-specific middleware. This division should make it easier to understand all those strange interactions that take place between the clients and the servers on the network.

The Transport Stacks Middleware

The transport stacks middleware consists of transport protocols—including TCP/IP, NetBIOS, IPX/SPX, DECnet, AppleTalk, OSI, and SNA/APPN—that provide reliable end-to-end communications across Wide Area Networks (WANs) and Local Area Networks (LANs). How do all these protocols seamlessly work together? They use the magic of LAN/WAN/LAN interconnect technology—such as routers, bridges, and gateways—that transport multiprotocol traffic across a campus or wide area network in an integrated fashion (see the following Briefing box). Groups can decide for themselves what protocols to run on their local networks and leave it up to the backbone providers to collect these protocols and route them across networks.

Figure 4-2 shows how bridges, routers, and gateways are used in a modern backbone network. As you can see, today's enterprise networks are made up of a combination of LANs, including Token Rings and Ethernets; WANs, including public and private packet switched networks that run X.25 and Frame Relay; and the bridge, routers, and gateways that provide the internetworking, multiprotocol "glue" that ties the LANs and WANs together (also see the following Briefing box on Bridges, Routers, and Gateways).

The Bridge/Router phenomenon is not the only area that experienced great progress. Modern operating systems—like OS/2, NetWare, Windows NT, and Unix SVR4—are becoming much more network friendly. They've introduced features that allow multivendor communication stacks and network adapters to easily plug into them. And they also make life easier for programmers by providing APIs that are stack independent.

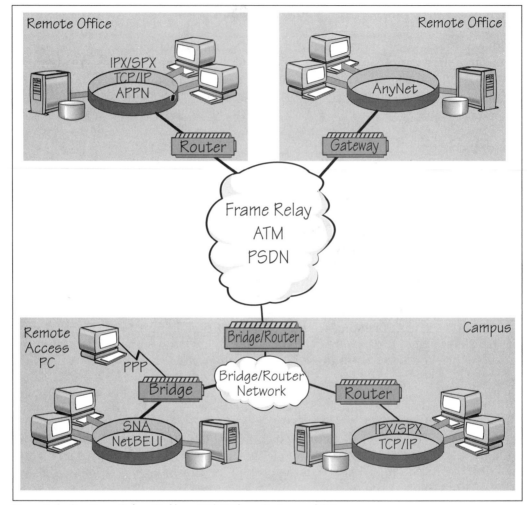

Figure 4-2. Creating a Modern Backbone With Bridges, Routers, and Gateways.

Here's a summary of some of the new operating system features that make that possible:

■ *The stack sandwich* provides the hooks for snapping multivendor protocol stacks into an operating system. To accommodate multivendor networks, modern operating systems must support multiple protocols, redirectors, and APIs. To do that effectively, the operating system must provide well defined interfaces between components. A modern operating system usually "sandwiches" the transport stacks between a transport-independent interface at the top of the stacks and a logical interface to the network device drivers at the bottom of the stacks (see Figure 4-3).

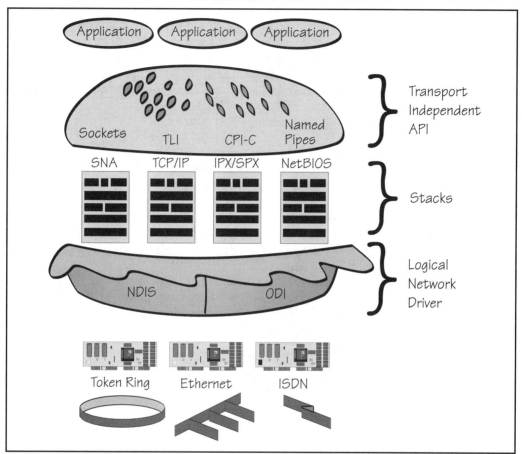

Figure 4-3. The Stack Sandwich.

■ *The logical network driver* provides a single interface to all the network adapters. This interface between the network adapter and the transport stacks is particularly important. The last thing vendors who provide transport stacks want is to write a driver for every possible network adapter. And, of course, network adapter vendors want to avoid having to interface to every possible stack. Microsoft/3Com's NDIS and Novell's ODI are the two most widely supported de facto standards for interfacing protocol stacks to network adapter device drivers. They do so by providing a logical network board that makes it easy to interface different network adapters with multiple protocol stacks (see Figure 4-3). Transport stack providers can use NDIS or ODI as the common interface to all network adapters. And network adapter vendors can use NDIS or ODI as the top layer for their network drivers. NDIS and ODI take care of sending and receiving data and managing the adapter card.

■ *The transport-independent APIs* sit on top of the transport stacks and allow developers to plug their programs into a single interface that supports multiple protocols. The Berkeley socket interface is becoming the premier choice on most operating system platforms for interfacing to multivendor multiprotocol stacks. Other choices include the *Transport Layer Interface (TLI)* used in NetWare and many Unix implementations; *CPI-C*, the modern SNA peer-to-peer API that can now run over both SNA and TCP/IP stacks; and *Named Pipes* that runs on top of NetBIOS, IPX/SPX, and TCP/IP stacks.

■ *The protocol matchmakers* allow applications written for a specific transport, such as SNA, to run across other networks, such as TCP/IP or IPX/SPX (see Figure 4-4). This strategy eliminates the need for gateways and works well with existing applications. For example, a Lotus Notes application written for NetBIOS could be made to run over SNA networks without changing a line of code. IBM's *AnyNet* product line currently offers protocol matchmakers for TCP/IP and SNA on the OS/2 and MVS platforms. IBM intends to add matchmakers for NetBIOS, IPX/SPX, and OSI. The formal IBM name for this matchmaker strategy is the *The Multiprotocol Transport Network (or MPTN)*. Several companies are in discussion with IBM about using MPTN, including Apple, HP, Oracle, and Ki Research.

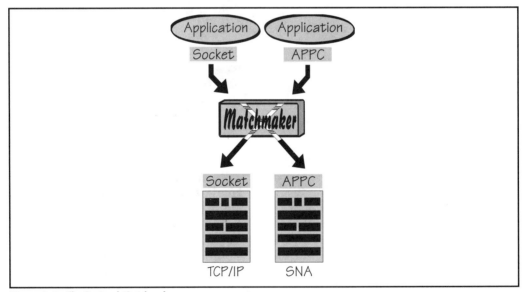

Figure 4-4. The Protocol Matchmaker.

In summary, today's network environment is a truly heterogeneous hodgepodge of protocols and media options. Network routers, gateways, and bridges insulate the application developer from having to worry about cabling, network adapters, or protocol transport choices. Multiprotocol API sets make it easier for service providers to develop client/server applications that run over multiple protocol stacks. And we're getting closer to the day when client/server programs can be plugged into any protocol stack (on any machine) almost as easily as appliances plug into electrical outlets.

Bridges, Routers, and Gateways

Briefing

Bridges are computers or devices that interconnect LANs using link layer routing information and physical addresses; protocols that do not support internetworking, like NetBIOS, are bridged. *Routers* interconnect LANs using protocol-dependent routing information. Routers create and maintain dynamic routing tables of the destinations they know. They are typically used with protocols such as TCP/IP, IPX/SPX, APPN, XNS, AppleTalk, and OSI. *Multiprotocol Routers* support different combinations of network layer protocols. *Bridge/Routers* are single devices that combine the functions of bridges and routers; they are quite popular today. *Gateways* are devices that perform brute force translations between protocols. They are used in situations where the backbone can only support one protocol, and all other protocols get translated to it.

Bridge/Routers started as a bottom-up phenomenon—they solved practical problems and were not part of a grand architecture. The Router products from Cayman Systems, Cisco, Wellfleet, IBM, DEC, and Novell can now encapsulate NetBIOS, AppleTalk, SNA, and IPX/SPX to allow only a single protocol to run on the backbone (usually IPX/SPX, APPN, or TCP/IP). The industry is still learning how to make these products work in environments that require the load balancing of traffic between links and the handling of high-priority traffic. Bridges use fixed path, one-route only schemes; only a few know how to re-route traffic to alternate paths when a link fails. While they can handle any LAN-based protocols, they do not perform very well when large amounts of broadcast packets are propagated throughout the network. But, the Bridge/Router industry is extremely competitive, and it will undoubtedly solve these problems. The industry is continuously introducing newer features and more robust models. For example, the newest routers use specialized protocols to determine the best paths for network traffic and can even perform load-balancing across multiple parallel paths.

Despite their popularity, bridges and routers are no panacea. Segmenting LANs with bridge and routers is a bandaid, not a long-term cure. When the widespread use of multimedia starts to dramatically increase our traffic loads, routers will become *incredibly expensive* bandaids. Routers will become much harder to manage and will introduce delays that are unacceptable for real-time data flows, like motion pictures. We anticipate that routers will eventually get replaced by ATM-based backbones, which we discuss later in this chapter. Of course, if you're in the router business, you may call these high-speed ATM switches the new routers of the mid-1990s. ❑

What's Missing?

The vision is nomadic, ubiquitous, client/server computing everywhere.

— *Tom Furey, 1993*

In order for the "ubiquitous network socket" to see the light of day, and for Figure 4-5 to become a reality, the following hurdles still have to be overcome:

Bringing the digital highway to the home: To do so requires a solution to the impedance mismatch (or bottleneck) created by the "last mile" of telephone cable that connects homes and offices to the long-distance service providers. In the US alone, telephone companies still own more than 100 million pairs of copper wire local loops. But, over the past decade, the long-distance carriers replaced their copper wire backbones with a network of superfast, high-bandwidth, low-tariff, fiber-optic cables. However, bringing these advantages into the home requires the upgrading of that last mile of local cable to fiber—a mind boggling expense.

But there's good news on the horizon in the form of two related technologies that promise to speed up the local loops without replacing the existing wiring: ISDN (see next Briefing box) and the ISDN-based T1 over copper connection (also known as HDSL). And if these don't work out, there's always the cable TV alternative.[1] Cable companies are already exploring the use of their coaxial cabling to include telephone services and connections to computer data networks such as the Internet. AT&T is also working on an adapter, called Sage, that may provide "universal access" into the home by plugging into both the existing telephone and cable networks. In addition, some cable operators (such as Time Warner) are installing fiber as a replacement for coax. And some local telephone companies are also expanding fiber beyond switching offices to the curbs of residential customers.

---

[1] In the US, the Telecommunications Infrastructure Act of 1993 (S 1086) proposes to free up regional telephone companies and cable companies to play into each other's territories, allowing them to offer "on ramp" connections to the information highway.

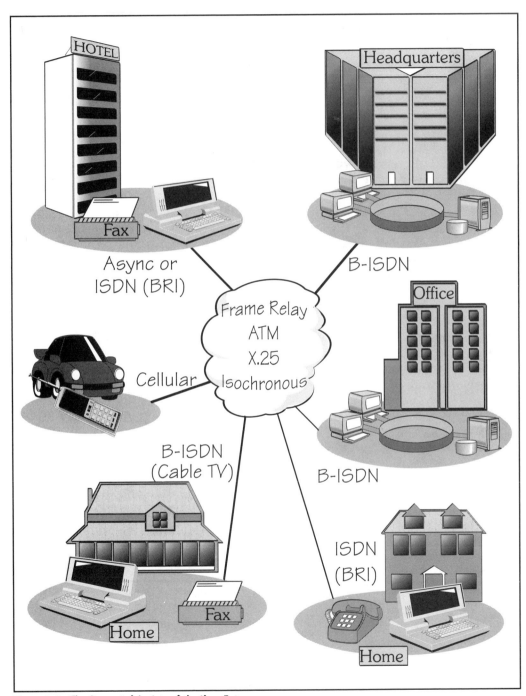

Figure 4-5. The Connected Society of the Near Future.

ISDN, B-ISDN, and ATM

Briefing

Integrated Services Digital Network (ISDN) is a digital telephony technology that supports the high-speed transfer of voice and data over telephone lines. The most prevalent ISDN service is the *Basic Rate Interface (BRI)*, also known as *2B + D*. This service works over regular telephone lines by creating two independent 64 Kb/s "B channels" for information (data or voice) and one 16 Kb/s "D channel" for signaling and placing calls. The Basic Rate telephone line is clocked at 192 Kb/s and uses time division multiplexing to allocate the two B and D channels; the extra 48 Kb/s is reserved. Basic Rate uses the standard 4-wire telephone jack that is used in homes and offices. A higher-capacity version of ISDN is also available; it is called the *Primary Rate Interface (PRI)*, or *23B + D*. PRI can deliver 1.544 Mb/s, but it is rarely used.

ISDN BRI is the digitization of the telephone line. It's an order of magnitude faster than anything you can do with a modem today. In addition, ISDN provides a lower-cost form of communication because it charges by connect time (like normal voice calls) rather than by the packet (like some PSDNs). Its higher speeds can reduce the connect time and save you some money. So why isn't everybody using ISDN? ISDN's acceptance depends on being able to "call out and reach anyone." To do that, all the central office switches involved in an ISDN connection must be digital. Today over 65% of US Centrex switches are ISDN-capable; Europe and Japan are further along. Forrester predicts that ISDN will become prevalent in 1995. According to Forrester, Pacific Bell, Bell Atlantic, Ameritech, US West, and Nynex will provide over 70% ISDN coverage at low cost by 1995. Southwestern Bell is the laggard, with less than 25% coverage. Mobile users with laptops should be able to use ISDN from their hotel rooms much before 1995. Forrester calls ISDN the LAN Outer Network (LON) because it extends the LAN's remote coverage, it provides decent bandwidth, it's reliable, it provides fast remote dial-up (1 second or less), and it's inexpensive (remote lines can be installed at a cost of $10 to $20 per month).

The proponents of ISDN feel it provides the ideal end-user entry point to the "data highway" because the telephone is ubiquitous. Another camp argues that 128 Kb/s does not provide enough bandwidth for multimedia and would rather go with coax (cable TV) and bypass ISDN (PRI or BRI). This is where an exciting technology called *Broadband ISDN or B-ISDN* comes into the picture. B-ISDN supports a bandwidth of 150 Mbit/s and above. It's an excellent candidate technology for the data highway because it can bring interactive voice, data, and video into the home using Cable TV's broadband channels. B-ISDN uses *Asynchronous Transfer Mode (ATM)* in both its connection-oriented and connectionless (also known as SMDS) modes. The B-ISDN standard defines an ATM adaptation layer (AAL) that is responsible for mapping data, voice, and video information to and from ATM-defined cell formats.

So what is ATM? It is the current darling of the network industry. ATM has the potential of revolutionizing networking at the LAN, WAN, campus Router, and home connection levels. ATM's high-speed, cell-based switching protocols permit the mixing of different traffic including data, voice, and video. Its system of transmitting small cells of information is flexible enough to work at capacities ranging from megabits to gigabits. ATM bandwidth is demand-based and scalable, meaning that each node can access the network at the speeds required by an application. ATM is the favorite building block technology for the construction of the digital highway. ATM can provide seamless networking and remove the current distinctions between LANs and WANs. Several telephone and cable TV companies, such as Time Warner, are installing ATM switching systems. However, many standards are still needed to make implementations of ATM interoperate.

Any of these approaches is better than what we have today: POTS (Plain Old Telephone Service). We wouldn't mind BRI using one B channel for data (or voice) while the other B channel is transmitting an image, fax, or movie, in the background. And it beats installing two telephone lines and dial modems. BRI will do fine until we get B-ISDN on ATM and live happily ever after in bandwidth heaven. ❏

Bringing the digital highway to the mobile user: Many alliances are being formed to create the ultimate network that will let users "communicate anywhere, anytime." The alliances are between various computer and telephone companies. Their aim is to glue together wired and wireless networks so that they can shoot high-speed data through the air to mobile users. RAM Mobile Data claims that it already can provide two-way wireless services to 90% of the U.S. urban population. RAM is expected to announce the availability of AT&T Mail and Lotus cc:Mail on RAM networks. ARDIS, the IBM/Motorola digital wireless network, is another contender. In 1994, Cellular-Vision plans to cover the New York city area with a 1 Gbit/s wireless network that supports multimedia and interactive television. AT&T spent $12.6 billion to acquire McCaw Cellular Communications to "round-out" its end-to-end wireless suite of offerings.

McCaw is testing an evolutionary technology called *Cellular Digital Packet Data (CDPD)* that allows data to be transmitted over the existing analog cellular network. CDPD can dynamically pick the open voice channels and use them for data traffic. Two warring digital alternatives to CDPD are also being proposed: *Time-Division Multiple Access (TDMA)* and *Code-Division Multiple Access (CDMA)*. Regardless of which technology is chosen, we expect cellular data networks to really start catching on.

Nomadic Martians

In September 1993, the US Federal regulators (FCC) cleared the way for a dramatic expansion of wireless services by allowing 200 MHz of government-held radio frequency to be auctioned to private developers. This is five times the spectrum originally allocated to the cellular phone industry. This action could conceivably lead to a day when wired phones are seldom used and are replaced by small mobile phones carried by nearly everyone at all times. Phone numbers will be individually assigned to individuals, not locations.

The FCC action includes the allocation of 40 MHz of spectrum bandwidth for LAN-based wireless office applications at frequencies between 1.85 GHz and 2.2 GHz, which can be supported by low-cost, low-power, small-cell, one-chip transceivers. This dedicated spectrum, called the *Personal Communication Services (PCS)*, will eliminate interference from other radio sources, including cellular phones, garage door openers, and security devices. PCS will help create private networks that incorporate different data-transmission methods and easily provide links at 32 kbit/s (or more). PCS will open up entire new industries based on low-cost and ubiquitous wireless technology for data transmissions.

But who will maintain order in the friendly skies? Currently, each wireless network provider is building its own "skyway." To bring order out of that chaos, the IEEE 802.11 committee was given the thankless task of creating standards for wireless networks. The standards are intended to cover the following areas: wireless modems, APIs, PCMCIA devices, data security in the sky, bridges from wired-to-wireless LANs, guidelines to prevent broadcast interference, and a media-access protocol for radio and infrared transmissions.

Bringing "isochronous" multimedia support to the digital highway: What is an isochronous network? It's a network that provides very low and predictable node-to-node delays (or latencies). Isochronous networks are capable of dealing with the steady, immediate delivery, and high-bandwidth requirements of multimedia technology. For example, networks that support desktop training videos or videoconferencing need to supply, on demand, 1.5 Mbits/s (or more) to each PC. We can accommodate some of that demand by exploiting the prioritized traffic services of existing Token Ring and Ethernet networks. Higher priority frames are assigned to the delay-sensitive traffic. But what we really need are high-speed networks with separate voice/video and data traffic channels (also called virtual circuits) that can guarantee a fixed delivery time for multimedia traffic (see next Briefing box).

Near completion is the *Fiber Distributed Data Interface* II (*FDDI II*), a virtual circuit standard that divides *FDDI's* 100 Mbit/s bandwidth into 16 separate circuits, each of which can be allocated to either data or isochronous traffic (see next Briefing box). ANSI is also working on a gigabit-speed version of FDDI called FFOL (for FDDI Follow On LAN). Two competing 100 Mbit/s Ethernet proposals were ratified by IEEE in July of 1993 in addition to a 16 Mbit/s isochronous Ethernet. Further on the horizon are Asynchronous Transfer Mode (ATM) networks that are being built from the ground up to handle voice, video, and data. Currently, FDDI products (over copper) sell for one-fifth the price of equivalent ATM offerings. Table 4-1 compares the contending high-speed network technologies.

Table 4-1. Comparing High-Speed Network Technologies.

Networks	Isochronous support	Bandwidth	Access Scheme	When
FDDI	No	100 MBit/s	Contention	Now
Synchronous FDDI	Yes	100 MBit/s	Contention (with Priority)	Now
FDDI II	Yes	100 MBit/s	Contention and Virtual Circuits	1994-5
FFOL	Yes	2.40 GBit/s	Contention and Virtual Circuits	1995
Ethernet II	No	100 MBit/s	Contention	1994-5
ATM	Yes	2.48 GBit/s	Pure Circuit Switch	1994-5

In conclusion, the transport elements of the middleware infrastructure are coming together at a fast pace. We have a pretty good idea of how everything will eventually interconnect with everything else. But interconnectivity is only a first step in the long road to ubiquitous client/server computing. In the next few sections, we explain how the NOS and service-specific middleware conspire to create a single system view on top of these raw transports. In other words, *the network is the computer.*

What's a Virtual Circuit?

Briefing

Virtual circuits are like the phone system. They get established when two nodes need to communicate, and relinquished after they're not needed. Because video and voice are carried over the network in streams within virtual circuits, delays are low and constant. For example, the Frame Relay Wide Area Network (WAN) packet switching technology uses virtual circuits to allocate bandwidth on demand and optimize the use of the existing bandwidth.

In contrast, today's LAN technology allocates bandwidth by *contention*. Everybody is bidding with everybody else to obtain the use of the broadcast medium. To get on the LAN, you must either wait for a token (Token Ring) or start broadcasting; you must be prepared to back off if you detect a collision (Ethernet). Contention methods cannot guarantee deterministic response times (or delays). It's a matter of luck, and things get worse around rush-hour. The situation can be improved by assigning priorities, but there's still contention within the same priority levels.

Some of the new isochronous LAN technologies propose a *hybrid* environment that allocates a certain amount of bandwidth to contention traffic and gives the rest to virtual circuits. For example, isochronous FDDI, FDDI II, FFOL, and Ethernet allocate a certain percentage of the network bandwidth to multiple 64 kbit/s virtual circuits and give the remainder to normal contention-based data.

However, *purist* technologies, like ATM, only provide virtual circuits. ATM uses high-speed, hardware-based, circuit-switching technology that is potentially capable of unleashing an awesome amount of isochronous bandwidth at very low cost (every node is given its own dedicated LAN segment into the switch). ❑

The Network Operating System Middleware

The Network Operating System (NOS) Middleware:

■ *Extends the local operating system's reach to include networked devices such as printers, file directories, and modem pools.* These are the classical functions provided by network operating systems such as NetWare 3.1 and LAN Server 3.0.

■ *Provides a distributed computing foundation that helps create a "single system" out of all the diverse resources distributed on the network.* This includes directory services that provide a way to find things on the network, "federated" naming services that allow things to be uniquely named, distributed security and authentication services, a single logon, network time, and many others. These global services provide the distributed software infrastructure required for creating "intergalactic" client/server applications that span across multiple organizations within a company or across companies. The trick is for that infrastructure to attain this level of cohesion and trust *without sacrificing the autonomy of local administrative units.* This infrastructure is starting to appear in products like NetWare 4.0, Banyan Vines, and the OSF Distributed Computing Environment (DCE).

■ *Supports the coordination of applications that are split across client/server lines.* Two types of client/server exchanges are supported: tightly- coupled request/reply interactions and loosely-coupled queue-based interactions. *Remote Procedure Calls (RPCs)* provide tightly-coupled interactions. The OSF *Distributed Computing Environment (DCE)* and the Sun/USL *Open Network Computing (ONC)* provide two different RPC infrastructures. *Message-Oriented Middleware (or MOM)* is used for loosely-coupled exchanges of work packets across multiple operating systems. These queues can be very important to laptop users who are not always connected to the client/server network.

The basic NOS infrastructure is currently in place. The challenge is for organizations and programmers to absorb this new paradigm. They will need to reevaluate the world in distributed, cooperative, client/server terms.

The Service-Specific Middleware

This is the most exciting area of client/server middleware. It deals with the avant-garde technologies that are not yet ripe for integration into the NOS. This is an area where the standards are still fluid and new structures are being discovered. It is also the area where all the new client/server applications are being created. We will look at five service-specific middleware standards:

- **Database middleware** allows clients to invoke SQL-based services across multivendor databases. The database middleware is defined by "de facto" standards such as ODBC, IDAPI, DRDA, RDA, Oracle Glue, and SAG's CLI. These standards define a call level interface for SQL and address some of the issues of multivendor SQL interoperability "on the wire."

- **Transactional RPC middleware** allows clients to invoke services across multiple transaction servers. TP Monitors allow the different servers to control their local resources and to cooperate with other TP Monitors when they need access to resources that are not local. The TP Monitors guarantee the integrity of all the activities within and across servers. The TP Monitor middleware consists of the transactional RPCs that allow clients to specify transactional boundaries and the interserver calls necessary to coordinate the multisite transaction. The "standards" in this area include Tuxedo's ATMI and /WS, Encina's Transactional RPC, and X/Open's TxRPC and XATMI.

- **Groupware middleware** allows clients to invoke services on a groupware server. This is a new area where middleware standards are being created almost every day. The middleware "du jour" is MAPI and VIM in the area of electronic mail, VIC for group calendaring, and the Lotus Notes APIs for almost everything else.

- **Object middleware** allows clients to invoke methods that reside on remote servers. The key middleware is the OMG's CORBA specification for interfacing to object request brokers (ORBs), the OMG's Object Services, and the ODMG-93 API set for interfacing to Object DBMSs.

- **Distributed System management middleware** allows managing stations to talk to managed services. The current standards in this area are SNMP and CMIP.

In summary, it is becoming almost feasible to place data where it is needed, regardless of vendor platform.

Server-to-Server Middleware

Middleware does not include the software that provides the actual service. It *does*, however, include the software that is used to coordinate inter-server interactions (see Figure 4-6). Server-to-server interactions are usually client/server in nature—servers are clients to other servers. However, some server-to-server interactions require specialized server middleware. For example, a two-phase commit protocol may be used to coordinate a transaction that executes on multiple servers. Servers on a mail backbone will use special server-to-server middleware for doing store-and-forward type messaging. But most modern software (even on operating system kernels) follows the client/server paradigm. And at least one TP Monitor (CSI/Bachman's Ellipse) goes as far as protecting the client's GUI state using the two-phase commit transactional discipline.

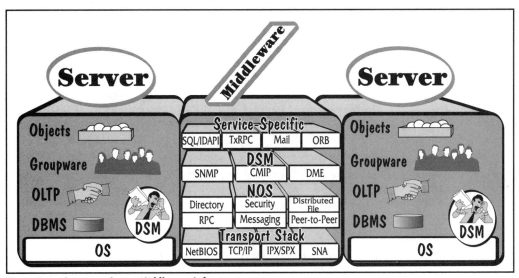

Figure 4-6. Server-to-Server Middleware Infrastructure.

THE STATE OF THE CLIENT/SERVER INFRASTRUCTURE

MIS is the only group who can understand the implications of extending communications and strategic systems to customers and employees.

> — *George Colony,*
> *President of Forrester Research Inc.*
> *(November, 1993)*

So what can we say about the state of the client/server infrastructure? The transport network is in place (with more coming). A vast physical "infozone" is starting to connect the separate worlds of computers, telephones, and cable TV. As George Colony observes, "Smart companies will take advantage of the connections to their customers, suppliers, and workers." This means that corporate enterprise networks will expand their coverage as the high-speed services reach out to smaller offices, homes, and mobile users.

The NOS distributed computing environment is more than adequate for creating applications that can span across multiple organizations and companies. We have a rudimentary infrastructure for managing client/server systems (based on the classical OSF DME model). The completed system management platform requires distributed object technology, which will not be available until late 1994 at the earliest.

The current crop of 32-bit commodity operating systems is quite capable of running the client and server sides of the equation. Our application server technology—including Database Servers, TP Monitors, Groupware, and Object Brokers—allows us to create very imaginative, high-quality client/server applications. And this is only the beginning; there is an awesome amount of application server technology on the horizon.

It would be ideal if a single operating system could run both the client and server sides of the equation. It would simplify the infrastructure and allow us to concentrate on building function. But this is like saying that the airline industry would be in better shape if it didn't have to deal with airports in 200 or more countries. Airlines created their industry in a multinational world, and we have to create ours in a multivendor, multiorganizational world where the diversity of hardware and operating systems is a fact of life.

The most difficult question is: How do you pick the client, server, and middleware building blocks that give you the biggest bang for the buck within the constraints of your budget? You're confronted with a wide variety of choices: the operating system, the GUI, the network protocol, the RPC, the NOS, the tools, and the database. And these are the easy choices. The more difficult choices are: Which competing technology is best: database servers, TP Monitors, groupware, or objects? When you get past these choices, you'll need to develop a mind-set that will help you seize the opportunities created by the client/server infrastructure. Using the airline analogy, now that we have the airports, planes, and control towers, where's the opportunity? For users, the opportunity is cheap transcontinental travel—and for entrepreneurs, the sky is the limit!

Part 2
Clients, Servers, and Operating Systems

An Introduction to Part 2

Now that you've got the "bird's eye" view of our planet, are you ready for some action? We've got a dangerous journey ahead. Did you bring your bullet-proof vests? Don't panic! You're in good hands. We're only going to cross an active war zone. No, it's not Yugoslavia. It's the client/server operating system wars, and they're just as dangerous. You'll feel the bullets coming right out of the book. But, don't worry. You'll live.

Part 2 is an overview of what clients and servers do in life and what they require from their operating systems. We'll briefly look at various OSs and see what they have to offer on both the client and server sides. There's no right or wrong when it comes to OSs—it's one big balancing act with hundreds of shades of gray. Everything is fuzzy and constantly in flux. If you make the wrong decision or ride the wrong client/server wave, you simply go broke (or take the next spaceship back to Mars). Some of the big players in client/server can afford to take a more secular view of OSs by simply porting to all the platforms. If you can afford to be secular, do it. Otherwise, you'll have to pick your OSs very carefully.

Chapter 5

Clients, Servers, and Operating Systems

---

*L*ook at every path closely and deliberately. Try it as many times as you think necessary. Then ask yourself, and yourself alone, one question...Does this path have a heart? If it does, the path is good; if it doesn't, it is of no use.

> — Carlos Castaneda,
> *The Teachings of Don Juan*

This chapter starts with a brief description of what typical clients and servers do in life. We then examine what each side of the client/server equation needs from an operating system. By the time you reach the end of this chapter, you should be better prepared to know what to look for in a client/server platform.

THE ANATOMY OF A SERVER PROGRAM

The role of a server program is to *serve* multiple clients who have an interest in a shared resource owned by the server. This section describes a day in the life of a typical server. Here's what a typical server program does:

■ *Waits for client-initiated requests*. The server program spends most of its time passively waiting on client requests, in the form of messages, to arrive over a communication session. Some servers assign a dedicated session to every client. Others create a dynamic pool of reusable sessions. Some provide a mix of the two environments. Of course, to be successful, the server must always be responsive to its clients and be prepared for *rush hour traffic* when many clients will request services at the same time.

■ *Executes many requests at the same time*. The server program must do the work requested by the client promptly. Clearly a client should not have to depend on a single-threaded server process. A server program that does not provide multitasking will run the risk of having a client hog all the system's resources and starve out its fellow clients. The server must be able to concurrently service multiple clients while protecting the integrity of shared resources.

■ *Takes care of VIP clients first*. The server program must be able to provide different levels of service priority to its clients. For example, a server can service a request for a report or batch job in low priority while maintaining OLTP-type responsiveness for high-priority clients.

■ *Initiates and runs background task activity.* The server program must be able to run background tasks triggered to perform chores unrelated to the main program's thrust. For example, it can trigger a task to download records from a host database during non-peak hours.

■ *Keeps running*. The server program is typically a mission-critical application. If the server goes down, it impacts all the clients that depend on its services. The server program and the environment on which it runs must be very robust.

■ *Grows bigger and fatter.* Server programs seem to have an insatiable appetite for memory and processing power. The server environment must be upwardly scalable and modular.

WHAT DOES A SERVER NEED FROM AN OS?

In distributed computing environments, operating system functions are either *base* or *extended* services. The base services are part of the standard operating system, while the extended services are add-on modular software components that are layered on top of the base services. Functionally equivalent extended services are usually provided by more than one vendor. There is no hard rule that determines what gets bundled in the base operating system and what goes into the extensions. Today's extensions are usually good candidates for tomorrow's base system services.

Base Services

It should be apparent from the previous description that server programs exhibit a high level of concurrency. Ideally, a separate task will be assigned to each of the clients the server is designed to concurrently support. Task management is best done by a multitasking operating system. Multitasking is the natural way to simplify the coding of complex applications that can be divided into a collection of discrete and logically distinct, concurrent tasks. It improves the performance, throughput, modularity, and responsiveness of server programs. Multitasking also implies the existence of mechanisms for intertask coordination and information exchanges.

Servers also require a high level of concurrency within a single program. Server code will run more efficiently if tasks are allocated to parts of the same program rather than to separate programs (these tasks are called coroutines or threads). Tasks within the same program are faster to create, faster to context switch, and have easier access to shared information. Figure 5-1 shows the type of support that servers require from their operating system. Let's go over the server operating system requirements.

- *Task Preemption*. An operating system with preemptive multitasking must allot fixed time slots of execution to each task. Without preemptive multitasking, a task must voluntarily agree to give up the processor before another task can run. It is much safer and easier to write multitasking server programs in environments where the operating system automatically handles all the task switching.

- *Task Priority*. An operating system must dispatch tasks based on their priority. This feature allows servers to differentiate the level of service based on their clients' priority.

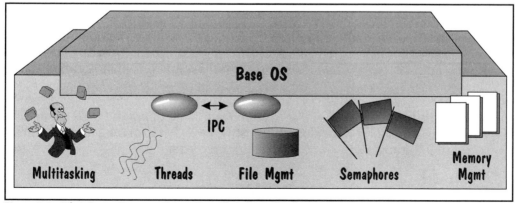

Figure 5-1. What Server Programs Expect From Their Operating System.

■ *Semaphores*. An operating system must provide simple synchronization mechanisms for keeping concurrent tasks from bumping into one another when accessing shared resources. These mechanisms, known as semaphores, are used to synchronize the actions of independent server tasks and alert them when some significant event occurs.

■ *Interprocess Communications (IPC)*. An operating system must provide the mechanisms that allow independent processes to exchange and share data.

■ *Local/Remote Interprocess Communications*. An operating system must allow the transparent redirection of interprocess calls to a remote process over a network without the application being aware of it. The extension of the interprocess communications across machine boundaries is key to the development of applications where resources and processes can be easily moved across machines (i.e., they allow servers to grow bigger and fatter).

■ *Threads*. These are units of concurrency provided within the program itself. Threads are used to create very concurrent, event-driven server programs. Each waiting event can be assigned to a thread that blocks until the event occurs. In the meantime, other threads can use the CPU's cycles productively to perform useful work.

■ *Intertask Protection*. The operating system must protect tasks from interfering with each other's resources. A single task must not be able to bring down the entire system. Protection also extends to the file system and calls to the operating system.

■ *Multiuser High-Performance File System*. The file system must support multiple tasks and provide the locks that protect the integrity of the data. Server programs typically work on many files at the same time. The file system must support large number of open files without too much deterioration in performance.

■ *Efficient Memory Management*. The memory system must efficiently support very large programs and very large data objects. These programs and data objects must be easily swapped to and from disk preferably in small granular blocks.

■ *Dynamically Linked Run-time Extensions*. The operating system services should be extendable. A mechanism must be provided to allow services to grow at run time without recompiling the operating system.

Extended Services

The extended services must provide the advanced system software that will exploit the distributed potential of networks, provide flexible access to shared information, and make the system easier to manage and maintain. It should also make it easier for independent software vendors (ISVs) and system integrators to create new server applications. Figure 5-2 shows some of the extended services server programs expect from their operating system. We will go over these expectations, starting from the bottom layer and working our way up. Some of these expectations read more like wish lists. They will eventually find their way into most operating systems.

- **Ubiquitous Communications**. The operating system extensions must provide a rich set of communications protocol stacks that allow the server to communicate with the greatest number of client platforms. In addition, the server should be able to communicate with other server platforms in case it needs assistance in providing services.

- **Network Operating System Extensions**. The operating system extensions must provide facilities for extending the file and print services over the network. Ideally, the applications should be able to transparently access any remote device (such as printers and files) as if they were local.

- **Binary Large Objects (BLOBs)**. Images, video, graphics, intelligent documents, and database snapshots are about to test the capabilities of our operating systems, databases, and networks. These large objects (affectionately called BLOBs) require operating system extensions such as intelligent message streams and object representation formats. Networks must be prepared to move and transport these large BLOBs at astronomic speeds. Databases and file systems must be prepared to store those BLOBs and provide access to them. Protocols are needed for the exchange of BLOBs across systems and for associating BLOBs with programs that know what to do when they see one.

- **Global Directories and Network Yellow Pages**. The operating system extensions must provide a way for clients to locate servers and their services on the network using a network directory yellow page type of service. Network resources must be found by name. Servers must be able to dynamically register their services with the directory provider.

- **Authentication and Authorization Services**. The operating system extensions must provide a way for clients to prove to the server that they are who they claim to be. The authorization system determines if the authenticated client has the permission to obtain a remote service.

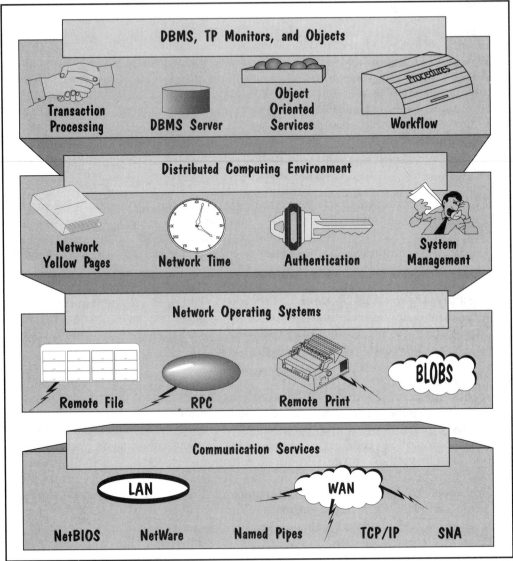

Figure 5-2. What Server Programs Hope to Get From Their Extended Operating Systems.

- *System Management*. The operating system extensions must provide an integrated network and system management platform. The system should be managed as a single server or as multiple servers assigned to domains. An enterprise view that covers multiple domains must be provided for servers that play in the big leagues. System management includes services for configuring a system, facilities for monitoring the performance of all elements, generating alerts when things break, distributing and managing software packages on client workstations, checking for viruses and intruders, and metering capabilities for pay-as-you-use server resources.

■ *Network Time*. The operating system extensions must provide a mechanism for clients and servers to synchronize their clocks. This time should be coordinated with some universal time authority.

■ *Database and Transaction Services*. The operating system extensions must provide a robust Multiuser Database Management System (DBMS). This DBMS should ideally support SQL for decision support and server-stored procedures for transaction services. The server-stored procedures are created outside the operating system by programmers. More advanced functions include a *Transaction Processing Monitor (TP Monitor)* for managing stored procedures (or transactions) as atomic units of work that execute on one or more servers.

■ *Object-Oriented Services*. This is an area where extended services will flourish for a long time to come. Services are becoming more object-oriented. The operating system will be required to provide "object broker" services that allow any object to interact with any other object across the network. The operating system must also provide object interchange services and object repositories. Client/Server applications of the future will be between communicating objects (in addition to communicating processes). Object groups will come together in loose associations to provide a service. The Object Management Group (OMG) is working on an architecture that allows objects to communicate across networks, hardware platforms, and operating systems.

As you can see extended does mean "extended." It covers the universe of current and future services needed to create distributed client/server environments. No current operating system bundles all the extended functions. Most can be purchased *a la carte* from more than one vendor.

THE ANATOMY OF A CLIENT PROGRAM

Client/Server applications are *client-centric*. The client side provides the "look and feel" for the services a system provides. All client applications have this in common: they request the services of a server. What makes client applications different is what triggers the requests and what Graphical User Interface (GUI), if any, is needed. Based on these differences, we can classify clients into three categories: *Non-GUI Clients*, *GUI Clients*, and *OOUI Clients* (see Figure 5-3).

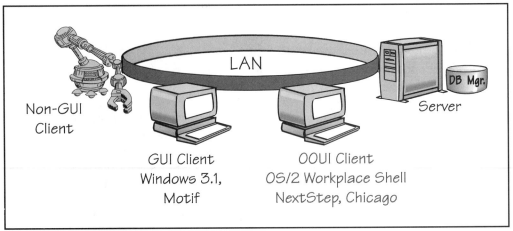

Figure 5-3. Three Client Types: Non-GUI, GUI, and OOUI.

Non-GUI Clients

Non-GUI client applications generate server requests with a minimal amount of human interaction (see Figure 5-4). Non-GUI clients fall into two sub-categories:

■ ***Non-GUI clients that do not need multitasking.*** Examples include automatic teller machines (ATMs), barcode readers, cellular phones, fax machines, smart gas pumps, and intelligent clipboards (future). These clients may provide a simple human interface in the request generation loop.

■ ***Non-GUI clients that need multitasking.*** Examples include robots, testers, and daemon programs. These clients often require very granular, real-time, event-driven multitasking services.

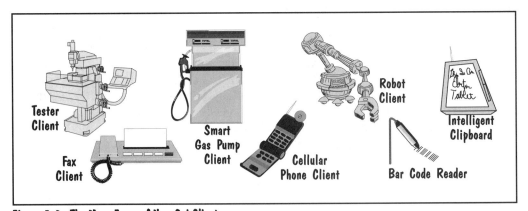

Figure 5-4. The Many Faces of Non-Gui Clients.

GUI Clients

Simple GUI Clients are applications where occasional requests to the server result from a human interacting with a GUI. The simple GUI interface is a good fit for mainstream, OLTP-type business applications with repetitive tasks and high volumes. They also make good front-end clients to database servers. Simple GUI client applications are graphical renditions of the dialogs that previously ran on dumb terminals. GUIs replace the "green screen uglies" with graphic dialogs, color, menu bars, scroll boxes, and pull-down and pop-up windows (see Figure 5-5). Simple GUI dialogs use the object/action model where users can select objects and then select the actions to be performed on the chosen objects. Most dialogs are serial in nature. This model of user interaction is predominantly used in Windows 3.X and OSF Motif applications. It is also known as the CUA 89 graphical model.

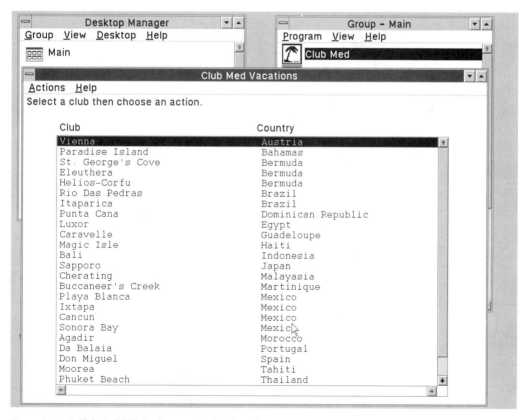

Figure 5-5. A Club Med GUI Application "Look and Feel."

Object-Oriented User Interface (OOUI) Clients

The *Object-Oriented User Interface (OOUI)* metaphor is used to provide what Microsoft Chairman Bill Gates calls *information at your fingertips*. This is a highly-iconic, object-oriented user interface that provides seamless access to information in very visual formats. OOUIs are used by information workers doing multiple, variable tasks whose sequence cannot be predicted. Examples include executive and decision-support applications, multimedia-based training systems, system management consoles, and stockbroker workstations. OOUIs have an insatiable appetite for communications. OOUI desktop objects need to communicate among themselves and with external servers. The communications are, by necessity, real time, interactive, and highly concurrent.

Examples of OOUIs are the OS/2 Workplace Shell, NextStep, and Macintosh. Current OOUIs provide a visual desktop metaphor (think of it as an arcade game) where related objects and programs can be brought together to perform a task. The desktop can contain multiple workplaces running concurrently (see Figure 5-6).

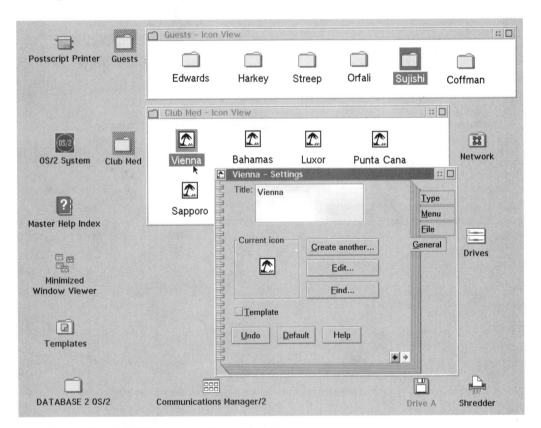

Figure 5-6. A Club Med OOUI Application "Look and Feel."

Each workplace may be running parallel dialogs, also called *modeless dialogs*, over parallel sessions with the server. With advanced multimedia-type applications, these parallel dialogs may be used to display images, video, multiobject folders, and voice annotated mail. Information is displayed to the user in the foreground windows, while background tasks are constantly moving information to and from servers. For example, the first page from a multimedia document is displayed in a window while a background task is busy prefetching the rest of the document from the server.

OOUIs focus on the objects required to accomplish a task. They provide folders, workareas, shadows, and associations that allow users to personalize their desktops and manage their objects. OOUIs provide a common metaphor for creating, copying, moving, connecting, and deleting any object on the desktop. One of the major features of OOUIs is the concept of multiple views of objects.

GUI VERSUS OOUI: A CLOSER LOOK

> *OOUIs allow users to work with objects that are representative of the environment they work in, rather than objects the computer understands.*
>
> — *Theo Mandel*
> *The GUI-OOUI War:*
> *Windows vs. OS/2 (VNR, 1994)*

The style of the user interface is an important issue for the client desktop. It defines the paradigm by which many applications can share a screen in a multitasking networked environment. Currently, the OS/2 Workplace Shell and NextStep are the best examples of "pure" OOUIs. The Macintosh is a hybrid—its "look and feel" is OOUI, but its underlying structure is mostly GUI. But Apple, with its OpenDoc strategy, is rapidly moving toward a document-centered OOUI approach. And the future Taligent and Chicago interfaces will be OOUIs.

OOUI: A New Paradigm for the Desktop?

The familiar GUI paradigm defines an *application-centered* user interface. This is the familiar Windows 3.X desktop in which a user interacts with a computer by starting an application from a list of programs (or icons representing them) displayed in a window. The OOUI paradigm, on the other hand, defines an *object-centered* user interface that lets users interact with the computer by manipulating visual business objects.

In an OOUI, the application is transparent to the user. The desktop is a collection of objects (icons) and windows associated with those objects, as opposed to GUIs, where the desktop is a collection of windows or icons representing windows associated with applications. In OOUI environments, the user interacts with objects rather than with the operating system or with separate programs. The interaction has the same look and feel across all tasks. The OOUI is a simulation of how users interact with objects in real life. It is a computer visual of the real-life situation.

OOUIs: Object Templates

In the OOUI environment, the users do not load programs. In fact, they're not even supposed to know what a program is. So how does anybody get any work done without programs running on a desktop? You work with objects, of course. OK, but how are these objects created? Where do they come from? Some OOUIs (for example, the Workplace Shell) provide some predefined system objects like clocks, games, shredders, and so on. The user supplements these objects with "user objects" that they create by cloning a template of an existing object. A *template* is object terminology for a cookie cutter. Instead of creating cookies, it creates identical objects. Where does the user get these templates from? The Workplace Shell provides a special folder called the *templates folder.* This folder is your "object factory." You "tear off" templates and drag them to the folder or desktop area where you want to work (see Figure 5-7). *Who creates these object templates?* The software component providers who create specialized *objectware* for a living.

So how does this objectware plug into the Workplace Shell? It is supplied to users in the form of a Dynamic Link Library (DLL) that gets placed in a subdirectory. After that is done, the new object class will automagically appear in the *templates folder* the next time it is opened. For the users, it's all fun and games from then on: *cookie cutting and cloning objects.*

Application Features: GUI Versus OOUI

The best way to compare GUIs and OOUIs is to put the two side-by-side and contrast some of their features. Let's go back to Figures 5-5 and 5-6, the GUI and OOUI vintages of our Club Med application.[1] By just looking at these two pictures, can you tell what the OOUI fuss is all about?

---

[1] The GUI Club Med was developed in the first edition of our book **Client/Server Programming with OS/2**. The OOUI Club Med was developed for the second and third editions of the same book. It's a true Workplace Shell application.

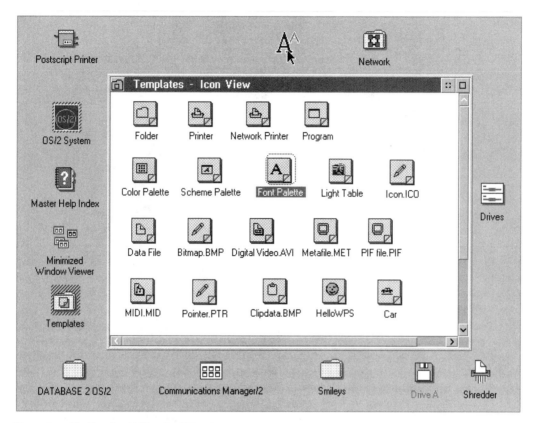

Figure 5-7. The Template Folder: An Object Factory.

■ The OOUI Club Med is an extension of the operating system's user interface. You can't tell where the application starts and the OS desktop ends. They appear to be seamlessly integrated.

■ The OOUI Club Med invites the user to manipulate the visual Club Med objects through drag-and-drop. For example, a transaction may be triggered by dragging a guest object to the shredder to delete it. Or, if we want to be kind, we'll drop it on the FAX machine icon to send a confirmation of the reservation.

■ The OOUI Club Med icon can be opened at any time to reveal a notebook view of the information inside it. The notebook control makes it possible to visually staple together many dialog windows and let the user find the information needed. This is a giant step forward for OLTP-type of applications.

■ The OOUI Club Med setup will reappear the way the user left it when the machine is turned on again. The desktop configuration is persistent.

■ The OOUI Club Med is very familiar, especially to kids. It feels like a video game. Kids feel quite at home with drag and drop, icons, and direct manipulation. The OOUI is a simulation of reality that they can easily recognize. Can we say the same about adults?

■ The OOUI Club Med can be extended to seamlessly work with any other OOUI object (with very little new code). We could easily think of mail-enabling it or allowing scanned pages to be dragged into the notebook view. The OLTP transaction is starting to look more like its real-world counterpart.

■ The GUI Club Med, on the other hand, is your typical WIMP (Windows, Icons, Mouse, and Pointer) interface. The icon is just there to represent the application to the desktop. You're not invited to play with it. You start the application by clicking on the icon. From then on, you're in menu land. The user is quite aware that there is a running Club Med application.

Table 5-1 provides a detailed summary of the features that distinguish OOUIs from GUIs.

Table 5-1. GUI Versus OOUI.

Feature	Graphical User Interface (GUI)	Object-Oriented User Interface (OOUI)
Application structure	A graphic application consists of an icon, a primary window with a menu bar, and one or more secondary windows. The focus is on the main task. Ancillary tasks are supported by secondary windows and pop-ups. Users must follow the rigid task structure (and may get trapped in a task). An application represents a task.	A graphic application consists of a collection of cooperating user objects. Everything that you see is an object. Each object is represented by an icon and has at least one view. Objects can be reused in many tasks. The application's boundaries are fuzzy. The user defines what's an application by assembling a collection of objects. These objects may come from one or more programs and are integrated with the desktop objects the system provides (like printers and shredders). The users can innovate and create their own "lego-like" object collections.
Icons	Icons represent a running application.	Icons represent objects that may be directly manipulated.
Starting an application	Users start applications before selecting an object to work with.	Users open the object on the desktop, which causes a window view of the object to be displayed.
Windows	Users open a primary window and then specify the objects they want to interact with. The same window can be used to display other objects.	A window is a view of what's inside an object. There is a one-to-one relationship between a window and an object.
Menus	Menus provide the primary method for navigating within an application.	Each object has a context menu. You navigate within an application or across applications by directly manipulating objects. The desktop functions as one big menu; icons represent the objects that you can manipulate.
Active application visual	Icons represent minimized windows of active applications.	Icons are augmented with the *in-use* emphasis to represent an active object.
Direct manipulation	An application may provide direct manipulation on an ad hoc basis.	Objects are created, communicated with, moved, and manipulated through drag-and-drop manipulation.
Creating new objects	Objects are created in an application-specific manner, usually through some form of copy mechanism or using the menu choices: new or open.	A templates folder contains a template for every object type. To create a new instance of an object, drag its template to where you want the new object to reside.

Table 5-1. GUI Versus OOUI. (Continued)

Feature	Graphical User Interface (GUI)	Object-Oriented User Interface (OOUI)
Actions	Choose object; then choose action from menu bar.	In addition to choosing actions from menus, a user can drag objects to icons to perform operations, for example, drag a file to a printer icon.
Containers	Text-based list boxes provide the primary form of containment.	In addition to list boxes, OOUIs provide container objects, including folders and notebooks. These in turn can contain other objects. Actions performed on container objects affect all the objects inside them.
Focus	Focus is on the main task.	Focus is on active objects and tasks.
Who is in Control?	Control alternates between the user and the application.	All the applications behave the same and the user acts as the conductor. Think of the user as the visual programmer of the desktop.
Product Examples	Windows and Motif.	OS/2 Workplace Shell, NextStep, Macintosh, and the future Chicago and Taligent.

WHAT DOES A CLIENT NEED FROM AN OS?

Each of the three types of clients described here place a different set of requirements on the operating system. These requirements are listed in Table 5-2. As you can see, all client applications need some mechanism to communicate service requests and files to a server. All three client categories will function best in a robust, multitasking environment. It is particularly important for the client environment to be robust because it is impossible for system providers to test the client software on all possible hardware/software combinations (you can't dictate what people run on their PCs). It is important to use an operating system that can protect programs from clashing and crashing. No client program should cause the system to hang (requiring a reboot).

GUI and OOUI clients work best with a thread-like mechanism for handling the background requests. By using separate threads for the user interface and background processing, the program can respond to user input while a separate thread handles the interaction with the server. This is how GUIs avoid the notorious "hourglass" icon, a sure sign that the computing environment is not keeping up with the human. Threads also help clients respond to asynchronous calls from a server (callback). Priority-based preemptive multitasking is also required to respond to multimedia devices and to create client applications where multiple dialogs are displayed in parallel.

Table 5-2. What Does a Client Need From an OS?

Requirement from an OS	Non-GUI Client		Simple GUI Client	OOUI Client
	Without Multitasking	With Multitasking		
Request/reply mechanism (preferably with local/remote transparency)	Yes	Yes	Yes	Yes
File transfer mechanism to move pictures, text, database snapshots	Yes	Yes	Yes	Yes
Preemptive multitasking	No	Yes	Desirable	Yes
Task Priorities	No	Yes	Desirable	Yes
Interprocess communications	No	Yes	Desirable	Yes
Threads for background communications with server and receiving callbacks from servers	No	Yes	Yes (unless you like the hourglass icon)	Yes
OS robustness including intertask protection and reentrant OS calls	No	Yes	Desirable	Yes
Window 3.X GUI (CUA '89 vintage) with menus, scroll bars, and so on	No	No	Yes	Yes
OOUI framework, object-based interactions, drag and drop, multimedia support, OS/2 Workplace Shell, or NextStep vintage	No	No	No	Yes

CLIENT/SERVER HYBRIDS

Another point to consider is that the industry is moving beyond the pure client/server model. This is because more intelligence (and data) is moving onto the client. Database clients keep snapshots of tables locally. TP Monitor clients coordinate multiserver transactions. Groupware clients maintain queues. Multimedia clients check-in and check-out folders. And distributed object clients accept requests from objects anywhere. These "new age" clients must provide a "server lite" function—an interim step toward fulfilling the post-scarcity vision of a full client and server function on every machine.

A "server lite" function is a thread, queue, or background process on the client machine that can accept *unsolicited* network requests—usually from a server. For example, a server may call its clients to synchronize locks on a long duration transaction, refresh a database snapshot, or recall a checked-out multimedia document. A "server lite" (as opposed to a full-blown server) does not need to support concurrent access to shared resources, load balancing, or multithreaded communications. We call clients that provide a "server lite" function *hybrids* (as opposed to pure).

The Future Is OOUI

Soapbox

An OOUI *utilizes a GUI for its set of componentry but adds to it significant semantic content on the meaning of objects and user gestures.*

— *John Tibbets*
Keynote Address, OOPSLA 1991

OOUIs are the up-and-coming trend in user interfaces. The next generation of Windows from Microsoft—Chicago and Cairo—is rumored to be "pure" OOUI. Why is Microsoft going OOUI when it has the world's most popular GUI product? Can the answer have something to do with "information at your fingertips" or is it related to multimedia data types? Taligent's interface is also rumored to be pure OOUI. And a future version of COSE will move the "unified" Unix desktop to OOUI (but not in the first release). So why is everybody moving to OOUI?

OOUIs provide a more natural front-end for client/server applications. They provide the *framework* for integrating objects from different vendors at the visual level. OOUIs are the visual part of the object paradigm. Visual objects will replace application suites as the way to integrate the desktop. Applications, as we currently know them, will no longer be built. Instead, software will be provided as object *components* that plug-and-play into an OOUI *framework*.

OOUIs offer many benefits to end users and to object component vendors. If you want to get the inside scoop on the "GUI versus OOUI," we recommend Theo Mandel's excellent book, **The GUI-OOUI War: Windows Versus OS/2** (VNR, 1994). You'll get a cognitive psychologist's viewpoint of how humans interact with computer user interfaces, and you'll also learn the relative "psychological" merits of OOUI versus GUI. Our opinion (we're on the Soapbox, remember) is that once you start using an OOUI, there's no going back to GUIs.

So why aren't OOUIs everywhere? This is Theo Mandel's answer: "Probably the biggest drawback to the OOUI is that it really requires a paradigm shift from many of today's GUI products. It is a strange situation, but because the popular GUIs don't mirror the real world very well, it takes time for users of these systems to get used to something that more closely matches the way they work in the real world. Strange but true!" ❑

BETTING YOUR BUSINESS ON AN OS PLATFORM

To choose an operating system platform, you must first decide which mass computer market (or culture) you're going to play in. A computer mass market provides distribution channels, a support infrastructure, user groups, mass publications, trade shows, complementary products, and large installed bases of users that are potential customers for your product. Here are the leading contenders:

■ **The PC world** includes all types of Intel-based machines that run DOS (and its variants), Windows 3.X, OS/2, Windows NT, and NetWare. PCs are ubiquitous in the business world.

■ **The Macintosh world** is strongly entrenched in certain sectors of the business world (among writers, illustrators, and marketing departments).

■ **The Unix world**, in all its variants and hardware platforms, is the world of engineering workstations and power users.

■ **The supermini world** includes DEC hardware and VMS-based solutions, the AS/400, scalable Unix systems like Sequent and Pyramid, and specialized systems like Tandem's NonStop computers.

■ **The mainframe world** is dominated by IBM's MVS hosts.

Going through the motions of picking a client/server platform is a good mental exercise. It helps sharpen our understanding of the issues and platform trade-offs. In the "real world," things are not black and white. There are no hermetically sealed computer worlds at the intergalactic client/server level. And very few machines started life as green-field client/server systems—most of the world's computers, even the PCs, are "legacy systems." You'll typically be dealing with heavy doses of platform mixing. Luckily, client/server middleware is starting to become the *cross-platform unifier.* So, once you're fully proficient with one platform, you'll be able to work with the next one without too much sweat. In the meantime, diversity is what makes client/server so much fun.

Chapter 6

Servers: Reaching for the Limits

All things...are aggregations of atoms that dance and by their movements create sounds. When the rhythm of the dance changes, the sound it produces also changes...Each atom perpetually sings its song, and the sound, at every moment, creates dense and subtle forms.

> — A Tibetan Lama,
> From Alexandra David-Neel's
> Tibetan Journey

In this chapter, we explore the question of server upward scalability. Most LANs in operation today have less than 50 clients. A normal PC server can handle these situations without too much effort. The trend, however, is to put more PCs on the LAN. At some point, we will have to answer the question: When does a server run out of steam?

SERVER SCALABILITY

What are the upper limits of servers? The limits really depend on the type of service required by their clients. One safe rule is that clients will always want more services, so scalable servers are frequently an issue. Figure 6-1 shows the different levels of escalation in server power. It starts with a single PC server that reaches its limits with the top-of-the-line processor and I/O power. The next level of server power is provided by superservers populated with multiprocessors. If that is not enough power, the client/server model allows you to divide the work among different servers. These multiservers know no upper limits to power. But they must know how to work together.

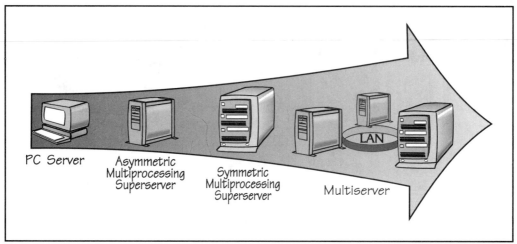

Figure 6-1. The PC Server Scalability Story.

RISC VERSUS INTEL

At the heart of each PC is at least one Intel microprocessor that is a key factor in determining how fast that machine will run. Will Intel deliver enough power to fuel servers? Or, is it time to move on to *RISC* (Reduced Instruction Set Computer) technology? RISC has traditionally been available only in the Unix workstation market such as Sun's SPARC and IBM's RS/6000 series. But this is now changing. Microsoft's Windows NT operating system supports Intel as well as the MIPS R4000 and Alpha. The IBM Microkernel will allow Taligent and the Workplace OS (with the OS/2 personality and others) to run on Intel and a variety of RISC engines. Tandem's NonStop systems use MIPS R4400s. Macintoshes are now offered on PowerPC. RISC architectures place only the most used instructions in hardware. This results in smaller chips that allow the introduction of a new generation of processors with double the performance every sixteen months, on average. Vendors of RISC microprocessors believe that they have an insurmountable advantage over Intel's Complex Instruction Set Computer (CISC) 80X86 family.

Intel, however, claims that it is working on three generations of microprocessors at the same time. Its Pentium processor uses a *superscalar RISC* technology that comes close to matching the performance of the best of today's RISC processors. Intel, which is outshipping all competitive microprocessors at a ratio of 100 to 1, is known for its continuous breakthroughs in process technology. Intel claims that it is accelerating the rate of its performance upgrades; it should be able to keep up with most of its RISC competitors. PC servers have indeed come a long way. For example, the power of a Pentium today is equivalent to that of a top-of-the-line mainframe, circa 1990. But this is not the entire story. We can do better than wait for future speed improvements in processor technology by exploiting multiprocessing and parallel architectures, which are the topics of the next section.

MULTIPROCESSING SUPERSERVERS

If you need more server power, you'll be looking at a new generation of *superservers*. These are fully-loaded machines; they include multiprocessors, high-speed disk arrays for intensive I/O, and fault-tolerant features. Operating systems can enhance the server hardware by providing direct support for multiprocessors. With the proper division of labor, multiprocessors should improve job throughput and server application speeds. A multiprocessor server is upwardly scalable. Users can get more performance out of their servers by simply adding more processors instead of additional servers. Multiprocessing comes in two flavors: asymmetric and fully symmetric (see Figure 6-2).

Asymmetric Multiprocessing

Asymmetric multiprocessing imposes hierarchy and a division of labor among processors. Only one designated processor, the master, can run the operating system at any one time. The master controls (in a tightly-coupled arrangement) slave processors dedicated to specific functions such as disk I/O or network I/O. A coprocessor is an extreme form of codependency where one processor completely controls a slave processor through interlocked special-purpose instructions. The coprocessor has unique special-purpose hardware that is not identical to the main processor. An example is a graphic coprocessor.

Symmetric Multiprocessing

Symmetric multiprocessing treats all processors as equals. Any processor can do the work of any other processor. Applications are divided into threads that can run concurrently on any available processor. Any processor in the pool can run the operating system kernel and execute user-written threads. Symmetric multiprocessing improves the performance of the application itself as well as the total throughput of the server system. Ideally, the operating system should support symmetric

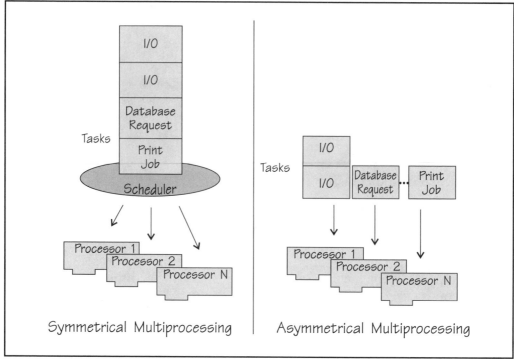

Figure 6-2. Symmetric and Asymmetric Multiprocessing.

multiprocessing by supplying three basic functions: a reentrant OS kernel, a global scheduler that assigns threads to available processors, and shared I/O structures. Symmetric multiprocessing requires multiprocessor hardware with some form of shared memory and local instruction caches. Most importantly, symmetric multiprocessing requires new applications that can exploit multithreaded parallelism. The few applications on the market that exploit SMP are SQL database managers such as Oracle7 and Sybase.

By the end of 1994, all the major 32-bit operating systems—including Unix, OS/2, and NT—will support symmetric multiprocessing (SMP). These operating systems will run on commodity superserver platforms; the hardware vendors have been gearing up for these OSs for quite some time. Microsoft's Windows NT Advanced Server supports up to 4 processors in SMP mode (vendor-specific drivers can support more). USL's UNIX System V Release 4 with multiprocessing extensions (SVR4MP) provides threads for parallel processing in SMP-based configurations. OSF, the other major Unix standard provider, is working on a multiprocessor microkernel based on Carnegie Mellon University's Mach kernel. Many proprietary or hardware-specific Unix multiprocessor offerings are currently available—including Sun's Sparcserver 600MP series, Banyan's VINES SMP, SCO's Unix MPX, Sequent Computers, and Pyramid Technology. In December 1993, IBM shipped the beta version of OS/2 SMP, which supports 16-processor SMP configurations on Intel.[1] IBM also demonstrated its Workplace OS running in SMP mode at Fall Comdex, 1993.

Beyond SMP, we see loosely-coupled, parallel computers like Tandem's NonStop systems and Oracle's NCube. Additionally, microkernels like Chorus may lower the barrier to entry into this select club. Their "shared-nothing" architectures eliminate the bottlenecks found in SMP architectures, allowing them to scale to hundreds or even thousands of processors, all working together.

MULTISERVERS: UNLIMITED SERVER POWER

Multiservers are used in environments that require more processing power than that provided by a single server system—either SMP or uniprocessor. The client/server model is upwardly scalable. When more processing power is needed, more servers can be added (thus creating a pool of servers). Or, the existing server machine can be traded up to the latest generation of PC superserver machine. Multiservers remove any upward limits to the growth of server power. This power can be provided by ordinary servers working in all kinds of ensembles. As we explain in later chapters, network operating system extensions like the *Distributed Computing Environment (DCE)* and TP Monitors like CICS, Encina, and Tuxedo provide the plumbing needed to create cooperating server ensembles.

---

[1] A future version of OS/2 SMP will support Intel's APIC chip. Intel will announce an SMP standard in 1994 based on APIC. Currently, each SMP port must be handcrafted for a PC superserver platform. An OS-independent standard for SMP interfaces to the hardware will help commoditize SMP-based superservers (at least on Intel hardware).

Is the Move to RISC Inevitable?

Soapbox

Commodity Intel-based servers supplemented with SMP are powerful enough to handle more than 90% of client/server application needs. These servers can run ordinary PC software and have a strong affinity with clients. The current breed of 32-bit OSs are finally taking advantage of the Intel hardware. It's not clear that there's a pressing need to move to RISC. The next step in servers and OSs will be support for megaclusters. Servers can also take advantage of loosely coupled multiservers using TP Monitor technology.

So where does RISC fit in this scenario? It will mostly be used for non-Intel applications that run natively on RISC. For example, Apple is in the midst of a huge software conversion to PowerPC exploitive applications. What is gained by going to RISC? Smaller chip footprints, less power consumption, and perhaps lower prices. If nothing else, it spurs some competition with Intel, which should help push prices down. IBM is reportedly developing a version of its PowerPC RISC chip that interprets X86 instructions and can run Intel Software at the same performance as a 66 MHz Pentium (Source: **PC Week**, February 14, 1994). If IBM succeeds, Intel may face some tough competition from the PowerPC. But according to PC Week, that won't happen till mid-1995; so don't hold your breath waiting. ❑

Chapter 7

The OS Wars

> *We love them all equally and we hate them all equally. Our strategy is operating system agnosticism.*
>
> — *Jim Manzi, Chairman of Lotus Corp.*
> *(March 22, 1993)*

Picking a client/server platform is not an easy task. New operating systems for the desktop seem to be sprouting like weeds, while older operating systems are fragmenting into mutant "sibling" variants. This is not necessarily bad news for the client/server architecture model, which thrives on diversity. However, it can be bad news if you're trying to develop a software product and you end up picking the wrong client/server platform.

If you think about it, the client/server market really has three key players—Novell, Microsoft, and IBM—and hundreds of niche players. The three key players are each trying to enlist the largest number of niche players to join their camp. Novell is a key player because it controls Unix, NetWare, and the low-end channel through a huge army of certified NetWare distributors. Microsoft controls the desktop (via DOS and Windows) and volume distribution channels. IBM controls the largest

sales and systems integration channel in the computer business, and its products cover every facet of client/server computing. Niche players include server vendors of all stripes, database vendors, middleware providers, horizontal application houses, system integrators, consultants, and so on.

Integration and Channels Are Key

Warning

The systems integration and distribution channels are very important to the success of client/server computing. This industry knows how to sell and support shrink-wrapped packages (commodities) and mainframes (the long sales cycle). We're having a very hard time selling client/server solutions that need some handholding and at the same time consist of commodity-like components. ❑

WHICH CLIENT?

The client is probably the single most important component in client/server. Whoever controls the client is, at least, halfway there. Will Microsoft control the client automatically because it controls today's desktop? You may remember from our client requirements in Chapter 5, "Clients, Servers, and Operating Systems," that client OSs need to be robust and multithreaded. Though ubiquitous, DOS and Windows do not make very good client platforms. Their poor little computer brains are too weak to give us what it takes to build universal clients and fulfill the vision of post-scarcity client/server computing where each machine is both a client and a server. For client/server computing to unleash its potential, we must move to 32-bit client platforms with full multithreaded support, robust memory management, and preemptive multitasking. Microsoft understands this and is working on Chicago. (NT is too resource-intensive for the average client. According to Forrester Research, the capacity of the typical corporate PC is 8 MBytes of RAM and 60 MBytes of hard disk; NT requires twice that amount.) Novell also understands this and is proposing the shrink-wrapped UnixWare—a heroic first try. And there is OS/2, which had an installed base of over 4 million at the end of 1993; this is the largest installed base of any 32-bit OS.

As you can see in Figure 7-1, OS/2 goes lower in the spectrum than any other 32-bit client platform, requiring just 6 MBytes of memory. It's hard for any operating system platform to beat OS/2's robust and seamless integration of all DOS, MS-Windows, and OS/2 environments in its Workplace Shell. In addition, OS/2's advanced 32-bit features, preemptive multitasking, and page-based virtual memory are ideal for multimedia applications. OS/2's main competition as a client platform comes

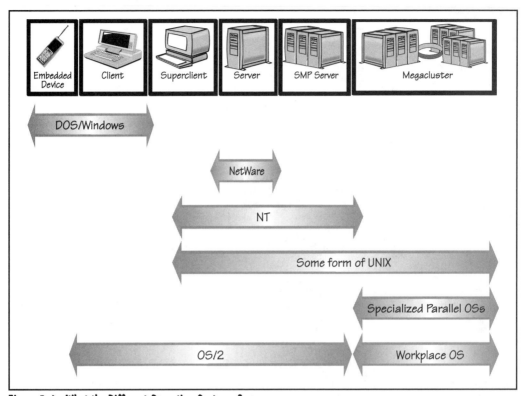

Figure 7-1. What the Different Operating Systems Cover.

from the extreme low end of the PC spectrum: DOS and Windows 3.X. DOS and Windows will continue to rule supreme in non-demanding client environments. Microsoft's Chicago (expected in 1995) will be OS/2's main challenger for dominance of the 32-bit client marketplace. The question is whether OS/2 can create an irreversible critical mass market share *before* Chicago ships, and then run a Chicago personality from within OS/2 *after* Chicago ships.

But what about desktop Unix? So far, the desktop has been almost a Unix-free zone. In an industry that numbers desktop systems in tens of millions, desktop Unix sales are in the noise level. At the end of 1993, the Solaris installed base stood at 15,000 copies; UnixWare stood at 30,000 (Source: **PC Week**, February 14, 1994). These numbers are not enough to attract vendors of desktop applications. You still can't call an 800 number or walk into your local Egghead store and buy standard Unix. Installing Unix is a chore; Unix SVR4.2 requires 93 diskettes (versus 18 for OS/2, which is still a lot). Unix is also tough to administer and can easily intimidate your average desktop user. And finally, Unix's limited market means that common desktop software, when available, is 2-3 times more expensive than standard PC software.

NextStep is a heroic effort to bring Unix to the desktop. Its user interface is even more OOUI-like than OS/2s Workplace Shell, and it has superb graphics to boot. However, NextStep's advanced capability does not come cheap. It requires a 486 (or above), 24 MBytes of RAM (for 16-bit color), 120 MBytes of disk space, and it retails for $795. So NextStep is not your average client platform, but it's nice.

WHICH SERVER?

Figure 7-1 shows that the competition is fierce on the server front. The most serious competitors in the low-end server range are NetWare 4.0, OS/2, NT Advanced Server, and the Unix on Intel variants. In the mid-range server front, the competition is Unix, OS/2 SMP, and NT (NetWare drops out because it does not provide SMP support). Finally, in the high-end server range, NT and OS/2 (without the Microkernel) drop out; but any mainframe or supermini worth its salt that can act as a server to PCs is a potential competitor. The most serious competitors are the RISC mainframe vendors that can provide massively parallel computing, scalability, and/or fault tolerance (for example, Tandem, Pyramid, Stratus, and Sequent). The new parallel, MVS-based IBM mainframes—with their transaction engines, enterprise-based system management, and large databases—are also formidable competitors.

NetWare as a Server

By a big margin, the largest server installed base belongs to Novell's NetWare. NetWare is a very fast, effective, well-supported file server. NetWare also makes a good database server for decision-support applications. There are NetWare-based DBMSs from nine popular database vendors. However, NetWare is running out of steam. To become a general-purpose application server vendor, Novell needs to find a way to open its server platform. To try to address this problem, Novell introduced *NetWare Loadable Modules (NLMs)* in NetWare 3.1, which are special name spaces set aside on the server that allow programmers to provide new system services (i.e., write applications). The NLM server modules you create get loaded by NetWare to manage these name spaces. Your NLMs, in effect, become part of the NetWare operating system kernel. Novell provides tools and a programming environment for the development of NLMs.

But while they open NetWare up to application development, NLMs have become the Achilles' heel of NetWare. They have been slow to catch on with third-party developers who are used to writing applications for conventional server operating systems such as Unix and OS/2. Here's some of the problems with NLMs that make it very difficult (if not impossible) to use NetWare as a general-purpose application server platform:

■ *Lack of memory protection.* NLM applications in NetWare 3.1 are not memory protected. They operate in Ring 0, which is reserved for the operating system. A bug in an application can bring the whole system down. The applications and the NetWare OS can conflict, causing NLMs to crash unpredictably and without resolution. NetWare 4.0 partially alleviates the problem by providing optional memory protection. Novell gives users the option of running NLMs outside of Ring 0 (with 20% performance degradation). The tradeoff is one of speed versus a slightly higher level of memory protection—if an application crashes in the "protected domain," it still brings down the Ring 3 applications but not NetWare itself. NT, OS/2, and all Unix variants provide bullet-proof memory protection.

■ ***Lack of memory management.*** NetWare treats all memory as one flat segment. It does not support virtual memory services, a standard service in conventional operating systems such as NT, OS/2, and Unix. The lack of virtual memory (that is, no support for paging code in and out of memory) limits the number of NetWare applications that can run on a server. Developers must worry about memory conflicts, which are always a real danger in NetWare.

■ ***Lack of preemptive multitasking.*** NetWare will not interrupt a running application to allow one with higher priority to run. A misbehaved application that runs for a long time (such as a batch job) can cause problems for everybody else. Developers are responsible for structuring and managing the priority of running tasks within the NLMs they create. NT, OS/2, and most Unix variants support preemptive multitasking.

■ ***Limited programming tools***. With NLMs, you are dependent on a Novell-specific programming environment. OS/2 and Unix support a very rich general-purpose programming environment with compilers available from all major vendors.

NLMs evolved as ad hoc tools that allow non-Novell vendors to extend the NetWare platform. They do not provide the robustness you expect from general-purpose operating systems such as OS/2 or Unix. According to Richard Finkelstein, NetWare's non-preemptive status puts too much of the burden on the application developer because it requires applications to be bug free, "a virtual impossibility with the complexity of software we are talking about."[1] To ease some of the NLM problems and help prevent conflicts between software, Novell established an NLM certification program. In general, it's not a good idea to run application NLMs on the same machine that provides the file or database servers. Some people even recommend that you only run one NLM on each server, but that's untenable.

Novell's acquisition of USL may be an admission that it needs a general-purpose programming platform such as Unix to become a major player in the application server market. With Novell as the proud owner of USL, NetWare is sure to become an integral part of Unix (or vice versa). But in the meantime, how will Novell position NetWare as an application development platform? They can't just openly say, "NLMs are bad for applications…move on to UnixWare."

---

[1] Richard Finkelstein is president of *Performance Computing, Inc.*, a Chicago-based database consulting firm.

NT as a Server

Windows NT Advanced Server makes an excellent departmental server platform. NT is Windows-friendly, secure, and scales up through SMP. It is also easy to install and use. NT Advanced Server is an attractively priced package that sets a new bar for PC servers. In many ways, NT is an ideal server system for PCs—it removes most of the system limits, supports symmetric multiprocessing, and provides a familiar user interface. The Win32 programming environment and tools are familiar to programmers versed in Microsoft tools. So we can expect to see some great server applications appear some day on the NT. There are a few issues with NT, though, when you start comparing it with rival server platforms like NetWare, Unix, and OS/2:

■ *NT Advanced Server is slow and bulky as a file server.* NT Advanced Server is slower than NetWare, Microsoft's LAN Manager, and IBM's LAN Server; it also eats up a lot more resources. **PC Week** (August 16, 1993) published benchmark results that show NT Advanced Server to be considerably slower than NetWare 3.11 as a file server, and it needed 4-8 MBytes more memory. According to *LANQuest LABs*, an independent test lab, IBM's OS/2 LAN Server 3.0 is 45% faster than NT Advanced Server.[2]

■ *NT's SMP does not scale well.* NT's version of SQL Server got good reviews as a high-performance database. However, when it came to Symmetric Multi-processing (SMP) scalability, *ZD Labs* discovered that NT running SQL Server can only deliver an 85% increase in throughput using a 4-CPU machine.[3] In this case, Microsoft makes both the operating system and the database server, so the two are optimally integrated. The 4-CPU results show that NT's SMP is far from delivering linear scalability, even with a thread-intensive application like SQL Server.

■ *NT does not support a command language.* System administrators found NT's lack of support for a batch command language to be a major nuisance.

■ *NT lacks support channels.* As a server, NT is competing in a marketplace where training, installation, support, system integration, and client/server skills are critical for the success of the product. An advanced server platform requires

---

[2] Source: **LANQuest** (October, 1993). According to the LANQuest report, "NT's performance fell off significantly after more than 100 users. Above this load, too few clients completed the test to produce valid results. Microsoft's LAN Man 2.2 on OS/2 was able to do 200 equivalent users, but fell apart at 300. OS/2's LAN Server was tested successfully at 300 and 400 users. Overall, OS/2's LAN Server 3.0 supported up to 4 times the number of users and 2.4 times the peak throughput of Microsoft Windows NT Advanced Server."

[3] Source: **PC Week** (September 13, 1993).

a long sales cycle and a lot of customer hand-holding. NT must learn how to coexist with every form of legacy system if it is to play a role in the enterprise. Who will provide all this system integration and support? This is an area where Microsoft is very weak. It has had practically no success with client/server or multiuser products. Microsoft's forte is shrink-wrapped products. In contrast, NetWare is supported by Novell's vast army of certified resellers who are very experienced at installing and supporting networks. OS/2 is supported by thousands of IBM system engineers who have some of the industry's best system integration skills. Unix can count on enormous pools of client/server specialists. There are more trained client/server consultants on SCO Unix alone than in all of Microsoft.

Microsoft promises to fix some of NT's shortcomings in a future upgrade called *Daytona*, expected in late 1994. In addition, Microsoft plans to deliver *Cairo* in 1995 as its strategic object-oriented server platform.

OS/2 as a Server

OS/2 also makes an excellent departmental server. It is a seasoned, 32-bit operating system with advanced multithreaded capabilities. OS/2 has been the incubator of some leading-edge server software such as Lotus Notes and the DSOM CORBA-compliant ORB. OS/2's database, middleware, and communications offerings are as rich as its Unix counterparts, but they are almost always easier to install, use, and manage. And, as a rule, they are much less expensive. OS/2 has a rich NOS environment that includes NetWare, DCE, LAN Manager, LAN Server, and a variety of Message Oriented Middleware (MOM) software. It is also one of the industry's best managed client/server platforms. As a mid-range server, OS/2's 16-processor SMP capability provides excellent scalability by making good use of threads and fully exploiting Intel hardware.

OS/2 on the IBM microkernel, with its support of multiclustered superservers, is a good candidate for replacing mainframes as a corporate backbone server. Of course, you'll have to wait until late 1994 or 1995 to get the high-end server features. But it may be worth the wait because the IBM Microkernel has some very powerful features (see the following Briefing box). So with all this seemingly exceptional functionality, what are OS/2's limitations as a server platform?

■ *Much of its high-end server functions are still "futures."* This includes C2 security, Unicode support (for internationalization), RISC support via the Workplace OS, and megaclusters.

■ *The system has its limits.* The largest file size OS/2 supports is 2 GBytes. Disk partitions are limited to 512 GBytes. These may appear like reasonable limits now, but they will hit us as we move into multimedia.

■ *There's room for improvement in the file system.* OS/2 doesn't support recoverable files with transaction protection; this feature is needed to protect data against system failures. NT, Unix, and even NetWare have this feature. Additionally, OS/2 doesn't have memory-mapped files, which treat all memory (disk and RAM) as one single address space. This feature is a double-edged sword: while it makes programming easier, it's also error-prone.

If we extend OS/2 to include the microkernel-based Workplace OS, then it appears, from a hardware viewpoint, that OS/2 has the potential to run any type of client or server application (from a laptop to clusters of superservers). OS/2 will be able to run its distributed object frameworks on top of this hardware. This will take some of the pain out of developing and maintaining client/server applications. Can OS/2 (with Workplace OS) emerge as the winner of both the client and server wars? The technology (and timing) is perfect. But OS wars are not won on technology alone. Both marketing and mindshare are key.

Do Microkernels Spell the End of OS Wars?

Briefing

Microkernels promise to provide new levels of portability in operating systems. In theory, they will allow applications written for different OSs to run on different hardware platforms by providing OS "personalities." So, everything runs on everything. To see how this works, let's look at the Mach-based IBM Microkernel for the Workplace OS family.

You can think of the Workplace OS family as a set of modular OS Legos that plug into a portable *microkernel*. The microkernel is an operating system whose inner guts were removed, thus leaving a raw skinny "kernel." But where did the "inner guts" end up? They were repackaged as modular components that can plug-and-play on top of the microkernel. These repackaged, "inner-gut" components include personality-neutral servers—such as device drivers, security services, file systems, memory managers, and network stacks—and personality servers that create an environment for running applications (see Figure 7-2).

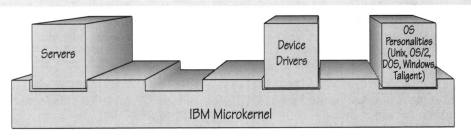

Figure 7-2. The IBM Microkernel Components.

The components work together by using a microkernel-based client/server messaging system. Clients request operating system services by invoking the services of a server (see Figure 7-3). The microkernel doesn't need to know whether the message comes from a local or remote process. Everything is kept loosely coupled, and the microkernel becomes the message-switch. The beauty is that all the clients and servers run as applications on top of the microkernel. Only the microkernel—about 50K lines of code—runs in the protected space. This makes all these services very portable.

The IBM Microkernel isolates the critical machine-dependent services from the OS components above it. As the name implies, personality-neutral servers can be shared by different operating system personalities (for example, OS/2 and Unix). This capability allows very flexible systems to be created on a single hard-

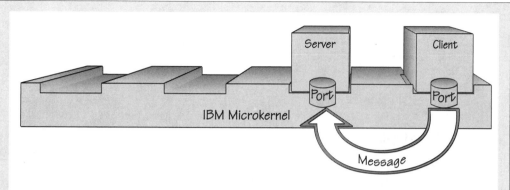

Figure 7-3. Microkernel Communications Via Ports and Messages.

ware platform. The clients for these services are typically the OS personalities, but they can also be other servers. For example, the memory manager may require the services of the file server. Leverage will be obtained by creating servers that can be reused across personalities.

The Workplace OS will run OS/2, DOS, Windows, Unix, OS/400, and Taligent applications. It does this by creating an operating system environment for each of these applications that executes the required OS services. This environment is called the operating system *personality server*. The personality servers map the OS calls to personality-neutral servers. They must also take care of any additional services required by an operating system environment.

The *dominant* personality server establishes the GUI (or OOUI) look for the entire machine. *Alternate* personalities can run their applications from the dominant personality. An alternate personality must be able to accept requests from the dominant personalities. For example, an OS/2 dominant personality will depend on Windows and Unix alternate personalities for running their respective applications. The trick is to make the alternate personalities fit seamlessly into the dominant personality's desktop. The Workplace OS intends to run the Workplace Shell—a personality-neutral server—as the seamless integrator of the desktop. Taligent will be offered as a dominant personality only. DOS and DOS/Windows will only be offered as alternate personalities. OS/2 and Unix will support both roles.

In summary, microkernels—including IBM's, OSF's Mach 3.0, and Chorus—may let you mix-and-match OS personalities and let them play on different hardware platforms. Everything will run on everything. You'll be able to logon to any machine and pick the OS personality that suits your taste and make it dominant; you can switch to subservient personalities when the need arises. It doesn't get any better. ❑

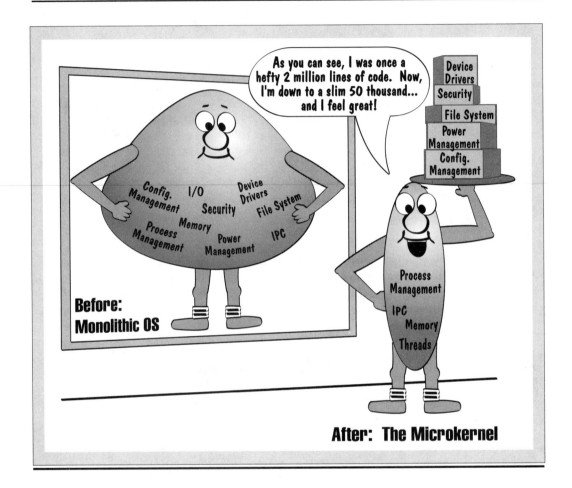

Unix as a Server

Most of the Unix variants make reasonable servers. Unix provides a seasoned, function-rich operating system that is scalable from the desktop to the supercomputer. Unix is the melting pot of the computer industry. Its close connection with universities makes it a great incubator of new ideas. Most of these ideas first appear on the commercial market as Unix extensions and variants. The Unix mainstream, on the other hand, moves a lot more cautiously. Unix can claim an army of trained programmers, integrators, and technicians.

The main problem with Unix has always been: Which Unix do you choose? At last count, there were over 40 variants of Unix on the market. Because Unix is a hardware independent operating system, an application should be able to run on any machine that supports Unix, from a PC to a Cray supercomputer. This server scalability story is very attractive, but it is not realistic. In the real world, what keeps this from happening are three factors: binary incompatibility, differences among the Unixes, and applications that are optimized for a particular operating system platform:

■ ***Lack of Binary Compatibility.*** The Unix world is different from the PC world where software comes in low-cost, shrink-wrapped floppy packages that can run on any PC clone that runs MS-DOS, Windows, or OS/2. Unlike these operating systems that are developed by one company and marketed on many types of hardware platforms, Unixes vary widely. There is still no broadly supported binary standard. Unix applications, at a minimum, have to be recompiled to be ported from platform to platform. This is a major headache and expense for software providers.

■ ***Functional Differences among the Unixes.*** There will always be differences among the Unixes: Vendors like to sell products, and functional differences are required to avoid relentless, no-win price wars. Even though X/Open's *Spec 1170*—which supports over 1,170 kernel APIs selected from the top 50 Unix applications—will be used to "brand" Unixes as such, it will only define the least common denominator functions. To get what you paid for out of a platform, you will likely need to use its extensions and lose portability.

■ ***Unix does not perform as well as a specialized operating system.*** Unix is a general purpose operating system. Unix applications are at a price/performance disadvantage against applications that were designed to take advantage of an optimized solutions-oriented operating system with a supporting hardware platform. For example, it is very hard for a database application ported to IBM's S/370 Unix (AIX) to outperform a DB2 or CICS application running on MVS, the S/370s native operating system. Or, Unix OLTP server applications on RISC cannot provide the overall price/performance of OLTP applications running on Tandem Computer's Nonstop Kernel, an operating system that is designed to exploit a loosely-coupled RISC multiprocessor network optimized for OLTP parallelism and high availability (no shared memory anywhere).

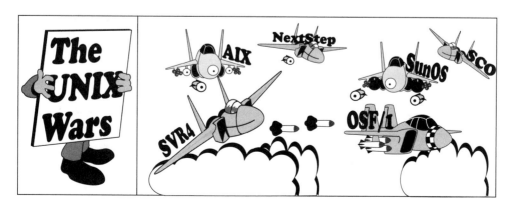

Dvorak's First Law of Client/Server

Soapbox

If you can run the same OS on both clients and servers—do it!

— John Dvorak

PC Magazine columnist John Dvorak's first law of client/server says: "If you can run the same OS on both clients and servers—do it!" Yes, it is true that client/server allows us to "mix and match," but it's simpler to avoid this. Running the same OS on both clients and servers makes LANs simpler to administer, and you can easily move programs (and functions) between clients and servers. In addition, the installation procedures, the file systems, and the interfaces to the operating system are the same on both the clients and the server. This familiar setting makes it easy for departments and small organizations to introduce client/server solutions.

Part 3
Base Middleware:
Stacks and NOSs

An Introduction to Part 3

Congratulations, you're still alive after going through the OS wars. Wasn't that exciting? Yes, Earth people are always fighting over one thing or another. That seems to be in their nature. But we're going to change the pace now and take you through some more secular terrain. Instead of fighting each other, the client/server vendors will now try to hide their differences behind a facade called the "single system image."

Now don't get us wrong. The folks you met in Part 2 are far from burying the hatchet. Instead, they're all trying to make everybody else's system look like their own. If they can't get rid of the other systems, the next best thing is to make them disappear (the politically correct term is to "make them transparent"). So how do they do that disappearing trick? By throwing layer upon layer of middleware until everything becomes one. Now that's magic!

Part 3 is about the base middleware that is used to create the "single system illusion." We will start with a brief tutorial on *Network Operating System (NOS)* middleware. You'll discover the "bag of tricks" NOSs use to create illusions that would put to shame the great Houdini himself—that's one of our better magicians who lived on Earth not too long ago. There were no NOSs in Houdini's time.

After exploring the NOSs, we go into the *stacks* middleware, which introduce their own repertoire of tricks. Eventually, nothing is what it appears to be. Everything gets deconstructed, reconstructed, and then repackaged so that it "appears to work" with everything else. But you'll know better, of course.

You'll soon discover that each vendor will be glad to sell you a different set of middleware products. Unfortunately, middleware does not extend its disappearing act to make the products themselves transparent. This is because middleware is a lucrative business in its own right. And when there's money to be made, nothing disappears. And we pay for the pleasure of seeing the heterogeneous world look like it's one happily integrated system. Yes, we pay for illusions on Earth. Look at our movie industry.

Finally, we will introduce you to some of the products you'll need to create the type of illusions that meet your fancy (or real needs). You can create almost any type of facade as long as you have the money to pay for it. Another important reason to look at products is to get a reality check of what's really there. The middleware vendors are practitioners of magic who, like all magicians, sometimes forget what's real. So it's essential to go behind the stage and see what's really there, at least in terms of product. We hope you'll enjoy the show.

Chapter 8

NOS: Creating the Single System Image

Single system image creates an illusion in the minds of users that all the servers on the network are part of the same system or behave like a single computer.

— Andrew Tanenbaum (1992) [1]

This chapter goes over the functions that the Network Operating System (NOS) middleware must provide to create a "single system image" of all the services on the network. As we explained earlier, this is really a Houdini-sized illusion that makes all servers of the world—we're talking about a multiserver, multiservice, multivendor, and multinetwork world—appear to the client as one big happy family. In a sense, the NOS middleware provides the glue that recreates the single system out of the disparate elements. It's a thankless job, but without it there can be no client/server computing. By the end of this chapter, you'll get a better appreciation of the "bag of tricks" that are used by clients and servers to create the *grand illusion*.

---

[1] Source: Andrew S. Tanenbaum, **Modern Operating Systems** (Prentice Hall, 1992).

NOS MIDDLEWARE: THE TRANSPARENT ILLUSION

NOSs are evolving from being a collection of independent workstations, able to communicate via a shared file system, to becoming real distributed computing environments that make the network *transparent* to users.

What Does Transparency Really Mean?

Transparency means fooling everyone into thinking the client/server system is totally seamless. It really means hiding the network and its servers from the users and even the application programmers. Here are some of the types of transparencies the NOS middleware is expected to provide as part of its "network disappearing act":

■ *Location transparency*—You should not have to be aware of the location of a resource. Users should not have to include the location information in the resource's name. For example, *Machine**directory**file* surfaces the name of the server machine. This is a transparency violation.

■ *Namespace Transparency*—You should be able to use the same naming conventions (and namespace) to locate any resource on the network. The whole universe is one big tree (see Figure 8-1). This includes every type of resource on any vendor's product.

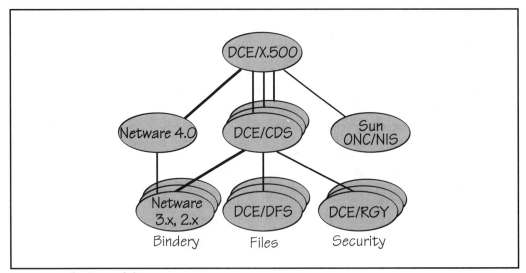

Figure 8-1. The Universal Namespace.

■ **Containment transparency**—You should be able to move resources on the servers without requiring any changes on the client. For example, you should be able to move a file from one subdirectory to another on the server and make it totally transparent to the client machines.

■ **Logon transparency**—You should be able to provide a single password (or authentication) that works on all servers and for all services on the network.

■ **Replication transparency**—You should not be able to tell how many copies of a resource exist. For example, if a naming directory is shadowed on many machines, it is up to the NOS to synchronize updates and take care of any locking issues.

■ **Distributed access transparency**—You should be able to work with any resource on the network as if it were on the local machine. The NOS must handle access controls and provide directory services.

■ **Distributed time transparency**—You should not see any time differences across servers. The NOS must synchronize the clocks on all servers.

■ **Failure transparency**—You must be shielded from network failures. The NOS must handle retries and session reconnects. It must also provide some levels of service redundancy for fault-tolerance.

■ **Administration transparency**—You should only have to deal with a single system management interface. The NOS must be integrated with the local management services.

The challenge for the NOS middleware is how to provide this high level of transparency *without sacrificing the autonomy of the local OS*.

NOS: Extending the Local OS's Reach

One of the functions of a NOS is to make the physical location of resources (over a network) transparent to an application. The early NOSs were in the business of virtualizing the file and printer resources and redirecting them to LAN-based file and print servers. These NOSs provided agents on the local machines—the *requesters*—that intercepted calls for devices and *redirected* them to servers on the LAN. The only way an application (or user) could tell the difference between a local or remote resource was from a pathname, which included its machine name. But aliases could be used to even hide the pathnames from the users. The NOS thus extends the local OSs device support transparently across the network. Practically anything that can be done on a local OS can be done remotely and transparently.

FYI

What's in a Name?

Briefing

In client/server systems, names must be unique within the context in which they are resolved (and used). You can think of a context as an autonomous naming authority. It's like the area code in the telephone system. A federated naming scheme (or *namespace*) is a conglomeration of independent naming authorities. In a federated namespace, each name must include its naming authority. For example, if you're within the US telephone naming authority, you can only call somebody in Switzerland by including the country code for Switzerland along with the person's telephone number. It's a tree-like (or hierarchical) naming scheme. If you create enough layers of hierarchy, you'll end up with a namespace that includes every communicating entity in the universe. ❑

The NOS allows applications written for the local OS to become networked without changing a line of code. Most NOSs allow clients that run on different OSs (such as DOS, Mac, and Unix) to share files and other devices. For example, a Mac client sees DOS files in the Mac format.

A new generation of network file servers promises to introduce even more transparency into the file systems. For example, the DCE *Distributed File Service (DFS)* provides a single image file system that can be distributed across a group of file servers (see Figure 8-2). The DFS file naming scheme is location-independent. Each file has a unique identifier that is consistent across the network. Files use the DCE global namespace just like the rest of the network resources. And the file system is integrated with the DCE security mechanisms.

DFS provides a *Local File System (LFS)* with many advanced features, including replication facilities that make the file system highly available. Fast response is achieved with a distributed cache. A snapshot of the file system can reside on the client, which can operate on files even if the server is down. Backups and file relocations can take place without making LFS unavailable. LFS also provides transactional log support. In case of a system crash, file records can be replayed to bring the system to a consistent state. LFS still has a few problems that need to be ironed out; but when it is ready, it will raise the bar for distributed file systems. DFS can work with other local file systems, such as NFS, or the Unix file system.

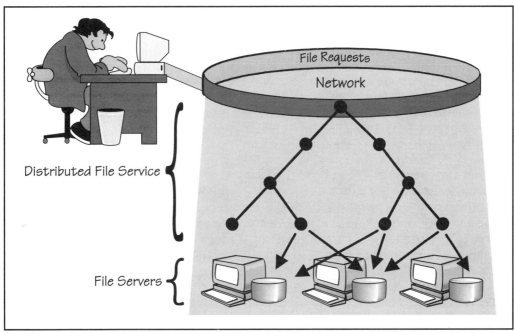

Figure 8-2. The New Generation: DCE's Distributed File Server.

A Tale of NOSs and OSs

Soapbox

Is a NOS an extension of the local OS? Or, is it a new type of distributed OS that simply grafts itself onto an existing OS? Or, is it simply middleware glue, which lives in a *no man's land* until it finds the right home? Or, is it "glue" that's working its way toward replacing the local OS? The answer is a bit of all of the above.

The early NOSs, like NetWare 2.X and LAN Manager, were mainly in the business of providing shared file and printer access to DOS machines. LAN Manager went one step further and created network extensions of Named Pipes, OS/2's local interprocess communication mechanism. With Windows NT, Microsoft went *all the way* and bundled the entire NOS (LAN Manager) with the OS. As far as Microsoft is concerned, the NOS is dead. Of course, Novell's fortunes depend on keeping the NOS separate from the OS. But when it comes to UnixWare, Novell does quite a bit of bundling itself—it currently incorporates both the Network File Server (NFS) and the NetWare client (two NOS functions) with the Operating System.

Sun Microsystems, the pioneer of the modern NOS, placed NFS in the public domain along with the Sun RPC and the *Network Information Service (NIS)*—formerly known as the yellow pages. NIS provides a secured network directory service that maps user names to encrypted passwords, as well as machine names to network addresses and other items. The NISs are replicated using a master/slave arrangement. DCE goes even further than Sun by providing an OS-independent layer of glue that includes distributed directory services, network security, RPC, threads, and distributed time. DCE is the epitome of *pure middleware*.

Eventually every resource will be virtualized. We won't be able to tell where anything resides. Clients can hide the location of the servers and make all resources appear to exist on the desktop. After all, the goal is to provide a fully transparent single system image of the universe. However, there are at least two ways to get to that goal: by introducing super NOSs (the DCE model), or by making the OSs do it all themselves (the NT model). In the meantime, until we find a smart OS that can really do *everything* for us, it is better to live with the NOSs—they provide us with more choices. ❏

Global Directory Services

Distributed applications will move information between people. To do that, they'll need a way to find people—a directory. And when applications and services—like messaging—all start using a single directory, then user management will be centralized, making your life easier.

— Jamie Lewis, Burton Group
(December 20, 1993)

The state of a client/server system is always in flux. Users join and leave the network. Services can be added and moved around at will. Data is always being created and moved around. So who keeps track of all this activity? How do clients find their servers in a constantly changing universe? Where is the single system image kept? It's kept in the NOS's directory service, of course (see Figure 8-3). This essential component tracks all the NOS's resources and knows where everything is. Without it, we would be lost. Ideally, a distributed directory should provide a single image that can be used by all network applications—including e-mail, system management, network inventory, file services, RPCs, distributed objects, databases, authentication, and security.

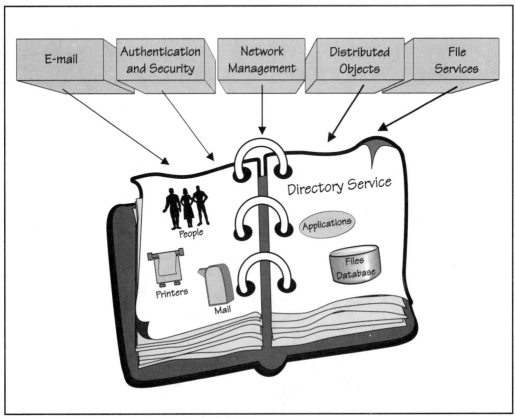

Figure 8-3. Global Directories: Keeping Track of NOS Resources.

In a modern NOS, the directory service is implemented as a distributed, replicated, object database. It is *distributed* to allow different administration domains to control their environment. It is *replicated* to provide high availability and performance where needed. Remember, if the directory is down, all the network activity comes to a grinding halt. Nothing can be found. It's an *object database* in the sense that everything that is tracked is an instance of an object class. Inheritance can be used to derive new object types.

A typical directory is implemented as a set of named entries and their associated attributes. For example, "MyServer" may be an instance of an application server type (or class). Its attributes can be: room number = 54, status = up, and CPU utilization = 54 percent. MyServer may also contain a list of the functions it exports and their interface definitions.

Modern NOS directories have APIs and user interfaces that allow programs (or humans) to locate entities on the network by querying on the name or attributes. For example, a program can issue a query to locate all the 1200-dpi printers that are not busy. If you know the name of an entity, you can always obtain its attributes. The directory service itself is a well-known address known to all the trusted users on the network (and sometimes even intruders).

How do directories maintain their autonomy in a global network environment? How do they let us create unique names on the network without bumping into each other? How do we accommodate legacy naming services? This is usually accomplished by introducing hierarchical namespaces like in a file system (see Figure 8-4). In each name, there is a *global component* and a *local component*. The global component is the name by which the local directory is known at the intergalactic level. The global component manages a federation of loosely-coupled local directories. The local component can then be named according to local conventions. In addition, a

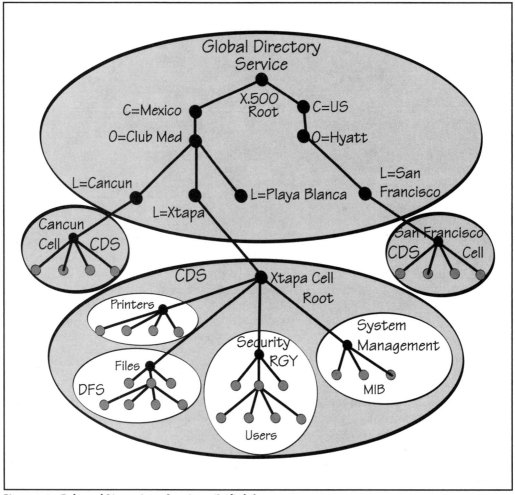

Figure 8-4. Federated Directories—Creating a Unified Namespace.

gateway agent can reside on each local directory and can forward queries for non-local names to a global directory (or naming service).

How are directories replicated? Typically, a directory maintains a master copy and read-only shadow replicas. Two types of synchronization schemes are used to refresh the replicas:

■ **Immediate Replication** causes any update to the master to be immediately shadowed on all replicas.

■ **Skulking** causes a periodic propagation (for example, once a day) to all the replicas of all changes made on the master.

In summary, the new generation of NOS directory services uses some of the most advanced distributed database and object technology to keep track of distributed system resources. The technology is flexible enough to manage and track today's coarser network entities—such as printers, users, programs, and servers—and the more fine-grained entities that are beginning to appear—such as distributed objects.

The X.500 Global Directory Standard

Briefing

Warning: This box is filled with TLAs (Three-Letter Acronyms).

The industry standard for global directories, X.500, is based on a replicated distributed database (see Figure 8-5). Programs can access the directory services using the X/Open Directory Service (XDS) API. The XDS APIs allow programs to read, compare, update, add, and remove directory entries; list directories; and search for entries based on attributes. The X/Open Management (XOM) API is used for defining and navigating through the information objects that comprise the directory. Think of XOM as an object metalanguage. Each object in an X.500 directory belongs to a class. A class can be derived from other classes. XOM provides an API for defining object classes and their attributes. XOM APIs also define basic data types such as string.

The X.500 client component—the Directory User Agent (DUA)—and server component—the Directory System Agent (DSA)—communicate using the Directory Access Protocol (DAP). Servers talk to each other using the Directory System Protocol (DSP). The DAP and DSP formats and protocols are defined in the X.500 standard and provide worldwide interoperability among directory services.

The X.500 standard was written to run on top of the OSI communication protocol. OSI is not very popular, so many implementations of X.500 cheat and use alternatives like TCP/IP or IPX/SPX. Regardless, X.500 is a standards success story. It is our best hope for finding things on intergalactic networks. Sorry for all the acronyms! ❏

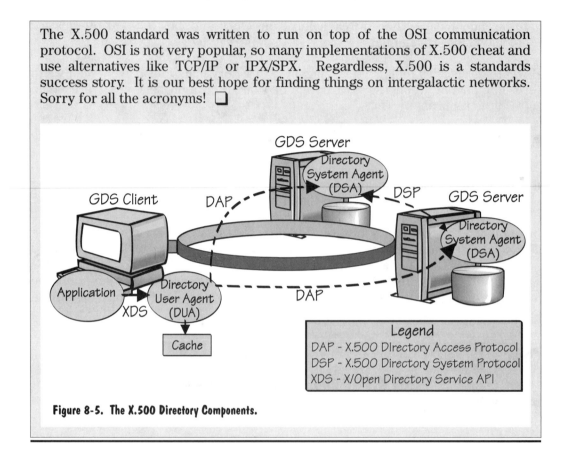

Figure 8-5. The X.500 Directory Components.

Distributed Time Services

Maintaining a single notion of time is important for ordering events that occur on distributed clients and servers. So how does a client/server system keep the clocks on different machines synchronized? How does it compensate for the unequal drift rates between synchronizations? How does it create a single system illusion that makes all the different machine clocks tick to the same time? With the NOS's distributed time services, of course.

Typically, the NOS addresses the problem of distributed time using two complementary techniques:

■ *It periodically synchronizes the clocks on every machine in the network.* The NOS typically has an agent on each machine—DCE calls it a *Time Clerk*—that asks *Time Servers* for the correct time and adjusts the local time accordingly. The agents may consult more than one Time Server, and then calculate the probable correct time and its inaccuracy based on the responses it receives. The agent can upgrade the local time either gradually or abruptly.

■ ***It introduces an inaccuracy component to compensate for unequal clock drifts that occur between synchronizations.*** The local time agents are configured to know the limits of their local hardware clock. They maintain a count of the inaccuracy factor and return it to an API call that asks for the time. The time agent requests a synchronization after the local clock drifts past an inaccuracy threshold.

As you can see, today's NOSs may have even surpassed the Swiss in their attention to intricate timing details.

Distributed Security Services

The client/server environment introduces new security threats beyond those found in traditional time-shared systems. In a client/server system, you can't trust any of the operating systems on the network to protect the server's resources from unauthorized access. And even if the client machines were totally secure, the network itself is highly accessible. Sniffer devices can easily record traffic between machines and introduce forgeries and Trojan Horses into the system. This means the servers must find new ways to protect themselves without creating a fortress mentality that upsets users.

To maintain the single system illusion, every trusted user must be given transparent access to all resources. How is that done when every PC poses a potential threat to network security? Will system administrators be condemned to spend their working lives granting access level rights to users, one at a time, for each individual application on each server across the enterprise? Let's find out what the NOSs have to offer.

Can We Obtain C2-Level Security on the LAN?

To date, no NOS has yet achieved C2 level security (but DCE may be coming close). C2 is a government security standard for operating systems which requires that users and applications be authenticated before gaining access to any operating system resource. To obtain C2 certification on a network, all clients must provide an authenticated user ID, all resources must be protected by access control lists, audit trails must be provided, and access rights must not be passed to other users that reuse the same items. Let's go over the security mechanisms a modern NOS can provide to meet (and even beat) C2 level security on the network.

- *Authentication: Are you who you claim to be?* In time-shared systems, the authentication is done by the OS using passwords. NOSs have to do better than that. Any hacker with a PC and network sniffer knows how to capture a password and reuse it. OK, so let's encrypt the password. Oh boy! Who is going to manage the secret keys and all that good stuff? Luckily, NOSs have an answer: *Kerberos*. Kerberos is the trusted third party that allows two processes to prove to each other that they are who they claim to be. It's a bit like two spies meeting on a street corner and whispering the magical code words that establish the "trust" relationship. Both parties obtain the magic words separately from Kerberos.

- *Authorization: Are you allowed to use this resource?* Once clients are authenticated, the server applications are responsible for verifying which operations the clients are permitted to perform on the information they try to access (for example, a payroll server may control access to salary data on a per-individual basis). Servers use *Access Control Lists (ACLs)* to control user access. ACLs can be associated with any computer resource. They contain the list of names (and group names) and the type of operations they are permitted to perform on each resource. NetWare's administration services, for example, make it easy for network managers to add new users to groups without having to specify access rights from scratch. NOSs can easily meet C2's ACL requirements.

- *Audit Trails: Where have you been?* Audit services allow network managers to monitor user activities, including attempted logons and which servers or files

Kerberos: "You Can't Trust Anyone"

Briefing

MIT's project Athena adopted the position that it is next to *impossible* to make sure each workstation on the network is secure. Instead, the MIT folks took it as a given that some "impersonation" would take place on the LAN and decided to protect themselves against it. The result was a software fortress called Kerberos that delivers a higher level of security than traditional passwords and access control lists. Kerberos automatically authenticates every user for every application. The Kerberos protocol, especially with the add-ons introduced by the OSF DCE, fulfills the authentication requirement of C2. It allows servers to trust their clients (mostly PCs) and vice versa. You must remember that we could always put a Trojan Horse on the server side, so the servers also need to prove their identity. ❑

are used. Audit services are a piece of the arsenal needed by network managers to detect intruders in their own organizations. For example, they can monitor all the network activity associated with a suspect client workstation (or user). Knowing an audit trail exists usually discourages insiders from tampering with servers using their own logon, but they can do it under somebody else's logon. Most NOSs support audit trails, and that should make the C2 accreditation people happy.

Also, many add-on tools are available to help secure a particular PC. For example, Mergent International's **PC/DACS** product (for DOS and OS/2) offers audit trails to monitor user activity and prevent system files (such as CONFIG.SYS and AUTOEXEC.BAT) from being altered—these are the files that start the security program. PC/DACS also offers some security against users who boot their PCs from the A: drive. In summary, it looks like "C2 security on a LAN" is well within the reach of a modern NOS, like OSF's DCE.

Can We Do "Better Than C2" on the LAN?

We need "better than C2" security when traffic moves over unsecured wide area networks. How can we guarantee that vital messages are not tampered with? You don't want the data in an electronic fund transfer to be intercepted and rerouted from your account to somebody else's. Modern NOSs, like the OSF DCE, provide at least two mechanisms for dealing with these type of situations:

■ ***Encryption*** allows two principals to hold a secure communication. Each principal must obtain a copy of a "session key" from a trusted third party (for example, a Kerberos server). This "session key" can then be used for encoding and decoding messages. Another approach is to use a public key encryption technique. But encryption may be an overkill in some situations: It introduces performance overheads and may be subject to governmental restrictions.

■ ***Cryptographic checksums***, a less extreme solution, ensure that data is not modified as it passes through the network. The sender calculates a checksum on the data, using a "session key" to encrypt it, and appends the result to the message. The receiver recalculates the checksum, decrypts the one received in the message using the "session key," and then compares the two. If they don't match, the message is suspect. Without the "session key," intruders will not be able to alter the data and update the checksum.

Single Logon Makes it Easier for the User

Users are already complaining about having to do multiple logons to different servers and resource managers. Modern NOSs provide the technology that allows a user to access any server resource from anywhere—including hotel rooms, offices, homes, and cellular phones—using a single signon. How's that done? With Kerberos-like security, of course. You simply log on once (see Figure 8-6) get authenticated, and then obtain a set of security tickets (also called tokens) for each server with which you want to communicate. All this activity is conducted under-the-cover by the NOSs security agents. No password is stored in the login script on the client, and no telephone callbacks are required. It doesn't get any easier, as long as you can remember your password.

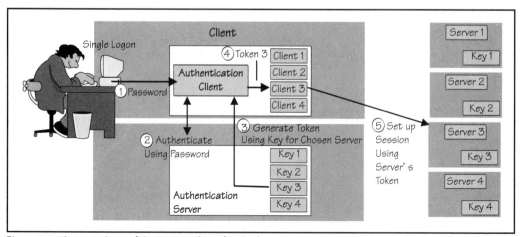

Figure 8-6. Logon to One and Get to Everything You Need.

Chapter 9

RPC, Messaging, and Peer-to-Peer

Good middleware protects the application from the different networking layers and even from the different sets of hardware.

— Leslie Yeamans,
VP System Strategies, Inc.
November, 1993

Client/server applications are split across address spaces, physical machines, networks, and operating systems. How do clients and servers talk to each other? How are the requests and responses synchronized? How are the dissimilar data representations on different computers handled? What happens if one of the parties is unavailable? You guessed it: The modern NOS is taking on a lot of these responsibilities. It comes with the territory. The purpose of the NOS is to make distributed computing transparent. This means it must create an environment that hides the nastiness of dealing with communication protocols, networks, and stacks.

All NOSs offer *peer-to-peer* interfaces that let applications communicate using "close to the wire" send/receive semantics. Most NOSs provide some form of *Remote Procedure Call (RPC)* middleware that hides "the wire" and makes any server on the network appear to be one function call away. An alternative type of model—message queuing or simply, *Message-Oriented Middleware (MOM)*—is gaining new converts. It turns out that messaging is incredibly helpful in situations where you do not want the clients and servers to be tightly synchronized. The current NOSs don't include MOM in their offerings. However, some very powerful product offerings are available from companies that specialize in this field. Let's take a closer look at what each type of interface has to offer.

PEER-TO-PEER COMMUNICATIONS

The peer-to-peer communication model is used to create both cooperative and client/server applications. The term "peer-to-peer" indicates that the two sides of a communication link use the same protocol interface to conduct a networked conversation. Any computer can initiate a conversation with any other computer. The protocol tends to be symmetric, and it is sometimes called "program-to-program." The peer-to-peer interface tends to be "close to the wire" in the sense that it does not fully mask the underlying network from the programmer. For example, the interface will surface transmission timeouts, race conditions, and network errors, and then leave it to the programmer to handle. We will have more to say about the peer-to-peer API offerings when we discuss stacks in the next chapter.

REMOTE PROCEDURE CALL (RPC)

RPCs hide the intricacies of the network by using the ordinary procedure call mechanism familiar to every programmer. A client process calls a function on a remote server and suspends itself until it gets back the results. Parameters are passed like in any ordinary procedure. The RPC, like an ordinary procedure, is synchronous. The process (or thread) that issues the call waits until it gets the results. Under the covers, the RPC run-time software collects values for the parameters, forms a message, and sends it to the remote server. The server receives the request, unpacks the parameters, calls the procedure, and sends the reply back to the client.

While RPCs make life easier for the programmer, they pose a challenge for the NOS designers who supply the development tools and run-time environments. Here's some of the issues they face:

- *How are the server functions located and started?* At a minimum, somebody's got to provide a run-time environment that starts a server process when a remote invocation is received, passes it the parameters, and returns the response. But what happens when multiple clients go after the same function? Is each function packaged as a process? Pretty soon you discover that an entire environment is needed to start and stop servers, prioritize requests, perform security checks, and provide some form of load balancing. It also becomes quickly obvious that threads are much better at handling these incoming requests than full-blown processes. And it is better to create a server loop that manages a pool of threads waiting for work rather than create a thread for each incoming request. What is really needed on the server side is a full-blown *TP Monitor*. This is, of course, a lot more function than what the current NOSs provide.

■ *How are parameters defined and passed between the client and the server?* This is something NOSs do quite well. The better NOSs provide a *Network Interface Definition Language (NIDL)* for describing the functions and parameters that a server exports to its clients. A *NIDL compiler* takes these descriptions and produces source code stubs (and header files) for both the client and server (Figure 9-1). These stubs can then be linked with the client and server code. The client stub packages the parameters in an RPC packet, converts the data, calls the *RPC run-time library*, and waits for the server's reply. On the server side, the server stub unpacks the parameters, calls the remote procedure, packages the results, and sends the reply to the client.

■ *How are failures handled?* Because both sides of the RPC can fail separately, it is important for the software to be able to handle all the possible failure combinations. If the server does not respond, the client side will normally block, time out, and retry the call. The server side must guarantee *only once semantics* to make sure that a duplicate request is not re-executed. If the client unexpectedly dies after issuing a request, the server must be able to undo the effects of that transaction. Most NOSs provide connection-oriented and connectionless versions of their RPCs. If you need a more robust environment, use the connection-oriented RPC.

■ *How is security handled by the RPC?* Modern NOSs make it easy to automatically incorporate their security features into the RPC. All you need to specify is the level of security required (authentication, encryption, etc.) and the RPC and security feature will cooperate to make it happen.

■ *How does the client find its server?* The association of a client with a server is called *binding*. The binding information may be hardcoded in the client (for example, some services are performed by servers with *well-known* addresses). Or a client can find its server by consulting a configuration file or an environment parameter. A client can also find its server at run time through the network directory services. The servers must, of course, advertise their services in the directory. The process of using the directory to find a server at run time is called *dynamic binding*. The easiest way to find a server is let the RPC do it for you. This is called *automatic binding*, meaning that the RPC client stub will locate a server from a list of servers that support the interface. Finally, clients may use a broadcast method to indicate that they want a particular service done. The

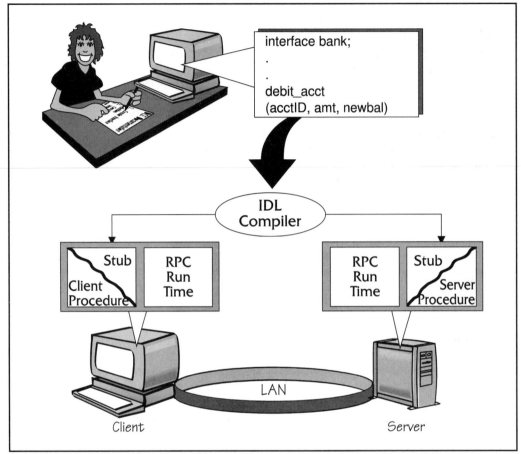

Figure 9-1. The Mechanics of an RPC Stub Compiler.

servers then respond by bidding for the job. While bidding sounds like a great idea, it is rarely used in practice.

- **How is data representation across systems handled?** The problem here is that different CPUs represent data structures differently (for example, *big-endian* versus *little-endian*). So how is data transparency achieved at the RPC level? To maintain machine-independence, the RPC must provide some level of data format translation across systems. For example, the Sun RPC requires that clients convert their data to a neutral canonical format using the *External Data Representation (XDR)* APIs. In contrast, DCE's *Network Data Representation (NDR)* service is multicanonical, meaning that it supports multiple data format representations. The client chooses one of these formats (in most cases, its own native data representation); tags the data with the chosen format; and then leaves it up to the server to transform the data into a format it understands.

In other words, the *server makes it right*. DCE assumes that in most cases the client and server will be using the same data representation, so why go through the translation overhead? Sun assumes that client MIPs are cheap, so it lets the client do the translation, which makes life easy for the server. With Sun, all clients look the same to the server: The *client makes it right*.

Figure 9-2 shows how the RPC mechanism all comes together. The scenario shows a simple seat reservation application. The seating server first starts up, advertises its location and service in the network directory, and begins its continuous cycle of receiving and servicing requests. A ticketing client keeps in its cache the location of the server. When a customer is ready to buy a ticket for a Madonna concert, an RPC is issued to reserve a seat. Notice how the client and server stubs cooperate to make that happen. It takes a lot of work to make that reservation for the Madonna concert. RPCs take away some of that drudgery.

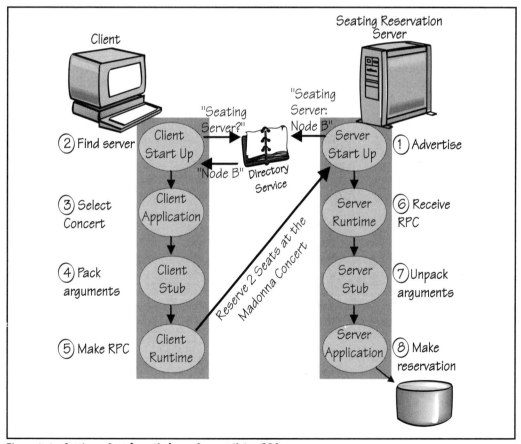

Figure 9-2. Getting a Seat for a Madonna Concert Using RPCs.

MESSAGING AND QUEUING: THE MOM MIDDLEWARE

Every DAD needs a MOM.

> — *The Message-Oriented Middleware*
> *(MOM) Consortium* [1]

"Every DAD needs a MOM" is the unofficial motto of the MOM Consortium. In this context, DAD stands for *Distributed Application Development* and MOM stands for *Message-Oriented Middleware.* We agree with the motto. MOM is a key piece of middleware that is absolutely essential for a class of client/server products. If your application can tolerate a certain level of time-independent responses, MOM provides the easiest path for creating enterprise and inter-enterprise client/server systems. MOM also helps create nomadic client/server systems that can accumulate outgoing transactions in queues and do a bulk upload when a connection can be established with an office server.

MOM allows general-purpose messages to be exchanged in a client/server system using message queues. Applications communicate over networks by simply putting messages in queues and getting messages from queues. MOM hides all the nasty communications from applications and typically provides a very simple high-level API to its services. A MOM Consortium was formed in mid-1993 with the goal of creating standards for messaging middleware. Members are product providers, including IBM (*MQSeries*), Covia (*Communications Integrator*), Peerlogic (*PIPES*), Horizon Strategies (*Message Express*), and System Strategies (*ezBridge*). So what can you do with MOM?

MOM's messaging and queuing allow clients and servers to communicate across a network without being linked by a private, dedicated, logical connection. The clients and servers can run at different times. Everybody communicates by putting messages on queues and by taking messages from queues (see Figure 9-3). Notice that the server sends back the reply via a message queue. Messaging does not impose any constraints on an application's structure: If no response is required, none is sent.

MOM products provide their own NOS services—including hierarchical naming, security, and a layer that isolates applications from the network. They use virtual memory on the local OS to create their queues. Most messaging products allow the sender to specify the name of the reply queue. The products also include some type of *format field* that tells the recipient how to interpret the message data.

---

[1] Source: **Information Week** (November 1, 1993).

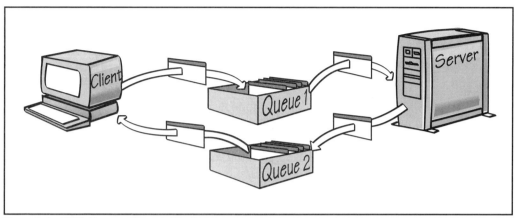

Figure 9-3. MOM: Two-way Message Queuing.

MOM-enabled programs do not talk to each other directly, so either program can be busy, unavailable, or simply not running at the same time. A program can decide when it wants to retrieve a message off its queue—there are no time constraints. The target program can even be started several hours later. Or, if you're using a laptop on the road, you can collect outgoing requests in a queue and submit them to the server when you get to a phone or to an office LAN. Messaging allows either the client or the server to be unavailable (see Figure 9-4).

Figure 9-4. MOM: Save Your Messages Until You Get to a Server.

Messaging queues are very versatile. You can use them to create one-to-many or many-to-one relationships (see Figure 9-5). In the figure, many clients are sending requests to one server queue. The messages are picked off the queue by multiple instances of the server program that are concurrently servicing the clients. The server instances can take messages off the queue either on a first-in/first-out basis or according to some priority or load-balancing scheme. In all cases, a message queue can be concurrently accessed. The servers can also use messaging filters to throw away the messages they don't want to process, or they can pass them on to other servers.

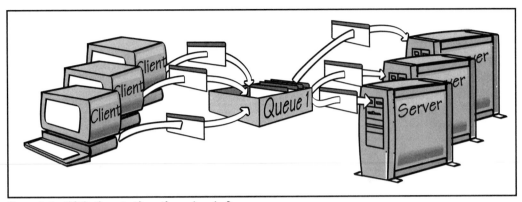

Figure 9-5. MOM: Many-to-Many Messaging via Queues.

Most MOM messaging products make available a single API set that runs on multiple operating system platforms. Most also provide *persistent* (logged on disk) and *non-persistent* (in memory) message queues. Persistent messages are slower, but they can be recovered in case of power failures after a system restart. In both cases, messages can be either copied or removed from a queue. A message queue can be *local* to the machine or *remote*. System administrators can usually specify the number of messages a queue can hold and the maximum message size.

Most messaging products provide a minimum level of fault-tolerance in the form of persistent queues. Some of the products provide some form of *transactional protection*, allowing the queue to participate in a two-phase commit synchronization protocol. And some may even reroute messages to alternate queues in case of a network failure.

MOM VERSUS RPC

Comparing the Messaging and RPC paradigms is like doing business via a telephone call versus exchanging letters or faxes (see Figure 9-6). An interaction using a telephone call is immediate—both parties talk to each other directly to conduct their business. At the end of the phone conversation, a unit of work is concluded. Conducting business via mail allows you to stage work, prioritize it, and do it when you're ready for it. You're in control of the workflow, not that ringing phone. On the other hand, it may be frustrating on the client side not to receive immediate feedback.

Table 9-1 compares the messaging and RPC architectures. Messaging is, of course, more flexible and time-tolerant than RPC. However, messaging only skews things in time and may create its own level of complications. In the telephone analogy (i.e., RPC), you complete the work as it arrives; you don't have to manage stacks of incoming letters (or faxes). Your clients are happy to get immediate service. When

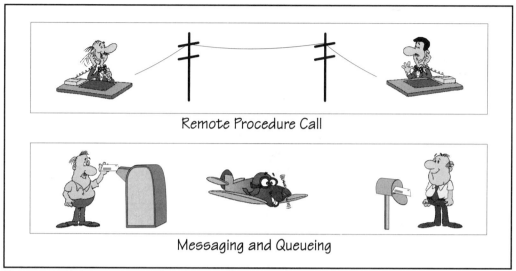

Figure 9-6. MOM Versus RPC: Do You Like Post Office or Telephones?

you close shop at the end of the day, you're all done with your work. In the mail analogy, letters may start to pile up, and clients may be polling their incoming mailboxes continuously, waiting for a response. We may have made life easier for the server at the expense of the client. On the other hand, messaging does free clients from being synchronized to their servers; this can be very liberating for mobile and home users.

Table 9-1. Comparing MOM and RPC.

Feature	MOM: Messaging and Queuing	Remote Procedure Call (RPC)
Metaphor	Post office-like.	Telephone-like.
Client/Server time relationship	Asynchronous. Clients and servers may operate at different times and speeds.	Synchronous. Clients and servers must run concurrently. Servers must keep up with clients.
Client/Server sequencing	No fixed sequence.	Servers must first come up before clients can talk to them.
Style	Queued.	Call-Return.
Persistent Data	Yes.	No.
Partner needs to be available	No.	Yes.

Table 9-1. Comparing MOM and RPC. (Continued)

Feature	MOM: Messaging and Queuing	Remote Procedure Call (RPC)
Load balancing	Single queue can be used to implement FIFO or priority-based policy.	Requires a separate TP Monitor.
Transactional support	Yes (some products). Message queue can participate in the commit synchronization.	No. Requires a transactional RPC.
Message filtering	Yes.	No.
Performance	Slow. An intermediate hop is required.	Fast.
Asynchronous processing	Yes. Queues and triggers are required.	Limited. Requires threads and tricky code for managing threads.

In summary, there's plenty of room for MOMs, RPCs, and peer-to-peer styles of communication on the modern NOS. Each distinctive style presents its own paradigm for conducting business. You'll end up choosing the style that provides the best fit for your particular needs.

CONCLUSION

As you may have surmised from this chapter, the NOS middleware pieces are of interest to all client/server apps. If you don't acquire the pieces "off-the-shelf," you'll have to recreate them in some shape or form. After all, a network is almost unusable without security, directory, and naming services. And everybody needs MOM, RPC, or peer-to-peer communications. The NOS creates a "gentle and civilized environment" on raw networks that lets you focus on your client/server business. The next chapter, on stacks, takes you closer to the network wire. After reading it, you'll get a better appreciation for the value-added provided by the NOS middleware.

Chapter 10

Stacks: Ubiquitous Communications

Therefore, ye soft pipes, play on.

— *Keats*

This chapter provides a brief overview of the transport stacks middleware. We cover the "big five" of networking: TCP/IP (with sockets), IPX/SPX (with TLI), NetBEUI (with NetBIOS), APPC/SNA (with CPI-C), and Named Pipes. Obviously, there's no way we can do justice to the communication stacks and their interface protocols in one chapter. Instead, we will give you a feeling for what the big five have to offer in terms of features and what makes them important.

WHAT'S A STACK ANYWAY?

The stacks middleware must provide "any-to-any" ubiquitous communications—including the communications stacks proper and the interface to the network adapters that drive local, wide-area, and wireless networks. In Part 1, we provided a brief glimpse of the communications infrastructure that's covering most of our planet. The transport stacks are the nervous system that make the physical networks come together.

Communications software vendors have tackled the problem of network complexity by breaking down complex protocols into layers (see the following Briefing box). Each layer builds on top of the services provided by the layers below it. Eventually, you get a *stack* of layers that looks like a birthday cake. Vendors sell their communication products as stack offerings that are architected to work together. In theory, each stack layer has a well-defined set of APIs and protocols so that it should be possible to mix-and-match different vendor offerings within the same stack. In practice, this is not the case. You buy an entire stack from a single vendor and pray that it works with the hardware.

The lowest layer of communication software belongs to the device drivers that provide an interface to several types of communication hardware adapters. The bottom of the stacks sits on top of the device drivers. The top of the stacks sits right below the NOS. The stacks and NOS are simply divisions that help us create a Survival Map. The *OSI Reference Model* defines seven layers of functions that a "complete" stack should ideally provide. To help you navigate through this chapter, we couldn't resist coming up with our own interpretation of where the most popular commercial stacks fit in the OSI reference model (see Figure 10-1). Remember, it's just a reference model. So take it in with a grain of salt. *Real* products don't have any notion of architectural boundaries or reference models—they just get a job done.

So what do stacks provide? At the lower layers, they interface to the hardware using the physical *Media Access Control (MAC)* protocols defined by the IEEE. The *Logical Link Control (LLC)* provides a common interface to the MACs and a reliable link service for transmitting communication packets between two nodes. The OSI *link* layer combines the LLC and MAC functions. On top of this layer is the *network* layer that allows packets to be routed across multiple networks. The *transport* layer sits on top of the network layer and provides some form of reliable end-to-end delivery service. The *session* layer deals with network etiquette—who goes first, who reconnects in case of failure, and synchronization points. On top of the session layer is a *presentation* layer that deals with data representation. Finally, the *application layer* provides network services and interfaces to an application.

The boundary between the stacks and NOS gets fuzzy at the upper layers. For example, is the peer-to-peer interface an application, presentation, or session layer service? Does it belong to the NOS or to the stacks? But, then, everything in client/server is a bit fuzzy.

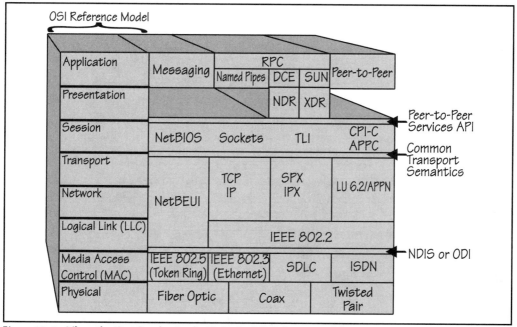

Figure 10-1. Where the Most Popular Stacks Fit in the OSI Reference Model.

FYI **Layering: Breaking Down Complexity**

Briefing

Layering is a software design technique used to break down complex programs into a hierarchy of services. Powerful new services can be provided by adding new layers on top of more primitive service layers. A service interface defines the services provided by an underlying layer to the layers above it.

Layering also provides an ideal framework for explaining and organizing the communications between two independent programs. Program-to-program communications is broken down into exchanges between the corresponding peer layers in each program. The following three concepts form the basis for the layered approach:

■ At each layer, client and server peers cooperate jointly to provide a service. Of course, one peer can end up doing all of the work, but the service is still considered to be a joint effort by the peers for that layer. The *protocol* is the contract the peers abide by. It specifies how the work is divided among the peers, the semantics of the message exchanges for that layer, and the handshake sequences.

■ Each layer builds on top of the services provided by the layers beneath it. A *service interface* specifies how a layer can obtain access to the services of the layer directly below it. The interface should hide all the nasty details of the workings of the underlying layer while providing a complete set of services.

■ Services become more abstract the higher the layer. For example, the lower layers may be concerned with the interfaces to the hardware or the operating system, while the higher layers may provide a more application-specific type of service, such as a file transfer.

Layering is quite popular in the area of data communications. There are several examples of layered protocol stacks in this chapter. ❑

STACK MIDDLEWARE

Some of the stacks we cover in this chapter are more complete than others. For example, SNA and IPX/SPX cover all the traditional layers. TCP/IP does not support a link layer and depends on sockets for its session and presentation services. NetBIOS does not provide a network layer. Named Pipes is a client/server protocol with RPC-like functions. However, all the Named Pipes implementations now include both the client and server sides—this means that it is also a peer-to-peer protocol. Named Pipes is just an interface layer that sits on top of other protocols (such as NetBEUI and IPX/SPX). In this section, we look at the services provided by each stack.[1]

TCP/IP and Sockets

TCP/IP—originally the network of choice for the government, the Internet, and the universities—is now increasingly finding its way into commercial environments. TCP/IP is particularly strong in enterprises that require internetworking between different LAN environments. The TCP/IP protocol runs on virtually every operating system platform. Over 300 vendors sell TCP/IP communications products, and that market is rapidly growing.

Internet Protocol (IP)

The network layer of the TCP/IP stack is provided by the **Internet Protocol (IP)**. It provides the basic mechanism for routing packets in the internet. IP is not a reliable communication protocol. It does not understand the relationships between packets and does not perform retransmissions. IP requires higher-level protocols such as TCP or UDP to provide a reliable class of service (see the following Briefing box).

TCP and UDP

The transport layer of TCP/IP consists of two protocols that provide end-to-end transport services:

■ *Transmission Control Protocol (TCP)* provides a reliable, session-based service for the delivery of sequenced packets across an internet.

■ *User Datagram Protocol (UDP)* provides a datagram service. Datagrams are unreliable but fast.

The TCP/IP protocol does not specify an application interface layer. However, sockets have emerged as TCP/IP's premier peer-to-peer API.

---

[1] You can get more of the gory details—including programming examples for NetBIOS, APPC, Named Pipes, TCP/IP, and NetWare—in our book, **Client/Server Programming with OS/2 2.1** (VNR, 1993).

Datagrams Versus Sessions

Briefing

Connection-oriented protocols—also known as *session-based protocols*, *virtual circuits*, or *sequenced packet exchanges*—provide a reliable two-way connection service over a session. Each packet of information that gets exchanged over a session is given a unique sequence number through which it gets tracked and individually acknowledged. Duplicate packets are detected and discarded by the session services.

The price you pay for this reliable class of service is the overhead associated with creating and managing the session. If a session is lost, one of the parties must reestablish it. This can be a problem for fault-tolerant servers that require automatic switchovers to a backup server if the primary server fails. The backup server needs to reestablish all the outstanding sessions with clients. In addition, sessions are inherently a two-party affair and don't lend themselves well to broadcasting (one-to-many exchanges).

Datagrams—also known as *connectionless protocols* or *transmit and pray* protocols—provide a simple but unreliable form of exchange. The more powerful datagram protocols such as NetBIOS provide broadcast capabilities. NetBIOS allows you to send datagrams to a named entity, to a select group of entities (multicast), or to all entities on a network (broadcast). Datagrams are unreliable in the sense that they are not acknowledged or tracked through a sequence number. You "transmit and pray" that your datagram gets received. The recipient may not be there or may not be expecting a datagram (you will never know). Novell literature estimates that about 5% of datagrams don't make it. You may, of course, design your own acknowledgement schemes on top of the datagram service. Some stacks (for example, LAN Server's Mailslots) provide an acknowledged datagram service.

Datagrams are very useful to have in "discovery" types of situations. These are situations where you discover things about your network environment by broadcasting queries and learning who is out there from the responses. Broadcast can be used to obtain bids for services or to advertise the availability of new services. Broadcast datagrams provide the capability of creating electronic "bazaars." They support the creation of very dynamic types of environments where things can happen spontaneously. In situations where the name of the recipient is not known, broadcast datagrams are the only way to get the message out. The cost of broadcast datagrams is that, in some cases, recipients may get overloaded with "junk mail." The multicast facility helps alleviate this problem because broadcast mail can then be sent only to "special interest" groups. The alternative to broadcast is the network directory services.

Datagrams are also very useful in situations where there is a need to send a quick message without the world coming to an end if the message is not received. The typical situation is sending control-like information, such as telling a network manager "I'm alive." It doesn't make sense to go through all the overhead of creating a session with the network manager just to say "I'm alive," and what if there are 500 nodes on the network? The manager will need 500 permanent sessions, an exorbitant cost in resources. This is where the datagram alternative comes in. With datagrams you can send your "I'm alive" message. And if the manager misses your message once, it will get another one when you send your next heartbeat (provided you're still alive). ❏

Sockets

Sockets were introduced in 1981 as the Unix BSD 4.2 generic interface that would provide Unix-to-Unix communications over networks. In 1985, SunOS introduced NFS and RPC over sockets. In 1986, AT&T introduced the *Transport Layer Interface (TLI)* that provides functionality similar to sockets but in a more network-independent fashion. Unix SVR4 incorporates both sockets and TLI. As it stands, sockets are far more prevalent than TLI in the Unix world. Sockets and TLI are very similar from a programmer's perspective. TLI is just a cleaner version of sockets. We cover TLI in the IPX/SPX stack section.

Support for sockets exists on a multiplicity of operating system environments, including MS-DOS, Windows, OS/2, UNIX, Mac OS, and most mainframe environments. The Windows socket API, known colloquially as *WinSock*, is a multivendor specification that standardizes the use of TCP/IP under Windows. The WinSock API is based on the Berkeley sockets interface. In the BSD Unix system, sockets are part of the kernel and provide both a standalone and networked IPC service. Non-BSD Unix systems, MS-DOS, Windows, Mac OS, and OS/2 provide sockets in the form of libraries. In Unix SVR4, sockets are implemented in terms of streams. Streams in SVR4 provide the mechanism for hooking external drivers to the kernel. It is safe to say that sockets provide the current "de facto" portable standard for network application providers on TCP/IP networks.

The three most popular socket types are *stream, datagram*, and *raw*. Stream and datagram sockets interface to the TCP and UDP protocols, and raw sockets interface to the IP protocol. The type of socket is specified at creation time. In theory, the socket interface can be extended, and you can define new socket types to provide additional services. A socket address on the TCP/IP internet consists of two parts: an internet address (IP_address) and a port number (see Figure 10-2). So what's an internet address? And what's a port number?

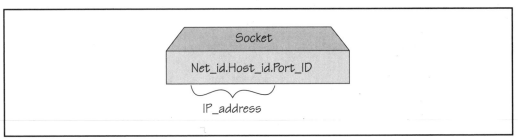

Figure 10-2. Socket = Internet Address (IP) + Port Address.

An *internet address* is a 32-bit number, usually represented by four decimal numbers separated by dots, that must be unique for each TCP/IP network interface card within an administered AF_INET domain. A TCP/IP *host* (i.e., networked machine) may have as many internet addresses as it has network interfaces.

A *port* is an entry point to an application that resides on a host. It is represented by a 16-bit integer. Ports are commonly used to define the entry points for services provided by server applications. Important commercial server programs—such as Oracle and Sybase DBMSs—have their own *well-known* ports.

Blocking Is Dangerous Under Windows

Briefing

The Windows client platform introduces the following problem for network programmers: How do you handle calls that block waiting for something to happen? With DOS, this is not a problem because a single program owns the entire machine; it can simply block the CPU and wait. This is not a problem for Unix and OS/2 because they support preemptive multitasking and threads. A blocking operation can be handled in OS/2 by a thread that relinquishes the use of the CPU until an event causes it to unblock. In the meantime, the thread that handles the user interface can keep up with user inputs. Under Windows, we have a difficult environment: a GUI interface that belongs to more than one program (and needs to remain interactive) without the benefit of preemptive multitasking or threads. So, in contrast to Unix and OS/2, a call that blocks under Windows is literally *blocking* the CPU. Every program on the machine— including the GUI—hangs until the call completes.

So how do programs under Windows work with protocols—such as sockets—that originated on preemptive multitasking OSs? How do they handle functions that block until they complete? They simply issue nonblocking calls and perform some form of cooperative polling around a **PeekMessage** loop waiting for the function to complete. For example, *WinSock* specifies that under Windows, a socket function that blocks must include a PeekMessage loop, which periodically yields the CPU. In addition, the specification forbids *any* network command (blocking or non-blocking) to be issued while a blocking command is in progress. So it's a bit of a mess. ☐

NetWare: IPX/SPX and TLI

Because Novell owns—depending on whose numbers you quote—between 50% and 75% of the network market, it follows that IPX/SPX, NetWare's native stack, must be the most widespread stack in the industry. IPX/SPX is also popular with network managers in large enterprises who are delighted with its internetworking capabilities. This means that IPX/SPX covers the entire spectrum, from PC LANs to enterprise LANs. IPX/SPX is an implementation of the *Xerox Network Services (XNS)* transport and network protocol. Banyan Vines is also an adaptation of XNS, but it uses a TCP/IP-like addressing scheme. XNS, developed by the Xerox PARC research institute, is a much cleaner architecture than the older TCP/IP protocol. It's ironic that XNS (in the form of IPX/SPX) is the world's most predominant stack. This is another example of a PARC technology that Xerox was not able to exploit.

The IPX/SPX network layer is provided by the *Internet Packet Exchange (IPX)* protocol. This is a "send and pray" datagram type of protocol with no guarantees. It is used as a foundation protocol by sophisticated network applications for sending and receiving low-overhead datagram packets over the internet. Novell's SPX builds a reliable protocol service on top of IPX. NetWare provides 12 API calls that can be used to obtain datagram services using IPX. The transport layer of IPX/SPX is provided by the *Sequenced Packet Exchange (SPX)* protocol, which provides a reliable connection-oriented service over IPX. The service consists of 16 API calls.

NetWare provides four peer-to-peer protocols on top of the IPX/SPX stack: Net-BIOS, Named Pipes, TLI, and the IPX/SPX APIs. These protocols are supported in the DOS, Windows, OS/2, and NLM environments. After its acquisition of USL, Novell now owns TLI—remember, that's the *Transport Layer Interface* designed by AT&T as the sockets replacement. The Novell **Programmer's Guide for C** (June, 1993), states that "Novell has adopted TLI as a standard for applications that need a transport layer."

An application written to TLI is, in theory, stack independent. It should run on IPX/SPX or TCP/IP with very few modifications. TLI is a modern implementation of Berkeley sockets, so it should be familiar to Unix programmers. Like sockets, TLI hides many of the time-consuming details associated with lower-level protocols (such as IPX/SPX). The TLI API consists of about 25 API calls.

NetBIOS and NetBEUI

NetBIOS is the premier protocol for LAN-based, program-to-program communications. Introduced by IBM and Sytek in 1984 for the IBM PC Network, NetBIOS now runs with almost no changes on Ethernets, Token Rings, ARCnets, StarLANs, and even low-cost serial-port LANs. NetBIOS is used as an interface to a variety of stacks—including IBM/Microsoft LANs (NetBEUI), TCP/IP, XNS, Vines, OSI, and IPX/SPX protocol stacks. Support for a NetBIOS platform exists on a multiplicity of operating system environments, including MS-DOS, Windows, OS/2, Windows NT, Unix, and some mainframe environments. NetBIOS is currently the de facto portable standard for network application providers. One of the many reasons for NetBIOS's success is its intuitive simplicity.

NetBEUI is the protocol stack that comes with IBM and Microsoft LAN products—including Windows for Workgroups, NT, LAN Manager, LAN Server, DB2/2, and SQL Server. It came to life as the original transport for NetBIOS commands. The literature often uses the term NetBIOS to refer to the combination of the NetBIOS interface and the NetBEUI stack.[2] This can be misleading. NetWare, for example, has nothing to do with NetBEUI, yet it uses NetBIOS as an interface to both IPX/SPX and TCP/IP. IBM and Microsoft use NetBIOS as an interface to both TCP/IP and NetBEUI. So be careful, especially when you read our books; we've been known to use NetBIOS and NetBEUI interchangeably.

NetBEUI offers powerful datagram and connection-oriented services. It also offers a dynamic naming service based on discovery protocols. NetBEUI's main weakness is the lack of a network layer. Its other weakness is the lack of security. The broadcast mechanism, used to dynamically "discover" names, can be a liability on an unsecured internet where it's not a good idea to expose names. Broadcasting names also causes unwanted traffic on the internet. Luckily, most bridges and routers have ways to filter the discovery packets and block them from propagating to other networks.

The NetBIOS services are provided through a set of commands, specified in a structure called the *Network Control Block (NCB)*. The structure also contains

---

[2] The confusion may have started with Microsoft's naming of NetBEUI. It stands for *NetBIOS Extended User Interface* (NetBEUI).

the parameters associated with the command and the fields in which NetBIOS will return information to the program. A command can be issued in either wait or no-wait mode. In the *wait* mode, the requesting thread is blocked until the command completes. In the *no-wait* mode, control is returned to the calling thread at the earliest time possible, usually before the command completes. When the command completes, the NetBIOS DLL places a return code in the NCB.

Named Pipes

Most LAN vendors support Named Pipes on MS-DOS, Windows, and OS/2. This includes Novell's NetWare, Banyan's Vines, and the LAN Manager/LAN Server family of products from IBM and Microsoft. Named Pipes are built-in networking features in both Windows NT and Windows for Workgroups. Unix support for Named Pipes is provided by LAN Manager/X (or Advanced Server for Unix). A very important benefit of Named Pipes, at least for Windows and OS/2 client/server programmers, is that they're part of the base interprocess communications service. The Named Pipes interface is identical, whether the processes are running on an individual machine or distributed across the network. Named Pipes run on NetBIOS, IPX/SPX, and TCP/IP stacks.

Named Pipes provide highly reliable, two-way communications between clients and a server. They provide a file-like programming API that abstracts a session-based two-way exchange of data. Using Named Pipes, processes can exchange data as if they were writing to, or reading from, a sequential file. Named Pipes are especially suitable for implementing server programs that require many-to-one pipelines. A server application can set up a pipeline where the receiving end of the pipe can exchange data with several client processes. Then it lets Named Pipes handle all the scheduling and synchronization issues.

The New SNA: APPC, APPN, and CPI-C

IBM is evolving SNA into a true distributed operating system that supports cross-network directory services, transparent network access to resources (such as servers, applications, displays, printers, and data), common data streams, and integrated network management. *Advanced Peer-to-Peer Network (APPN)* is the network infrastructure responsible for this "true distribution." APPN creates an SNA internet without the mainframe-centric hierarchy of traditional SNA configurations. The mainframe is just another node on the internet. APPN allows LU 6.2 SNA applications, using APPC or CPI-C APIs, to take full advantage of peer networks. It also greatly simplifies SNA configuration, provides better availability through dynamic routing, makes it easier to maintain SNA networks, and meets the flexibility requirements of modern networks.

APPN is becoming *another* de facto routing protocol standard. In September 1993, Cisco buried the hatchet with IBM and chose to support the APPN standard for routing SNA packets. Previously Cisco, the market leader in IP routers, was proposing a scheme for "tunneling" SNA traffic over IP backbones called *Advanced Peer-to-Peer Internetworking (APPI)*. Other major router vendors—including Wellfleet, Ungermann-Bass, 3Com, N.E.T, Crosscom, and IBM's 6611—are also going with APPN. The result is that router vendors are standardizing on APPN to route SNA traffic.

Advanced Program to Program Communication (APPC) is IBM's architected solution for program-to-program communication, distributed transaction processing, and remote database access across the entire IBM product line. Using APPC or CPI-C, a program can converse through one of SNA's 50,000 installed networks with peers located anywhere in the world. These peers can run on PCs, RS/6000s, AS/400s, S/38s, and S/370s, as well as on many non-IBM host platforms. An application program, called a *Transaction Program (TP)*, uses the APPC or CPI-C APIs to communicate with other TPs on systems that support APPC/SNA. APPC's weaknesses include the lack of support for datagrams, broadcast, and multicast services. The APPC model is inherently conversational. APPC's other weakness is the lack of a consistent API across all platforms.

Common Programming Interface for Communications (CPI-C) builds on top of APPC and masks its complexities and irregularities. Every product that supports APPC has a slightly different API. CPI-C fixes that problem. Writing to the CPI-C API allows you to port your programs to other SNA platforms, such as S/370 and AS/400. Networking Services/DOS (NS/DOS) provides CPI-C/APPC for DOS and Windows using less than 140 KBytes of memory. From a programmer's perspective, APPC provides a *verb with control-block* API, while CPI-C provides a consistent *call-based* API on top of APPC (see Figure 10-3). The CPI-C API is common across different operating systems and programming languages. IBM provides CPI-C language bindings for all its SAA compilers. APPC offers interoperability and

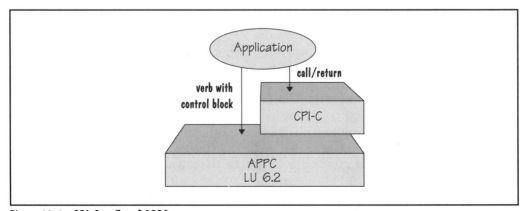

Figure 10-3. CPI-C on Top of APPC.

platform-specific optimizations. CPI-C offers *both* portability and interoperability, but it gives up some of the platform-specific features of APPC. And, of course, CPI-C programs can talk to APPC partners.

The X/Open consortium has licensed the CPI-C interface from IBM; so have several other companies (including Novell and Apple). In addition to *all* the IBM platforms, CPI-C APIs are provided by Insession Inc. (for Tandem Computers), Systems Strategies (for Unix), Rabbit Software (for DOS), and DCA Inc. (for DOS and OS/2). Apple has announced planned support for CPI-C on Macintosh. Bull, Brixton, and HP are working on Unix versions. Microsoft is working on a Windows version— CPI-C is one of the four SNA APIs supported by the *WinSNA* standard.

In summary, it looks like CPI-C is becoming *another* important "de facto" (and possibly "de jure") API standard for peer-to-peer communications. With the Any-Net/2 multiprotocol common transport (also known as MPTN), CPI-C applications are to run unchanged on a broad selection of transport stacks—including TCP/IP, and SNA today—and OSI, IPX/SPX, and NetBIOS in the near future (see Figure 10-4).

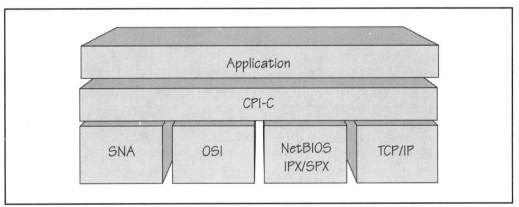

Figure 10-4. CPI-C: A Stack-Independent API (Source: IBM Blueprint for Networking, March 1992).

The CPI-C API consists of about 40 calls; APPC consists of over 60 calls. Most of these calls deal with configuration and services.

Conclusion

A NOS will typically support the peer-to-peer APIs that work with its native stack (NetWare, for example, supports IPX/SPX) and emulate some of the other popular APIs—NetWare, for example, supports NetBIOS, Named Pipes, TLI, and Sockets on top of IPX/SPX. The modern thinking is that the NOS should provide a stack-independent protocol that works on any transport, as well as stack-specific APIs that are made to work on top of other stacks.

A stack-independent API leads to a least common denominator solution. This can be very limiting. Over the years, each peer-to-peer API set introduced its own unique flavors of communication semantics. For example, NetBIOS is very good with broadcast (one-to-all) and multicast (one-to-some) communications. APPC is a master of robust conversations. Named Pipes makes it very easy to write client/server (many-to-one) applications. A least common denominator approach ends up supporting simple session-based conversations between two parties (one-to-one). As a result, we believe that the different APIs will be with us for a long time to come.

This concludes our *brief* overview of the underlying principles behind NOS and Stacks middleware. The next step is to look at some representative products that provide NOS and Stack solutions. We must warn you that there are an overwhelming number of products, from hundreds of vendors, that fall into that category. We will only cover a few selected products to give you a feel for what type of solutions are available. Since this is an **Essential Client/Server Survival Guide** we'll try to point out the most essential products.

Chapter 11

LAN Server and NetWare: The NOS Classics

---

*C*hoosing a NOS can seem like part blind luck, part mysticism—just like the feeling when you step into a casino. The NOS newcomer must learn the rules of each network offering and discover which vendor requires the steep ante, which game is most likely to pay off at high odds, and which best suits the situation.

— *PC Magazine (October 26, 1993)*

In this chapter, we very briefly cover *NetWare* from Novell and *LAN Server* from IBM, the number one and number two bestselling NOSs. We've already introduced NetWare in Part 2, so we'll begin our discussion with LAN Server.

IBM LAN SERVER

The IBM LAN Server is the most widely used OEM variant of Microscft's *LAN Manager*, popularly known as *LAN Man*. LAN Man makes the network an integral part of OS/2; it also provides interoperability with MS-NET and PC-LAN worksta-tions running MS-DOS and Windows. *LAN Manager/X* extends the platform to UNIX System V. LAN Man is also bundled with *Windows NT Advanced Server*. In addition, *Windows for Workgroups* is a peer-to-peer subset of LAN Man. The IBM LAN Server is fully compatible with LAN Man at the API and functional levels. LAN Server supports LAN Man clients (and vice versa). Both utilize the same security system, and the same applications will run on both platforms. LAN Server 3.0 is a 32-bit version of LAN Man that takes full advantage of OS/2, making it the fastest PC NOS in the industry. LAN Server is IBM's "strategic" network operating system product and is developed independently from Microsoft.

With LAN Server, you can write your own network application services as simple OS/2 programs. Your programs can use OS/2's native Named Pipes protocol to communicate with DOS, Windows, NT, and OS/2 clients; one server can support up to 1000 client workstations. Your programs can also take advantage of all the built-in server features such as network security, audit trails, domain-based multi-server management, and fault-tolerance.

IBM's contractual rights to Microsoft's LAN Man code end with the current version of the code. IBM intends to continue to evolve LAN Server toward full interoperability with NetWare. In addition, LAN Server will continue to interoperate with its LAN Man siblings. Most importantly, LAN Server will implement the powerful OSF Distributed Computing Environment (DCE).

NETWARE VS. LAN SERVER

NetWare 4.0, as a server platform, offers the same kind of services as LAN Server. Both server platforms are essentially equivalent in the following areas: file and print services, disk duplexing, disk mirroring, Uninterruptible Power Supply (UPS) support, multiserver domain administration, audit trails, alerts, security features, login scripts, multiple adapter support, Named Pipes support, and remote IPL capabilities for DOS, Windows, and OS/2 clients. NetWare and LAN Server can both be installed and upgraded remotely. And both platforms can support, in theory, a maximum of 1000 clients.

So What Does NetWare Do Better Than LAN Server?

For starters, it allows you to create monstrous files that can span across multiple disk drives. NetWare can work with a gargantuan amount of total disk storage: 32 Terabytes versus LAN Server's not too shabby 48 Gigabytes. NetWare directly supports Unix clients, while LAN Server relies on third parties. Bean counters are in love with NetWare's meticulously built-in accounting services, which can be used to charge clients for any service used. And NetWare's *Systems Fault Tolerance III (SFT III)* gives you fault tolerance using replicated servers. NetWare 4.0 introduces powerful new features such as the X.500-based directory services, authentication services via encrypted key technology, burst-mode technology for increasing the speed of data transfer over Wide Area Networks, and file-by-file compression. It also has built-in routing capabilities for IPX/SPX, TCP/IP, and AppleTalk protocols.

The feature that really makes NetWare wonderful is its multifaceted, chameleon-like file server that can be made to look like everybody else's favorite file system. The NetWare file server stores everybody's files in its own "private-label" Novell format. But depending on what the client wants, NetWare can apply the right magic to make its files resemble MS-DOS FAT, OS/2 HPFS, Sun NFS, or Macintosh AFP. This is how NetWare allows Windows, OS/2, Mac, Unix, and DOS clients to access the same files.

So What Does LAN Server Do Better Than NetWare 4.0?

It provides some unique features—such as the file replication service, the network time service, multimedia, multiprocessing, and the remote execution of commands—and it is able to accept commands from NetView. LAN Server, like NetWare 4.0, is gearing up to become an enterprise server platform. Unlike NetWare, LAN Server will be based on an "open" DCE platform for its cell directory, X.500 global directory, Kerberos-based authentication, RPC, network time, and DME-based system management.[1] Both the DCE Toolkit for OS/2 and LAN NetView's implementation of DME's Network Management component are commercially available.

LAN Server is the industry's first NOS to support isochronous multimedia traffic on ordinary LANs. It does this by taking advantage of the priority service on network adapters: Token Ring or Ethernet. It then uses this service to reserve bandwidth for time-dependent multimedia streams. Using the priority service on Token Ring provides nearly 90% bandwidth utilization. LAN Server's multimedia *Resource Reservation Subsystem (RRS)* prioritizes and synchronizes multimedia stream movement on the network with the disk subsystem. RRS detects multimedia data automatically and runs applications unchanged. For maximum performance, RRS requires an IBM *LAN Streamer* Token Ring card on the server side (see Figure 11-1). The clients can use ordinary 16 Mbit/s adapters. LAN Streamer supports multiple queues, allows direct transfers from the server cache to the adapter memory, and can reserve up to 90% of the network bandwidth for priority multimedia data.

But, what makes LAN Server really *great* is its programming platform. It is safe to say that most of the world's great server applications have yet to be written. LAN Server, because of its affinity to OS/2, provides an ideal platform for creating those

---

[1] NetWare is semi-proprietary: Its RPC is based on Sun's RPC; its directory service is "X.500-like," but it does not interoperate with other X.500 directories; and its authentication service and system management are proprietary.

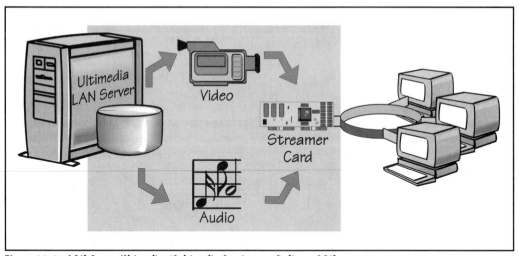

Figure 11-1. LAN Server Ultimedia: Multimedia Services on Ordinary LANs.

applications. When you're programming in the LAN Server environment, you can use any OS/2 software package. LAN Server applications can use OS/2's preemptive multitasking, threads, interprocess communications, memory protection, dynamic link library facilities, and demand-paged virtual memory. The LAN Server API package has very consistent semantics because it was designed from the outset as an extension of the OS/2 API set. NetWare, by contrast, added functions piecemeal as the product matured. The OS/2 connection also gives you access to dozens of compilers, programmer productivity tools, Case tools, DBMSs, ODBMSs, ORBs, image and multimedia application enablers, communication stacks, and device drivers for almost anything that can be controlled by a PC.

Chapter 12

DCE: The Postmodern NOS

By 1994, the OSF DCE will be established as the industry standard for client/server computing (0.8 probability).

— *Gartner Group (January, 1993)*[1]

The dominance of single-vendor software architectures is fading as corporations move into the multivendor world of client/server and enterprise networks. Open Systems is the current buzzword for creating a new world order in distributed computing. The OSF *Distributed Computing Environment (DCE)* is emerging as the de facto standard for client/server computing in an "open" multivendor NOS environment. According to OSF, more than 100 vendors are currently building DCE products, although very few are on the market yet.

DCE is important because it provides the most comprehensive NOS solution for integrating multivendor servers in a *heterogeneous* client/server environment. Although there are some partial NOS solutions for the heterogeneous server

---

[1] Source: **Gartner Research Note**, SAP-222-087 (January 20, 1993). If you're reading this book, it must be 1994 or later. So how good is the Gartner 1993 prediction?

environment, no existing product matches DCE's integration technology. This is because DCE was built on top of the industry's "best-of-breed" commercial NOS technology.

DCE allows a client to interoperate with one or more server processes on other computing platforms, even when they are from different vendors with different operating systems. In addition, DCE provides an integrated approach to security, naming, and interprocess communications. All these pieces are used to create a coherent heterogeneous client/server environment. DCE is the best architectural example of an intergalactic *postmodern NOS*. It is intended to become the "mother of all NOSs."

WHAT IS DCE?

The DCE from the Open Software Foundation (OSF) is probably the most significant open systems standard for heterogeneous client/server interoperability. DCE consists of an integrated set of technologies that make it easy to create, use, and maintain applications in a distributed environment. DCE provides the plumbing that enables secure access to distributed resources wherever they are and on whatever operating system they run. In essence, DCE creates an open NOS environment that spans multiple architectures, protocols, and operating systems. The X/Open standards consortium is including the DCE specifications in Version 4 of its *X/Open Portability Guide (XPG)*. The importance of DCE is that *almost* every computer manufacturer is planning to support it (see the following Soapbox).

Who's Not On Board?

Soapbox

As we go to press, Sun, whose RPC was rejected by OSF, has not endorsed DCE. Sun is offering its *Open Network Computing (ONC)* as the alternative to the OSF DCE. A number of third parties are planning DCE ports to Sun platforms. In addition, Novell does not fully embrace DCE but IBM is rumored to be developing NLM versions of DCE. Finally, Microsoft is only implementing parts of DCE (mostly by reverse-engineering the OSF implementation) because it does not want to pay royalties to OSF. Other than these "big three," everyone else seems to be on board the DCE ship. ❏

DCE is the result of a multitechnology and multivendor open selection process. OSF identifies requirements and solicits technologies from the computer industry at large through an open bidding process. The OSF then picks the best submissions and integrates the technology into core software layers for resale by others. OSF member companies receive the core code in "snapshots" that can be integrated into their products. The DCE Release 1.0 package contains more than 1.1 million lines of C code, documentation, and a set of functional tests. Note that DCE is not just for Unix. Its purpose is to facilitate the creation of distributed applications and to enable the transparent sharing of resources across a variety of networks, operating systems, and vendors.

DCE provides key distributed technologies, including a remote procedure call, a distributed naming service, a time synchronization service, a distributed file system, network security service, and a threads package (see Figure 12-1). These six key technologies will be incorporated by IBM (into MVS, AIX, DOS/Windows, and OS/2), DEC (into VMS, Ultrix, OSF/1, and ACE), HP (into HP/UX, Domain, and OSF/1),

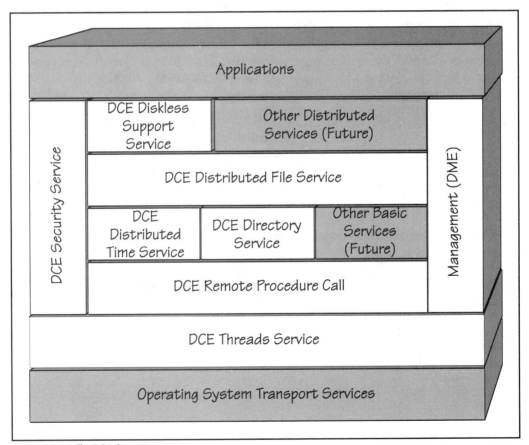

Figure 12-1. The DCE Components.

Gradient (into MS-DOS), Cray (into Unicos), Siemens (into SINIX), and Tandem (into Guardian and Integrity). DCE will also interoperate (at the RPC level) with Atlas, the competing open standard for distributed computing from the now defunct Unix International. The sections that follow contain a brief summary of the main DCE components, including their origins.

DCE RPC

OSF adopted the Apollo RPC with some enhancements from DEC (the multithread server). DCE provides an *Interface Definition Language (IDL)* and compiler that facilitate the creation of RPCs. The IDL compiler creates portable C code stubs for both the client and server sides of an application. The stubs are compiled and linked to the RPC run-time library, which is responsible for finding servers in a distributed system, performing the message exchanges, packing and unpacking message parameters, and processing any errors that occur.

The most powerful feature of the DCE RPC is that it can be integrated with the DCE security and name services. This integration makes it possible to authenticate each procedure call and to dynamically locate servers at run time. Servers can concurrently service RPCs using threads. The RPC mechanism provides protocol and network independence.

The DCE RPC does not support transactions. To do that means adding context information in the RPC messages that identify the transaction (and its status) on behalf of which the RPC is doing the work. It also means providing semantics for bracketing transactions (i.e., begin transaction and end transaction). There are currently two competing approaches for adding transactional support to the DCE RPC:

■ X/Open has defined a transaction interface called *TxRPC* that is intended to be used with the DCE RPC.

■ Transarc's Encina product provides its own DCE-based transactional RPC component, including a C-based precompiler.

The OSF DCE SIG TP Working Group is getting ready to issue a TP Requirements RFC that specifies the X/Open API with a DCE-based transaction protocol. Transarc is expected to respond.

DCE: Distributed Naming Services

OSF adopted the DCE distributed naming services from DEC's DECdns product and Siemens' DIR-X X.500 services. The DCE naming services allow resources such as programs, servers, files, disks, or print queues to be identified by user-oriented names in a special-purpose distributed database that describes the objects of interest. Object names are independent of their location on the network.

DCE divides the distributed environment into administrative units (or domains) called *cells*. A DCE cell is a combination of client and server workstations. The cell's domain is defined by the customer. A cell usually consists of the set of machines used by one or more groups working on related tasks. The cell size is dictated only by how easy it is to administer. At a *minimum*, a DCE cell must have one cell directory server and one security server.

As shown in Figure 12-2, the DCE directory service consists of two elements: *Cell Directory Service (CDS)* and *Global Directory Service (GDS)*. This two-tier

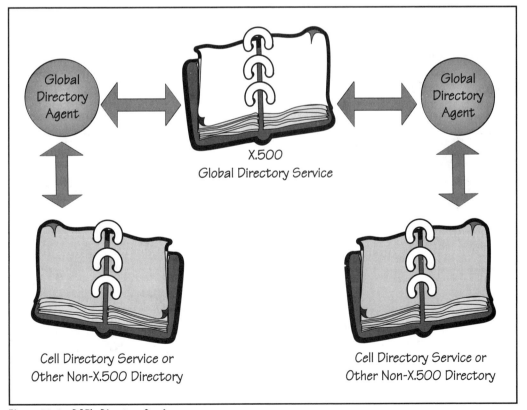

Figure 12-2. DCE's Directory Services.

hierarchy provides local naming autonomy (at the cell level) and global interoperability (at the intercell level). Global access is provided using X.500's "intergalactic" naming system or with TCP/IP's Internet *Domain Name System (DNS)*. All the names in the DCE system taken together make up the DCE *namespace*, which looks like a hierarchical file system. The DCE namespace is used by the different DCE services. For example, the security service uses a part of the namespace to maintain its information on user accounts and principals. The DFS file system uses another part of the namespace for the file system.

DCE: Distributed Time Services

OSF adopted this technology from DEC's DECtds time server product. The Time Service provides a mechanism for synchronizing each computer in the network to a recognized time standard. The DCE Time Service provides APIs for manipulating timestamps and for obtaining universal time from public sources such as the Traconex/PSTI radio clock.

DCE requires at least three Time Servers; one (or more) must be connected to an *External Time Provider*. The Time Servers periodically query one another to adjust their clocks. The External Time Provider may be a hardware device that receives time from a radio or a telephone source. DCE uses the UTC standard, which keeps track of time elapsed since the beginning of the Gregorian calendar—October 15, 1582.

FYI

What Does a Time Server Do?

Briefing

The Time Server is a node that is designated to answer queries about the time. A DCE LAN provides at least three Time Servers; one (or more) must be connected to an *External Time Provider*. The Time Servers query one another to adjust their clocks. The External Time Provider may be a hardware device that receives time from a radio or a telephone source. If no such source is available, the system administrator's watch may do. The commonly used time format in the industry is the UTC standard, which keeps track of time elapsed since the beginning of the Gregorian calendar—October 15, 1582. This time is adjusted using the Greenwich time zone differential factor (for example, -5 hours in New York City). ❑

DCE: Distributed Security Services

Kerberos—A three-headed dog that guarded the gates of Hades.

— Greek Mythology

OSF adopted MIT's Kerberos authentication system and enhanced it with some HP security features. Kerberos, a protocol that Machiavelli would have loved, is based on total mutual distrust. The MIT folks who built it named it after a three-headed mythological monster that guarded the gates of Hades (i.e., Hell). Why would anyone want to crash the gates of Hell? We'll let security administrators answer that one. The Kerberos monster consists of three "heads," all residing on the same secured server: the Authentication Server, Security Database, and Privilege Server. The MIT three-headed monster gives network administrators the heavy-duty security needed to keep "intruding hackers" from crashing into the network's gates.

DCE's network security services provide authentication, authorization, and user account management. *Authentication* validates that a client, typically a user or program, is who or what it claims to be. This validation is accomplished through the secure communications capability provided by the RPC and the Kerberos ticketing mechanism. Each DCE machine must run a security agent.

The DCE *security server* is a physically secured server that stores security-related information such as names and associated passwords. Each DCE cell must have a security server; it is usually a dedicated machine. A cell may have replicated security servers for backup. The DCE *login facility* enables users (DCE calls them *principals* or *units of trust*) to establish their identity by authenticating themselves

using a password. The DCE security system never sends a password in "clear text" across the network.

The security agent works with the authenticated RPC to provide secure access to all the DCE services—not just authentication. The RPC mechanism hides all the complexity of the security system from the user. It obtains the tickets, provides encryption when needed, and performs authenticated checksums if the policy requires it. Under-the-covers, both the RPC client and server must mutually authenticate one another by exchanging tickets (little secrets) with a trusted third party (the Kerberos server). Each party trusts the Kerberos server to identify the other party on the network. This is called *trusted third-party secret-key encryption*. In addition, information is timestamped so that the usefulness of a ticket expires within a relatively short period of time, measured in hours.

Authorization comes after authentication; it determines whether the authenticated client has permission to access a resource. DCE supports authorization through Access Control Lists (ACLs). Each DCE implementation that uses ACLs must implement an ACL manager that controls access to services and resources managed by it (DCE provides sample code that shows how to create an ACL manager). *Data integrity* is provided by DCE using cryptographic data checksums to determine whether a message was corrupted or tampered with while passing through the network. In addition, *data privacy* can be ensured by encrypting data that is transferred across a network.

In summary, DCE solves the problems associated with user authentication in distributed networks. Passwords are never sent *in the clear*. The security database (DCE calls it the *registry*) can be propagated across trusted servers. DCE's Kerberos, in addition to solving the authentication problem, helps with the authorization issue. And better yet, the whole scheme can work on heterogeneous systems. No other NOS can match DCE when it comes to security.

 DCE and Access Control Lists

Briefing

Modern NOSs, like the OSF DCE, provide a set of APIs that allow servers to create and manage their ACLs. The DCE NOS also provides hooks that help the clients present their authorization credentials to the server applications. DCE calls it the *Privilege Attribute Certificate (PAC)*—a security-server issued ticket the client must present to the server. PACs contain authorization information specific to the client, such as the groups it belongs to. DCE provides a set of server APIs that can read the information contained in the PACs and match them with the information in the ACLs. ❏

The Battle Between Public and Private Keys

Soapbox

A potential weakness of DCE is its security model, which is based on Kerberos, derived from the DES. Rymer notes that many IBM competitors, notably Novell and Microsoft, have openly scorned DES in favor of RSA public key encryption.

> — Andy Reinhardt, Byte Magazine
> (November, 1993)

What John Rymer really said:

NetWare 4.0 uses encryption primarily to authenticate users and sessions. By contrast, OSF offers the option of securing DCE by encrypting messages. IBM also has a general cryptography architecture [DES] that makes encryption services available to application builders.

> — John R. Rymer, Network Monitor
> (May, 1992)

What's going on here? It appears that Andy is confusing two issues: encryption and authentication. We'll clear up this confusion by first giving you a quick level set on public keys, private keys, DES, and RSA. Then we'll speculate on why Novell rejected Kerberos.

Encryption has been used to protect information for at least 4000 years. Today, the two predominant approaches to electronic encryption are based on private cypher keys and public cypher keys:

■ The ***private key*** approach uses a single key to encrypt or decrypt information. Each pair of users who need to exchange messages must agree on a private key and use it as a cypher to encode and decode their messages. This method works well, as long as both sides maintain the secrecy of the private key. It's their shared "little secret."

■ The ***public key*** approach uses two keys: a public key and a private key. The public key may be listed in directories and is available for all to see. You encrypt your message with your private key and the recipient uses your public key to decode it. In addition, anybody can send you an encrypted message by using your public key as a cypher (you decode it with your private key). This way, you don't even have to know who the sender is. Again, all this works well, as long as you keep your private key secret.

The *Data Encryption Standard (DES)* is based on this public key approach and has been the official US national cryptographic standard since 1977. DES was originally proposed by IBM as a 128-bit cypher, but the NSA (the U.S. spy agency) insisted that it be trimmed to 56 bits before accepting it as the basis for the national cryptographic standard—the NSA didn't want an algorithm that they could never break. DES has been the encryption algorithm of choice for the U.S. government for doing interbank electronic fund transfers and for most commercial users. In all its years of service, there has not been a reported case of DES cracking. A machine performing one DES decryption per microsecond would take 2000 years to crack a given key. The DES algorithm enables 72 quadrillion possible keys.

Kerberos uses an encryption cypher based on DES. As far as keys go, Kerberos uses a shared, session-specific, private key approach. Remember, Kerberos maintains a list of each client's password (or private key). Because it knows all the private keys (or passwords), Kerberos can generate an encrypted session key that convinces a recipient that the sender is really authentic. The recipient decrypts the session key using its private key, and is satisfied that only Kerberos could have encrypted it using its password. As a result, it accepts the shared session key. And, the sender is happy because it knows the recipient must be authentic because it was able to decipher the encrypted session key issued by Kerberos.

RSA is a public key algorithm invented at MIT. RSA stands for the initials of its three inventors. It is considered the public key algorithm of choice and is used mostly for authentication. RSA can also be used for encrypting very short messages. The problem is that RSA is too slow for encrypting longer messages and requires DES to do that. If the encryption is done in software, DES is about 100 times faster than RSA. In hardware, DES is between 1000 and 10,000 times as fast, depending on the implementation (Source: Stang and Moore, **Network Security Secrets**, IDC Books, 1993).

So why would anybody want RSA? Because it lets you encrypt messages without the prior exchange of secrets (or tokens) and it provides an unforgeable electronic signature (see Figure 12-3). Only you can know your private key—there is no "trusted third party" like Kerberos. An RSA signature can be binding in legal courts because there can be no fingerpointing. And if you loose control of your private key, you're the only one to blame. It takes 2 billion years of computer time to break an RSA key. One of the problems with RSA is that the private key part must be delivered to each node on the network without breaching security. They need something like Kerberos to do that.

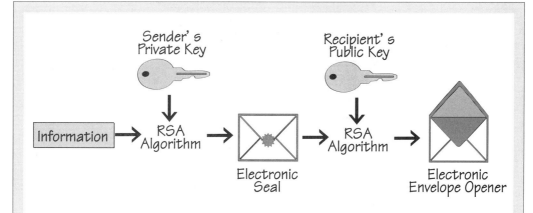

Figure 12-3. Public Keys: The Sealed Digital Envelope.

So with this explanation behind us, let's go back to the Novell, DCE, and Kerberos controversy. Novell does not support encrypted messages; therefore, it does not need DES. But when it came to authentication, Novell chose not to use Kerberos because it felt RSA did the job. It did not require a "trusted security server" that could become a bottleneck in large networks. However, the DCE implementation of Kerberos avoids that problem by replicating the security servers and the password databases. The level of DCE security (and therefore number of exchanges with Kerberos) is based on user-defined policy. It is very hard to imagine a session-level RPC authentication being slower than an RSA encryption/decryption cycle (especially when you factor in the query to the public key server).

The only advantage RSA provides over DCE's version of Kerberos is the "unforgeable" electronic signature. But as far as we know, all the Kerberos security loopholes were eliminated in the HP-augmented version DCE uses. We've never heard of anybody breaking DCE Kerberos, but can it be used in courts? Even though Kerberos does not totally eliminate fingerpointing, somebody should take a Kerberos-authenticated signature to court and find out.

In summary, the DCE version of Kerberos scales well and provides fool-proof authentication. DES is needed for encrypted messages regardless of whether you're using RSA or Kerberos. So why did Novell reject Kerberos? Perhaps Novell, like Microsoft, did not want to pay the OSF licensing fees for the augmented DCE version of Kerberos. Of course, the Novell marketing literature could always claim that NetWare provides electronic signatures that can stand in a court of law. ❑

Distributed File System (DFS)

For its distributed file server, OSF chose the *Andrew File System (AFS)* from Transarc (and Carnegie Mellon University) and the diskless client from HP (also based on AFS protocols). The DCE *Distributed File System (DFS)* provides a uniform namespace, file location transparency, and high availability. DFS is log-based and thus offers the advantage of a fast restart and recovery after a server crash. Files and directories can be replicated (invisibly) on multiple servers for high availability. A cache-consistency protocol allows a file to be changed in a cache. The changes are automatically propagated to all other caches where the file is used, as well as on the disk that owns the file. The DFS file system APIs are based on the POSIX 1003.1a (portable OS interface). DFS is interoperable with Sun's NFS, giving NFS sites an easy migration path to the more function-rich DFS file server.

DFS provides a single image file system that can be distributed across a group of file servers. The DFS file naming scheme is location-independent. Each file has a unique identifier that is consistent across the network. Files use the DCE global namespace just like the rest of the network resources. And the file system is integrated with the DCE security and RPC mechanisms. Because DFS fully exploits the DCE services, it can be administered from any DCE node, which helps keep costs down in a widely distributed system.

Threads

OSF chose the Concert Multithread Architecture (CMA) from DEC. This portable thread package runs in the user space and includes small wrapper routines to translate calls to a native kernel-based thread package (like OS/2 or Mach threads). Threads are an essential component of client/server applications and are used by the other DCE components. The DCE thread package makes it possible to provide granular levels of multitasking on operating systems that do not provide kernel-supported threads. The DCE thread APIs are based on the POSIX 1003.4a (Pthreads standard). The DCE threads also support multiprocessor environments using shared memory. DCE provides a semaphore service that helps threads synchronize their access to shared memory.

OSF's DCE Releases

The following is a chronology of the DCE releases from OSF:

- **Release 1.0**, shipped 1Q '92, is a developer's toolkit.

- **Release 1.0.1**, shipped 3Q '92, is a production release.

- **Release 1.0.2**, shipped 2Q '93, fixed hundreds of bugs and integrated DFS into DCE.

- **Release 1.0.3**, shipped December 1993, fixed more bugs. This maintenance release focused on providing an industrial-strength version of the Distributed File System.

- **Release 1.1**, due in September 1994 (it slipped from 4Q '93), is a major DCE release that adds a ton of new function. It will have faster, tighter code and will be easier to manage. The RPC may incorporate the dynamic invocation feature from CORBA and may be more ORB-friendly. We expect to see some load balancing on the server side of the RPC and better availability features. The new auditing and accounting features will help with system management; the DCE environment will be able to track its events. The naming services will support double-byte character sets (for international language support). The release promises to make DCE industrial-strength. These features will not appear in commercial implementations until some time in 1995.

The DCE releases are for OSF members such as IBM, Tandem, DEC, and HP. The members must then take the OSF release code and port it to their respective platforms and do whatever it takes to create a product. You should expect a product lag of at least six months.

How to Profit From DCE

Soapbox

The intergalactic NOSs are creating brave new possibilities for client/server application developers. There are no limits to the possible system ensembles that can be built on top of an architectural base, such as the one DCE provides. The winners in the software development game will be those who learn how to harness that architectural power and use it to create exciting new software packages. Just think of all the personal agents and network gnomes that can roam through the DCE universe and do all sorts of interesting stuff.

You can think of "intergalactic" distributed architectures (such as DCE) as large shopping malls that rent you space on which to run your software. You create the shops, boutiques, and even department stores that physically reside in the mall. You depend on the mall owners to provide parking, common grounds, and a pleasant environment for shoppers. The key is to figure out what services and boutiques will thrive in that mall. You'll have to discover the software server equivalents of bookstores, restaurants, record stores, jewelers, clothing boutiques, hairdressers, and large department stores.

All you need to open shop in this client/server shopping mall is a PC running software components, such as the ones described in this book. The pieces are starting to come together, and there is enough to get you started. The point we're making is that there is a very low barrier to entry in this business. Anybody with a fully-loaded PC can play in it and compete effectively. So now that you don't have to worry about the plumbing, lighting, or parking, you have more time to concentrate on what the shoppers in the mall (the clients) really need in terms of services and goods. The ultimate mall will be created using distributed objects on top of DCE's intergalactic services. This is the topic of Part 7. ❑

Part 4
SQL Database Servers

An Introduction to Part 4

Ah! You're still with us, so you must have enjoyed the "single system illusion" in the last part. NOSs and stacks are great—there can be no client/server computing without them. But the real hot area in client/server today is in SQL databases. Have you Martians heard about Database Valley? That's a strip of highway south of San Francisco where database companies are creating a new California Gold Rush. But in the new Gold Rush, they mine SQL instead of gold.

So pack your luggage: We're heading west. What? You Martians don't have cowboy boots? No problem. They wear sneakers in Database Valley. You won't need mining gear, either. All the modern mining is done on computer screens by looking at SQL tables and relational calculus. The guy who discovered the gold, a guru named Codd, is a mathematician. Yes, an abstract mathematician created a new Gold Rush with tables. No, the tables are not made of gold. They're computer creations that point to other tables and store and organize information. In this part, we're going to visit the gold country and understand how putting SQL databases on client/server networks could have created such a commotion.

Even though all these new database barons live within a few miles from each other, they all speak different SQL dialects. They can't understand each other. And the biggest barons are always charging ahead with new features that bring in more gold. So how do they ever work together? By throwing tons of middleware onto networks. These folks have agreed to create loosely coupled database federations fueled by middleware. The more ambitious are now proposing to pull all the world's data into warehouses that transform it into information. The warehouses could turn into perpetual gold-generating machines.

The plan for Part 4 is to first look at what this SQL stuff is all about: What standards are being created? What awesome new extensions are the barons concocting? We then look at the middleware needed to create the database federations. With all this preparation behind us, we can look at these fabulous warehouses—the new gold-mining machines. We close with an overview of some representative products that give us some form of reality check. When you deal with gold rushes and California dreams, you really need reality checks.

Chapter 13

SQL Database Servers

At *present the majority of existing client/server-based software is to be found in the area of databases, and it is here that the greatest challenge to any corporation currently lies.*

— *Richard Finkelstein,*
President of Performance Computing

This chapter covers SQL databases from a client/server perspective. SQL servers are the dominant model for creating client/server applications. SQL server vendors—including Oracle, Sybase, Informix, Ingres, and Gupta—have almost become household names. Why is SQL so popular from a client/server connectivity perspective? Can relational databases hold the fort against newer models of client/server computing—including object databases, distributed object managers, and groupware? Are TP Monitors needed, or can we do just fine with the stored procedures provided by the database vendors? In this chapter, we give you a snapshot of where things are in database-centric client/server computing. This sets the stage for answering these questions later in the book.

Our plan for this chapter is to first look at the magic of SQL and the relational model from a client/server perspective. We go over the standards—including SQL-89,

SQL-92, and SQL3. We conclude with the important SQL "extensions" that add active intelligence to tables—including stored procedures, rules, and triggers.[1]

THE FUNDAMENTALS OF SQL AND RELATIONAL DATABASES

Perhaps the most important trend among database servers of any size is the emergence of SQL as the *lingua franca* for the manipulation, definition, and control of data. SQL, now an ISO standard, is a powerful set-oriented language consisting of a few commands; it was created as a language for databases that adhere to the *relational model*.

SQL's Relational Origins

The relational model of database management was developed at IBM's San Jose Research Lab in the early 1970s by E.F. Codd. SQL—pronounced "sequel"— originally stood for Structured Query Language; now the acronym is the name. It was also developed by IBM Research in the mid-1970s to serve as an "English-like" front-end query language to the System R relational database prototype. Even though the SQL language is English-like, it is firmly rooted in the solid mathematical foundation of set theory and predicate calculus. What this really means is that SQL consists of a short list of powerful, yet highly flexible, *commands* that can be used to manipulate information collected in tables. Through SQL, you manipulate and control *sets* of records at a time. You tell the SQL database server what data you need; then it figures out how to get to the data.

The relational model calls for a clear separation of the physical aspects of data from their logical representation. Data is made to appear as simple tables that mask the complexity of the storage access mechanisms. The model frees you from having to concern yourself with the details of how the data is stored and makes the access to data purely logical. Using SQL statements, you only need to specify the tables, columns, and row qualifiers to get to any data item.

Oracle Corporation was the first company to offer a commercial version of SQL with its Oracle database in 1979. In the early 1980s, IBM came out with its own SQL products: SQL/DS and DB2. Today, over 200 vendors offer SQL products on PCs, superminis, and mainframes. Most of these products incorporate the SQL-89

---

[1] In spite of its length, this chapter is not a general introduction to programming with SQL. Here's a shameless advertisement: You'll find a lengthy introduction to SQL and 400 pages of detailed SQL programming examples in our book, **Client/Server Programming with OS/2 2.1** (VNR, 1993).

standard features, some include SQL-92 features, and a few have even implemented their proprietary versions of SQL3 functions.

SQL has become the predominant database language of mainframes, minicomputers, and LAN servers; it provides the focus for a market-share battleground. The emergence of SQL client tools that can work across servers is heating up the competition even more, making SQL a horizontal industry where you can "mix-and-match" front-end tools with back-end servers.

What Does SQL Do?

The SQL language is used to perform complex data operations with a few simple commands in situations that would have required hundreds of lines of conventional code. Physicists might call SQL "the grand unified theory of database" because of the multifaceted roles it plays. Here is a partial list of roles:

- ***SQL is an interactive query language for ad hoc database queries.*** SQL was originally designed as an end-user query language. However, modern graphical front-ends to SQL databases are much more intuitive to use. And they do a good job hiding the underlying SQL semantics from end users.

- ***SQL is a database programming language.*** It can be embedded in languages such as C, C++, and COBOL to access data or it can be called using the X/Open callable interface API set. Vendors, like Sybase and Oracle, even offer SQL-specific programming languages. SQL provides a consistent language for programming with data. This raises programmer productivity and helps produce a more maintainable and easy to change system.

- ***SQL is a data definition and data administration language.*** The data definition language is used to define simple tables, complex objects, indexes, views, referential integrity constraints, and security and access control. All the SQL-defined objects are automatically tracked (and maintained) in an active data dictionary (that is, system catalogs). The structure and organization of a SQL database is stored in the database itself.

- ***SQL is the language of networked database servers.*** It is being used as a universal language to access and manipulate all types of data. For example, the IBM Information Warehouse uses SQL as the network access standard for both relational and non-relational data (like IMS and Indexed files). Even the object database vendors are adopting a derivative of SQL as a query language for objects.

■ ***SQL helps protect the data in a multiuser networked environment.*** It does that by providing good reliability features such as data validation, referential integrity, rollback (undo transaction), automatic locking, and deadlock detection and resolution in a multiuser LAN environment. SQL also enforces security and access control to database objects.

SQL provides a number of advantages to system builders because the same language that is used to define the database is also used to manipulate it. The SQL language makes it easy to specify product requirements in an unambiguous manner. This helps communications between customers, developers, and Database Administrators (DBAs).

The ISO Standards: SQL-89, SQL-92, and SQL3

Although many commercial implementations of SQL have existed since 1979, there was no official standard until 1986, when one was published jointly by the American National Standard Institute (ANSI) and the International Standards Organization (ISO). The 1986 standard was revised in 1989 to introduce referential (and check constraints) integrity; it is now known as *SQL-89* or ANSI SQL. In late 1989, a separate ANSI addendum for Embedded SQL was added to SQL-89.

SQL-89

The SQL-89 standard was an "intersection" of the SQL implementations of that time, which made it easy for existing products to conform to it. SQL-89 was a watered-down SQL that made the term "SQL compliant" almost meaningless. Vendors (like Gupta, Oracle, and XDB) would usually add DB2 (or SAA) compliance to their checklist of compliances. And even that didn't mean too much, at least in terms of creating a unified SQL.

SQL-92

The ISO *SQL-92* (also called SQL2), ratified in late 1992, is over five times the length of the original SQL-89 standard. SQL-92 standardizes many of the features previously left to the implementor's discretion (i.e., the loopholes) and is essentially a superset of SQL-89. C.J. Date estimates that it's going to take a big implementation effort to bring the current relational databases to SQL-92 standards. To get around that problem, ISO suggests a staged approach with three levels of compliance: entry, intermediate, and full. To help you understand where you're at, the SQL-92 standard introduces the concept of a *flagger*—a program that examines the source code and "flags" all SQL statements that do not conform to SQL-92.

What's New in SQL-92?

Details

Incidentally, the word "relation" does not appear anywhere in the standard. And the word "database" is used only informally (it is formally replaced by "SQL data"). This is a relational database standard?

— **C.J. Date (May, 1993)**

This section provides a quick summary of what's new in SQL-92 for readers who are already familiar with SQL and the previous SQL-89 standard. If you're not familiar with SQL, first read this chapter and then come back to this box.

The previous SQL-89 standard supports the SQL Data Definition Language (DDL) for creating tables, indexes, views, and referential integrity constraints. The standard also supports GRANT/REVOKE security privileges. The SQL-89 Data Manipulation Language (DML) consists of the SELECT, INSERT, UPDATE, and DELETE commands. COMMIT and ROLLBACK are used for transaction management. A cursor mechanism provides row-at-a-time navigation. The SQL-89 Embedded SQL addendum defines the mechanism for embedding SQL statements in FORTRAN, COBOL, PL/I, and Pascal.

The "new" SQL-92 standard supports all the SQL-89 features and adds the following features:

- **SQL agents**—these are defined as programs or interactive users that produce SQL statements. In the previous standard, SQL statements were associated with Authorization IDs (an ambiguous concept).

- **SQL client/server connections**—before performing any database operations, a SQL agent must ask the SQL client code to CONNECT to some SQL server. A connection establishes a SQL session. SQL-92 supports concurrent connections (or sessions) but only one can be active at a given time. Agents can explicitly switch between connections using the SET CONNECTION command.

- **More granular transaction controls**—using the SET TRANSACTION command, we can specify a transaction as read-only or read/write. A read-only transaction cannot change the state of the database. In addition, we can set the *isolation level* (i.e., the level of automatic lock protection) for a given transaction to *read-uncommitted*, *read-committed*, *read-repeatable*, or *serializable*.

■ **Standardized catalogs for describing the structure of a database**—a catalog, in the new standard, is a collection of *SQL-schemas* describing "one database." The schemas are SQL tables that describe the structure of base tables, views, privileges, constraints, etc. Each SQL-session has one *cluster* of catalogs describing all the data available to that session.

■ **Embedded SQL support for new languages**—including C, Ada, and MUMPS.

■ **Support for dynamic SQL**—including dynamic cursors and the typical commands (with minor surprises) that have been used by most database vendors to generate SQL code at run time.

■ **Support for new data types**—including BLOBs, VARCHAR, DATE, TIME, and TIMESTAMP.

■ **Support for temporary tables**—including local and global tables. Temporary tables are used as working storage and are automatically dropped at the end of a session. Think of them as memory variables created using the SQL DDL statement with the TEMPORARY attribute.

■ **Support for join operators**—including outer join, union join (no matching), cross join (all combinations), and inner join. All of these joins are supported with special operators in the FROM clauses of queries. SQL-89 did not specify mechanisms for creating the different types of joins.

■ **Standardized error codes and diagnostics**—the use of SQLCODE is not recommended any more; the preferred approach is to use SQLSTATE, which contains a five-character text string with standard values for the different error conditions. A GET DIAGNOSTICS statement was introduced to return more error information.

■ **Domain checks and constraints**—including domain constraints (acceptable values), assertions, and base table constraints. Constraints are rules that a user defines to restrict the values of what goes into the table columns. Any constraint can be defined to be immediate or deferred.

■ **Miscellaneous improvements**—including new string functions, scrollable cursors, commands for altering and dropping objects, refinements to the referential integrity model, support for data type conversions, improvements in revoking privileges, and a CASE statement.

Some of the "new" SQL-92 features are already implemented in existing database products. However, be prepared for a few surprises in almost every area, regardless of how familiar they may seem. ❏

SQL3

Even though it may take vendors many more years to become fully SQL-92 compliant, a new 1000-page SQL3 draft is already in circulation. The specification will be broken into four documents: SQL/CLI, Persistent Stored Modules (or SQL/PSM), SQL/Bindings (with application languages), and SQL3, which covers everything left over. Each document will progress independently—it's a multipart standard. SQL3 adds many new features to an already bloated SQL-92 standard. But we don't expect SQL3 to be ratified until the latter part of the decade. Just to calibrate you, it took three years before the early SQL-92 draft, which appeared sometime in 1989, became a standard. However, it's important to get a cursory understanding of what's being proposed in the SQL3 standard to get an idea of where SQL is heading (see Figure 13-1).

Figure 13-1. The Evolution of the SQL Specification.

The most important new features in the SQL3 draft are the Object SQL features—including encapsulation, methods, user-defined data types, and inheritance. The SQL3 spec refers to these functions as *MOOSE*, which stands for *Major Object-Oriented SQL Extensions*. We will return to Object DBMSs in Part 7.

SQL3 is also developing the specification for stored procedures, triggers, and user-defined functions. It will probably incorporate a revised version of the X/Open SQL *Callable Level Interface (CLI)*, which supports stored procedures. In addition, SQL3 may also include specifications for multimedia SQL (SQL/MM). The ISO group commissioned to look at the implications of "full text" data for SQL expanded its charter to include the more general issue of multimedia data—including full text, digitized audio, video clips, spatial and seismic data, and other forms of real-life data structures. SQL/MM, like MOOSE, will use abstract data types to define the operations supported on each multimedia object type. Unlike today's BLOBs, abstract data types provide methods to manipulate each of the multimedia data types. Providing the storage is the easy part; the harder part is providing the methods and enough multimedia-specific data fields that allow us to do something meaningful with these BLOBs (like rotating or playing them). As DEC's Jim Melton, one of the key SQL3 strategists, puts it, "BLOBs and objects are two very different animals."

The SQL3 draft also contains suggested SQL improvements—including persistent (or "held") cursors that remain open after a commit, new join types, temporary views, user-defined roles in security, column specific privileges, and a better definition of how to update views. It also deals with esoteric topics—including syncpoints over sessions, subtables and supertables, and asynchronous SQL statement execution.

WHAT DOES A DATABASE SERVER DO?

In a database-centric client/server architecture, a client application usually requests data and data-related services (such as sorting and filtering) from a database server. The database server, also known as the SQL engine, responds to the client's requests and provides secured access to shared data. A client application can, with a single SQL statement, retrieve and modify a set of server database records. The SQL database engine can filter the query result sets resulting in considerable data communication savings.

A SQL server manages the control and execution of SQL commands. It provides the logical and physical views of the data and generates optimized access plans for executing the SQL commands. In addition, most database servers provide server administration features and utilities that help manage the data. A database server also maintains dynamic catalog tables that contain information about the SQL objects housed within it.

Because a SQL server allows multiple applications to access the same database at the same time, it must provide an environment that protects the database against a variety of possible internal and external threats. The server manages the recovery, concurrency, security, and consistency aspects of a database. This includes controlling the execution of a transaction and undoing its effects if it fails. This also includes obtaining and releasing locks during the course of executing a transaction and protecting database objects from unauthorized access.

Most SQL servers provide, at a minimum, SQL-89 level functionality. Most servers also include some SQL-92 features, but to our knowledge no vendor has yet implemented a fully compliant SQL-92 server. Quite a few servers offer proprietary versions of SQL3 stored procedures, triggers, and rules. Some server engines (for example, Ingres) have implemented some form of SQL Object extensions.

So what is a SQL server? It's a strange hybrid mix of standard SQL and vendor-specific extensions. The leading database-only vendors—including Sybase, Oracle, Informix, and Ingres—have a vested interest in extending their database engines to perform server functions that go far beyond the relational data model. The more diversified system software vendors—including IBM, DEC, Tandem, and Novell—are inclined to stick with SQL standards and offload the non-standard procedural extensions to NOSs (like DCE), TP Monitors, Object Databases, and Distributed Object Managers. Finally, some of the smaller database vendors—including Gupta, XDB, and Watcom—are making their mark by creating "best-of-breed," standard-compliant implementations of SQL.

In this section, we briefly go over the architecture of database servers. We then review some of the major features they provide—including shared data access, transactional protection, referential and domain integrity, and database catalogs.

SQL Database Server Architectures

Figures 13-2, 13-3, and 13-4 show three server architectures that databases use to handle remote database clients: process-per-client, multithreaded, and hybrid. Here are the trade-offs of the three approaches:

■ *Process-per-client architectures* provide maximum bullet-proofing by giving each database client its own process address space. The database runs in one or more separate background processes. The advantages of this architecture is that it protects the users from each other, and it protects the database manager from the users. In addition, the processes can easily be assigned to different processors on a multiprocessor SMP machine. Because the architecture relies on the local OS for its multitasking services, an OS that supports SMP can transparently assign server processes to a pool of available processors. The disadvantage of process-per-client is that it consumes more memory and CPU resources than the alternative schemes. It can be slower because of process context switches and interprocess communications overhead. However, these problems can easily be overcome with the use of a TP Monitor that manages a pool of reusable processes. Examples of database servers that implement this architecture include DB2/2, Informix, and Oracle6.

■ *Multithreaded architectures* provide the best performance by running all the user connections, applications, and the database in the same address space. This architecture provides its own internal scheduler and does not rely on the local OS's tasking and address protection schemes. The advantage is that it conserves memory and CPU cycles by not requiring frequent context switches. In addition, the server implementations tend to be more portable across platforms because they don't require as many local OS services. The disadvantage

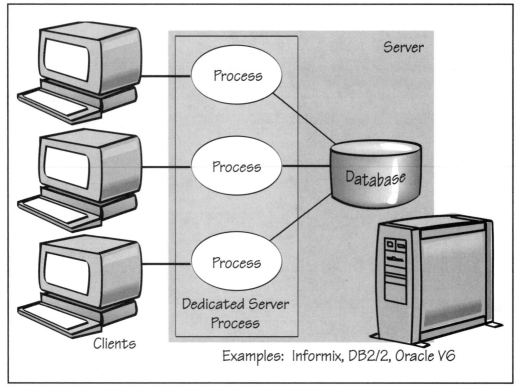

Figure 13-2. Process-per-Client Database Server Architecture.

is that a misbehaved user application can bring down the entire database server and all its tasks. In addition, user programs that consist of long-duration tasks (for example, long queries) can hog all the server resources. Finally, the preemptive scheduling provided by the server tends to be inferior to the native OS's scheduler. Examples of database servers that implement this architecture include Sybase and SQL Server (but SQL Server uses Windows NT's SMP scheduler instead of the one provided by Sybase).

■ *Hybrid architectures* consist of three components: 1) multithreaded network listeners that participate in the initial connection task by assigning the client to a dispatcher; 2) dispatcher tasks that place messages on an internal message queue, and then dequeue the response and send it back to the client; and 3) reusable shared server worker processes that pick the work off the queue, execute it, and place the response on an out queue. The advantage of this architecture is that it provides a protected environment for running the user tasks without assigning a permanent process to each user. The disadvantages are queue latencies. While this architecture, appears on the surface to be good, its load balancing is not as good as that provided by a TP Monitor. In fact, the queues may get in the way of the TP Monitor's own scheduling algorithms. The

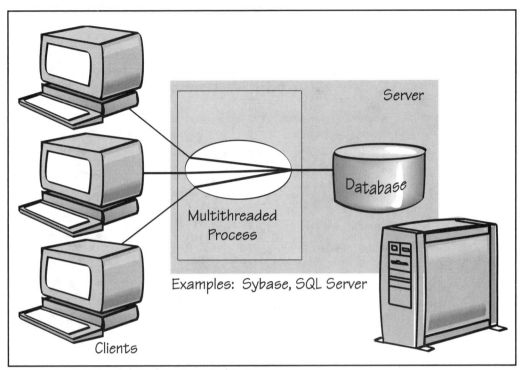

Figure 13-3. Multithreaded Database Server Architecture.

first database server to implement this architecture is Oracle7. According to Rich Finkelstein, you can expect anywhere from 20% improvements to 20% degradation of performance between Oracle V6 and Oracle7.

So which architecture is best for client/server? It's a tough choice. The process-per-client architectures perform poorly when large number of users connect to a database, but they provide the best protection. The multithreaded architectures can support large number of users running short transactions, but they do not perform well when large queries are involved. They also do not provide bullet-proof protection. Hybrid architectures are, in theory, very promising. But are they better than using a TP Monitor with a process-per-client database server? As a rule of thumb, these architectures don't matter much if you're just doing simple LAN-based decision support. However, they do matter if you're planning to create a bullet-proof OLTP system. If you're planning the latter, we suggest that you check references carefully and go for the maximum amount of bullet-proofing.

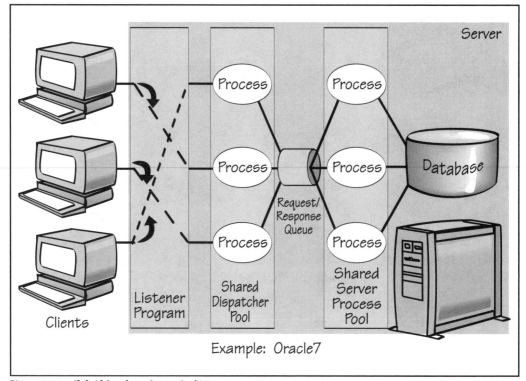

Figure 13-4. Hybrid Database Server Architecture.

STORED PROCEDURES, TRIGGERS, AND RULES

Relational databases now have built-in procedural extensions—including stored procedures, triggers, and rules. These extensions are very useful but extremely non-standard. So why are database servers moving into the procedural turf? What are these extensions and what new services do they provide? We answer the first question with an opinionated Soapbox. The contents of this section attempt to answer the second question.

What Is a Stored Procedure?

Many database vendors are now offering an RPC-like mechanism for database. This mechanism is sometimes referred to as "TP lite" or "stored procedures." A stored procedure is a named collection of SQL statements and procedural logic that is compiled, verified, and stored in the server database. A stored procedure is

Look Who's Cheating

Soapbox

Relational database vendors are cheating big time. They're adding all sorts of procedural extensions to SQL that deviate from the original vision of a "pure declarative language for relational data." Database purists used to scoff at procedural languages for being "relationally incomplete and insecure."

So what are today's newest and hottest SQL extensions? They are procedural constructs of all types—including stored procedures, triggers, rules, and proprietary scripting languages. So instead of keeping the data separate from the code, the relational vendors have simply brought the code to the database. Not only do databases store procedures, but they have also given them the keys to the data kingdom. Procedural constructs, as you will find out in this section, are simply taking over the database.

So the current message we're getting from the relational vendors is: "Procedures are OK as long as they're *ours* and we get to store them on *our* databases." But we believe database vendors are stepping out of their territory. They should stick to managing the data and leave the procedural extensions to the NOS RPCs, MOMs, TP Monitors, Object Databases, and Distributed Object Managers (DOMs). Of course, what will happen instead is that everybody will step into everybody else's turf; most client/server systems will become hybrids of some sort. ❑

typically treated like any other database object and registered in the SQL catalog. Access to the stored procedure is controlled through the server's security mechanisms.

Stored procedures accept input parameters so that a single procedure can be used over the network by multiple clients using different input data. The client invokes a remote procedure and passes it the parameters required to do a job. A single remote message triggers the execution of a collection of stored SQL statements. The result is a reduction of network traffic (compared to remote SQL) and better performance. Table 13-1 shows the results of a TPC-like benchmark we ran on a DB2/2 database to compare the performance of dynamic SQL, static SQL, and two flavors of stored procedures. The results explain why stored procedures are so attractive—they're much faster in client/server situations than the other SQL alternatives.

Table 13-1. Server Network Performance.[1]

LAN Database Servers		LAN Stored Procedures	
Dynamic SQL (RDS/NETBIOS)	Static SQL (RDS/NETBIOS)	Application Remote Interface (RDS/NETBIOS)	Roll-Your-Own Named Pipes (NetBIOS)
2.2 TP1s/sec	3.9 TP1s/sec	10.9 TP1s/sec	11.6 TP1s/sec

1. The benchmarks are from our book: **Client/Server Programming with OS/2 2.1, Third Edition** (VNR, 1993). The book contains about 100 pages of code for running these benchmarks. The benchmarks were run on a slow 486-class machine; they do not represent the best-case performance of DB2/2.

The concept of stored procedures was pioneered by Sybase in 1986 to improve the performance of SQL on networks. Stored procedures are used to enforce business rules and data integrity; to perform system maintenance and administration functions; and to extend the database server's functions. However, the primary use of stored procedures (in all of its variations) is to create the server side of an application's logic. The encapsulation features of stored procedures are well suited for creating performance-critical applications known as Online Transaction Processing or *OLTP*. These applications typically: 1) receive a fixed set of inputs from remote clients; 2) perform multiple precompiled SQL commands against a *local* database; 3) commit the work; and 4) return a fixed set of results (see Figure 13-5).

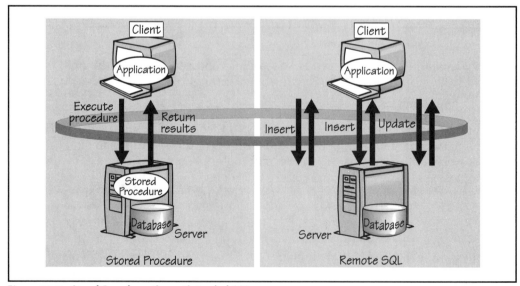

Figure 13-5. Stored Procedures Versus Networked SQL.

In other words, a stored procedure is a database-centric, RPC-like SQL entity that is persistent, shared, and has a name. It reduces network traffic, improves response times, and provides an object-oriented flavor of database service that is well suited for OLTP applications. Stored procedures also provide better *site autonomy* because the remote modification of tables can only occur through locally executing programs. If the tables change, you don't need to recompile all your remote applications. In general, stored procedures provide better distribution of intelligence than static or dynamic remote SQL.

Static and Dynamic SQL

Briefing

Static SQL statements are defined in your code and converted into an access plan at program preparation time. The SQL statement is known before your program is run. The database objects need to exist when precompiling static SQL statements. You can think of static SQL as being a compiled form of the SQL language. Static SQL is a performance enhancement feature.

Dynamic SQL statements are created and issued at run time. They offer maximum flexibility at the expense of execution speed. You can think of dynamic SQL as an interpretive form of the SQL language. The database objects need not exist when precompiling dynamic SQL statements. The compilation of dynamic SQL statements is done at run time and must be repeated every time the same statement gets executed again.

Static SQL is used for writing highly optimized transaction programs. Dynamic SQL is used for writing general database programming utilities and by GUI front-end tools that need to create ad hoc queries. ❏

Stored Procedures Versus Static and Dynamic SQL

Table 13-2 compares the client/server functional characteristics of stored procedures with other forms of SQL programming. You can see that stored procedures offer many advantages.

Table 13-2. Stored Procedures Versus Static and Dynamic SQL.

Feature	Stored Procedure	Remote SQL	
		Embedded Static	Dynamic
Named function	Yes	No	No
Shared function	Yes	No	No
Persistently stored on server	Yes	Yes	No
Input/output parameters	Yes	No	No
Tracked in catalog	Yes	Yes	No
Procedural logic	Within object	External	External
Flexibility	Low	Low	High
Abstraction level	High	Low	Low
Standard	No	Yes	Yes
Performance	Fast	Medium	Slow
Tool-friendly	No	No	Yes
Client/Server shrink-wrap friendly	Yes (call procedure)	No (messy)	Yes (CLI calls)
Network messages	1 request/reply for many SQL commands	1 request/reply per SQL command	1 request/reply per SQL command

So, What's Wrong With Stored Procedures?

One drawback of stored procedures is that they provide less ad hoc flexibility than remote dynamic SQL. In addition, stored procedures may perform very poorly if their plans are not refreshed (rebound) to take advantage of the optimizer statistics—dynamic SQL creates a fresh plan with every execution. Another drawback is that there is no transactional synchronization—i.e., two-phase commit—between stored procedures; each stored procedure is a separate transaction.

However, the main drawback of stored procedures is that they're totally non-standard. This results in a number of problems. No two vendor implementations are alike. The language for describing the stored procedures and their functionality vary from server to server; stored procedures are not portable across vendor platforms. There is no standard way to pass or describe the parameters. It is difficult for database tools to create and manage stored procedures. Dealing with the parameters is very messy (there is no standard interface definition language or stub compiler tool).

Alternatives to Stored Procedures

Soapbox

OK, we'll admit it. Stored procedures are better than the embedded SQL alternative. But now that you've seen what these stored procedures are all about, you may agree with us that they're not a panacea, and they're certainly not the only game in town. Stored procedures (or "TP lite") will face some stiff competition from other types of RPC-like extensions, which offer more sophisticated functions and are further along in their standardized implementations. For example, NOSs and Transaction Monitors have their own architectures for implementing function that is equivalent to the database stored procedures. You've already encountered the NOS's DCE RPC and the MOM implementations in Part 3. In Part 5, we'll go over the "TP Heavy" implementation of stored procedures. You'll discover that Transaction Monitors provide an OS-like environment for scheduling and managing transactions. Transaction Monitors execute stored procedures "in style" by providing message queuing, load balancing, routing, nesting, and two-phase commit synchronization. In addition, distributed object managers are defining their own versions of stored procedures (i.e., method invocations) through the CORBA standard. ❑

Which Stored Procedure?

The following examples illustrate some of the differences in vendor implementations of stored procedures:

■ **Sybase and SQL Server** stored procedures can return multiple rows, but they do not support cursors. They require the use of Transact-SQL, a proprietary procedural language, to create the stored procedures, which are compiled and stored in the catalog. The procedures are invoked using the SQL EXECUTE command and passing it the name of the stored procedure and server on which it resides.

■ **Oracle7** stored procedures only return a single row, but they support cursors. They require the use of PL/SQL—a proprietary procedural language. The procedures are invoked by following the procedure or function name with a database link that points to the remote server.

■ **IBM's DB2/2** implements stored procedures as ordinary DLL functions written in standard programming languages. The stored procedures (DLLs) reside on the same server as the database, but they are not stored within the database.

The procedures are executed by issuing an Application Remote Interface (ARI) command that uses two buffers (of type SQLDA) to pass self-describing parameters.

■ **Gupta's SQLBase** allows a set of SQL commands (known as a *command chain*) to be stored on the server and later executed. SQLBase does not support procedural extensions within the command chain. Three SQL extended commands—STORE, EXECUTE, and ERASE—are used to manage the command chains.

■ **Informix** won't let you share stored procedures between transactions.

The list of vendor differences goes on. The bad news is that SQL-92 does not address stored procedures; SQL3 does, but we won't see it soon enough.

Triggers and Rules

Triggers are special user-defined actions—usually in the form of stored procedures—that are automatically invoked by the server based on data-related events. Triggers can perform complex actions and can use the full power of a procedural language. A *rule* is a special type of trigger that is used to perform simple checks on data. Both triggers and rules are attached to specific operations on specific tables. In other words, an event tells you something happened to the database; a trigger or rule is an event handler you write to take the proper action in response to that event (see Figure 13-6).

Triggers and rules are typically used to perform tasks related to changes in tables, such as auditing, looking for value thresholds, or setting column defaults. Enabled triggers or rules are executed whenever a table is updated by a SQL DELETE,

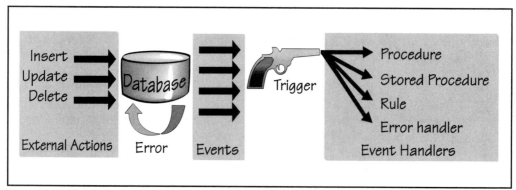

Figure 13-6. The Mechanics of SQL Triggers.

INSERT, or UPDATE command. A separate trigger or rule can be defined for each of these commands, or a single trigger may be defined for any updates to a table.

In general, triggers can call other triggers or stored procedures. So what makes a trigger different from a stored procedure? Triggers are called implicitly by database generated events, while stored procedures are called explicitly by client applications. Server implementations of triggers are extremely non-standard and vendor-specific. Here are some examples of vendor implementation differences:

■ **Sybase and SQL Server** support only one trigger per INSERT/UPDATE/DELETE operation.

■ **Ingres** supports multiple triggers, but the execution of the triggers is non-deterministic.

■ **Oracle7** supports up to 12 triggers per table. It does that by allowing you to specify for each INSERT/UPDATE/DELETE the following: a *before trigger* that fires before the SQL statement executes, and an *after trigger* that fires after the SQL statement executes. In addition, Oracle lets you specify the number of times a trigger fires. *Row-level triggers* fire once for each updated row; *statement-level triggers* fire once for the entire SQL statement, even if no rows are inserted, updated, or deleted. Both can be defined to be active simultaneously. Oracle7's implementation of triggers is close to the SQL3 draft standard (but it's not fully compliant).

■ **Informix** supports before and after triggers and more than one trigger per operation; it uses the column numbers to determine the sequence of trigger firings.

Triggers are written in proprietary SQL procedural extensions. Different implementations limit what triggers can do. For example, Oracle7 will not let you issue commits or rollbacks from within a trigger. Triggers and rules are also used, in a very *non-standard* manner, by Sybase (prior to System 10) and by SQL Server to enforce referential integrity. For example, a trigger associated with a particular table is invoked when data in the table is modified or updated. However, trigger-enforced referential integrity has many drawbacks, and very few database servers use it (see the following Warning box). Instead, most servers implement the SQL-89 defined *declarative referential integrity* standard. In summary, triggers are extremely non-standard, and the situation will not improve until SQL3 becomes a standard.

The Pitfalls of Referential Integrity

Warning

Trigger-enforced referential integrity is non-standard, error-prone, and difficult to implement and maintain. Triggers require programming efforts to implement referential integrity; declarative integrity doesn't. Because a server has no way of knowing that a trigger is being used for referential integrity, it cannot do anything to help optimize it. For example, a transaction that adds 100 new parts to a trigger-enforced relationship between a supplier and parts table will cause the trigger to be executed 100 times. It will check the same key value each time; the execution of triggers is not deferrable. In contrast, a server-enforced referential implementation would check the value only once for the entire transaction.

In addition, referential triggers are hard to document (and query) because they consist of procedural code. In contrast, declarative integrity provides better documentation and clarity by using catalog-based standard DDL SQL statements. Finally, some trigger implementations only support three triggers (or fewer) per table, which may not be enough to exhaustively cover all the referential constraints and rules that need to be enforced. ❏

Chapter 14

SQL Middleware and Federated Databases

A *client/server database is a waste of hardware and software if there's no way to access its data.*

— Joe Salemi (1993) [1]

How does a SQL database client access data that's on multivendor database servers? With database-specific middleware, of course. Why not use straight SQL? Because it's not that simple. A heavy dose of *middleware* is needed to smooth over the different SQL dialects and extensions, network messaging protocols, and vendor-specific "native" APIs. It's sad to report that after eight years of intense standardization efforts, SQL clients cannot talk to SQL servers without layer upon layer of middleware. The best we can do today is to allow a "federation" of loosely-coupled, autonomously-owned, multivendor database servers to communicate using a "least common denominator" approach. The industry calls this compromise *federated database systems*.

---

1 Source: Salemi, **Client/Server Databases** (ZD Press, 1993).

This chapter looks at the middleware that's needed to make SQL clients and servers work across multivendor, heterogeneous, database networks—or more simply put, federated databases. How well does this middleware provide a "single database illusion" in a federated world?

To create the "single database illusion," the middleware must make two sets of customers happy: 1) the developers of applications and front-end tools who need a single OS-independent SQL API to get to any database server; and 2) the MIS connectivity people who must make the disparate desktop clients talk to the "federated" database servers on their enterprise networks. The middleware must address difficult issues such as: How does a client program issue multivendor SQL calls? How do federated database desktops interoperate with federated database servers? Can all this be done transparently?

The good news is that the answer to all these questions is a qualified *yes*. Remote access to federated databases is currently one of the hottest new product areas. It's an area that's also getting a lot of attention from the people who create our industry standards, both *de facto* and *de jure*. The bad news is that there are lots of "standards" and hot products from which you can choose. Another piece of bad news is that this middleware cannot be used to create production-strength, federated databases—it does, however, provide an adequate foundation for decision support systems.

SQL MIDDLEWARE: THE OPTIONS

Based on our previous definition, middleware starts with the API on the client side that is used to invoke a service, and it covers the transmission of the request over the network and the resulting response. Middleware does not include the software that provides the actual service. So the questions we need to answer are: What API do SQL database servers provide to clients? And how is the request/reply exchanged with the server? As you will discover, there are too many answers to both of these questions.

Before going into detailed answers, let's first create a common mindset that will help us understand the solutions. We'll start with SQL "Nirvana"—these are the integrated single-vendor offerings. We then look at the problems created in a multivendor, federated SQL environment. Next we give you a quick overview of the two leading architectures for smoothing over the federated database discrepancies. Finally, we give you our two cents worth on what *federated* SQL Nirvana should include.

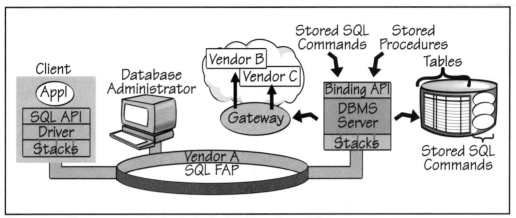

Figure 14-1. The Components of a Single-Vendor SQL Client/Server Offering.

SQL Nirvana: The Single Vendor Option

If a single vendor SQL solution can fulfill all your shared data needs, consider yourself *very* lucky. All you need to do is read this section and then move on to the next chapter. Figure 14-1 shows what a typical single-vendor middleware solution currently provides:

- ■ *A vendor-proprietary SQL API that works on a multiplicity of client platforms.* Most vendors support DOS, Windows, and OS/2 clients; quite a few also support Macintosh and some Unix variants. Most vendor APIs support SQL-89 with proprietary extensions. Some of the vendor APIs use *Embedded SQL (ESQL)*, and others support a call-level interface (CLI). More on that later in this chapter.

- ■ *A vendor-proprietary SQL driver.* This is a thin client run-time element that accepts the API calls, formats a SQL message, and handles the exchanges with the server. The format of the SQL message and the handshake are known, affectionately, as the FAP, which stands for *Format and Protocols*. The SQL FAPs are typically vendor-defined.

- ■ *FAP support for multiple protocol stacks.* As a result of user pressures, most vendors now support multiple protocol stacks. Some vendors bundle the stacks with their drivers; others support a common transport interface (like Sockets or Named Pipes) and require that you provide your own stacks. At the server side, the vendor typically provides "listeners" for the different stacks. However, some vendors provide their own internal protocol gateways. For example, Oracle7 on Unix translates IPX/SPX packets to TCP/IP on the server side.

■ *Gateways to other vendor databases.* Some vendors provide gateways that make other vendors' databases look like their own. For example, Oracle, Sybase, Ingres, Gupta, and XDB all provide gateways to DB2. Most vendor-supplied database gateways only provide an intersection of the features supported by the two databases (i.e., the least common denominator). This means that most vendor-supplied database gateways only support dynamic SQL. They are only good for simple data extracts and queries—not for transaction processing (also see the following Soapbox). Most vendor-supplied gateways require two database engines: the vendor's own database, which acts as a middle tier on the gateway server; and the "foreign" database. The middle-tier database server provides a directory of connected databases, catalog services, and handles the shipping and routing of "foreign" requests.

■ *Client/Server database administration tools.* Most vendors will let you manage and administer the database from a remote workstation using a graphical user interface. You have a single point of management for the middleware, the clients, and the servers, as long as they're from the *same* vendor.

■ *Front-end graphical application development and query tools.* These help you create visual interfaces to the database server. Of course, each vendor supplies GUI tools for its own database servers. Most third-party tools do a good job for a particular database (see the following Warning box).

Tools: Not All Databases Are Equal

Warning

The SQL database server peculiarities and extensions create major headaches for the vendors of multiplatform client/server database tools. As a result, the support of server extensions tends to be highly uneven. Most tool vendors usually do an excellent job supporting their "preferred" server platform, they do a mediocre job on the second platform, and they do an atrocious job for the rest of the platforms (they provide almost no support for server-specific extensions). Let's face it: front-end tool vendors have their cup full just trying to keep up with the graphical engines on which they run—Windows, Motif, Macintosh, and the OS/2 Workplace Shell—and they can only deal with so many server idiosyncrasies. The current darling of the tool vendors is Sybase because its own tools are comparatively weak. However, each database server has its GUI tool specialists. With over 120 GUI tool vendors out there, many are trying to stay alive by becoming best-of-breed for a particular database server (i.e., specializing). ❏

Vendor Gateways: Are They Just a Bandaid?

Soapbox

A vendor gateway solution is not really open. It ties you into the vendor's database offering, and you get whatever gateway connectivity the vendor chooses to implement. Typically, the vendor will not support the smaller platforms (and if they do, support is very spotty). The vendor also has no incentive to create a level playing field for their competitor's databases. Everybody supports data extracts from DB2 and DEC's Rdb; but what incentive does Oracle have to provide gateways to Sybase and Ingres (or vice versa)?

In all fairness, Sybase, Oracle, and Informix are trying to make their gateways more "open" by exposing some of the internal programming interfaces. For example, the Sybase *Open Data Server (ODS)* and the corresponding Microsoft *Open Data Services (ODS)* are general-purpose, event-driven server APIs that can be used by third parties to create gateways. The OS/2-based MDI *Database Gateway for DB2* was developed jointly by Micro Decisionware and Microsoft using ODS as their gateway base. The MDI OS/2 gateway translates Sybase (DB-Library) or ODBC client API calls to DB2 calls. The clients run on DOS, Windows, or OS/2, and use Named Pipes to communicate to the MDI gateway server, which in turn uses an APPC stack to talk to the mainframe (see Figure 14-2). MDI supports, in addition to DB2, Teradata and SQL/DS.

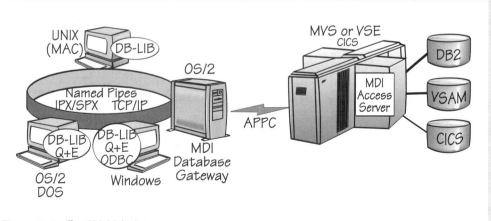

Figure 14-2. The MDI OS/2 Gateway.

Some gateways go out of their way to "compensate" for missing functions on the "foreign" database engines. For example, the MDI gateway provides a mainframe component called the *DB2 CICS Access Server.* It uses the CICS TP Monitor to simulate Sybase stored procedures on DB2 (but it doesn't come cheap; count on paying between $24k and $70k for that convenience). Oracle7 and Ingres gateways support some level of two-phase commit for updating foreign data, but it's still a least common denominator approach.

In our opinion (this is a Soapbox), if you're already locked into a single vendor database solution, then you might as well enjoy the convenience provided by the vendor's gateway. It's good for occasional decision-support access to foreign databases. And it's highly convenient because you use the same APIs and middleware to get to that foreign data almost transparently. However, you're at the total mercy of your vendor, and it locks you in deeper. But given the chaotic state of "open database middleware," locking yourself into a single vendor solution may not be such a bad idea (you'll understand why after you finish reading this chapter). For most large enterprises, a single vendor database solution is not in the cards. They have too many diverse database management requirements that go all the way from PC-based decision support systems to high-volume OLTP production data. ❑

SQL Nightmare: The Multivendor Option

Figure 14-3 shows what happens when you move into a multivendor database world. Here's the short list of obvious inconsistencies that you will immediately face:

■ *Different SQL APIs* make it a nightmare to write a common set of applications. Even if common API semantics were magically to show up later in this chapter, we still need a way to deal with all the proprietary SQL extensions.

■ *Multiple database drivers* eat up precious memory space on the client machines (especially for DOS). Can these drivers use the same protocol stacks or do we need duplicate stacks? If multiple stacks are needed, how will they share the LAN adapter? Who do we call when a problem occurs?

■ *Multiple FAPs and no interoperability* means that the database protocols from the different vendors are simply sharing the LAN; they cannot talk to one another.

■ *Multiple administration tools* means that database administrators must familiarize themselves with a set of managing workstations, each of which have their own semantics and user interfaces.

We have not even addressed some of the thornier issues, such as federated database joins, federated commits, or concurrent access to federated data.

The federated middleware solutions concentrate on simple SQL access to a federated database—one connection at a time. More ambitious schemes, such as RDA and DRDA, aim at creating a federated environment that matches the power of a single-vendor distributed database approach. But they're far from accomplishing that goal. The best we can do today is focus on the issues of submitting simple SQL statements against one federated database at a time.

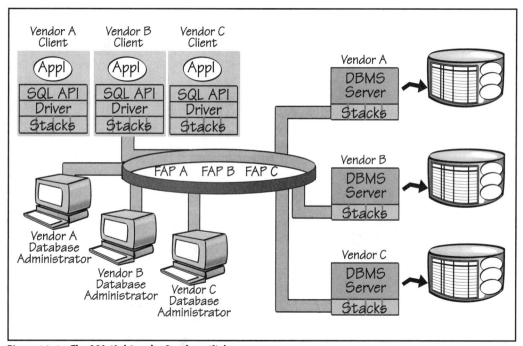

Figure 14-3. The SQL Multivendor Database Nightmare.

Middleware Solution #1: The Common SQL Interface

The first step towards regaining some level of sanity in a federated database environment is to *standardize on a common SQL Interface* (see Figure 14-4). The idea is to create a common SQL API that is used by all the applications and then let the server differences be handled by the different database drivers. This is, of course, easier said than done. Here are the problems:

■ **Which SQL API to standardize on?** You'll soon discover that there are many SQL "standard APIs" on the table. How are stored objects on the server defined and invoked (remember the stored procedures and static SQL)? Should we use a call-level API or the ISO-defined embedded SQL? How do we deal with the non-standard SQL extensions? Will the common interface be slower than the native vendor implementation?

■ ***Multiple drivers are still required.*** Should the drivers reside on the client or on the server side? Who provides the drivers to the "common APIs"? What's the incentive for the vendors to support a "common" driver over their own "native" driver? Can the drivers coexist on the same stacks or on the same LAN adapters?

■ ***Multiple managing stations and multiple FAPs are still required.*** We haven't solved those problems; we just made them invisible to the developer. So the system administration people are still not happy.

Later in this chapter, we will go over the contending schemes for creating a common SQL interface—including Embedded SQL, the SAG CLI, IDAPI, ODBC, Oracle Glue, X/Open, and the EDA/SQL API.

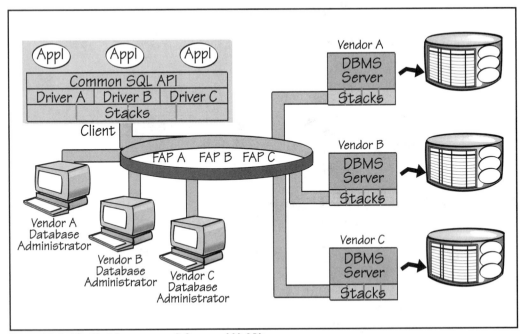

Figure 14-4. The First Convergence: A Common SQL API.

Middleware Solution #2: The Open SQL Gateway

Let's assume that we have all magically agreed on a common SQL interface. What is the next middleware improvement that can be *realistically* accomplished to better articulate the federated database environment? Figure 14-5 shows a middleware solution that's currently in vogue: *the open gateway.* The idea is to standardize on one (or most likely two) open industry FAPs, supply a common client driver for the FAP, and develop a gateway catcher for each server. The gateway catcher will "catch" the incoming FAP messages and translate them to the local server's native SQL interface. The good news is that the industry has at least three "common" FAPs to choose from: the ISO/SAG RDA, IBM's DRDA, and EDA/SQL. Later in this chapter we will spend some time looking at the trade-offs of the three approaches.

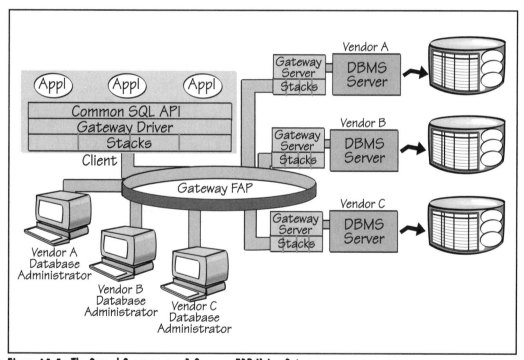

Figure 14-5. The Second Convergence: A Common FAP Using Gateways.

Middleware Solution #3: Federated Nirvana

Let's assume that we have both the common FAP and the common API. What else is needed to create a federated SQL environment that provides the same level of completeness as the single vendor implementation? Figure 14-6 shows what this

Part 4. SQL Database Servers

"ideal" would look like. Notice that we've removed the gateway catchers, which improves server performance, reduces cost, and simplifies maintenance. And, we've created a single database administration interface.

To eliminate the gateway catchers, the common FAP must either support a superset of all the SQL dialects or it must tolerate native SQL dialects (meaning that it must allow pass-throughs). The SQL vendors must also agree to replace their own private FAPs with the common FAP.

The database administration facility will be the last proprietary stronghold to fall. There is just too much variety in the database server implementations to create a common interface. Even if we solved the technological issues, there are still some thorny political issues to be resolved. For example, is there a single point of administration control in a federated database environment? IBM's *DataHub*, an OS/2-based tool, is an example of a federated (but single-vendor) database administration tool. DataHub provides a set of integrated database management functions for DB2/2, DB2/MVS, DB2/VM, DB2/6000, and SQL/400. The database management products from *EcoSystems* are also beginning to address these issues. Finally, the database vendors are working on a DBMS MIB that defines database configuration and control parameters to SNMP management stations.

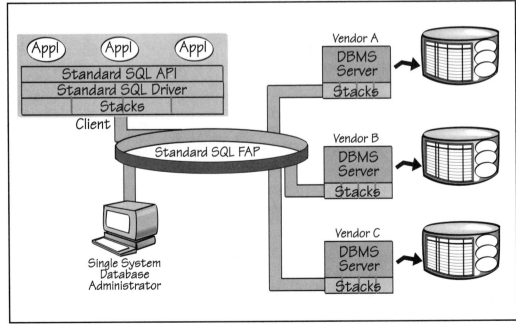

Figure 14-6. The Third Convergence: Direct Implementations of the Common FAP.

WILL THE REAL SQL API PLEASE STAND UP?

How do you access SQL data? Can an application transparently access a system of federated databases? Can an application built for one SQL database be deployed on another? What's the state of the SQL data access standards? The answers, as you will discover in this long section, are a fuzzy yes, no, and maybe.

The early SQL architects felt it was very important to keep the SQL programming language neutral. In fact, SQL was created as a higher-level declarative language that was to isolate us from low-level procedural constructs. Remember, it was designed as an end-user query language. But to create applications that use SQL, it became obvious that SQL constructs needed to be integrated within existing programming languages. Incidentally, "SQL first" people view this process as extending SQL with procedural capabilities, while programmers think of it as providing an interface to SQL services. Two competing approaches are currently in vogue for supporting SQL from within programming languages: *embedded SQL*, and the SQL *Call-Level Interface (CLI)*. Figure 14-7 shows the two approaches.

This section looks at the SQL interface from the point of view of how it helps create a federated middleware solution. We will first look at embedded SQL because it is an ISO standard. We then look at the CLI alternatives, including the SAG CLI and

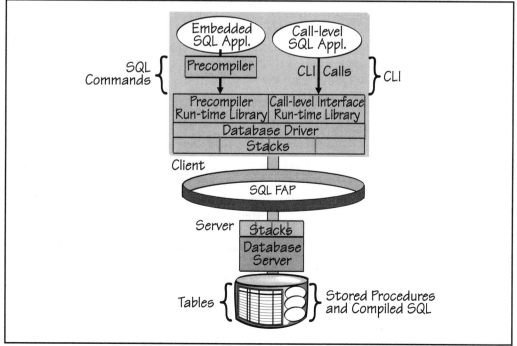

Figure 14-7. SQL APIs Come in Two Styles: CLI and ESQL.

some of its more famous mutants: ODBC, IDAPI, Oracle Glue, and the X/Open SQL CLI. We will defer the discussion of the EDA/SQL CLI to the gateway section.

The SQL-92 Embedded SQL (ESQL)

Embedded SQL (ESQL) is an ISO SQL-92 defined standard for embedding SQL statements "as is" within ordinary programming languages. The SQL-92 standard specifies the syntax for embedding SQL within C, COBOL, FORTRAN, PL/I, Pascal, MUMPS, and ADA. Each SQL statement is flagged with language-specific identifiers that mark the beginning and end of the SQL statement. This approach requires running the SQL source through a precompiler to generate a source code file that the language compiler understands. As an example, for the C-language an embedded SQL statement must start with the **EXEC SQL** keyword pair and end with a semicolon (;). These bracketed statements will be processed by the precompiler and anything else in your source code will be passed through unchanged.

From a client/server packaging perspective, the biggest hurdle with ESQL is that the target database must be known (and available) when the program is being developed. This makes it hard to target a client program to a database at run time. In addition, the installation process involves binding applications to each server database they connect to—a process that may be too complicated for the "shrink-wrapped" client/server software market. Finally, precompilers have traditionally been tied to a particular database product; you must recompile your embedded SQL code for each vendor's database server. The same features that make precompilers so popular with IS shops and corporate developers have turned into liabilities for the providers of shrink-wrapped client/server software.

The SQL Call Level Interfaces (CLIs)

The alternative to Embedded SQL is to use a callable SQL API for database access. An API does not require a precompiler to convert SQL statements into code, which is then compiled and bound to a database. Instead, an API allows you to create and execute SQL statements at run time. In theory, a standard API can help you write portable applications that are independent of any database product. Of course, in practice things are not that simple. In this section, we go over the SAG CLI and some of its more famous mutants: ODBC, IDAPI, Oracle Glue, and the X/Open SQL CLI.

The SAG CLI

In 1988, 44 database vendors created a consortium called the *SQL Access Group (SAG)*, which was to provide a unified standard for remote database access. The original goal of the SAG charter founders—Tandem and DEC—was to accelerate the pace of remote SQL standard development and put in place a multivendor SQL solution that would allow any SQL client to talk to any SQL server. Tandem and DEC were very interested in an open set of multivendor front-end tools for enabling their SQL databases. So they drove the SAG effort, which resulted in one of the industry's most successful "open standards."[2]

SAG focused its efforts on two separate undertakings: 1) An interoperability standard that allows any database client to talk to any database server "at the wire" by using common message formats and protocols, and 2) A SQL *Call Level Interface (CLI)* that defines a common API set for multivendor databases. This section focuses on the SAG CLI; we will return to the SAG interoperability standard in the middleware section.

The *SAG SQL CLI* is a vendor-independent set of APIs for SQL databases; it can be used by applications without requiring a SQL precompiler. In theory, a SQL CLI lets you access any database through the same programming interface. Currently, the SAG CLI only supports *dynamic SQL* and provides functions that correspond to the SQL-89 specification. SAG provides common SQL semantics (and syntax), codifies the SQL data types, and provides common error handling and reporting. SAG defines a common set of system catalogs including the table structures they use. SAG's connection management service allows SQL clients to specify connections to remote database servers. The three connection commands defined by SAG—CONNECT, SET CONNECTION, and DISCONNECT—are now part of the SQL-92 standard.

The SAG APIs allow you to connect to a database through a local *driver* (3 calls), prepare SQL requests (5 calls), execute the requests (2 calls), retrieve the results (7 calls), terminate a statement (3 calls), and terminate a connection (3 calls). In December 1993, SAG released a new "preliminary" version of its CLI; the final specification is due later in 1994.

The Microsoft ODBC CLI

Microsoft's *Open Database Connectivity (ODBC)* Windows API standard for SQL is a greatly extended version of the SAG CLI. ODBC defines about 54 API calls; 23

---

[2] The early efforts of Jim Gray (then associated with Tandem Computers, and now with DEC) and of Jeri Edwards (Tandem Computers) led to the formation of the SAG consortium.

(the core APIs) are based on the SAG CLI. Some of the Microsoft extensions are generic; others are specific to the Windows environment. ODBC defines three *conformance levels* for its drivers: core (i.e., SAG), level 1, and level 2. Each of these levels is a superset of the previous level and corresponds to the class of ODBC functions supported by an ODBC database driver (see the next Briefing box). Applications are responsible for making sure that an ODBC driver supports a conformance level. Microsoft provides an ODBC SDK to help developers create database-specific drivers. Some vendors—including IBM for the DB2/6000, Tandem for NonStop SQL, Ingres, and Informix—provide ODBC drivers for their SQL servers (see Figure 14-8).

In addition, third parties—such as Q+E Software—are offering ODBC driver suites on Windows, OS/2, and Unix that run against a variety of database servers. IBM's DB2 CLI (see X/Open CLI section) is almost identical to the ODBC API, which makes it easier to port ODBC-compliant Windows applications to OS/2 and Unix.

ODBC has many drawbacks. The most serious one is that the specification is controlled by Microsoft and it is constantly evolving. ODBC drivers are difficult to build and maintain. The current drivers are buggy and have different ODBC conformance levels, which are not well documented. The ODBC layers introduce a lot of overhead (especially for SQL updates and inserts) and are never as fast as the native APIs.

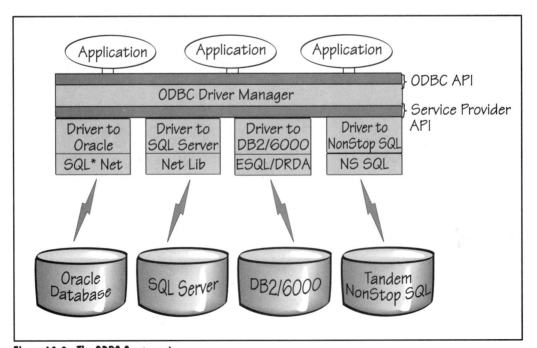

Figure 14-8. The ODBC Components.

FYI

What's a Database Driver?

Briefing

CLIs—including ODBC, IDAPI, and SAG—require the use of intelligent database drivers that accept a CLI call and translate it into the native database server's access language. With the proper driver, any data source application can function as a CLI-server and be accessed by the front-end tools and client programs that use the CLI. The CLI requires a driver for each database to which it connects. Each driver must be written for a specific server using the server's access methods and network transport stack. In the future, X/Open and SAG plan to provide a standard driver-to-server protocol, called the Remote Data Access (RDA); it will work with a variety of transport stacks to provide platform independence among database servers (more on that later in this chapter).

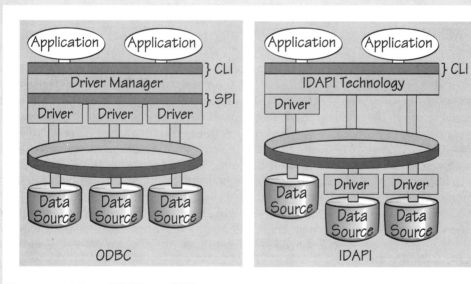

Figure 14-9. Drivers: ODBC Versus IDAPI.

Microsoft's ODBC provides a driver manager that routes an ODBC CLI-call to a particular driver (see Figure 14-9). The driver manager talks to the driver through an ODBC-defined *Service Provider Interface (SPI)*. IDAPI goes a step further by providing a networked SPI-like interface, which allows the drivers to reside on a "gateway" machine. This can be very helpful in situations where multiple client workstations need to access multiple servers, each requiring a separate driver. All the driver combinations can reside on a single "gateway" server instead of on every client machine. CLIs may support different levels of compliance; it's up to the driver writer to select the level of compliance provided in an implementation.

Drivers may usually be obtained from database and front-end tool vendors. They are also bundled with some client/server applications that require them. Some database server companies are bundling ODBC (and very soon IDAPI) drivers with their databases and not charging more for it. Drivers may also be purchased from a new-breed of "middleware for middleware" companies. For example, Q+E Software provides a suite of drivers (priced at $199) for more than 15 database servers. Database vendors are not interested in doing drivers unless they have to. As a result, some vendors, such as Informix and Gupta, are directly referring customers who need drivers to Q+E. However, purchasing drivers from a third party introduces one more complication in an already complicated loop. On the other hand, "middleware for middleware" vendors may find themselves becoming the single point of support and contact for federated database integration using CLIs. ❑

The IDAPI CLI

In February 1993, Borland, IBM, Novell, and WordPerfect introduced a working draft of yet another SAG-based CLI called the *Integrated Database Application Programming Interface (IDAPI)*. IDAPI supports two types of access methods to databases: a SQL CLI based on the SAG CLI, and a record-at-a-time navigational CLI based on Borland's NAV/CLI. The NAV/CLI is used to interface to Xbase and ISAM databases. IDAPI supports advanced SQL features, including cross-database joins, concurrent scrollable cursors on different servers, and query language conversions. These features allow a desktop client to dynamically correlate information from several databases at once. IDAPI promises to introduce less overhead than ODBC. In addition, IDAPI-compliant applications will be able to access ODBC-compliant databases. One of IDAPI's main strengths is that its drivers can reside on the server side, giving clients access to a shared set of database drivers, typically on a gateway server (see Figure 14-9).[3]

IDAPI is key to Borland's strategy. It serves as the unifying interface between Borland's tools—including Quattro and ObjectVision—and its three PC database products: Paradox, dBase, and InterBase. IBM intends to support IDAPI on both OS/2 and AIX. Novell and WordPerfect have pledged to support IDAPI in future releases of their products. In addition, Q+E Software intends to create IDAPI driver suites for Windows, OS/2, and Unix that work with a variety of database servers. In November 1993, Borland claimed that the IDAPI initiative had more than 65

---

[3] The IDAPI working specification may be obtained by calling 1-800-344-4394.

companies behind it. However, as we go to press, no IDAPI drivers are available, and Borland has still not released an SDK for creating them.

Oracle Glue

As the most recent entrant in the SQL "standard" CLI sweepstakes, Oracle announced that its *Glue* would work with everything—including ODBC, IDAPI, Sybase DB LIB, dBase, Paradox, Apple's DAL, and e-mail (see Figure 14-10). Unlike its SQL*Net V2 product, Glue was announced as an Oracle-independent product. A specification document is available that explains how all this will come together. According to Oracle, "Glue fills the gap with an API that's adaptable, portable, and integrated enough to glue the data to the desktop."

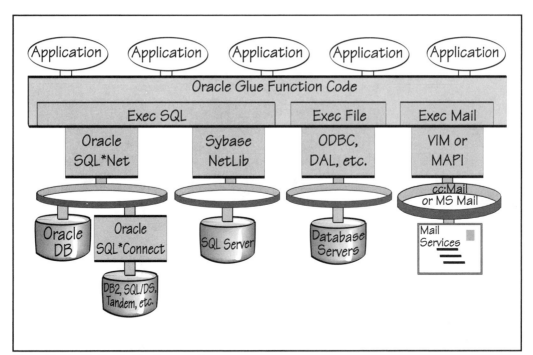

Figure 14-10. The Oracle Glue Components.

The Glue API is invoked through four function calls that can be embedded in application scripts and source code: *execsql* accesses DBMSs; *execfile* works with file servers and Xbase engines; *execmail* accesses mail systems; and *execlink* links applications to Personal Digital Assistants (PDAs). In other words, Glue is supposed to be the universal interface for every type of data-oriented middleware. Glue will even access IBM databases through the *Oracle Open Gateway* for DRDA. Oracle has plans to make Glue available on Windows, Windows NT, OS/2, Macintosh System

7, and various Unix platforms. Unfortunately, the April '93 release of the Glue product only supported Oracle's native APIs.

The X/Open CLI

To counter all these CLI extensions, X/Open became the official "guardian" of the SAG CLI, which is now called the *X/Open CLI*, to differentiate it from IDAPI and ODBC.[4] The X/Open CLI is focused on SQL-89. The next revision is expected to cover the SQL-92 extensions. Figure 14-11 shows an IBM-supplied *DB2 CLI driver* that conforms to the X/Open API (with some extensions) and supports DOS, OS/2, and AIX clients. The DB2 CLI driver translates CLI calls to the native ESQL calls supported by DB2/2.

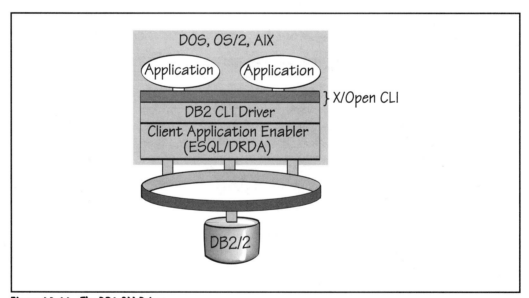

Figure 14-11. The DB2 CLI Driver.

CLI Versus ESQL

Table 14-1 compares the CLI and ESQL capabilities. In general, today's crop of SQL CLIs are flexible but slow. They can only be used for decision-support systems.

---

[4] The X/Open CLI is documented in the SQL *Common Application Environment (CAE)* specification that is part of the XPG4 package published in late 1992. The CLI spec can be purchased from either X/Open or SAG.

Higher performance systems will require the use of either stored procedures or static embedded SQL. A CLI, like ODBC, may cheat and let you invoke a vendor-specific stored procedure using pass-throughs (you specify the stored procedure name and server as parameters in the EXECUTE SQL API call). X/Open will eventually specify a CLI stored procedure call based on SQL3. But don't hold your breath waiting. In any case, CLIs are still too slow when compared to the performance of native APIs. And as long as vendors don't implement the CLI natively (see the next Soapbox), this will remain the case.

Table 14-1. The X/Open CLI Versus ISO ESQL

Feature	X/Open SQL Call-Level Interface (CLI)	ISO SQL-92 Embedded SQL (ESQL)
Requires target database to be known ahead of time	No	Yes
Supports static SQL	No (future)	Yes
Supports dynamic SQL	Yes	Yes
Supports stored procedures	No (future)	No (future)
Uses the SQL declarative model	No	Yes
Applications must be precompiled and bound to database server	No	Yes
Easy to program	Yes	No
Easy to debug	Yes	No
Easy to package	Yes	No

Which CLI?

Soapbox

Use native (direct) APIs whenever possible. Standard APIs (e.g., ODBC) should be considered as a last resort...not the first.

— *Richard Finkelstein (November, 1993)*

The reason Finkelstein doesn't like "standard" CLIs is that they require too many levels of translations before they reach the native APIs. Any type of layering scheme requires release level synchronizations between the different components, which all come from different vendors. As can be expected, vendors will first support their native API sets and then worry about the "standard CLIs." This means the CLIs will not be synchronized with the latest releases of the database engines and drivers. In addition, the CLI approach on top of database drivers adds layers of complexity. For example, debug is far more complicated. You can expect a lot more fingerpointing between vendors when the NOS, API libraries, database drivers, native OSs, and database engines all have to be in sync for things to work.

But the million dollar question is: Why can't vendors—like Oracle, Sybase, and IBM—make the X/Open CLI the "native API" of their respective databases? The answer is that each database engine offers a unique set of extensions to native SQL; these extensions require a different set of APIs to invoke their services. Will vendors ever offer a non-extended version of SQL? Of course not—they're out there trying to differentiate their product! So by definition, the common CLI will always be a "least common denominator" approach that is not optimized for a particular database. Database vendors are not likely to reveal their future "extended plans" to standards bodies, so common CLIs will always trail behind the SQL engine's native API capabilities. And forget portability because even the "standard CLIs" have escape clauses (or pass-throughs) that defeat that goal. The bottom line is that any program that takes advantage of the advanced capabilities of a database engine will not be database-neutral. So much for standards! ❏

What About the Proprietary SQL Languages?

Both the CLI and ESQL approaches let you use your favorite procedural language for writing code. The alternative is letting the SQL vendors introduce new procedural languages for SQL. This is precisely the approach taken by the two leading database vendors: Sybase and Oracle.[5] Sybase requires that you use its proprietary *Transact-SQL* language; Oracle gives you a choice between standard ESQL precompilers or *PL/SQL*, Oracle's own proprietary language.

The benefits of using a vendor-specific proprietary language is that, in theory, all your SQL programs (including the procedural logic) will automatically port to all the platforms these vendors support; you don't have to concern yourself with precompilers and compilers for each platform. But be careful—this is not always the case. The price you pay is vendor lock-in. It's the classic trade-off.

---

[5] This approach is not limited to Oracle and Sybase. Ingres provides its proprietary *Ingres/4GL* and Informix supports its own *Stored Procedure Language (SPL)*.

The following is a brief description of two vendor-specific SQL programming environments and what they can do for you:

- **Sybase Transact-SQL** supports a vendor-specific SQL dialect, which, prior to Sybase 10, did not even support cursors and many of the standard SQL-92 features. However, Transact-SQL includes powerful proprietary extensions that let you create stored procedures, triggers, and rules. *System stored procedures* are used to supplement the server management commands. The execution of a stored procedure on a server can be delayed for up to 24 hours with the *WAITFOR* option. The language supports conditional logic and the declaration and initialization of variables. Error handling in Transact-SQL is cumbersome because the programmer must check the error status after each SQL statement; there is no provision for calling exception handlers automatically when an error occurs.

- **Oracle PL/SQL** also supports a modified SQL dialect that is based on the SQL-92 standard. PL/SQL can be used in triggers, stored procedures, or as blocks of SQL statements sent to the server to be executed all at once so as to reduce network traffic. PL/SQL can be used within a host language, such as C or COBOL, or from within one of Oracle's client tools, such as SQL*Forms. PL/SQL provides conditional logic and lets you assign values to variables. In addition, it supports event-driven error handlers; you can use the standard error handler or override it with one you supply. Oracle7 allows you to group PL/SQL procedures within *Stored Packages*. Packages are managed using the regular SQL DDL statements (CREATE, ALTER, and DROP). Objects within a package can be *visible*, which means that they are callable from outside the package, or *hidden*, which means they can only be called from within the package.

In summary, the success of SQL has opened up a plethora of non-standard languages. You'll have to make the decision of which one fits your needs best. You also have the choice of using a standard procedural language with a SQL precompiler. Some database servers, like DB2/2, let you write stored procedures using any language that creates a DLL and supports a SQL precompiler.

OPEN SQL GATEWAYS

In this section, we look at "open SQL gateways" that translate the SQL calls into an industry-standard common *Format and Protocol (FAP)*. The FAP provides the common protocol between the client and the server. As we explained earlier in this chapter, the gateway acts as the broker that translates client API calls into the FAP format, transports them, and then maps them to the appropriate server calls (and vice versa). The open gateway must provide (or support) a standard SQL Interface (CLI or ESQL). It must also be able to locate remote servers and provide catalog services without requiring an intermediary database server. The open gateway must also provide tools for creating the server side of the gateway.

We will look at the three contending architectures (or products) for common gateways: ISO/SAG *Remote Data Access (RDA)*, IBM's *Distributed Relational Data Access (DRDA)*, and IBI's *EDA/SQL*—an open gateway that currently supports more than 50 database server platforms. Gateways are a temporary fix until vendors agree on a common FAP and implement it *natively* on their servers. So we will look at which of the contending FAPs has the best chance of becoming this common standard.

RDA and DRDA: More Than Just Gateways

Briefing

DRDA and RDA are more than just gateway protocols. They both provide end-to-end architectures for creating true federated distributed databases. Most gateways simply pass a SQL statement to a remote database system, generally treating each SQL statement as a separate transaction. DRDA and RDA aim at supporting multisite transactions (though RDA isn't quite there yet). Some gateways handle the character conversion but don't have all the sophisticated features provided by DRDA and RDA for creating common data representations. Gateways typically link two locations; DRDA and RDA are built to support data backbones (with multiple entry and exit points). ❑

IBI EDA/SQL

Enterprise Data Access/SQL (EDA/SQL), from Information Builders, Inc. (IBI), is a family of open gateway products that uses SQL to access over 50 relational and non-relational database servers—an industry record. EDA/SQL is a component of IBM's *Information Warehouse* decision-support solution. In addition, IBI has developed, with Microsoft, an ODBC driver for EDA/SQL gateway servers. EDA/SQL is a continuation of IBI's 10-year experience in developing gateway code primarily for read-only query access. IBI does not provide a database server; the company is focusing on the "glue" business.

Figure 14-12 shows the EDA/SQL components. Here's what they do:

■ *API/SQL* is another "common" CLI that uses SQL-89 as the standard database access language. API/SQL will pass-through SQL calls that it does not recognize. The calls can be issued asynchronously—meaning the client application does

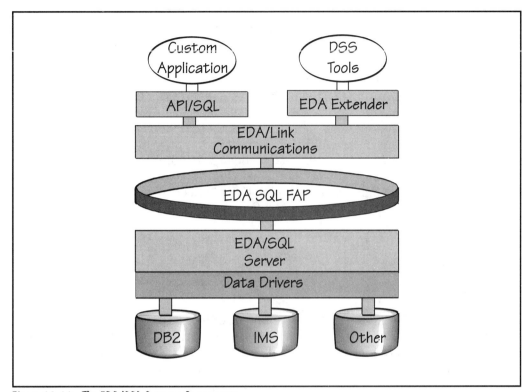

Figure 14-12. The EDA/SQL Gateway Components

not have to block waiting for the call to complete. It lets you query the status of any pending requests. The API/SQL also provides an RPC call that can be used to invoke CICS transactions or user-written procedures. API/SQL is available on DOS, Windows, OS/2, OS/400, AIX, Sun/OS, VAX/VMS, HP-UX, MVS, VM, Wang/VS, and Macintosh.

■ **EDA/Extenders** are utilities that allow API/SQL calls to be issued from within existing products that support some form of dynamic SQL. You can think of the extenders as "redirectors" of SQL calls. Of course, the calls get redirected to API/SQL, which then routes them through the gateway network. Extenders are provided for many popular applications—such as Lotus 1-2-3—and for database front-end tools that work with popular databases (relational or nonrelational). Many popular client tools are being delivered "EDA-enabled" out of the box.

■ **EDA/Link** supports over 12 communication protocols including NetBIOS, Named Pipes, SNA, TCP/IP, and DECnet. EDA/Link provides password verification and authentication, and handles message format translations. It lets you create communications profiles using pop-up menus. The stacks it supports vary with different client/server configurations.

- *EDA/Server* is a multithreaded catcher that typically resides on the target database server machine. It receives client requests and translates them into server-specific commands. If the target database is relational, it passes the ANSI-compliant SQL directly to the *EDA/Data Driver*. If the target database is not relational, SQL requests are passed through the *Universal SQL Translator*, which maps the SQL syntax of the incoming request into the data manipulation language that is specific to that server's driver. EDA/Server also handles security, authentication, statistics gathering, and some system management. EDA/Servers are available for MVS, VM, OS/2, RS/6000, DEC VAX (VMS), HP-UX, SUN (OS), and Pyramid. On October 12, 1993, IBI announced additional EDA/Servers for the following platforms: OS/400 Database Manager, CICS on MVS, and DB2 and IMS via DRDA. It also announced an EDA/SQL "Transaction Server" for CICS and IMS using EDA/SQL RPCs.

- *EDA/Data Drivers* provide access to data in over 50 different formats. These drivers take care of any variations in syntax, schema, data types, catalog naming conventions, and data representation. A specific data driver must be installed for each data source you need to access.

As a parting note, EDA/SQL is an excellent piece of middleware for decision support systems and data extractions. However, it does not provide the robust transactional support needed for production-type database access. Its FAP is not a candidate for replacing existing vendor-specific middleware. Let's look at RDA and DRDA alternatives to understand why this is the case.

ISO/SAG RDA

The ISO RDA is an emerging standard for universal data access based on the little-used OSI stack. One of SAG's goals is to port (and extend) the RDA FAP to the TCP/IP protocol. RDA provides functionality that is equivalent to the SQL-89 and SQL-92 (entry) specifications. RDA is *not* very tolerant of SQL deviations. The server will reject any SQL command that does not conform to an RDA-defined SQL subset. However, SAG may allow some cheating with pass-through commands.

The current version of RDA only supports dynamic SQL. RDA allows a client to be connected to more than one database server at a time, but it does not support a two-phase commit protocol to synchronize updates on multiple databases. An RDA client may issue asynchronous requests to a server whenever it desires; it does not have to wait for pending requests to complete.

RDA defines a set of SQL catalog tables that are based on the SQL-92 standard; it does not tolerate any catalog deviations. RDA returns error codes using the SQL-92 SQLSTATE return codes. It also supports the SQL-92 subset of SQLCODE return values. All other return codes are rejected. RDA supports a *repetition count* mechanism that lets any operation be repeated one or more times—for example, multirow fetches. Each repetition may use a different set of inputs.

RDA requires that all data exchanged between the client and the server be converted to a common "canonical" format. This means that all data is converted twice—once by the sender and once by the receiver. The benefit is that everybody needs to learn only one common conversion format. The disadvantage is that multiple conversions may result in the loss of data precision and can impact performance, especially when both the client and server use the same protocol.

RDA uses the ISO *Abstract Syntax Notation One (ASN.1)* to define the messages and then encodes (or tags) their contents using the ISO *Basic Encoding Rules (BER)*. BER uses a type/length/value tagging scheme to convey a value. Each data item must be individually tagged, so if a query generates a result set of 20,000 rows, each field in each of the 20,000 rows must be tagged—that's a lot of tagging overhead.[6]

What's coming next? RDA is working on defining a two-phase commit protocol that's based on the *ISO Transaction Processing (ISO TP)* standard. It's also waiting on the final SQL3 specifications for stored procedures before it can incorporate them into RDA. The committee is looking at providing static SQL support along lines that are similar to DRDA packages.

IBM DRDA

IBM's long-term distributed database strategy is known as the *Distributed Relational Database Architecture*, or simply *DRDA*. IBM is promoting DRDA as the standard for federated database interoperability. A number of influential database and gateway vendors—including Oracle, Sybase, Micro Decisionware, IBI, Informix, XDB, Ingres, Borland, Cincom, Progress, Novell, and Gupta—have announced support for DRDA. Six of these vendors have already announced (or are shipping) DRDA-based products. According to IBM, over 100 DRDA-exploitative applications are being developed by different companies using existing products (mostly OS/2's DDCS/2).

DRDA's goal is to provide an interoperability standard for fully distributed heterogeneous relational database environments. To do that, DRDA defines the protocols (or FAPs) for database client-to-server and server-to-server interactions. In DRDA terminology, a client is called an *Application Requester (AR)*, and a database

---

6 For a more complete explanation of RDA's tagging overhead, refer to Richard Hackathorn's excellent book, **Enterprise Database Connectivity** (Wiley, 1993).

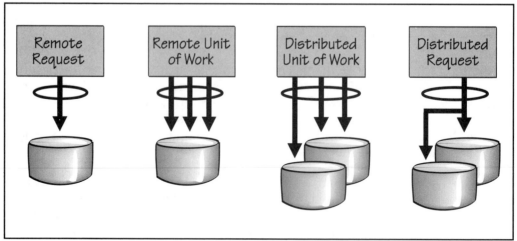

Figure 14-13. DRDA's Four Types of Database Transactions.

server is an *Application Server (AS)*. The AR-to-AS protocol is used for the typical client/server interactions. The AR-to-AR protocol synchronizes transactions that span across multiple SQL servers; it also used to route SQL commands from server to server.

Figure 14-13 shows the four levels of database transactions defined by DRDA:

■ **Remote request** means one SQL command to one database. This is used mostly for issuing queries among dissimilar systems.

■ **Remote unit of work** means many SQL commands to one database. This is your typical client-to-single-server transaction. The client can connect to one database server at a time, issue multiple SQL commands against that server's database, issue a commit to make the work permanent, and then switch over to another database server to start a subsequent unit of work.

■ **Distributed unit of work** means many SQL commands to many databases but each command goes to one database. This is your typical multiserver transaction. DRDA handles the multisite synchronization, security, and data integrity functions (two-phase commit). It locates remote data sites and coordinates requests (including the update of data) at several locations in a single transaction.

■ **Distributed request** means many SQL commands to many databases, but each command can execute against multiple databases. With this capability, DRDA can service single requests that span multiple sites, such as a *multisite JOIN*. It can also distribute a single query across multiple servers to improve performance through parallelism.

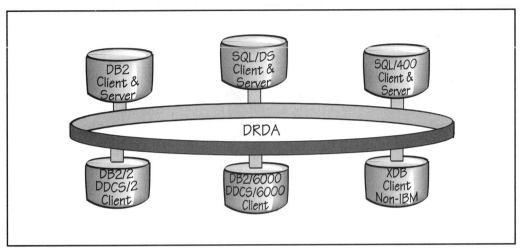

Figure 14-14. IBM's DRDA Implementations.

How much of this architecture is implemented in real products today? The best way to find out is by looking at IBM's own database server products (see Figure 14-14). After all, DRDA's *primary* goal is to allow IBM's own "heterogeneous" database servers to interoperate.

DRDA Features

What type of additional functions does DRDA provide? It mainly handles the thorny network and code portability issues, including:

- ■ *SQL Message Content and Exchange Protocol:* DRDA handles the negotiations between clients and servers for supported server attributes. It only does message translations when needed. There is no concept of a canonical message format; instead, it is a "receiver makes it right" protocol. This means that if data needs to be converted, it is only done once. And no conversion is done if a client and server use the same formats. DRDA uses DDM, an intermediate messaging language, to mediate SQL exchanges across unlike machines; DRDA takes care of dissimilar data representations, catalog structures, and command syntax conversions. DRDA does not tag every field in every row in a multirow result set. Instead, it creates a single descriptor for the entire result set. All these features help reduce network traffic and improve performance.

- ■ *Transport Stack Independence:* DRDA supports the MPTN interface, which means that it can run on top of APPC/APPN or TCP/IP (the two protocols currently supported by AnyNet) for client/server communications. DRDA handles data blocking, security, authentication, server routing, and generates alerts for both network and database failures.

- **Multiplatform Program Preparation:** DRDA supports under-the-cover, multiplatform program preparation. A program is created locally; its output can be distributed to multiple servers using a remote BIND utility. The BIND process produces executable SQL code (called packages or plans) on the servers.

- **Static or Dynamic SQL Support:** A DRDA client can invoke the SQL statements on the server one at a time by identifying a package and the statement within it. In addition to dynamic SQL, packages make it possible to execute precompiled static SQL statements on the servers (including support for cursors).

- **Common Diagnostics:** DRDA returns status information upon completion of each SQL command. DRDA provides a standard set of return codes in the SQLSTATE field (based on the SQL-92 standard). Database specific return codes are still provided in the SQLCODE field. IBM's OS/2 based DataHub product provides an integrated system management approach to DRDA databases. It performs database management tasks across multiple sites. It can trace a transaction through the database network and provide status.

- **Common SAA SQL Syntax:** DRDA recommends the use of SAA SQL for application portability across platforms. SAA SQL is a subset of SQL-92 (with some extensions). DRDA also supports target-specific SQL commands for situations when it is more efficient to use SQL extensions. In other words, if the client knows that a server supports certain SQL commands, it can issue the calls and DRDA will convey them to the server. Who says you can't have your cake and eat it too?

IBM is licensing both the DRDA specifications and the code to interested parties for a nominal fee. At least six major vendors have licensed the DRDA code. IBM is also adopting the X/Open CLI.

DRDA or RDA?

So why does this industry need two standards? Aside from the political and business issues, there are some compelling technical reasons for choosing DRDA over RDA (see Table 14-2). Many vendors will support both DRDA and RDA. Indeed, many vendors who have announced their intent to support DRDA have also committed to support RDA. Even IBM has made a statement of intent to support RDA (as well as DRDA) should it become the ISO standard. The good news is that some of these vendors will create "gateways" between DRDA and SAG/RDA. And, as usual, this business always has at least two standards for everything!

Table 14-2. RDA Versus DRDA.

Feature	ISO RDA	IBM DRDA
Support for dynamic SQL	Yes	Yes
Support for static SQL and persistent SQL packages	No	Yes
Support for standard SQL (ISO-92 subset)	Yes	Yes
Tolerance for SQL Dialects including dissimilar:		
■ SQL Commands	No	Yes
■ Catalogs	No	Yes
■ Error Codes	No	Yes
Overall performance and efficiency:	Poor	Good
■ Number of format conversions per message for common client and server	2 (to/from canonical)	0 (not needed)
■ Number of format conversions per message for unlike client and server	2 (to/from canonical)	1 (receiver makes it right)
■ Multirow tagging	Every row is tagged.	One tag description per result set
■ Multirow fetches	Using repeated command	Using single row fetch with updateable cursors or multirow fetches.
Two-phase commit and multisite distributed updates	No	Yes
Asynchronous Requests	Yes	No
Easy for vendors to implement	Yes	Not so easy. OS/2 sample code helps.
Transports	OSI and TCP/IP	APPC/APPN and TCP/IP
Integrated management	No	Yes (using DataHub)
Accounting information	No	Yes

Table 14-2. RDA Versus DRDA. (Continued)

Feature	ISO RDA	IBM DRDA
Data encoding	ISO BER/ASN.1	IBM DDM and Compound Object Formats.
Who's behind it?	40 vendors	15 vendors
De jure standard	Yes	No

CONCLUSION

The success of SQL has opened up a plethora of interface and middleware "choices." You'll have to make the decision on which one fits your needs best. As we see it, SQL (with its extensions) will remain vendor-specific for a long time to come. If you're using SQL databases for mission-critical applications, the "mix and match" of SQL database servers can only spell trouble. You might have to accept some form of vendor lock-in, in return for the convenience of getting more SQL power, better support, platform portability, and finding somebody to blame. The situation is better for decision-support systems and information warehouses. There, you have a much better chance of working with data from mulivendor database platforms. The current SQL federated database middleware can easily support these kinds of "non-mission-critical" applications. More on that in the next chapter.

Chapter 15

Warehouses: Information Where You Want It

With the new generation of desktop applications, the real database is often perceived to be a personal database that extracts its necessary contents from a myriad of data sources. This trend is causing the fragmentation of enterprise data into numerous isolated presentation-centered islands.

— Richard Hackathorn (1993)[1]

This chapter provides an overview of the technology used to create *information warehouses*—one of the most exciting new developments in client/server databases. "Warehouses" provide the foundation technology for creating intelligent clients that look like Danny De Vito's desktop in the movie *Other People's Money.* For those of you who haven't seen this movie, Danny's closest associate was an information-hungry PC that literally lived on real-time data, which it grabbed (or got fed) from multiple sources. Danny's PC would continuously grab data, massage it, and present it in dynamic formats—including trends, animations, simulations, and 3-D business graphics—that were relevant to Danny's interests. Danny, of course, was in love with that PC, which he used to make all his investment decisions and lots of

---

[1] Source: Richard D. Hackathorn, **Enterprise Database Connectivity** (Wiley, 1993).

money. The poor machine even had to wake him up every morning with an analysis of how his investment portfolio was doing.

WHERE IS THAT OLTP DATA KEPT?

Modern businesses live on data. The total quantity of data on computers currently doubles every five years. With the proliferation of client/server (and multimedia) technology, we expect data to double at least once a year in the future. So who is creating all this data? The answer is modern institutions in the course of conducting their everyday business. The computerized production systems that collect and consume this data are called OLTP systems—these are true data factories that run around the clock.

What Is OLTP?

Database-centered client/server applications fall into two categories: *Decision Support Systems (DSS)* and *Online Transaction Processing (OLTP)*. These two client/server categories provide dramatically different types of business solutions. These differences need to be understood before we can appreciate what data warehouses have to offer.

OLTP systems are used to create applications in all walks of business. These include reservation systems, point-of-sale, tracking systems, inventory control, stockbroker workstations, and manufacturing shop floor control systems. These are typically mission-critical applications that require a 1-3 second response time 100% percent of the time. The number of clients supported by an OLTP system may vary dramatically throughout the day, week, or year, but the response time must be maintained. OLTP applications also require tight controls over the security and integrity of the database. The reliability and availability of the overall system must be very high. Data must be kept consistent and correct.

In OLTP systems, the client typically interacts with a Transaction Server instead of a Database Server. This interaction is necessary to provide the high performance these applications require. Transaction servers come in two flavors: *OLTP Lite* provided by stored procedures, and *OLTP Heavy* provided by TP Monitors. In either case, the client invokes *remote procedures* that reside on a server. These remote procedures execute as transactions against the server's database (more on this in Part 5). OLTP applications require code to be written for both the client component and for the server transactions. The communication overhead in OLTP applications is kept to a minimum. The client interaction with the transaction server is typically limited to short, structured exchanges. The exchange consists of a single request/reply (as opposed to multiple SQL message exchanges).

Is Client/Server Creating New Islands of OLTP?

In the old days, OLTP applications ran on expensive mainframes that stored massive amounts of data, provided minimum downtime, and were the pride of the enterprise and the MIS shops. Today, the top-of-the-line OLTP applications—such as airline reservations, banking, stock markets, airport control towers, and hospitals—still run on expensive superservers and mainframes and are still controlled by the MIS shops. However, today any department with enough budget to buy a few PCs, hook them on a client/server LAN, and hire a programmer (or consultant) can create its *own* OLTP application. Software packages are also becoming available off-the-shelf. In other words, database-centric client/server technology has lowered the barriers of entry for creating private or department-owned OLTP systems. These systems are giving the departments total autonomy and control over the applications they create and the data they gather. At the extreme, an entire OLTP system can run on a single-user desktop database; all the data collected can be kept private (in other words, outside the reach of the enterprise). We all know how easy it is to create ad hoc database systems on stand-alone PCs using spreadsheets and simple database tools.

In general, all the data collected by an OLTP system is of direct use to the application and people that are creating this data. They understand exactly what this data means. And they know how to use it to solve their immediate day-to-day production problems. The application typically provides a sophisticated graphical interface to view and manipulate the data with transactional controls. The members of the organization understand how the data is structured. They can create sophisticated built-in reports and manipulate the data for their production uses.

What happens if somebody outside the direct OLTP group needs this data? How do they know what data is available? Where do they find it? How do they access it? What format will it be in? And, what will it mean? The last thing the OLTP people want is to give outsiders access to their precious production systems. These outsiders often don't really know what they want, and they may be issuing long ad hoc queries that can slow down the entire production system, corrupt the data, and create deadlocks.

In the old days, the outsiders could ask their MIS representatives to deal with their MIS counterparts that controlled production data to give them an indication of what data was available and how to get to it. With the proliferation of the private one-person and departmental OLTP solutions, even MIS doesn't know what data is available anymore. The data in the enterprise is fragmented, and we've gone back to islands of data processing. Data ends up being all over the place: on the client that originates it, on the departmental server, on one of many federated servers, or on the enterprise server. There is no integrated view.

One of the great attractions of client/server and PCs is the autonomy they provide. Most of us feel disassociated with enterprise data and would prefer local control of our resources. In many cases, our new-found freedom causes us to withdraw into our own little production turfs and ignore the needs of the larger community. We've created a dichotomy between the departmental (or personal) needs and the needs of the organization or larger community. We've also created a dichotomy between production data and informational data.

So who are these "outsiders" we're trying to keep off our turf? They're the people who comb through data looking for patterns, trends, and informational nuggets that can help them make better decisions. Creating barriers to data is like creating barriers to trade. If they can't get to our data and we can't get to theirs, then everybody loses. Precious data is kept out of the reach of those who may need it most.

INFORMATION AT YOUR FINGERTIPS

How do we preserve the local autonomy of production systems and yet allow access to outsiders? How do we make sure the outsiders don't impact the production systems? What data is made available to those outsiders? What data is kept private within the production system? Who owns the shared data? Who can update it? Should we allow direct access to production data or copy it to another database? How is extracted data maintained and refreshed? We'll answer all these questions in this chapter. But first let's look at the informational needs of these outsiders and understand how decision-support systems differ from OLTP production systems.

Information Hounds

Let's give a name to these "outsiders" who want to consume our information. They range from those with compulsive appetites for data—like the character played by Danny De Vito in the movie *Other People's Money*—to those with occasional needs—such as a student researching a term paper. What shall we call them? How about *decision makers*? Or, would you prefer *information hounds*? Let's settle on *information hounds* because it captures the role millions of us will soon be able to play with database warehouse technology. Anyone with a PC connected to an information warehouse will be able do the same types of things the Danny De Vito character did.

Of course, the first to consume this technology are business people making strategic decisions—pricing and market analysis—that depend on the availability of timely and accurate data. The ability to access information and act on it quickly will become increasingly critical to any company's (or individual's) success. Raw data becomes information when it gets into the hands of someone who can put it in context and use it. The data is the raw ingredient, which makes all this possible. There are many parallels between the manufacturing and distribution of goods and the manufacturing and distribution of information. High impact, high value decision making involves risk. Making decisions using old, incomplete, inconsistent, or invalid data puts a business at a disadvantage versus the competition.

Information is becoming a key component of every product and service. For example, analysts use information to spot the trends and shifts in buying patterns of consumers. Information sleuthing is an iterative process. The sophistication of queries increases as the information hound grasps more of the nuances of the business problem. The hound needs the ability to access information for multiple combinations of "what if" situations.[2]

An example may help explain the value of timely information. An unnamed apparel manufacturer was having problems reconciling the fast-moving fashion season with a distribution system that replenished stock based on what was forecast. The manufacturer decided to adopt a different technique and put in a system that collected daily sales information from the point-of-sale registers. The company also invested in analysis tools for knowledge workers and executives who needed to watch the daily sales. As a result, the manufacturer was able to cut costs by $47 million, resulting in a profit increase of over 25%. So timely information is highly valuable to some people.

What Is a Decision Support System?

Decision-Support Systems (DSS) are used to analyze data and create reports. They provide the business professional and information hounds with the means to obtain exactly the information they need. A successful decision-support system must provide the user with flexible access to data and the tools to manipulate and present that data in all kinds of report formats. Users should be able to construct elaborate queries, answer "what if" questions, search for correlations in the data, plot the data, and move it into other applications such as spreadsheets and word processor documents. Decision-support systems are not generally time-critical and can tolerate slower response times. Client/Server decision support systems are typically not suitable for mission-critical production environments. They have poor integrity controls and limited multitable access capabilities. Finding information may involve large quantities of data, which means that the level of concurrency control is not very granular; for example, a user may want to view and update an entire table.

Decision-support systems are built using a new generation of screen-layout tools that allow non-programmers to build GUI front-ends and reports by painting, pointing, and clicking. Point-and-click query builders take the work out of formulating the question.

---

[2] We are indebted to Dick Lockert of IBM Atlanta for sharing some of his deep insights on how information is used in warehousing applications.

What Is an Executive Information System?

Executive Information Systems (EIS) are even more powerful, easy-to-use, and business-specific than DSS tools. And they're certainly more expensive, which may explain why the "executive" attribute is in the name. In any case, distinctions between EIS and DSS are becoming less clear. The EIS tools have recently expanded their scope and offer a broader range of functions at the enterprise level. Dick Lockert, an information guru, makes a case that the "E" in EIS can now stand for "Enterprise" rather than "Executive" as such systems now have hundreds of users with many roles such as executive, manager, and business analyst. Another phrase to describe these evolving DSS/EIS systems is *Management Support Systems (MSS)*. If you prefer, let's simply call them the Danny De Vito tools.

Regardless of what they're called, these tools are creating a huge market. The IDC market research firm projects a combined EIS and DSS tools marketplace of $9.9 billion in 1996. These new-breed tools allow information hounds to perform deeper levels of analysis on totally up-to-date, real-time data that is obtained from internal business systems—such as OLTP-driven financial, personnel, and customer information systems—and external data sources—such as Dow Jones and Reuters.

Because the Danny De Vito tools were originally designed for executives, all information is presented in highly visual forms. Extraneous details are filtered out to suit the user's needs. These tools offer unique features—including "hot spot" finders, "slice and dice," "goal seekers," "drill-downs" to related information—and the more mundane features—including graphs, charts, statistical analysis, trends, queries, reports, and project management. They specialize in presenting information using visual metaphors that make it easy to navigate and sift through tons of data. Some of the better tools are used to discover late-breaking news on competitors, suppliers, government legislation, market research, economic conditions, or the latest stock market quotes. Examples of EIS and DSS tools include Comshare's *Commander Desktop*, Gupta's *Quest*, Trinzic's *Forest and Trees*, OpenBooks Software's *OpenBooks*, SAS Institute's *SAS System*, Intelligent Office's *TRACK*, IBM's *PAS/2*, and Lotus tools via *Datalens*.

Comparing Decision Support and OLTP Systems

As shown in Table 15-1, decision-support applications can be created directly by end users. Network administrators are still needed to help set up the client/server system, and Database Administrators (DBAs) may help assemble collections of tables, views, and columns that are relevant to the user (the user should then be able to create decision-support applications without further DBA involvement). The design of client/server systems for OLTP is a lot more involved; consequently, it requires a large amount of custom programming effort. We discuss OLTP system requirements in Parts 5 and 9.

Table 15-1. Comparing the Programming Effort for Decision Support and OLTP.

Client/Server Application	Client	Server	Messages
Decision Support	Off-the-shelf decision support tool with end-user programming. Canned event handlers and communications with the server.	Off-the-shelf database server. Tables usually defined for OLTP application. The DBA creates flexible views to make user autonomous.	SQL messages that are being standardized for multivendor interoperability.
OLTP	Custom application. GUI tool lays out screen, but the event handlers and remote procedure calls require programming at the C level.	Custom application. Transaction code must be programmed at the C level. The database is off-the-shelf.	Custom messages are optimized for performance and secure access.

Production Versus Informational Databases

Table 15-2 compares the database requirements of OLTP and decision-support systems. We need to understand the differences to get some better insights into what data warehousing can do for information hounds. The key points of difference is that decision-support data needs to be stable at a snapshot in time for reporting purposes. Production databases reflect the up-to-the-minute state of the business in real-time. Information hounds typically don't want the data changed so frequently that they can't get the same answer twice in a row. So informational copies may be updated less frequently.

Decision support data—or *informational data*—is collected from multiple sources; production data is collected by OLTP applications. The raw data that decision support systems extract from production databases is not normally updated directly. However, information hounds have a high requirement to tailor the informational database to their specific needs. This process is called "derived data enhancement." The informational database may contain derived data that records changes over time and summaries. Information hounds are rarely interested in a specific past event. They're always looking at summaries and trends.

Table 15-2. Database Needs: OLTP Versus DSS.

Feature	OLTP Database Needs	Decision Support Database Needs
Who uses it?	Production workers.	Information hounds.
Timeliness of data	Needs current value of data.	Needs stable snapshots of data frozen in time. Refresh intervals are controlled by user. May need occasional access to current value data.
Frequency of data access	Continuous throughout workday. Work-related peaks may occur.	Supports knowledge workers and managers.
Data format	Raw captured data.	Multiple levels of conversions, filtering, summarization, condensation, and extraction.
Data collection	From single application.	From multiple sources including archival data.
Data source known?	Yes, most of it is generated by single application.	No, it comes from different databases.
Timed snapshots versions	No, continuous data. Single version.	Yes, you can key off a snapshot's date/time. Each snapshot is a version unless you overwrite it during refresh.
Data access pattern	Multiple users updating production database.	Mostly single-user access. Intense usage on an occasional basis. For example, when a report is due.
Can data be updated	Current value is continuously updated.	Read-only, unless you own the replica.
Flexibility of access	Inflexible, access to data via precompiled programs and stored procedures.	Very flexible via a query generator.
Performance	Fast response time is a requirement. Highly automated, repetitive tasks.	Relatively slow.
Data requirements	Well understood.	Fuzzy. A lot of detective work and discovery.
Information scope	Finite. Whatever is in the production database.	Very vast. Data can come from anywhere.

THE INFORMATION WAREHOUSE

The "data warehouse" in the client/server environment is the repository of data for decision-support processing.

— *W.H. Inmon (1993)* [3]

Bill Inmon is credited as being the "father of the data warehouse," a concept he started writing about as far back as 1981. Inmon argues that "one cornerstone of client/server applications is the notion of the difference between and separation of operational and decision support processing." In September 1991, IBM announced its *Information Warehouse* framework, an event that "sparked much interest in the industry." In October 1993, IBM announced a series of new products, which make it very practical to create highly customized "Information Warehouses" on PCs, departmental servers, or mainframes. Many other commercial offerings—including various decision-support tools, Sybase 10's replicated server, Oracle7's replication facility, Teradata, Ingres' Replica Manager, MDI Database Gateway, Red Brick, Prism Solutions' Warehouse Manager, Evolutionary Technologies Extract ToolSuite, Trinzic Corp's InfoPump, and DEC's Data Distributor—provide different facets of a warehouse solution.

What's an Information Warehouse?

Bill Inmon and vendors like Teradata define a *warehouse* as a separate database for decision support, which typically contains vast amounts of information. Richard Hackathorn defines a *warehouse* as "a collection of data objects that have been inventoried for distribution to a business community."[4] In our own modest definition, "a warehouse is an active intelligent store of data that can manage information from many sources, distribute it where needed, and activate business policies." In the next section, we present IBM's definition. Hopefully, one of these definitions will ring a bell for you.

IBM's Information Warehouse

IBM defines its *Information Warehouse* as a framework consisting of four components: an informational database, open SQL access, automated copy management, and an information catalog (see Figure 15-1). These four components are supplemented by an open EIS tools strategy. An explanation of these components follows.

---

[3] Source: W.H. Inmon, **Developing Client/Server Applications** (QED, 1993).
[4] Source: Richard D. Hackathorn, **Enterprise Database Connectivity** (Wiley, 1993).

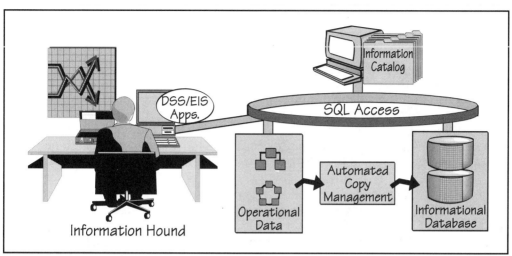

Figure 15-1. The Components of IBM's Information Warehouse.

■ ***The informational database*** is a relational database that organizes and stores copies of data from multiple data sources in a format that meets the needs of information hounds. Think of it as the decision-support server that transforms, aggregates, and adds value to data from various production sources. IBM, in contrast to Inmon, does not preclude housing the information database on the same server as the production database. Inmon sees the warehouse as a huge database. In contrast, IBM's informational database can be a personal database on a PC, a medium-sized database on a local server, or a very large database on an enterprise server. IBM's tools support all these environments.

■ ***Open SQL access*** is used to access all databases, whether they're relational or non-relational. IBM supports three SQL APIs: EDA/SQL's CLI, the X/Open CLI, and DRDA's ESQL. IBM encourages an open DSS and EIS tool strategy around these APIs. It also has made alliances with the major tool vendors. IBM's framework does not preclude an information hound from directly accessing a production database. In contrast, purists like Inmon feel that decision-support applications should only be able to access the informational database. IBM provides SQL access to everything and leaves the implementation decision to its customers.

■ ***Automated copy management*** manages the copying of data across databases as defined by the information hound. The hound defines, using SQL SELECT statements, the tables that need to be copied, the source and destination platforms, and the frequency of updates. *Refresh* involves copying over the entire table; *update* only propagates the changes to all the replicas. Everything can be automated or done manually.

■ *The information catalog* helps the information hound find out what data is available on the different databases, what format it's in, and how to access it. The information catalog gets its "data about data" (or metadata) by discovering which databases are on the network and then querying their catalogs. It tries to keep everything up-to-date. The information hound finds out what's available by consulting the information catalog. Some estimates claim that information hounds in large enterprises spend 80% of their time gathering data and 20% of the time analyzing it. The hounds don't even know the names of the objects they're looking for, where they're located, and how to access them. The information catalog helps alleviate those three problems.

In summary, IBM's Information Warehouse provides a level playing field for all the providers of decision-support tools and components. They've defined SQL as the "lingua franca" of decision support, which is nice, and they defined the components that are needed to automate data gathering. In October 1993, IBM announced *DataGuide/2*—an information catalog that runs on OS/2. Another OS/2 product, *DataHub/2*, is used as the copy manager for all the IBM databases. A third OS/2 product, *FlowMark/2*, can be used with DataHub/2 to further automate multistep processes that transform and move the data. Any relational database—for example, DB2/2—can be used as the information store. Finally, hundreds of DSS and EIS tools that use SQL can participate in this framework.

IBM is the first to admit that information warehouses are too ad hoc and customer-specific to be provided as a single shrink-wrapped solution. The next best thing for everybody is a framework that helps articulate this industry so that we can all contribute a piece of the solution. We think the Information Warehouse framework meets the needs of the OLTP people, while giving information hounds more freedom than ever to get to the information they need. This helps explain why this particular IBM "architecture" was so well-received in the industry.

What's Being Automated?

If you think about it, IBM's Information Warehouse provides a framework for automating all aspects of the decision-support process. Instead of asking the database administrators (DBAs) what information is available, the information hounds can now directly consult the *information catalog*. Of course, like all good DBAs, the information catalog obtains its data definitions from the catalogs of the various database servers.

Instead of asking the DBAs to perform copies of the data, the hounds simply use the *copy manager* to do that. The copy manager keeps the informational databases automatically refreshed (or updated) with changes from the source database. A *workflow manager* can orchestrate the multistep movement of data through the network. For each step of the process—and there can be many steps—the workflow manager knows which tool to invoke and what to do next. Finally, the *information database* is a normal SQL database that replaces all the private schemes that have been used by information hounds to store copies of their favorite data extracts. The Information Warehouse makes it easy for the hounds to get to their data and removes the overburdened DBAs from the loop (now they can focus their attention on the OLTP side of the house).

Replication Versus Direct Access

With the spread of client/server technology and loosely coupled federated databases, it becomes impractical from many perspectives—performance, security, availability, debt-to-history, and local control—to create a single centralized repository of data. Replicated data management will increasingly be used to remove the capacity, performance, and organizational roadblocks of centralized data access.

Automated copy management—or the management of replicated data—becomes a key technology for sharing data in a federated database environment. Decision-support applications using data warehouses are perfect candidates for replicated data technology. These applications usually tolerate a certain amount of obsolescence—the politically correct term is *volatility*—in their data. Data replication for decision support minimizes the disruption of production systems and allows you to tailor the informational databases to fit your needs.

On the other hand, *direct data access* is required by applications—mostly production OLTP—that cannot tolerate any "volatility" in their data. These applications require "live data" that reflects the state of the business. This type of live data is obtained in distributed situations using one of four approaches:

■ *Using federated databases that support synchronous (or continuous) replication of data*—the target databases must be synchronized within the same transaction boundary as the primary (or source) database. A target database that allows a user to directly update it is called a *replica*. To maintain a single-site update policy, the replica that gets updated becomes the new source database and must immediately propagate its updates. In general, synchronous replicated technology is a risky proposition in federated database environments. It requires support for two-phase commit protocols across heterogeneous databases.

■ *Using a centralized database server*—all the data is kept on one highly-scalable and fault-tolerant server. This solution, if it fits your organizational needs, will give you the least amount of headaches.

- *Using a single vendor's distributed database multiserver offering—* notice that we did not say multivendor because this technology is still full of holes (see the following Briefing).

- *Using a TP monitor to front-end multivendor database servers—*the database servers must support X/Open's XA protocol to be managed by a TP Monitor. As you will find out in Part 5, this technology can be very attractive in many situations.

In summary, there's a need for both kinds of data access: replicated and direct. The issues of direct access are well understood by the industry; many commercial solutions are available. On the other hand, the management of replicated data within an Information Warehouse framework is opening up exciting new opportunities. As more PCs become multimedia-enabled, we will start seeing federations of informational databases that include: the desktop client where local information is captured and viewed; the local server, which provides overflow storage; and global servers that collectively contain an infinite amount of information and storage. Efficient replication and copy management becomes the glue that ties together these new federations of databases.

The Distributed Database Model

Briefing

Our feedback shows that the user community is still more ready for replication today than for multiple site update—except for the adventurous.

> — *Marilyn Bohl, VP of Engineering, Ingres (November, 1993)*

Standard *off-the-shelf* commercial distributed database packages will provide, when they fully blossom, transparent access to data on a network. The distributed database keeps track of the location of data on the network, and it will route your requests to the right database nodes, making their location transparent. To be fully distributed, a database server must support multisite updates using a transactional two-phase commit discipline (see Figure 15-2). It should allow you to join data from tables that reside on several machines. It should also *automatically* update data in tables that reside on several machines.

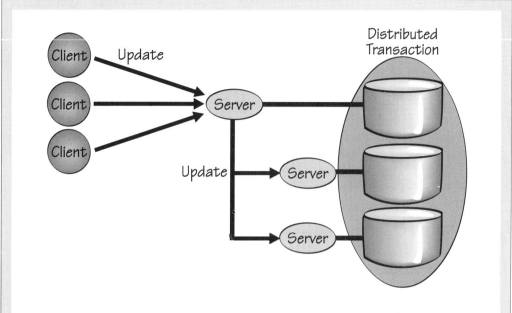

Figure 15-2. The Distributed Database Model.

Distributed databases make it easy to write distributed applications without having to first decompose your applications. With *true* distributed databases, the location of the data is completely transparent to the application. The chief advantage of a distributed database is that it allows access to remote data transparently while keeping most of the data local to the applications that actually use it. The disadvantages of a distributed database are:

■ They currently do not work in heterogeneous database environments. As a result, you're locked into a single vendor solution.

■ They poorly encapsulate data and services. You cannot change a local database table if it is being used by other sites.

■ They require too many low-level message exchanges to get work done. Distributed databases exchange messages at the SQL level. This is not as efficient as using stored procedures or RPCs managed by a TP Monitor.

■ They are very slow over long wide-area networks. Two-phase commits are very expensive in terms of messages sent, and it is difficult to join tables located on different computers and achieve good performance.

- They are very hard to administer. If one machine is not available, all the distributed transactions associated with it cannot execute. In contrast, with replicated databases, data can be accessed even if one server node is down.

The alternative to distributed databases are *federated* databases, which are more easily adaptable to today's organizational realities. We also believe that eventually millions of desktop machines will come with a standard database. When you start dealing with millions of databases, you're much better off with loose federations that are synchronized using distributed object managers or a new breed of personal TP Monitors—but, now we're talking about the "post-scarcity" client/server scenario. ☐

The Mechanics of Data Replication

It's very common for business people to routinely populate their spreadsheets with data extracted from external sources. The process (see Figure 15-3) consists of the following manual steps: 1) Extract data using a query, 2) Copy the results to a diskette file, 3) Copy the diskette file to the machine with the spreadsheet program, and 4) Import the file into the local database (or spreadsheet). This technique, called *manual extract*, is primitive, labor intensive, and error prone.

Figure 15-3. Getting to the Data Manually.

In this section, we look at the mechanics for the total automation of this extract process (see Figure 15-4). The copy mechanics deal with the following issues: How is the extract specified? How is data from multiple sources blended? Can data be transformed as part of the copy? Who orchestrates the copy process? How is data copied into the informational databases? How are the copies refreshed? How tightly synchronized are the replicas (or extracts) with the source? When can the replicas be updated? What are the transactional boundaries of a copy?

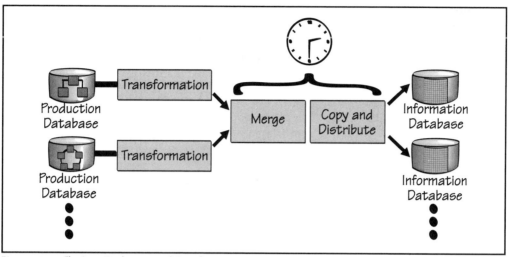

Figure 15-4. The Data Replication and Transformation Process.

Refresh and Updates

The informational databases are populated with data that originates from the various production databases. Typically, the data is copied or extracted using one of two techniques:

■ **Refresh** replaces the entire target with data from the source (see Figure 15-5). This works well when you are moving small amounts of data, which have low requirements for frequency of update (i.e., the data has low volatility). It is also used for doing initial bulk loads to the target database.

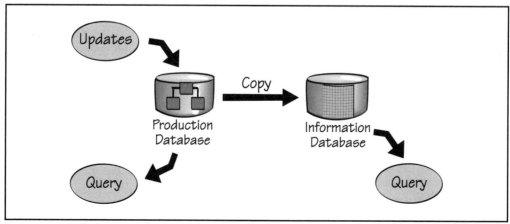

Figure 15-5. Replication via Refresh.

■ *Update* only sends the changed data to the target (see Figure 15-6). Updates can be either *synchronous*, which means that the target copy is updated in the same commit scope as the source table, or they can be *asynchronous*, which means that the target table is updated in a separate transaction than the one updating the source. Synchronous updates are useful in production environments for creating replicated databases that provide high availability. Asynchronous updates are useful in data warehousing situations. You get to specify the level of synchronization that you want to maintain between the source and the target and the interval of updates. This means that you get to control the level of data obsolescence you can tolerate.

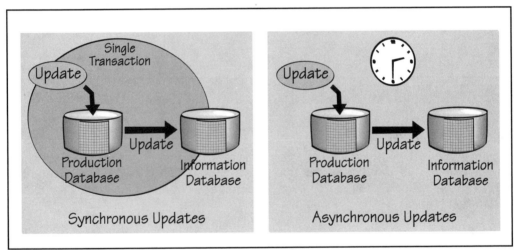

Figure 15-6. Replication via Synchronous and Asynchronous Updates.

Staging the Updates

Some of the warehouse products allow you to finely control the frequency of updates. IBM's Information Warehouse lets you specify the intervals at which you want *asynchronous update* data sent from the source to one or more targets. The changes to the source tables are captured in one or more *staging tables* for subsequent propagation to target tables (see Figure 15-7). At the intervals you specify, all the target databases in the system are updated simultaneously from the staging area.

To be more precise, the *data capture* component takes changed data from the database log and stores it in the *data staging tables* (see Figure 15-7). The *apply* component then takes the data from the staging tables and applies those changes to the target copies.

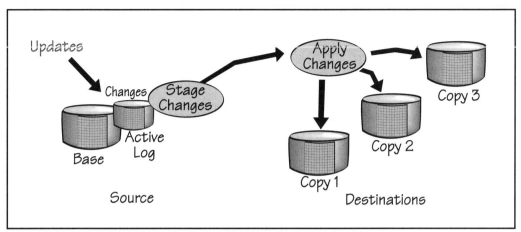

Figure 15-7. Staging: Copying from the Log.

Staging provides users with a consistent view of the data across the copies. It reduces contention on the production database—the copy tool does not interfere with production applications.

Cleaning the Raw Data

One of the attractive features of replicating data in warehouses is that you can control, enhance, and transform the "raw" data before storing it in the target databases. A well-designed warehouse lets you "filter and clean" raw data from production databases and store it in a form that's suitable for your informational needs. In other words, data warehouses are not simply passive collectors of data—they're in the business of creating value-added data from raw data.

As part of the copy, a warehouse translates data from its original raw formats (which may vary widely) into a single common format that's consistent for the informational application. The related data from multiple sites is combined and merged so that the "copy" becomes a single logical database. During this process, data may also be *enhanced*; that is, empty fields may be filled in or records extended. The data may be timestamped and stored in snapshots that capture a moment in time for historical trend analysis. The copy process also takes care of any data format conversions for different targets.

Some of the more sophisticated warehouses may apply user-defined specialized functions to the data to forecast trends; that is, fill in future values or create on-the-fly video presentations. They will also be able to convert data into formats that are appropriate to the decision support, spreadsheet, and multimedia viewing tools on the client machines. In other words, the sky is the limit when it comes to value-added warehousing functions.

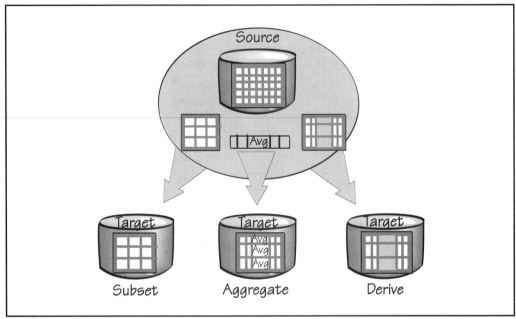

Figure 15-8. Upgrading the Raw Data: Subsets, Aggregates, and Derived Functions.

To give you an idea of what can be done today, let's take a closer look at the transform functions provided by IBM's Information Warehouse (see Figure 15-8). Using the OS/2 DataHub copy functions, the Information Warehouse lets you specify *subsets*, *aggregates*, and *derived functions* that you can automatically apply to data as it is copied between DB2 to DB2, DB2 to DB2/2, and DB2/2 to DB2/2 (refresh only) databases. We explain what this means:

■ **Subsets** allow you to transmit only the rows and columns that are of interest to your informational applications. You use SQL once to define your subsets to the copy tool, and these subsets will be performed automatically as part of the copy. In addition, different views of the same source data can be delivered to different copy targets. Multitable joins can also be used to define the copy transforms.

■ **Aggregates** allow you to transmit only the aggregations of data such as averages, sums, maximums, and so on. Again, you specify this once using SQL, and the copy tool will perform the aggregate every time a transfer takes place.

■ **Derived functions** allow you to specify data that does not exist but is the result of some calculation (or function) on data that does exist. For example, a new column of data may be defined on the target database that is the sum of two columns on the source database. The new column will automatically get created and updated as part of the automated copy process.

In addition to cleaning and merging the data, these functions can help you reduce the network traffic between the targets and the destinations because you only copy the data you want.

True Replicas

Replicas are *copies* of data, that may be updated (see Figure 15-9). When this happens, the updated replica must find a way to resynchronize its state with the original primary database. Normally, updates only take place on a single designated replica, and the primary server must abstain from doing any non-replica generated changes. In other words, the site of update shifts from the primary to the replica. The replica starts off with a full image of the primary database and sends all subsequent updates to the primary, either continuously or on a periodic basis. The primary database is then in charge of propagating the changes it receives to its target databases using the normal processes. The single-site update constraint may be relaxed by using *check-out* versions of replicated data—a technology that is widely used in Object Databases and will be covered in Part 7.

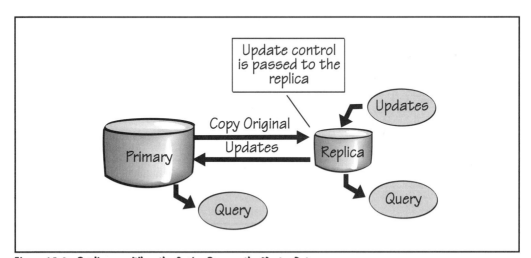

Figure 15-9. Replicas, or When the Copies Become the Master Data.

Ingres implements a database that allows both the master and the replicas to be separately updated and uses a *conflict resolver* to synchronize the data. When the changes in the replica are applied against the master an *update collision detector* resolves conflicts using one of four user-specified policies: the oldest update has priority, the most recent update has priority, a user-specified action is applied, or all replication is halted. Warning: True replicas can corrupt data.

The Future Warehouses

Information Warehouses will pop up everywhere. We expect most personal computer users to have private data warehouses with hot links to information sources all over the globe. We expect large data warehouses to play an important role as data stores for the information highway. Both Oracle and IBM are investing heavily into database-managed video on demand technology. The replication technology that was presented in this chapter is an embryonic version of what can be done. In addition to moving tabular data, we'll soon be moving BLOBs of video and sound from the large data warehouses in the sky to our private and departmental warehouses (and vice versa). The EIS/DSS technology will help us distill massive amounts of data into a few visual pieces of information that we can quickly understand and use. We expect to see personal versions of these currently expensive tools sell in the volume market for $50 (or less). In addition to business information, we expect the warehouses to package tons of information that deal with personal, educational, and consumer topics.

There's Still Money To Be Made in Database

Soapbox

This concludes our conceptual introduction of SQL Database servers. It was a long tour, which is to be expected from a technology that accounts for the majority of client/server applications that are in production today. Database technology is still in its prime. SQL database servers are becoming commodity items and are now learning how to coexist in federated database arrangements. Mission-critical database systems will continue to be sold in packages that superbly integrate scalable fault-tolerant hardware with software. The new areas of growth will be in the mass markets for database-oriented products. What does it mean to put an information warehouse inside each desktop and mobile laptop? Who will keep these warehouses fed with continuous real-time information? What tools will help us digest all this information in real time?

Yes, there are still fortunes to be made in database technology. Database companies—including Sybase, Oracle, Gupta, Informix, Tandem, IBM San Jose, and Ingres—are transforming Silicon Valley (where your authors live) into "Database Valley." And they did it all with some relational and SQL technology from IBM research. We predict (this is, after all, a Soapbox) that the marriage of "data warehouses" and "information highways" will create opportunities in database that dwarf anything we've seen so far. So the best is yet to come. And we certainly expect our valley to be called Database Valley by the end of the decade. ❑

Part 5
Client/Server Transaction Processing

An Introduction to Part 5

So what did you Martians think of the new California gold country? Oh, you want to start panning for SQL gold. Yes, it's a great business—but they do have earthquakes in California. And we have some other great opportunities to show you. For example, Part 5 is about transaction processing and TP Monitors, another important area of new client/server opportunity. Why? Because client/server computing can't live on shared data alone. The programs that operate on that data are just as important. To create effective client/server solutions, we need the software equivalent of a symphony conductor. That's the guy who waves the little wand to orchestrate all the musical instruments so that they play together.

So where is this client/server software conductor? What little wand can be used to orchestrate programs that don't even know about each other? How do we get these programs to act in unison when it takes tons of NOS and middleware just to get them to talk to each other? We've got news for you: The software conductor exists, and it is called a *TP Monitor*. The wand these software conductors use are called *transactions*. Using these transactions, a TP Monitor can get pieces of software that don't know anything about each other to act in total unison.

No, we're not selling snake oil; TP Monitors have solid credentials—they've been used for many years to keep the biggest of "Big Iron" running. In the mainframe world, a TP Monitor is sold with every database. The folks there discovered that without that conductor, they just had some very "inactive" data. If they needed TP Monitors on these single-vendor mainframes, we need them even more on client/server networks where every piece of software only knows how to play its own tune.

Without a conductor, don't expect any client/server music. Yes, an occasional jazz ensemble may spontaneously create music, but it's becoming the exception. We're being deluged with new software every day, and we can't just depend on good luck and Jazz. We need to hire a software conductor for the network. And eventually, every desktop will have a personal software conductor.

So get your tuxedos out—we're going to the symphony. What? You didn't bring them? No problem. The TP Monitor people are not very formal these days; they, too, have discovered sneakers. The plan for Part 5 is to first explore *transactions*. Transactions are to TP Monitors what SQL is to relational databases—it's the commodity that brings it all together. You'll discover that transactions come in all types: flat, chained, nested, long-lived, and sagas. But all transactions have one thing in common: They have ACID properties. What's that? We'll tell you soon. It's good stuff. Eventually, all our software will be ACID-ized.

With transactions in the bag we're ready for TP Monitors: What do they do? What do the new client/server models look like? What kind of standards do they follow? We'll answer all these questions and more. You'll discover that the conductor may save you enough money to more than pay for itself. What a business! The SQL

database servers are making gold—the TP Monitors help you save enough so that some of that gold gets diverted your way. Does this mean you don't move to California? We're not sure yet. The database people are making moves that suggest they may want to keep all the gold in their valley. They've invented something called *TP-Lite*—or "miniconductors" for their databases. You've already encountered some elements of TP-Lite: stored procedures, triggers, and SQL transactions. We'll go over the TP-Lite versus TP-Heavy "miniwar." Do you still have your helmets from the OS wars?

Chapter 16

The Magic of Transactions

> *The idea of distributed systems without transaction management is like a society without contract law. One does not necessarily want the laws, but one does need a way to resolve matters when disputes occur. Nowhere is this more applicable than in the PC and client/server worlds.*
>
> — *Jim Gray (May, 1993)* [1]

Transactions are more than just business events: They've become an application design philosophy that guarantees robustness in distributed systems. Under the control of a TP Monitor, a transaction can be managed from its point of origin—typically on the client—across one or more servers, and then back to the originating client. When a transaction ends, all the parties involved are in agreement as to whether it succeeded or failed. The transaction becomes the contract that binds the client to one or more servers.

---

[1] Source: Jim Gray, "Where is Transaction Processing Headed?" **OTM Spectrum Reports** (May, 1993).

In this chapter we first go over the so-called ACID properties that make transactions such desirable commodities in client/server computing. We then explain the *flat transaction*, which is the workhorse of all the commercial transaction systems—including TP Monitors, Database Managers, transactional file systems, and message queues. The flat transaction is not without its shortcomings; we look at these in some detail and suggest some workarounds. Finally, we go over some of the proposed alternatives to the flat transaction including sagas, chained transactions, and nested transactions.

THE ACID PROPERTIES

Transactions are a way to make ACID operations a general commodity.

— Gray and Reuter (1993) [2]

A transaction is a collection of actions embued with ACID properties. In this case, ACID—a term coined by Andreas Reuter in 1983—stands for Atomicity, Consistency, Isolation, and Durability. Here's what it means:

■ **Atomicity** means that a transaction is an indivisible unit of work: All of its actions succeed or they all fail; it's an all-or-nothing proposition. The actions under the transaction's umbrella may include the message queues, updates to a database, and the display of results on the client's screen. Atomicity is defined from the perspective of the consumer of the transaction.

■ **Consistency** means that after a transaction executes, it must leave the system in a correct state or it must abort. If the transaction cannot achieve a stable end state, it must return the system to its initial state.

■ **Isolation** means that a transaction's behavior is not affected by other transactions that execute concurrently. The transaction must serialize all accesses to shared resources and guarantee that concurrent programs will not corrupt each other's operations. A multiuser program running under transaction protection must behave exactly as it would in a single-user environment. The changes to shared resources that a transaction makes must not become visible outside the transaction until it commits. Again, this is how the consumer of the transaction sees it.

---

[2] Source: Jim Gray and Andreas Reuter, **Transaction Processing Concepts and Techniques** (Morgan Kaufmann, 1993). This 1000-page book is the Bible of transaction processing. It gives some great insights into the motivation behind transaction processing written by two of the original gurus who have pioneered this field.

■ *Durability* means that a transaction's effects are permanent after it commits. Its changes should survive system failures. The term "persistent" is a synonym for "durable."

A transaction becomes the fundamental unit of recovery, consistency, and concurrency in a client/server system. Why is that important? Take a simple debit-credit banking operation. You'd like to see all credit made to *your* account succeed. Any losses would be unacceptable (of course, any unexpected credits are always welcome). This means you're relying on the application to provide the integrity expected in a real-life business transaction. The application, in turn, relies on the underlying system—usually the TP Monitor—to help achieve this level of transactional integrity. The programmer should not have to develop tons of code that reinvents the transaction wheel.

A more subtle point is that all the participating programs must adhere to the transactional discipline. A single faulty program can corrupt an entire system. A transaction that unknowingly uses corrupted initial data—produced by a non-transactional program—builds on top of a corrupt foundation.

In an ideal world, *all* client/server programs are written as transactions. ACID is like motherhood and apple pie. It's necessary—and you can't have too much of it.

OK, enough preaching. Let's take a look at how software transactions model their business counterparts.

TRANSACTION MODELS

When should a transaction start? When should it end and have its effects made accessible to the outside world? What are appropriate units of recovery in case of failures? Can computer transactions mirror their real-world counterparts? To answer these questions, we will look at the *flat transaction*, go over its shortcomings, and take a quick peek at the proposed extensions.

So What's a Flat Transaction?

Flat transactions are the workhorses of the current generation of transactional systems. They're called flat because all the work done within a transaction's boundaries is at the same level (see shaded area in Figure 16-1).

The transaction starts with *begin_transaction* and ends with either a *commit_transaction* or *abort_transaction*. It's an all or nothing proposition—there's no way to commit or abort *parts* of a flat transaction. All the actions are

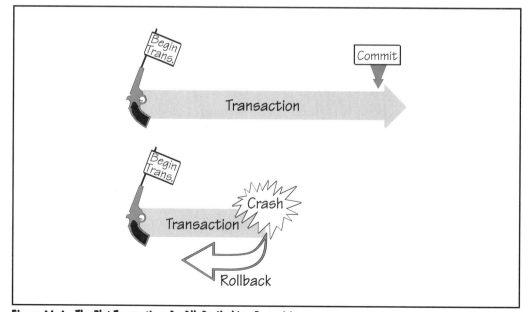

Figure 16-1. The Flat Transaction: An All-Or-Nothing Proposition.

indivisible, which is what we wanted in the first place. Table 16-1 compares the commands used in different TP Monitors to delineate the transaction boundaries.

Table 16-1. Comparing Flat Transaction Delimiters for Major TP Monitors (Adapted from OTM Spectrum Reports; February, 1993).

System	Transaction Delimiter		
	Start	**Commit**	**Abort**
Tuxedo	TPBEGIN	TPCOMMIT	TPABORT
Top End	tx_begin	tx_commit	tx_rollback
Encina RPC	transaction	onCommit	onAbort
X/Open	tx_begin	tx_commit	tx_rollback
OSI TP	C-BEGIN	C-COMMIT	C-ROLLBACK
Tandem RSC	Begin_Transaction	End_Transaction	Abort_Transaction
CICS	SYNCPOINT	SYNCPOINT	SYNCPOINT or ROLLBACK

We Like Our Transactions Flat

Soapbox

The major virtue of the flat transaction is its *simplicity* and the ease with which it provides the ACID features. Thousands of commercial applications were created using the very simple concept of a flat transaction. Historically, the flat transaction was first developed for banking applications—it provides an excellent fit for modeling short activities.

But as the transactional discipline begins to permeate all facets of computing, we're discovering that the flat transaction model does not provide the best fit in all environments. Millions of lines of code have been written to compensate for its shortcomings. The model is particularly weak when it comes to handling business transactions that span over long periods of time—days or even months. It's somewhat weak in the area of batch jobs. And it's a nuisance in situations that require partial rollbacks without throwing away an entire transaction's work—the rigid "all-or-nothing" application of the ACID principle gets in the way.

For political reasons, flat transactions using two-phase commits are usually not allowed to cross intercorporate boundaries—asynchronous MOM may be the preferred approach in such situations. We're also experiencing difficulties with the flat model in client/server environments where client "think time" is part of the transaction loop. There are workarounds for each of these problems, but they require writing some custom code. Wouldn't it be nice if we could extend the transaction model to automatically take care of all these situations for us?

It turns out that computer scientists everywhere are frantically searching for a "unified theory" of transactions that covers all the complex real-life situations and yet still maintains the ACID properties and the simplicity of the flat model. As a result, the academic literature is flooded with new transaction models that have esoteric-sounding names like Sagas, Chained, Promises, ConTracts, Check-Revalidate, Long-Lived, Multilevel, Migrating, Shopping Cart, and Anarchic and Non-Anarchic Nested Transactions.

With the exception of Non-Anarchic Nested Transactions—implemented in Transarc's Encina—none of these esoterics have found their way into commercial products. They make great reading and are always very clever. However, it's turning out not to be easy to extend the transactional model and still do ACID simply. And the jury is still out when it comes to nested transactions—they may be too difficult to manage in normal commercial applications.

At the risk of sounding too conservative, we still feel there's a lot of life left in venerable flat transactions. They can be used "as is" in over 90% of commercial client/server applications. And writing a *little* bit of code around them doesn't particularly bother us—at least we can get them to do exactly what's needed. We feel (remember, this is a Soapbox) it's more important to keep pushing the flat transaction discipline into every known program so that they can all participate in TP-Monitor coordinated transactions.

Transactions are here to help simplify our applications and give us better control over the environment in which they run. Some of the proposed extensions may create more problems than they solve. In any case, as Gray and Reuter point out, "no matter which extensions prove to be the most important and useful in the future, flat transactions will be at the core of all the mechanisms required to make these more powerful models work." ❑

Baby Stepping With Flat Transactions

A typical flat transaction does not last more than two or three seconds so as not to monopolize critical system resources such as database locks. As a result, OLTP client/server programs are broken into short transactions that execute back-to-back to produce results (see Figure 16-2). We call this effect transaction *baby stepping*—or getting work done by moving in "baby steps" from one stable state to the next.[3]

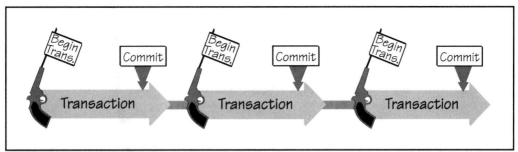

Figure 16-2. Back-to-Back Flat Transactions.

The Distributed Flat Transaction

Can a flat transaction run on multiple sites and update resources located within multiple resource managers? Yes. Even though a high level of parallelism may be involved, as far as the programmer is concerned, it's still just a flat transaction (see Figure 16-3). The programmer is not aware of the considerable amount of "under-the-cover" activity that's required to make the multisite transaction appear flat. The transaction must travel across multiple sites to get to the resources it needs. Each site's TP Monitor must manage its local piece of the transaction. In addition, one of the TP Monitors must coordinate the actions of all its fellow TP Monitors. This is usually done using a *two-phase commit* protocol, which coordinates the transaction's commit or abort across multiple sites (see the following Details box).

---

[3] The term "baby step" is adapted from the recent movie, "What About Bob?" Richard Dreyfus played the role of a psychiatrist who advocated baby stepping as a cure-all.

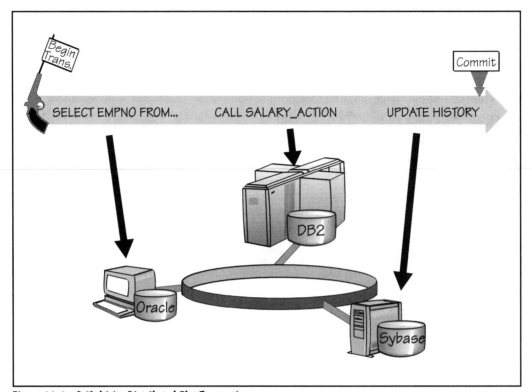

Figure 16-3. A Multisite Distributed Flat Transaction.

What's a Two-Phase Commit Protocol?

Details

The two-phase commit protocol is used to synchronize updates on different machines so that they either all fail or all succeed. This is done by centralizing the decision to commit but giving each participant the right of veto. It's like a Christian marriage: You're given one last chance to back out of the transaction when you're at the altar. If none of the parties present object, the marriage takes place.

It should come as no surprise by now that each commercial implementation introduces its own variation of the two-phase commit protocol. As usual, they don't interoperate. And, of course, there are standards bodies that are trying to make it all work together. In December 1992—after a five-year development cycle—ISO published its *OSI TP* standard that defines very *rigidly* how a two-phase commit is to be implemented (see Figure 16-4). Let's go over the mechanics of this protocol:

1. ***In the first phase of a commit***, the *commit manager* node—also known as the *root node* or the *transaction coordinator*—sends *prepare-to-commit* commands to all the *subordinate* nodes that were directly asked to participate in the transaction. The subordinates may have spawned pieces of the transaction on other nodes (or resource managers) to which they must propagate the prepare-to-commit command. It becomes a transaction tree, with the coordinator at the root.

2. ***The first phase of the commit terminates*** when the root node receives *ready-to-commit* signals from all its direct subordinate nodes that participate in the transaction. This means that the transaction has executed successfully so far on all the nodes and they're now ready to do a final commit. The root node logs that fact in a safe place (the information is used to recover from a root node failure).

3. ***The second phase of the commit starts*** after the root node makes the decision to *commit* the transaction—based on the unanimous yes vote. It tells its subordinates to commit. They, in turn, tell their subordinates to do the same, and the order ripples down the tree.

4. ***The second phase of the commit terminates*** when all the nodes involved have safely committed their part of the transaction and made it durable. The root receives all the confirmations and can tell its client that the transaction completed. It can then relax until the next transaction.

5. ***The two phase commit aborts*** if any of the participants return a *refuse* indication, meaning that their part of the transaction failed. In that case, the root node tells all its subordinates to perform a rollback. And they, in turn, do the same for their subordinates.

The X/Open XA specification defines a set of APIs that work with the underlying OSI TP protocol. In order to participate in an XA-defined two-phase commit, TP Monitors and resource managers (like databases and message queues) must map their private two-phase commit protocols to the XA commands. They must also be willing to let somebody else drive the transaction—something they're not accustomed to doing. The XA specification allows participants to withdraw from further participation in the global transaction during Phase 1 if they do not have to update resources. In XA, a TP Monitor can use a one-phase commit if it is dealing with a single resource manager. We'll have a lot more to say about XA in the next chapter.

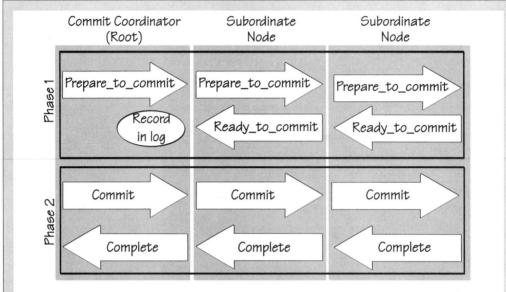

Figure 16-4. The Mechanics of the OSI TP Two-Phase Commit.

The two-phase commit protocol is by no means perfect. Here are some of its more serious limitations:

- ***Performance overhead***, which is introduced by all the message exchanges. The protocol has no way of discerning valuable transactions that need this kind of protection from the more tolerant transactions that don't need protection. It generates messages for all transactions, even read-only ones.

- ***Hazard windows***, where certain failures can be a problem. For example, if the root node crashes after the first phase of the commit, the subordinates may be left in disarray. Who cleans up this mess? There are always workarounds, but it's a tricky business. It helps to have some fault-tolerant hardware somewhere in the system, and preferably coordinating the transaction.

In the June 1993 ISO meeting, a number of suggestions were introduced on how to improve the two-phase commit protocol—including single-phase commits, read-only optimizations, overlapped transactions, implicit prepares, and delegated commits. We don't expect to see any of these proposals in a final draft soon. However, the *delegated commit* proposal is of practical interest in client/server applications. It means that a transaction originating from an unreliable platform—such as a cellular notebook—can delegate the commit coordination to an alternate node. Most of today's TP Monitors don't allow their clients to coordinate transactions. They prefer to do it for them. "Delegated commit" makes the process more democratic. ❏

The Limitations of the Flat Transaction

The "all-or-nothing" characteristic of flat transactions is both a virtue and a vice.

— ***Gray and Reuter (1993)***

So when does the all-or-nothing nature of the flat transaction become a liability? Mostly, in situations that require more flexibility than the all-or-nothing approach. The following are examples of business transactions that require a more flexible approach:

■ ***Compound business transactions that need to be partially rolled back.*** The classical example is a complex trip that includes travel arrangements, hotel reservations, and a car rental (see Figure 16-5). What happens if you simply want to cancel the car reservation but preserve the rest of the reservations? You can't do that within a flat transaction—the entire reservation is rolled back. It's an all-or-nothing proposition. This means you must give up the hotel and plane reservations just to get rid of the car—a real nuisance. The hotel/car reservation problem is used to justify the need for nested or chained transactions. But flat

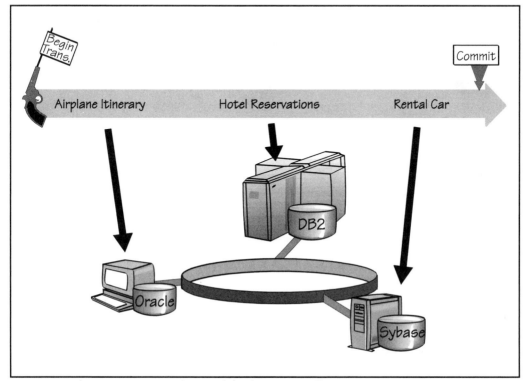

Figure 16-5. Flat Transactions: One Change and You Have to Start All Over.

transaction advocates could make a case that the hotel/car transaction should be broken down into separate hotel and car transactions. In other words, use multiple flat transactions to simulate the compound one.

■ ***Business transactions with humans in the loop.*** This is a classical GUI client/server transaction where a set of choices are presented to the user on a screen, and the server must wait for the decision. In the meantime, locks are held for those records that are on the tube. What happens if an operator that's viewing some airline seats decides to go to lunch? How long are the seats locked out? If it's executed as a single flat transaction, the seats will be held as long as that user is thinking or eating. Nobody else can get to those seats. This is obviously not a very good way to run a business. The solution is to split the reservation into two transactions: a query transaction that displays the available seats, and a reservation transaction that performs the actual reservation (see Figure 16-6). Of course, the existence of the seats must be revalidated before the update. If the seat is gone, the user must be notified. These extra steps mean more work for the programmer.

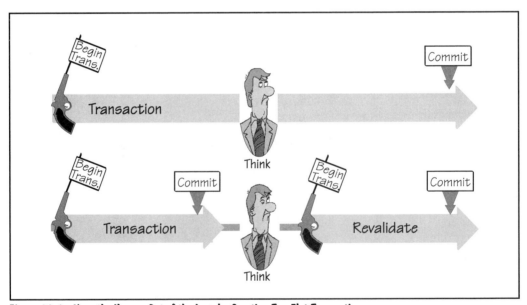

Figure 16-6. Keep the Human Out of the Loop by Creating Two Flat Transactions.

■ ***Business transactions that span over long periods of time.*** These are your typical engineering Computer-Aided Design (CAD) transactions that may require CAD-managed components to be worked on for days and passed from engineer to engineer (see Figure 16-7). The CAD transaction must be able to suspend itself and resume after shutdowns, preserve ongoing work across shutdowns, and know where it left off and what needs to be done next. In essence, it becomes a workflow manager. Obviously, flat transactions must be augmented by a workflow program to handle such long-lived work. This is an area where alternative transactional models—including object database check-in check-out transactions, replica management, and workflow—look very promising.

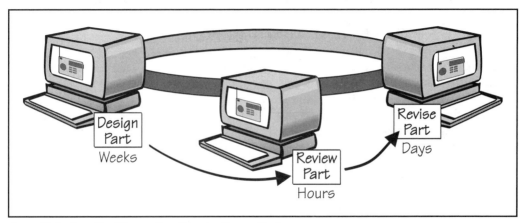

Figure 16-7. Long-Lived Transactions Spanning Days or Weeks.

■ ***Business transactions with a lot of bulk.*** The classical problem here is: How do you handle one million record updates under transactional control (see Figure 16-8)? Must the entire transaction be rolled back if a failure occurs after record 999,999 is updated? Yes, it's all-or-nothing if you're using a single flat transaction to do the million updates. On the other hand, if you make each update a separate transaction, it is much slower—a million separate commits are required—and where do you restart after the failure? This is an area where syncpoints or chained transactions have been proposed as a solution. But the solution may slow you down because it introduces more commits and maybe some restart code. We think you may be better off restarting an occasional flat transaction then going with the alternatives. After all, how often can a bulk transaction fail?

Figure 16-8. Flat Transaction: It Failed—Restart That Million Update Job.

■ ***Business transactions that span across companies.*** The problem here is a political one. Very few companies will allow an external TP Monitor (or database) to synchronize in real-time a transaction on their systems using a two-phase commit. The more politically correct solution may be to conduct an intercompany exchange using loosely coupled transactional message queues. A MOM solution allows organizations to split the unit of work into many transactions that can be executed asynchronously, processed on different machines, and coordinated by independent TP Monitors within each company (see Figure 16-9). You lose instantaneous consistency, but you're able to maintain arm's length controls between companies. From a software perspective, we ended up breaking a single two-phase commit flat transaction into three independent flat transactions that execute on company A's TP Monitor, MOM, and company B's TP Monitor. The MOM transaction ensures that the transaction has safely made it from company A's computer to company B's computer. We're assuming that MOM provides a durable queue that gives you "D" in ACID at commit time.

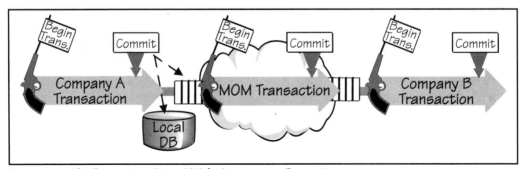

Figure 16-9. Flat Transactions: Using MOM for Intercompany Transactions.

In summary, most of the flat transaction's problems come from the rigidity imposed by the all-or-nothing discipline in situations that require more flexibility. You can work around most of these problems by breaking down transactions into smaller units and developing the control code that synchronizes the several smaller transactions. It's a trade-off: You can write one long transaction that can fail in a big way, or several smaller ones that fail in smaller ways. The designer, as usual, must perform a balancing act.

The Alternatives: Chained and Nested Transactions

Most of the proposed alternatives to the flat transaction are based on mechanisms that extend the flow of control beyond the linear unit of work. Two of the most obvious ways to extend the flow of control are by chaining units of work in linear sequences of "mini" transactions—the chained transaction or Saga—or by creating some kind of nested hierarchy of work—the nested transaction. Each of these two basic approaches have many refinements.

The solution to the long-lived transaction requires some form of control flow language for describing activities that evolve in time. This is more or less the model proposed in some of the more recent research literature under names such as *ConTracts, Migrating Transactions*, and *Shopping Cart Transactions*. None of these models are available in commercial applications. We feel that the best commercial solutions available today for long-lived transactions are in workflow managers and object databases, which we cover in Parts 6 and 7. So we will defer this discussion until then.

Syncpoints, Chained Transactions, and Sagas

The chained transaction, as the name implies, introduces some form of linear control for sequencing through transactions. The simplest form of chaining is to use *syncpoints*—also known as savepoints within a flat transaction that allow periodic saves of accumulated work (see Figure 16-10). What makes a syncpoint different from a commit? The syncpoint lets you roll back work and still maintain a live transaction. In contrast, a commit ends a transaction. Syncpoints also give you better granularity of control over what you save and undo. The transaction can be broken into a series of activities that can be rolled back individually. But the big difference is that the commit is durable while the syncpoint is volatile. If the system crashes during a transaction, all data accumulated in syncpoints is lost.

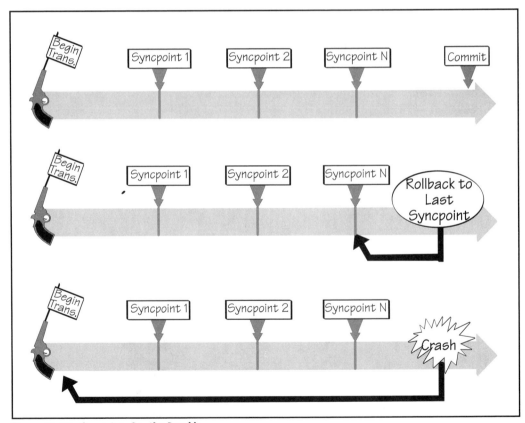

Figure 16-10. Syncpoints Are Not Durable.

Chained transactions are a variation of syncpoints that make the accumulated work durable. They allow you to commit work while staying within the transaction (i.e., you don't give up your locks and resources). A commit gives you the "D" in ACID without terminating the transaction (see Figure 16-11). But what you lose is the ability to roll back an entire chain's worth of work. There's no free lunch.

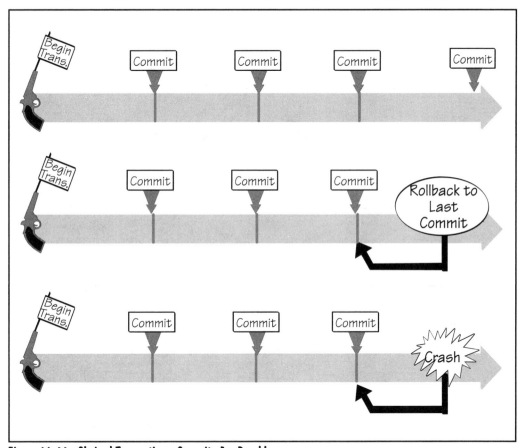

Figure 16-11. Chained Transactions: Commits Are Durable.

Sagas extend the chained transactions to let you roll back the entire chain, if you require it (see Figure 16-12). They do that by maintaining a chain of compensating transactions. You still get the crash resistance of the intermediate commits, but you have the choice of rolling back the entire chain under program control. This lets you treat the entire chain as an atomic unit of work. You can now have your cake and eat it too.[4]

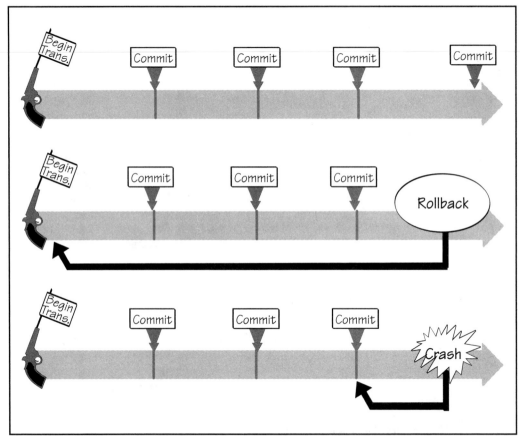

Figure 16-12. Sagas: Commits Are Durable but Can Be Rolled Back.

---

[4] The term Saga was first suggested by Bruce Lindsay of IBM Almaden Research. The concept was fully developed by Hector Garcia-Molina and K. Salem in 1987.

Nested Transactions

Nested Transactions provide the ability to define transactions within other transactions. They do that by breaking a transaction into hierarchies of "subtransactions," very much like a program is made up of procedures. The main transaction starts the subtransactions, which behave as dependent transactions. A subtransaction can also start its own subtransactions, making the entire structure very recursive (see Figure 16-13).

Each subtransaction can issue a commit or rollback for its designated pieces of work. When a subtransaction commits, its results are only accessible to the parent that spawned it. A subtransaction's commit becomes permanent after it issues a local commit and all its ancestors commit. If a parent transaction does a rollback, all its descendent transactions are rolled back, regardless of whether they issued local commits.

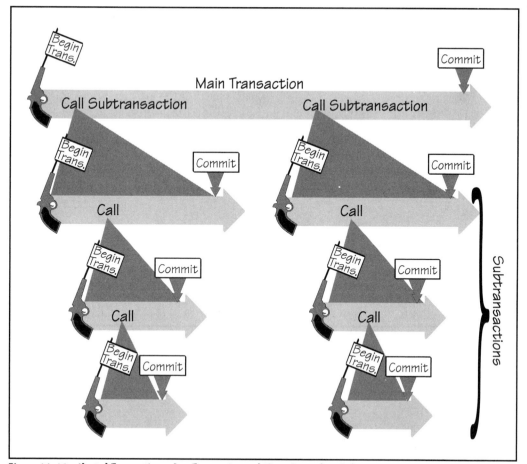

Figure 16-13. Nested Transactions: One Transaction and Many Dependent Subtransactions.

The main benefit of nesting is that a failure in a subtransaction can be trapped and retried using an alternative method, still allowing the main transaction to succeed. Nesting helps programmers write more granular transactions. The only commercial implementation of nested transactions we know of is the Encina TP Monitor. Encina's Transactional C allows you to declare the nesting directly in your code where it starts resembling regular procedure invocations. We still feel nesting may be an overkill that creates more problems than solutions. Of course, now that the Encina TP Monitor is on the market, you'll have your chance to prove us wrong.

Conclusion

Transactions are important because they give ordinary programs ACID qualities without writing a line of messy code. All you need to do is say begin and end transaction—and suddenly the magic appears. In the next chapter, we explain how the magic wand of TP Monitors provides the robust mechanisms that keep these transactions running under all sorts of conditions. We also noted that transactions are now being used to represent more complex business activities. Eventually, our transactions will be extended beyond their flat origins to cover some of these more complex business activities. The more pressing need is to permeate the simple flat transactions into all our client/server programs and "ACIDify" them. ACID is the best antidote to the inherent complexity in distributed systems.

Chapter 17

TP Monitors: Managing Client/Server Transactions

TP Monitors make a silk purse out of a sow's ear—they turn mundane operating systems into fast, highly reliable transaction engines.

> — Jeri Edwards, Director,
> Transaction Processing Development,
> Tandem Computers (February, 1994)

TP Monitors specialize in managing transactions from their point of origin—typically on the client—across one or more servers, and then back to the originating client. When a transaction ends, the TP Monitor makes sure that all the systems involved in the transaction are left in a consistent state. In addition, TP Monitors know how to run transactions, route them across systems, load-balance their execution, and restart them after failures.

One of the great appeals of a TP Monitor is that it is the overseer of all aspects of a distributed transaction, regardless of the systems or resource managers used. A TP Monitor can manage resources on a single server or multiple servers, and it can cooperate with other TP Monitors in federated arrangements. Future TP Monitors may reside on every client machine to bring desktop resources—such as the user interface, local data warehouses, or personal agents—within a distributed transaction's reach.

In this chapter we explain in some detail what TP Monitors are and what functions they perform. We go over X/Open's model for how TP Monitors interact with other resource managers in an open environment. We conclude with a list of benefits that TP Monitors provide. We felt this list was needed because the benefits of TP Monitors are not well understood in the PC LAN and Unix worlds. TP Monitors are either treated with awe and left to the "High-Priests" of computer science, or they are dismissed as antiques. Neither is true. TP Monitors are fun to program, and they create transactional magic on ordinary client/server networks. But enough talk; this isn't a Soapbox.

TP MONITORS

TP Monitors first appeared on mainframes to provide robust run-time environments that could support large-scale OLTP applications—airline and hotel reservations, banking, automatic teller machines, credit authorization systems, and stock-brokerage systems. Since then, OLTP has spread to almost every type of business application—including hospitals, manufacturing, point-of-sales retail systems, automated gas pumps, and telephone directory services. TP Monitors provide whatever services are required to keep these OLTP applications running in the style they're accustomed to: highly reactive, available, and well managed. With OLTP moving to client/server platforms, a new-breed of TP Monitors is emerging to help make the new environment hospitable to mission-critical applications.

What's a TP Monitor?

It should come as no surprise that our industry has no commonly accepted definition of a TP Monitor. We'll use Jeri Edwards' definition of a TP Monitor as "an operating system for transaction processing." This definition captures the essence of a TP Monitor. So what does an operating system for transaction processing do in life? How does it interface with the rest of the world? What services does it provide? We'll answer all these questions. In a nutshell, a TP Monitor does two things extremely well:

■ **Process management** includes starting server processes, funneling work to them, monitoring their execution, and balancing their workloads.

■ **Transaction management** means that it guarantees the ACID properties to all programs that run under its protection.

TP Monitors and OSs: The Great Funneling Act

Historically TP Monitors were introduced to run classes of applications that could service hundreds and sometimes thousands of clients (think of an airline reservation application). If each of these thousands of clients were given all the resources it needed on a server—typically a communication connection, half a MByte of memory, one or two processes, and a dozen open file handles—even the largest mainframe server would fall on its knees (see Figure 17-1). Luckily, not all the clients require service at the same time. However, when they do require it, they want their service *immediately*. We're told that the humans on the other end have a "tolerance for waiting" of two seconds or less. TP Monitors provide an operating system—on top of existing OSs—that connects in real time these thousands of impatient humans with a pool of shared server processes.

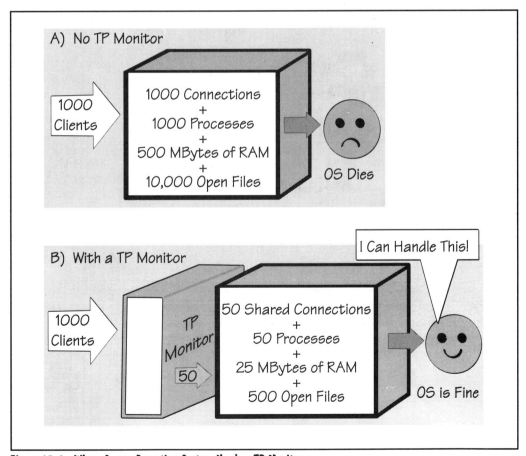

Figure 17-1. Why a Server Operating System Needs a TP Monitor.

How Is the Great Funneling Act Performed?

The "funneling act" is part of what a TP Monitor must do to manage the server side of a user-written OLTP application. In PC environments, the server side of the OLTP application is typically packaged as a DLL that contains a number of related functions. The TP Monitor assigns the execution of the DLL functions to *server classes*—these are groups of processes or threads that are prestarted, waiting for work. Each process or thread in a server class is capable of doing the work. The TP Monitor balances the workload between them.

When a client sends a service request, the TP Monitor hands it to an available process in the server class pool (see Figure 17-2). The server process dynamically links to the DLL function called by the client, invokes it, oversees its execution, and returns the results to the client. After that completes, the server process can be reused by another client. The operating system keeps the already loaded DLLs in memory, where they can be shared across processes. It doesn't get better!

In essence, the TP Monitor removes the process-per-client requirement by funneling incoming client requests to shared server processes. If the number of incoming client requests exceeds the number of processes in a server class, the TP Monitor

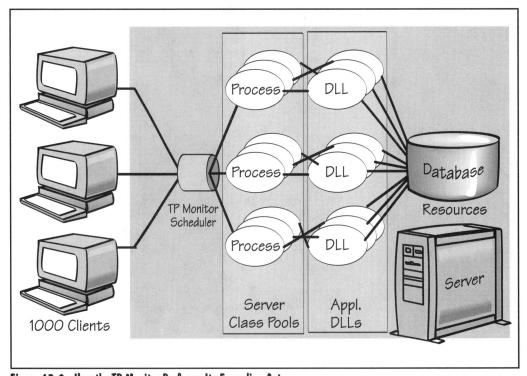

Figure 17-2. How the TP Monitor Performs Its Funneling Act

may dynamically start new ones—this is called *load balancing*. The more sophisticated TP Monitors can distribute the process load across CPUs in SMP environments. Part of the load balancing act involves managing the priorities of the incoming requests; the TP Monitor does that by running some high priority server classes and dynamically assigning them to the VIP clients.

TP Monitors and Transaction Management

The transaction discipline was introduced in the early TP Monitors to ensure the robustness of multiuser applications that ran on the servers. These applications had to be bullet-proof and highly reliable if they were going to serve thousands of users in "bet-your-business" situations. TP Monitors were developed from the ground-up as operating systems for transactions. The unit of management, execution, and recovery was the ordinary transaction and the programs that invoked them. The job of a TP Monitor is to guarantee the ACID properties while maintaining high transaction throughput. To do that, it must manage the execution, distribution, and synchronization of transaction *workloads*.

With TP Monitors, the application programmers don't have to concern themselves with issues like concurrency, failures, broken connections, load balancing, and the synchronization of resources across multiple nodes. All this is made transparent to them—very much like an operating system makes the hardware transparent to ordinary programs. Simply put, TP Monitors provide the run-time engines for running transactions—they do that on top of ordinary hardware and operating systems.

TP Monitor Client/Server Interaction Types

Ordinary operating systems must understand the nature of the jobs and resources they manage. This is also true for TP Monitors—they must provide an optimized environment for the execution of the transactions that run under their control. This means they must load the server programs, dynamically assign incoming client requests to server processes, recover from failures, return the replies to the clients, and make sure high-priority traffic gets through first.

So what kind of assumptions do TP Monitors make about their client/server transaction interaction types? They typically fall into one of four categories: conversational, RPC, queued, and batch (see Figure 17-3). The batch transactions typically run in low-priority mode. RPC and conversational transactions usually involve a human user that requires immediate attention; they run in high-priority mode. MOM-based queued-transactions can be of either type.

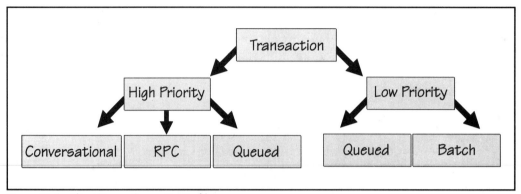

Figure 17-3. Client/Server Transaction Profiles.

In addition, TP Monitors must be prepared to communicate with all the resource managers on which the transaction executes—whether they're on the same machine or across a network. When the resource managers are across networks, the TP Monitor synchronizes the transaction with the remote TP Monitors using a two-phase commit.

Transactional RPCs, Queues, and Conversations

On the surface, transactional client/server exchanges appear to use the traditional NOS communication models: queues, RPCs, and conversational peer-to-peer communications. This is not so. They're using highly-augmented versions of these traditional communication mechanisms. However, most of the value-added elements are made transparent to the programmer—they look like ordinary exchanges bracketed by start and end transaction calls. The transactional versions augment the familiar NOS exchanges with the following value-added extensions:

■ They piggyback *transactional delimiters* that allow a client to specify the begin-transaction and end-transaction boundaries. The actual commit mechanics are usually *delegated* to one of the server TP Monitors because the client is assumed to be unreliable.

■ They introduce—under-the-cover—a three-way exchange between a client, server, and TP Monitor (the transaction manager). A new transaction is assigned a unique ID by the coordinating TP Monitor. All subsequent message exchanges between the participants are tagged with that transaction ID. The message exchanges allow the TP Monitor to keep track of what Jim Gray calls the "dynamically expanding web" of resource managers participating in a distributed transaction. TP Monitors need that information to coordinate the two-phase commit with all the participants in a transaction.

■ They embed transaction state information within each of the messages exchanged. This information helps the TP Monitor identify the state of the distributed transaction and figure out what to do next.

■ They allow a TP Monitor to enforce *exactly-once* semantics—this means that the message only gets executed once.

■ The TP Monitor guarantees that a server process is at the receiving end of the message. Traditional RPCs and MOMs do not worry about this kind of stuff— they assume that a program will "automagically" appear on the receiving end.

As you can see, there's a lot more going on here than a simple RPC or MOM exchange. The literature calls these enhanced services *Transactional RPC (TRPC)*, *Transactional Queues*, and *Transactional Conversations*. The distinguishing factor is that all resource managers and processes invoked through these calls become part of the transaction. The TP Monitor is informed of any service calls; it uses that information to orchestrate the actions of all the participants, enforce their ACID behavior, and make them act as part of a transaction. In contrast, traditional RPCs, messages, and queue invocations are between separate programs that are not bound by a transaction discipline. Table 17-1 summarizes the differences between transactional communication mechanisms and their traditional NOS equivalents.

Table 17-1. Transactional Versus Non-Transactional Communications.

Feature	Traditional MOM, RPC, and Conversations	Transactional MOM, RPC, and Conversations
Who participates?	Loosely-coupled client/server programs.	Transactionally bound client/server and server/server programs. The message invocation causes the recipient program to join the transaction.
Commit synchronization	No	Yes
Only-once semantics	No	Yes
Server management on the recipient node.	No. It's just a delivery mechanism.	Yes. The process that receives the message is started, load-balanced, monitored, and tracked as part of the transaction.

Table 17-1. Transactional Versus Non-Transactional Communications. (Continued)

Feature	Traditional MOM, RPC, and Conversations	Transactional MOM, RPC, and Conversations
Load balancing	Using the directory services. The first server to register becomes a hot-spot. No dynamic load balancing is provided.	Using the TP Monitor's sophisticated load-balancing algorithms. Can spread work across SMP machines and dynamically add more processes to cover hotspots of activity.
Supervised exchanges	No. Exchanges are simply between the client and the server. The exchanges are transient. No crash-recovery or error management is provided. You're on your own.	The TP Monitor supervises the entire exchange, restarts communication links, redirects messages to an alternate server process if the first one gets hung, performs retries, provides persistent queues and crash-recovery.

Examples of commercial implementations of a TRPC include the Encina Transactional RPC and CICS OS/2's External Call Interface (ECI). Examples of conversational transactional interfaces include Tuxedo's ATMI, Tandem's RSC, and APPC's Syncpoint features. MQSeries is an example of a transactional implementation of an "open" MOM queue. Some TP Monitors also include their own bundled versions of recoverable queues—in Encina's case it is RQS, and in Tuxedo it is /Q; CICS uses transient queues.

TRANSACTION MANAGEMENT STANDARDS: X/OPEN DTP AND OSI-TP

TP Monitors need standards because they're the ultimate glue software. The applications they coordinate could be running on different platforms with access to different databases and resource managers. These applications are most likely developed using different tools. And they have absolutely no knowledge of each other. The only way to make these disparate pieces come together is through "open standards" that specify how a TP Monitor interfaces to resource managers, to other TP Monitors, and to its clients.

Most of the standards activity around TP Monitors comes from two sources: the International Standard Organization (ISO)—the OSI-CCR and OSI-TP specifications—and X/Open's *Distributed Transaction Processing (DTP)* specifications. The ISO-OSI standards specify the message protocols (i.e., FAPs) that allow TP Monitors to interoperate. The OSI-TP specification, which we covered in the last chapter, is the most important of these standards; it defines, among other things, the two-phase commit protocol. X/Open has taken the lead in defining the APIs within a general framework for transaction processing. Together, X/Open DTP and OSI-TP form the foundations for "open transaction management." This section covers the X/Open DTP.

The X/Open DTP Reference Model—Vintage 1991

The X/Open DTP model is a software architecture that allows multiple application programs to share resources provided by multiple resource managers, and allows their work to be coordinated into global transactions.

— *X/Open, DTP Reference V2*
(December, 1993)

In 1991, the X/Open XTP group published the *Transaction Processing Reference Model*, which has achieved wide acceptance in the industry. The primary purpose of this model is to define the components of a transaction-based system and to locate the interfaces between them. The 1991 model defined three components: application programs, transaction managers, and resource managers (see Figure 17-4). In X/Open's definition:

■ A *resource manager* is any piece of software that manages shared resources—for example, a database manager, a persistent queue, or transactional file system—and allows the updates to its resources to be externally coordinated via a two-phase commit protocol.

■ A *transaction manager* is the component that coordinates and controls the resource managers. The transaction manager and resource manager communicate via X/Open's *XA interface* published in 1991. The transaction manager use xa_* API calls to interact with the resource managers; the resource managers use ax_* API calls to interact with the transaction manager. For example, the transaction manager issues an *xa_start* to tell a resource manager to join a new transaction. It issues *xa_prepare*, *xa_commit*, and *xa_rollback* to tell a resource manager to perform a two-phase commit. And it issues *xa_end* to tell the resource manager to leave this transaction. XA defines some additional calls for performing the recovery of "in-doubt" transactions. In the reverse direction, a resource manager issues an *ax_reg* call to register its presence dynamically with the transaction manager.[1]

---

[1] X/Open allows resource managers to become associated with a global transaction only after the application directly calls them. They use the *ax_reg* call to dynamically register their presence.

■ An ***application program*** uses the general APIs supplied by a resource manager (for example, SQL), but issues the transaction bracketing calls directly to the transaction manager via X/Open's *TX interface* published in 1992. An application calls *tx_begin* to start a transaction, *tx_commit* to commit it, *tx_rollback* to abort it, and *tx_set_transaction_controls* to set the chaining mode. Transactions can be chained or unchained (the default mode). The *tx_info* call returns information about the global context of a transaction. It is important to note that in the X/Open model, the application decides when it wishes to participate in a transaction; the TX interface drives the XA interface when managing a global transaction. In theory, this allows an application to be developed independently of the TP Monitor target environment.

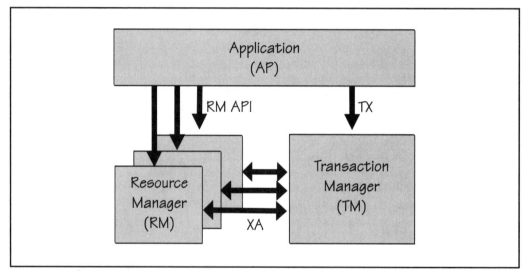

Figure 17-4. The X/Open 1991 Transaction Processing Reference Model.

The 1991 X/Open model only deals with programs talking to their local resource and transaction managers. The transaction can only execute within a single transaction manager's domain. It does not cover how an application requests resources that are on remote nodes and how these remote nodes join the transaction.

The X/Open DTP Reference Model—Vintage 1993

In December 1993, X/Open issued Version 2 of its Distributed Transaction Reference Model that adds a fourth component to the model: the *communication resource manager*. This component controls communications between distributed applications (see Figure 17-5). X/Open also defined a superset of XA called *XA+*

that defines the interface between the communication resource managers and the transaction manager. This interface lets the transaction manager know which remote resource managers the transaction is visiting and supports global transaction information flows across transaction manager domains. XA+ is still an X/Open snapshot; it will eventually supersede XA.

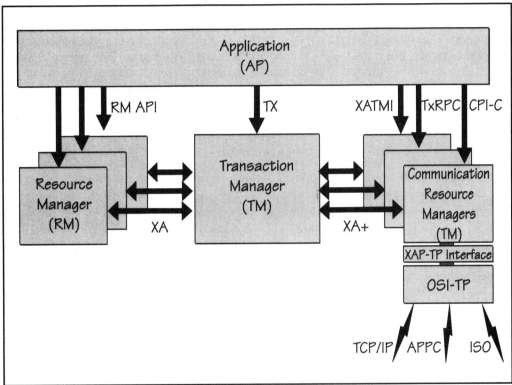

Figure 17-5. The X/Open 1993 Transaction Processing Reference Model.

At the application level, X/Open is in the process of defining *three* interfaces between applications and communication resource managers:

- **TxRPC** is a transactional version of the DCE RPC. An RPC call can either have *transaction-mandatory* or *transaction-optional* attributes that are specified through the IDL. The underlying mechanism for TxRPC is a technology from DEC called *Remote Task Invocation (RTI)* that uses OSI-TP to do the two-phase commit. TxRPC is still in the X/Open snapshot phase (also see the following Soapbox).

- **CPI-C V2** is a peer-to-peer conversational interface based on CPI-C and APPC. An IBM-led working group is in the process of extending CPI-C to support OSI-TP semantics. A preliminary spec is expected in mid-94.

■ **XATMI** is a client/server conversational interface based on Tuxedo's *Application/Transaction Management Interface (ATMI)*. The interface allows you to issue a single request/response using the *tpcall* API. Or it can be used in general conversation mode through the *tpconnect, tpsend, tprecv* calls. This interface is in the X/Open snapshot phase.

The target upper-layer protocol for each of these APIs is the OSI-TP FAP. Below the OSI-TP FAP, communication resource managers can support multiple transport protocols—including TCP/IP, ISO, and APPC. Of course, proprietary protocols may be used between homogeneous transaction manager domains. The use of OSI-TP is mandatory for communications between heterogeneous transaction manager domains. In theory, we should be able to achieve some level of multivendor interoperability (this is, after all, the idea behind all these standards). However, note that X/Open does not address the relationship between the different communication APIs—for example, it says nothing about an XATMI application being able to exchange messages with a CPI-C application via the X/Open specified communication resource managers.

Figure 17-6 shows how a global transaction exchange may be conducted. The application on the left node interacts with the remote resource via its communications resource manager. The transaction manager on the node where the request originates acts as the commit coordinator using the services of the communications resource manager. The commit coordinator is the *root* transaction monitor and the remote monitor is a *subordinate*.

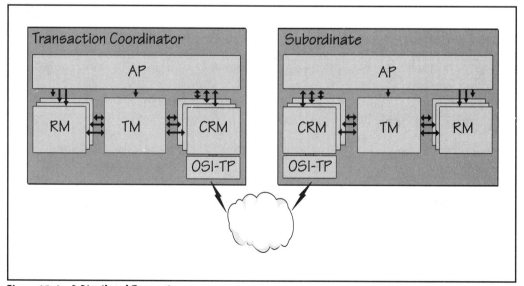

Figure 17-6. A Distributed Transaction.

Of course, more than two nodes may participate in an exchange. Global transactions that operate across distributed transaction managers are managed using trees of transaction manager relationships (see Figure 17-7). The example shows B to be the *superior* to both C and D, but it is a *subordinate* of A, which acts as the commit coordinator. During the two-phase commit, the superior manages the commitment coordination of its subordinates and reports the results up the chain.

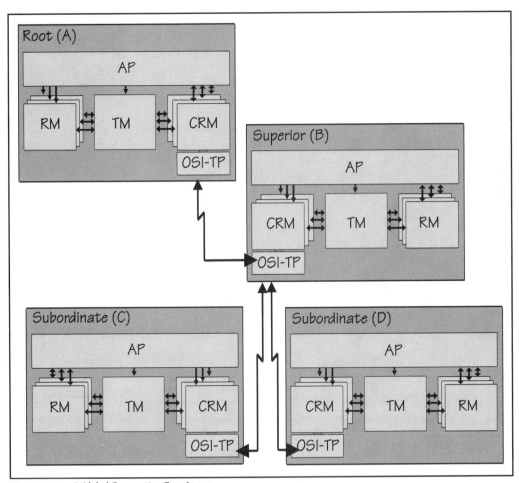

Figure 17-7. A Global Transaction Tree Structure.

Why Three Interface Standards?

Soapbox

So why do we need three interfaces at the application level? Wouldn't a single API make more sense from the portability and interoperability perspectives? We think so, but the "official" X/Open line is that they each bring their own rich set of interapplication communication paradigms. A more likely explanation is that the committee put together a specification that would make its three warring contingents—DCE, CICS, and Tuxedo—happy. This is how most standards are born!

By the way, there's more coming. X/Open is currently looking at adding a message queuing interface. Three base proposals were submitted for consideration: MQI (IBM), /Q (Tuxedo), and RQS (Encina). In addition, there's OSI-MQ. So perhaps we may get four more "standard" interfaces that will make everybody else on the committee happy. And a glaring omission is that nobody's defined a thin client interface that can issue a "delegated commit" and let the closest TP Monitor take it over from there. This may also lead to a few more interfaces!

And while we're on this Soapbox, note that OSF is not necessarily endorsing the X/Open TxRPC—remember, it's the one that's based on DCE. OSF's DCE SIG TP Working Group is issuing a Request for Technology for a "DCE-based" transactional RPC that is *not* based on OSI-TP. Transarc is expected to respond to this with a proposal that incorporates its own two-phase commit technology over different transports—yet another potential standard in the making. Where does it all end? ❏

What the Transaction Standards Do Not Address

The X/Open standard does *not* address many issues that are of practical importance to TP Monitors; for example:

- Process management including starting processes, registering processes, balancing workloads among processes, and so on.
- Configuration, installation, and monitoring of transaction processing systems.
- Security.
- Naming and directory services.
- System management and operator interfaces.
- Fault-tolerance.
- Desktop originated transactions. At a minimum, X/Open should address the issue of thin clients and delegated commits.

The X/Open model *does* address a very small but important subset of a TP Monitor: The transaction interfaces and how transactions are declared. However, it does not address the inner core: *transaction processing*. Yet, we need to standardize a lot of this inner core so that federated TP Monitors can become a reality.

Alternatives to the Standards

The alternative is to standardize on a single vendor's TP Monitor platform—preferably one that runs on many OSs and interoperates with a wide variety of resource managers. For example, IBM offers a "CICS on everything" solution—with CICS provided on MVS, AIX, HP-UX, OS/2, OS/400, and possibly NT. Tuxedo is being ported to all the Unix platforms and to Tandem Computers' highly-scalable Pathway environment. IBM and Transarc are also porting Encina to as many platforms as money and time permits.

The benefits provided by this single-vendor approach are:

- You can pick and choose and even "mix-and-match" resource managers (such as databases). You can do that because most TP Monitors and database managers now support XA and XA+ interfaces.

- Your applications are easier to manage because you're dealing with a single point of management.

- Your applications are easier to port (on your TP vendor's other supported OS/hardware platforms) because you get a large number of portable API calls. Your applications can take advantage of a much larger number of services than those provided in a least common denominator portability approach.

The negatives of this single-vendor approach are:

■ Your applications are not portable across TP Monitor platforms.
■ Your applications may not interoperate with other TP Monitors.
■ You're locked into a single vendor TP Monitor solution.

It's the typical "catch-22" of client/server computing: single vendor lock-in with peace of mind, or multivendor openness but waiting for up-to-date standards and broader functionality.

DO YOU NEED A TP MONITOR?

Because TP Monitors may be unfamiliar to many of our readers, we will go over a list of benefits that TP Monitors offer to client/server applications. Even though TP Monitors were originally introduced to serve very large "mission-critical" applications, the new versions are well-suited for handling client/server applications that span from a few nodes to thousands of nodes. Eventually, we believe that a TP Monitor component will reside on every workstation that's connected to a network—not just servers.

Here's a list of benefits that can be obtained from using the current crop of client/server oriented TP Monitors:

■ *Client/Server application development environment.* Increasingly, visual tool vendors are directly supporting RPCs and making the TP Monitor transparent to the developers. IDL-defined RPCs are easier to integrate with front-end tools than proprietary stored procedures. On the server side, TP Monitors provide general-purpose server shells (server classes) that run your RPCs. The TP Monitor introduces an event-driven programming style on servers by letting you associate RPCs (event handlers) with server events. In addition, the TP Monitor run-time environment enforces the ACID discipline without requiring any specialized code other than begin/end transaction. You can think of a TP Monitor as providing a pre-built framework that helps you build, run, and administer a client/server application (you don't start from ground zero). TP Monitors—augmented with open vendor GUI tools—provide an excellent platform for developing robust, high-performing, client/server applications quickly.

■ *Firewalls of protection.* In a client/server world, it is important to protect yourself from everything that can go wrong in the distributed environment. TP Monitors implement "firewalls" between applications and resource managers and between applications themselves. TP Monitors support tightly-coupled firewalls—such as two-phase commits or loosely-coupled firewalls such as those provided by transactional queues. The firewall unit of protection is the ACID transaction.

- *High availability.* TP Monitors are designed to work around all types of failures. The permeation of ACID principles throughout all components helps create self-healing systems. TP Monitors, at all times, are aware of the state of all the client/server resources that are under their control. With ACID you can detect a failure exactly where it happens. A TP Monitor can then restart a failed process or switch over to a process on another node in the event of hardware failures. Architectures with no single point-of-failure are achievable.

- *Load balancing.* TP Monitors specialize in process management and support both static and dynamic load balancing techniques. TP monitors support the prioritization of requests and can *dynamically* replicate server processes on the same server node or on different nodes. In the static case, a pool of server classes may be scheduled to handle certain peak loads (for example, between work shifts) and then scaled down to support other job mixes during the day. The TP Monitor's load balancing software is an excellent match for today's new breed of SMP server hardware.

- *MOM Integration.* TP Monitors complement MOMs very well. Together they can provide support for long-lived transactions and workflow type of applications. TP Monitors can act as the transaction coordinator for work that is exchanged through transactional queues. The queued events can trigger server processes managed by the TP Monitor.

- *Scalabilty of function.* TP Monitors encourage you to create modular reusable procedures that encapsulate resource managers. With a TP Monitor, you export the function call and not the data itself. This means that you can keep adding new function calls and let the TP Monitor distribute that function over multiple servers. TP Monitors allow you to create highly complex applications by just adding more procedures. The TP Monitor guarantees that procedures that know nothing about each other will work together in ACID unison. In addition, the TP Monitor lets you mix resource managers—meaning that you can always start with one resource manager and then move to another one while preserving your investments in the function calls. All functions—even legacy ones—join the TP Monitor managed pool of reusable procedures. In other words, TP Monitors let you add heterogenous server resources anywhere without altering the existing application architecture. The Standish Group calls this "matrix scalability."

- *Reduced system cost.* With TP Monitors you can save money. According to the Standish Group, TP Monitors may result in total system cost savings of greater than 30%—depending on system scale—over a more database-centric approach. In addition, the Standish Group research shows that significant "development time" savings—up to 40% or 50%—can be achieved. In addition, the funneling effect of TP Monitors can result in large savings in the acquisition of resource managers. This is because database vendors charge by the number of active users; funneling cuts down on that number, which equates to lower license fees. For example, the Standish Group estimates that with a TP Monitor you can save between 69% (on a 16-user Oracle) and 62% on a (128-user Oracle). TP Monitors, with their load balancing, also provide better performance using the same system resources; this means that you can run your application on less expensive hardware. Finally, TP Monitors don't lock you into a vendor-specific database solution, which makes the acquisition process more competitive adding to cost savings (instead, they lock you into a TP Monitor single vendor solution).

Chapter 18

TP-Lite or
TP-Heavy?

It is not part of Oracle's declared strategy to build a transaction manager because there are already plenty of known players out there who specialize in this area—Tuxedo, Top End, CICS, plus the Encina Monitor to come.

— *Jnan Dash, VP of Database Planning,*
Oracle (May, 1993) [1]

You may recall from Part 4 that the SQL database managers are also in the business of managing transactions across their own resources. Some database-centric advocates argue that database transactions with stored procedures is all that's needed in the area of transaction management. They call their approach *TP-Lite*.

In contrast to database managers, TP Monitors extend the notion of transactions to *all* resources, not just data-centric ones. TP Monitors track the execution of functions on a single server or across servers on the network—their approach is called *TP-Heavy.* We will go over the current industry debate between TP-Lite and

---

TP-Heavy. As Jim Gray puts it, "Your problems aren't over by just embracing the concept of RPC or even TP-Lite."

And while these two TP camps are debating, the majority of the PC-centric (and Unix) client/server world is *TP-Less*. There is very little awareness in the PC world today of what transaction management is and why it's even needed. However, transaction management is second nature to most IS people who are "downsizing" from mainframe environments. These folks won't deploy an OLTP application on PC LANs without some kind of TP Monitor. As a result they're creating demand for a new breed of LAN-based TP Monitors. The Standish Group says revenue from the so-called *open OLTP* systems will jump to $6 billion in 1994, which is about double 1993's estimated $3.1 billion; it is expected to reach $21.7 billion by 1996. Even if these numbers are overly optimistic, they still say that a big client/server OLTP market is in the making.

The TP Monitor vendors must be getting the message because they're delivering a new breed of "open" TP Monitor products on Unix—including Tuxedo, Encina, CICS/6000, and Top-End—and OS/2—including CICS and Encina. In addition, some products—for example, Bachman's newly acquired Ellipse client/server tool—now include an embedded TP Monitor.

In this chapter we cover the TP-Lite versus TP-Heavy debate. It's important to understand what's missing from database-centric transaction processing. And, of course, there will be a Soapbox that tells you which side of that debate we're on. As Jim Gray puts it, "TP is where the money is: both literally (most banks are TP systems) and figuratively (CICS has generated more revenues than any other piece of software)." So it may be worth exploring which type of TP system—Lite or Heavy—is best for client/server needs.

THE ORIGINS OF TP-LITE

> *My transaction hopes are pinned on the impact of the distribution of processing—when it is realized that data is not everything and that process is just as important.*
>
> — Jim Gray (May, 1993)

In the good old days of mainframes, the divisions were clear: Database servers focused on managing data, while TP Monitors focused on managing processes and applications. The two sides stayed out of each other's turf and kept improving on what they did best. It was a classical win/win situation where everybody prospered. This happy coexistence came to an end in 1986, when Sybase became the first database vendor to integrate components of the TP Monitor inside the database engine.

Sybase Breaks the Truce

How did Sybase do it? You may recall from Part 4 that Sybase funnels all client requests into a multithreaded single-process server. It's an N-to-1 funnel. This may be called a case of *funnel overkill* because the database and user applications share the same address space—a sure invitation for disaster.

But Sybase did not stop with funneling; it also became the first database vendor to introduce stored procedures and triggers—two functions that definitely belong on the procedural side of the house. With its new architecture, Sybase became the uncontested champion of the database benchmarking wars. Of course, most database vendors were quick to follow suit. By now, most of them provide some level of funneling and support for stored procedures in their database engines. Application developers and tool vendors were quick to exploit the benefits of stored procedures, and the *TP-Lite* client/server architecture was born.

Given the popularity of database servers on PC LANs, does this mean TP Monitors are dead? Are they just an anachronism from the mainframe days? Is TP-Lite integrated with database the new platform of choice for application servers and OLTP? The answers to all these questions must, of course, be no; we didn't write an entire part on TP Monitors for nothing. So let's first review the facts in a cool, analytical manner. Then we'll jump on the Soapbox and throw in some opinions as to where all this is heading.

What Is TP-Lite?

TP-Lite is simply the integration of TP Monitor functions in the database engines. Currently only a few of the TP Monitor functions are integrated, including function shipping, some level of funneling, single-function transaction management, and RPC-like calls. It is not clear if the database vendors plan to reinvent the wheel and develop all the missing TP Monitor functions in TP-Lite. There's still a long list of unimplemented functions; the TP Monitor people have a ten-year headstart.

What Is TP-Heavy?

TP-Heavy are TP Monitors as defined in this chapter. The new generation of *TP-Heavy* products for client/server LANs includes CICS, Encina, Tuxedo, Tandem's Pathway, Top End, and DEC's ACMS. All these TP Monitors support the client/server architecture and allow PCs to initiate some very complex multiserver transactions from the desktop. All these products are supported by open visual builder tools that let you create the front-end separately from the back-end.

TP-Heavy includes all the functions defined in this chapter—including process management, load balancing, global transaction synchronization, interfaces to multiple resource managers, and error recovery.

TP-LITE VERSUS TP-HEAVY

TP-Lite systems may not solve all the world's problems, but they solve many simple ones. According to Ziph's law: most problems are simple.

— *Jim Gray, High Performance*
Transaction Workshop (September, 1993)

We won't have an OLTP environment manufactured by a single vendor (TP-Lite), but rather an OLTP environment that comprises of a mosaic of services (TP-Heavy). I think TP-Heavy will win.

— *Alfred Spector, High Performance*
Transaction Workshop (September, 1993)

The competition between TP-Lite and TP-Heavy is painfully unequal. It's like comparing a Harley-Davidson motorcycle with a bicycle. TP-Lite can best be defined by what it lacks, which is a long list of functions. In a nutshell, TP-Lite functions don't execute under global transaction control, there is no global supervisor, and the process management environment is very primitive. TP-Lite server functions only work with a single resource manager (the local database), and they don't support any form of ACID nesting. Like a bicycle, these functions are perfect fits for certain environments. But it's important to understand what you're missing because you'll rarely see it mentioned in the database marketing literature.

TP-Lite Versus TP-Heavy: Scope of the Commit

A *TP-Lite* stored procedure is written in a database-vendor proprietary procedural language—PL/SQL, Transact SQL, and so on—and is stored in the database. A stored procedure is a transactional unit, but it can't participate with other transactional units in a global transaction. It can't call another transaction and have it execute within the same transaction boundary. As shown in Figure 18-1, if stored procedure A dies after invoking stored procedure B, A's work will automatically get rolled back while B's work is committed for posterity. This is a violation of the ACID all-or-nothing proposition. This limitation causes you to write large transactions that put everything within the scope of the commit. It doesn't help the cause of modularization or writing reusable functions.

In contrast, *TP-Heavy* procedures are written using standard procedural languages. They can easily provide all-or-nothing protection in situations like the one shown in the right-hand side of Figure 18-1. For TP-Heavy, dealing with global transactions is second nature.

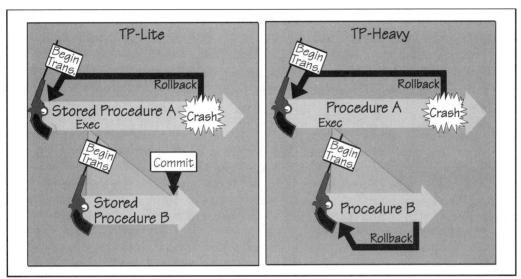

Figure 18-1. TP-Lite Versus TP-Heavy: Scope of the Commit.

TP-Lite Versus TP-Heavy: Managing Heterogeneous Resources

A *TP-Lite* stored procedure can only commit transaction resources that are on the vendor's database or resource manager (see Figure 18-2). It cannot synchronize

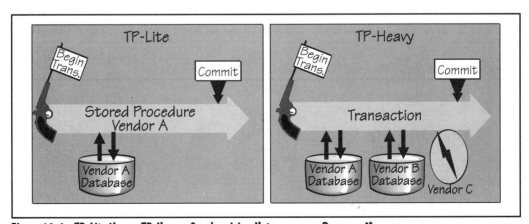

Figure 18-2. TP-Lite Versus TP-Heavy: Synchronizing Heterogeneous Resource Managers.

or commit work that is on a foreign—local or non-local—database or resource manager. In contrast, *TP-Heavy* procedures can easily handle ACID updates on multiple heterogeneous resource managers within the scope of a single transaction.

TP-Lite Versus TP-Heavy: Process Management

A *TP-Lite* stored procedure gets invoked, executed under ACID protection (within a single-phase commit), and *may* then be cached in memory for future reuse. That's about it. In contrast, *TP-Heavy* processes are prestarted and managed as server classes (see Figure 18-3). If the load on a server class gets too heavy, more processes are automatically started. Server classes support priorities and other class-of-service attributes. Server processes have firewalls around them so that the programs that run within them don't interfere with each other. If a server class process dies, it is restarted or the transaction can be reassigned to another server process in that class. The entire environment runs under the constant supervision of the TP Monitor. The server class concept helps the TP Monitor understand what class of service is required by the user for a particular group of functions. It's an intelligently managed environment.

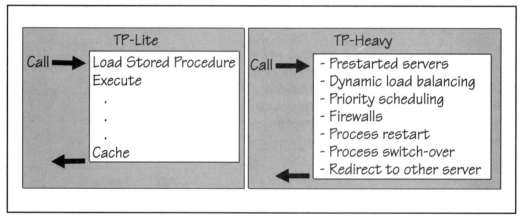

Figure 18-3. TP-Lite Versus TP-Heavy: Process Management.

TP-Lite Versus TP-Heavy: Client/Server Invocations

The *TP-Lite* stored procedure invocation is extremely non-standard. Vendors provide their own proprietary RPC invocation mechanism. The RPCs are not defined using an IDL. And they're not integrated with global directory, security, and authentication services. The communications links are not automatically restarted, and they're not under transaction protection. In addition, TP-Lite does not support MOM or conversational exchanges.

In contrast, the *TP-Heavy* environment is very open to different communication styles (see Figure 18-4). The RPC can use DCE as its base. MOM transactional queues can easily be integrated into the global transaction. Most TP Monitor vendors also support APPC/CPI-C for peer-to-peer communications.

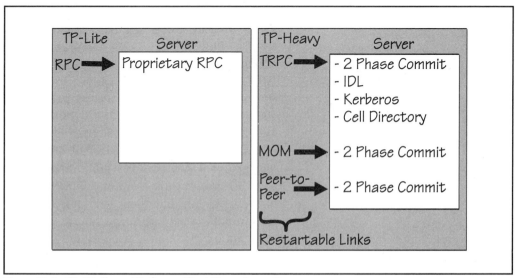

Figure 18-4. TP-Lite Versus TP-Heavy: Client/Server Invocation.

TP-Lite Versus TP-Heavy: Performance

TP-Lite stored procedures are much faster than networked static or dynamic SQL. However, they don't perform as well as TP-Heavy managed procedures, especially under heavy loads. According to the Standish Group, "today, virtually all standardized transaction processing benchmark results (e.g. TPC-A) are executed with a TP Monitor managing the application services in front of a database." Essentially the TP Monitor offloads the database server by multiplexing client requests. It acts as a funnel on top of whatever funnel the database may have already put in place.

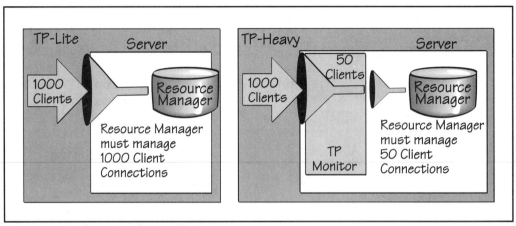

Figure 18-5. TP-Heavy Funneling Into TP-Lite.

Let's see how this can help even the "over-funneled" Sybase Server. In the example shown in Figure 18-5, instead of seeing 1000 clients, a Sybase multithreaded server is made to think it's dealing with 50 clients. The Sybase database server sees a reduced number of database clients, and acts more responsively as a result. The same story applies to other vendors' databases, some more than others. Figure 18-6 shows you how dramatic some of these numbers can be—the benchmarks were run on the same hardware with an Informix database engine (with and without a TP Monitor). In addition, significant cost savings can be achieved because fewer database resources are needed to support a given workload (the Informix example makes the point).

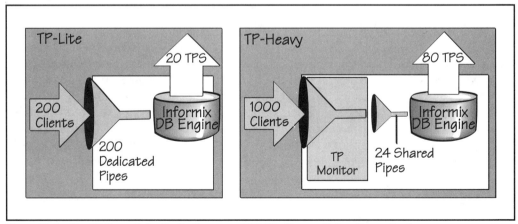

Figure 18-6. How TP-Heavy Helps the Performance of TP-Lite (Source: Unisys Corporation).

Conclusion

The database companies are primarily database-centric; it is unlikely they will solve the complete breadth of the problem.

> — *Alfred Spector, CEO Transarc Corp.*
> *(November, 1993)*

TP-Heavy products were created to meet the process management requirements of mission-critical OLTP environments. They tend to be very robust and have excellent system management facilities. TP-Lite products are newcomers in the area of process management and haven't had time to develop mature field-tested products. It takes years of product incubation to develop the right facilities in areas such as online distribution of new processes, remote debugging, built-in statistics, administration tools, and automatic switch-overs during failures (and later reconciliations). See the Soapbox below for a stronger opinion.

So Is It TP-Lite or TP-Heavy?

Soapbox

TP-Lite or TP-Heavy? Most likely neither. The debate about the need for a TP Monitor is only interesting in the short term, since today's transactional infrastructures are inappropriate for supporting business process re-engineering.

> — *Gartner Group (November 22, 1993)*

Rome wasn't built overnight and neither were TP Monitors. And as far as we can see, TP Monitors have a huge head start over TP-Lite in the area of process management. TP-Lite doesn't even come close to managing environments where a transaction spans across machines or resource managers (i.e., the so-called multidomain transactions). TP-Heavy provides global management and allows multivendor resource managers (including databases) to be plugged into the system; it gives us choice. You can then depend on TP-Heavy to make the "mosaic" whole. In contrast, TP-Lite provides an entry-level, single-domain, single-server solution for transaction processing.

So TP-Lite, like a bicycle, is quite useful in situations where you're dealing with a single vendor database and a small to medium number of users (let's say fewer than 50). And, as bicycles teach us the joy of being on wheels, TP-Lite will teach thousands of programmers the joy of transaction programming. TP-Lite is ideal in entry-level situations because it's less complex; you only have to deal with one server component: the database. The TP-Lite vendors also understand how to market to the client/server world—a very important advantage.

However, TP-Heavy technology is extremely important to the future of client/server computing. Think about what you could do with a Harley-Davidson instead of a bicycle. TP Monitors let us mix together components in all sorts of wild combinations; at the same time, they guarantee that everything comes together like clockwork. In other words, TP Monitors let us do the mix-and-match that is the forte of an open client/server world. Unfortunately, the TP monitor vendors are having a very hard time selling this message. They still use a lot of antique terminology that sounds very foreign to the PC LAN culture.

TP-Heavy vendors should focus on putting a "friendly" version of a TP Monitor on every desktop and in every 32-bit operating system. Gartner (see previous quote) would like to see transaction processing move to the next phase and start worrying about workflow—the topic of Part 6. We wholeheartedly agree, and think they should also move to objects. But given the current mindset of the TP-Heavy vendors, we'll be lucky just to get a TP Monitor on an occasional PC or Unix LAN server. They don't have the volume channels or the right packaging for their products, and they can't get beyond their "selling to MIS" origins. Yet MIS and the rest of us can greatly benefit if every PC on the network were ACID-ized. Wouldn't it be nice if every PC could participate in a global transaction? We believe that most exchanges in the "post-scarcity future" will be in the form of global transactions.

The situation may improve dramatically after Novell introduces "red box" versions of Tuxedo in mid-1994. CICS OS/2 V2 is also an excellent client/server product (the previous version was almost useless). It could do very well in the mass market, if only it could lighten up on the heavy "CICS-speak" that permeates throughout it. Encina—with its nested transactions, transactional RPC, and DCE NOS base—is the epitome of the postmodern TP Monitor. But it remains to be seen if any of these products can create a mass market that puts TP-Heavy back into the driver seat. If they fail because of poor marketing, database companies will not only steal the show but also end up having to reinvent the transaction wheel. ❑

Part 6
Client/Server
Groupware

An Introduction to Part 6

Well, if you Martians think that ACID transactions and TP Monitors were fun, wait until you see groupware. Oh, by the way, we have an Earthling game for you to play—its called the blind men and the elephant. We're going to put some blindfolds on you and let you guess what groupware is. The winner gets a night on the town. Are you ready?

OK, so what's groupware? Martian number one says "it's e-mail." Martian number two thinks it's a multimedia "document store." And Martian number three says they're both wrong: "it's clearly workflow." Do we have any more takers? Does anybody think it's got something to do with electronic conferencing? How about group calendaring and scheduling? As you can see from the cartoon, the groupware elephant is all of the above. OK, so you all won a night on the town. Do you need a party guide? We have a volunteer.

Part 6 is about this amorphous client/server category called groupware; it's amorphous because it's so new, and we don't yet fully understand its potential. The groupware proponents claim that their technology allows us to create new classes of client/server applications that are unlike anything we've seen on mainframes or minis. It does that by enabling the people-to-people elements in client/server communications. The PC revolution was built around *personal* computing; groupware may create an analogous software revolution around *interpersonal* computing. Yes, of course it includes Martians. So where is Groupware Valley? You Martians are always one step ahead of us.

We'll start by defining groupware. (Don't laugh: we really *can* do it.) We then go over what makes groupware different from SQL databases and TP Monitors. Next, we explore the constituent technologies that make up groupware—including multimedia document processing, workflow, e-mail, conferencing, and group calendaring and scheduling. However, with groupware, the whole is more than the sum of the parts, so we need to explore where that synergy comes from. We conclude with Lotus Notes, the most popular groupware product.

Chapter 19

Client/Server Groupware

Our groupware technology can serve to alienate and isolate people, or it can serve to forge a community. It is our choice.

— Carol Anne Ogdin,
Deep Woods Technology (August, 1993) [1]

Client/server groupware is a collection of technologies that allow us to represent complex processes that center around collaborative human activities. It builds on five foundation technologies: multimedia document management, workflow, e-mail, conferencing, and scheduling. Groupware is not another downsized mainframe technology; it's a genuinely new form of computing. It provides an excellent example of how client/server technology can be used to extend the computing envelope into uncharted territory. Of course, this also means that groupware doesn't neatly fit into predefined software categories. So we'll have some explaining to do.

---

[1] Source: **GroupWare'93 Proceedings** (August, 1993).

Our plan for this chapter is to first define groupware and the problems it solves. We'll then place groupware in the client/server model we've been building throughout this book. This won't be easy—groupware is an elusive concept that's continuously redefining its role as well as its relationship to the more established technologies. In addition, no single groupware product incorporates all the technology pieces. After we get a working definition, we'll look at the foundation technologies and how groupware combines the pieces within a client/server setting.

WHY IS GROUPWARE IMPORTANT?

People don't talk about operating systems; they simply assume they're there. Eventually, groupware will evolve the same way.

> — **Esther Dyson,**
> **Editor of *Release 1.0* (December, 1993)**

The Workgroup Technologies market research firm believes the groupware market will grow to almost $2.9 billion by 1996 from a modest $430 million in 1993. Lotus Notes—an amorphous groupware product that escapes definition—has sold more than 500,000 licenses to 2,000 companies. Notes revenues have soared more than fourfold—from $21 million in 1991 to an estimated $90 million in 1993. That's not counting the sizeable mini-industry which has developed around Notes. So what's causing all this sudden interest in groupware? According to David Coleman, editor of the newsletter "GroupTalk," the rapid growth is occurring because groupware can transform a company by changing the way people communicate with each other and, as a result, change the business processes. For example, groupware may be used to automate customer service and make a company more responsive. Groupware also has the potential to flatten organizations and remove layers of bureaucracy (see the following Soapbox).

Groupware allows direct contributors—wherever they may be—to collaborate on a job using client/server networks. We anticipate the growth of "virtual corporations" that get formed by unaffiliated groups of people to collaborate on a particular project. Groupware helps manage (and track) the product through its various phases; it also allows the contributors to exchange ideas and synchronize their work. It keeps track of the "collective memory" of the group.

Groupware, in many cases, allows departments to develop and deploy their own applications. Anyone who can create a simple spreadsheet can learn how to create a Lotus Notes application—few programming skills are required. The ability for departments to develop and create their own client/server groupware applications is leading to phenomenal returns on investment. Lotus quotes an independent study of 17 Notes customers that shows that their initial investment was recovered in three months (average). The groupware phenomenon—like spreadsheets or Macintosh Hypercards—is self-feeding. The difference is that groupware is a self-feeding client/server application; it is networked and interpersonal. Most groupware products also support open APIs that allow third parties (and IS shops) to add new functions on top of the foundation.

Soapbox

Groupware and Reengineering

Are we investing in groupware to infuse the organization with collaborative energy? Or are we investing primarily to staunch the bleeding?

— *Michael Schrage, Fellow,*
MIT Sloan School (September, 1993)

Bureaucracy in most organizations is very resilient; it will take a lot more than groupware to get rid of it. In fact, groupware can be misused to automate bureaucracy and make it more permanent. The current "reengineering" movement thinks it has found the problem: We've been applying Ford's assembly-line processes to business operations. We need to rethink the way we work—that is, reengineer the process. We wish them luck. Hopefully, they'll leave a few jobs behind after the reengineering.

The reengineering movement asserts that throwing technology into a poorly performing process won't help. We agree; nobody can quarrel with the fact that it doesn't make sense to automate a process that shouldn't be there in the first place. However, groupware is a secular technology; it can automate any type of process, including bad ones. You can use it to automate inefficient processes and make them more "efficiently inefficient." Or you can automate the reengineered structures and shoot to attain the order of magnitude improvements the gurus preach about. But we'll probably see a great deal of misuse of the technology until people learn this lesson. It's a lot more effort to rethink the way we work than to throw a shrink-wrapped package of groupware at it. Groupware vendors will make the same amount of revenue either way, but the value of their products to the companies that buy it will be radically different. ❑

What Is Groupware?

If you were to put twelve groupware experts in a room, you would get twenty definitions.

— **David Coleman (August, 1993)**

In a contest for the most fuzzily defined client/server software category, "groupware" would be the hands down winner. Over 200 products call themselves groupware. So let's cut the suspense and propose the following working definition: "Groupware is software that supports the creation, flow, and tracking of non-structured information in direct support of collaborative group activity."

There are other terms used as synonyms for groupware—collaborative computing, workgroup computing, and the academic-sounding "computer supported cooperative working." Groupware is the easiest of these terms to remember; vendors like the way it sounds because of the "ware" attached to it. So groupware it is.

Our definition implies that groupware is involved in the management of both information and activities. The "million dollar" question is: What makes groupware different from database managers and TP Monitors? For a change, we have some ready and straightforward answers.

HOW IS GROUPWARE DIFFERENT FROM SQL DATABASES?

Using an RDBMS to support documents is like teaching an elephant to fly.

— **Frank Ingari, VP Marketing, Lotus (February, 1993)**

The relational databases we covered in Part 4 deal with highly structured data that is accessed using SQL. They are excellent for managing applications that require high concurrency controls—including locking and isolation features—that are needed for immediate updates. They also provide excellent ad hoc query facilities. In contrast, groupware deals with highly unstructured data—including text, image, graphics, faxes, mail, and bulletin boards. Groupware provides the tools to capture this data at the point of entry and organize it in a nebulous thing called a *document*. You can think of a document as the container of diverse types of information. The document is to a workgroup what a table is to a SQL database: It's a basic unit of management. Groupware helps end users create document databases. It can move these documents via electronic mail and database replicas. And it provides everything you need to query, manage, and navigate through document databases. Documents are the currency of groupware.

Using OLE, DDE, OpenDoc, or native editors, groupware lets you view the components of the documents by launching the tools that created them in the first place. This means that if the document contains an image, movie, or sound clip, the groupware software will find it for you and let you view it. But can't we do that kind of stuff using SQL database BLOBs? Absolutely not (see the following Soapbox). SQL databases are great for providing access to structured data that's organized in table formats, but when it comes to multimedia and non-structured data, they're almost hopeless. Groupware-style document management fills this gap very well.

What About BLOBs?

Soapbox

In their current form, BLOBs are a lousy tool for handling advanced datatypes. They buy little or no leverage over storing data in a flat file. The RDBMS acts as little more than a very expensive flat file server.

— *Wayne Duquaine, Sybase,*
HPTS Workshop (September, 1993)

A BLOB, at least in a SQL database, is nothing more than up to four GBytes of uninterpreted binary data. All the rich semantic information is buried in the binary headers that the SQL database couldn't care less about. The headers describe the various sub-types and components that make up the BLOB including the data type (image, voice, text, and so on), the compression type, and the various indexes. The SQL database throws back at the application all the navigation tasks that are required to move through the BLOB's components.

SQL does not specify a self-describing data standard for BLOBs. Determining what's in the BLOB has to be reinvented by each application. GUI tools are left blind and clueless as to what each BLOB contains and how it should be processed. When it comes to BLOBs and multimedia, a SQL database is just a glorified and expensive file server with no value added. In contrast, the groupware document servers have made great strides toward providing some kind of a multimedia client/server solution. ❑

How Is Groupware Different From TP Monitors?

The TP Monitors we covered in Part 5 deal with management of transaction processes across client/server networks. So how do they compare with groupware? When it comes to document stores, TP Monitors can complement groupware software very well. The TP Monitor treats the document store like any other resource manager. If it supports a two-phase commit, the TP Monitor will gladly coordinate a distributed transaction that includes the document store. However, TP Monitors and groupware compete in the area of workflow. We believe that the groupware workflow is a much more developed technology than the TP Monitor long-lived transaction (but it's less protected).

The current workflow model—and groupware in general—is not transaction-oriented in the ACID sense. Groupware is good at reflecting the changing states of information over time, but it does not do very well when it comes to reflecting the current state of the data in real time. For example, groupware (and workflow) does not use two-phase commits to synchronize distributed changes across resource managers. It would be nice if TP Monitors and groupware combined efforts to infuse workflow with ACID properties (if it can be done). We cover workflow later in this chapter.

THE COMPONENTS OF GROUPWARE

As we said earlier, groupware builds on five foundation technologies: multimedia document management, workflow, e-mail, conferencing, and scheduling (see Figure 19-1). Groupware achieves its magic by combining these technologies and creating new synergy. The technology for multimedia document management and workflow comes from electronic document imaging systems; e-mail and scheduling

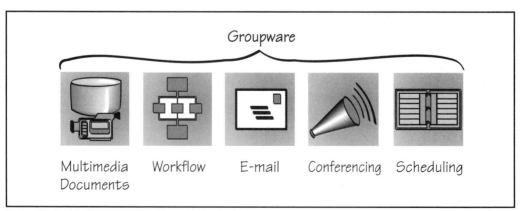

Figure 19-1. The Groupware Constituent Technologies.

come from office automation; and conferencing is native to groupware. Before we get into groupware proper, let's quickly review what these component technologies have to offer.

From Electronic Imaging to Multimedia Document Management

Groupware document management technology has its roots in electronic imaging. If we want to be purists, electronic imaging is just another form of special-purpose groupware. Of course, electronic imaging people—who have created a huge multi-billion dollar industry—can make the claim that groupware is just an imaging spin-off. In either case, we need to look at electronic imaging because it's an important client/server industry that is a precursor to groupware.

Electronic imaging started small. In the 1960s many businesses replaced large information paper warehouses with microfilm and computer-aided retrieval systems. By the mid-1980s, the appearance of PCs, LANs, scanners, compression boards, and optical disk juke-boxes allowed the automation of image storage as well as the data-centered tracking systems that locate those images. The new technologies made the online storage and display of images economical. In some applications, the cost savings associated with reduced staff and faster online access to documents (in seconds rather than days) justified the incremental expense for the new client/server systems. It costs $25,000 to fill a four-drawer paper file cabinet and $2,160 annually to maintain it. More importantly, 3 percent of paper is lost; the average cost to recover a document is $120. It is estimated that 3 billion paper documents are buried in US businesses alone; it's those kind of numbers that gave birth to the electronic imaging industry.

Electronic Imaging Client/Server Architecture

Electronic imaging systems are inherently database-oriented, client/server applications (see Figure 19-2). The client PCs capture and manipulate the images; they serve as front-ends to the data stored in image servers. The client PC typically does the following:

- The scanner attached to the client's PC digitizes the image through a process similar to that of a fax machine. (Not so coincidentally, fax machines sometimes serve as remote scanners.)

- After being digitized, the image is displayed and checked for quality; it is rescanned if necessary.

- While the image is displayed, information is extracted from it by an operator who enters the data in the fields of a GUI form. At a minimum, the document is assigned a simple index and identification code so that it can be retrieved later. More sophisticated (and costly) applications automate the extraction of information from the image into the GUI form using intelligent character recognition or bar-code readers.

■ The images are compressed by software or a hardware coprocessor and then sent to the server where they get stored.

■ The client can always access the documents in the server and visually display them. An image can be reviewed, printed, faxed, annotated with red lines or electronic notes, and so on.

The server side of an imaging application manages a shared database of images. Image servers typically store all the structured information in an SQL database; the document itself (i.e., the BLOB) is stored in a file server. Large image servers can handle 200,000 documents or more per day. Images are big: the average compressed digitized image weighs in at about 75 to 100 KBytes, but they can be as large as 2.5 MBytes for medical X-rays and engineering drawings. Consequently, many imaging applications may require terabytes of online storage.

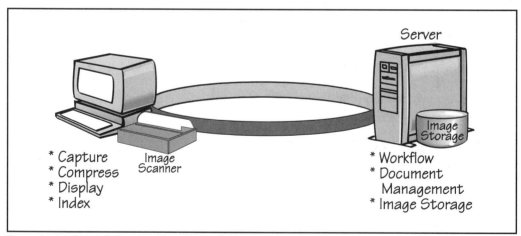

Figure 19-2. Electronic Imaging Client/Server Systems.

The image servers manage the workflow, security, image indexing (or metadata), and the pointers to the file systems where the BLOBs are physically stored. Here are some of their key functions:

■ Servers manage electronic renditions of file cabinets, which contain drawers and folders comprising documents. A document comprises a series of multimedia pages.

■ Workflow automates the movement of documents by moving them from one business operation to the next according to customer-defined rules and routes. Rules are used by the image server to control the routing, which may be based on document content, age, priority, workload balancing, external events, the day you need a document, database triggers, and other user-defined criteria.

■ User profiles and work queues are created and maintained on the server to specify the type of work users receive.

■ Reporting facilities allow managers to monitor the volume and types of work-in-process in the system, and to note its progress.

■ Documents are stored on various media; the server moves them around to optimize the delicate trade-off between storage cost and performance.

Groupware Multimedia Document Management

The groupware document management paradigm is a generalization of the electronic imaging file cabinet. For example, the basic unit of storage in groupware, such as Lotus Notes, is the *document*. A Notes document has an extremely flexible structure; it can be tagged with properties such as *client*, *region*, and *subject*. A Notes document can have any number of BLOB-like *attachments* (or embedded objects). Notes supports a compound document architecture, which means that it can handle multiple data types—including text, images, graphics, voice clips, and video.

Related collections of Notes documents are stored in *databases* that can then be indexed and retrieved by any of the documents' properties, or by the actual contents of the documents. It also supports full-text indexing. Notes created its own document database technology from scratch; unlike the image vendors, it does not build on top of existing file and SQL database servers. We're dealing with a *new* groupware-specific, document-centric, multimedia-enabled, database technology.

Workflow: What Is It? Where Does It Come From?

Imagine submitting a home mortgage application and having it go through in a matter of hours. Workflow is the "up and coming" client/server technology that can be used to automatically route events (and work) from one program to the next in structured or unstructured client/server environments (see Figure 19-3). The "classical" workflow paradigm is a river that carries the flow of work from port to port and along the way value gets added. Workflow defines the operations that must be visited along the way and what needs to be done when exceptions occur. The

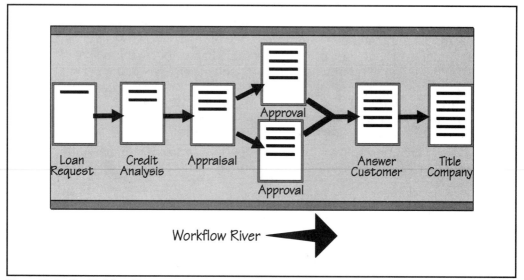

Figure 19-3. The Workflow River.

original work item may be merged with other work, transformed, or routed to another workflow. It's quite a dynamic environment. Some workflows may be fuzzy and not understood very well; others are deterministic and highly repetitive. In all cases, these workflows are there to help us collaborate in getting work done.

To appreciate what workflow is all about, you must understand its origins. Workflow technology has its historical roots firmly planted in the world of image management and computer-integrated manufacturing technology. FileNet Corporation—an imaging vendor—was a pioneer of this technology in 1984. FileNet and other electronic imaging companies—including Viewstar, Sigma, and IBM's ImagePlus—discovered that workflow could be used to automate the high-volume, formerly paper-based processes (see Figure 19-4).

Workflow is especially applicable to "paper factories," meaning large offices that routinely process documents representing business transactions (for example, loans, claims processing, and tax returns). Paper to these factories is what raw material is to manufacturing: "grist for the mill" that produces the organization's product. When the paper became an electronic image, workflow automated the movement of documents from one image processing operation to the next. Both the workflow controller and the work are electronic renditions of real-life factory constructs.

The imaging workflow systems are costly, rigid, centralized, and typically require a highly-skilled IS professional to do the design and integration. These systems tend to be proprietary and cannot interface well with other applications. On the positive

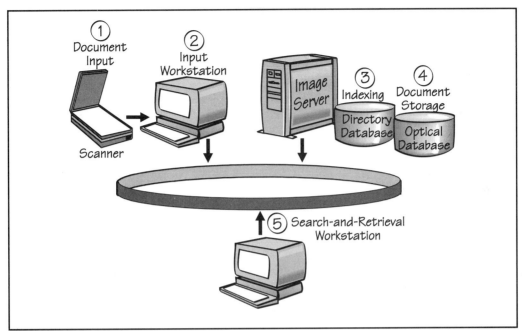

Figure 19-4. Workflow in Electronic Imaging Systems.

side, they can handle very large workloads and have excellent built-in security and version controls. They are very good at scheduling document-related tasks and tracking them to completion. The cost of such systems start at $5,000 per seat.

The New Workflow Systems

Groupware introduces a new breed of client/server workflow software for the masses. The new workflow packages go beyond their imaging counterparts in the following areas:

- **Support for ad hoc user needs.** The new workflow packages address both structured and unstructured process automation needs. They can automate well-understood processes as well as more nebulous ones.

- **Low-cost.** The new workflow packages sell at PC software prices—expect to pay between $100 to $500 per seat.

- **Integration with other applications.** The new workflow packages can integrate with existing applications by either spawning a process, or sending them some type of message-based event notification when their intervention is needed (using DDE, e-mail, and so on). Applications can also call the workflow manager to participate in or initiate a workflow process.

■ ***Programming with visual metaphors.*** The new workflow packages support drag-and-drop iconic manipulations for creating workflows and defining business rules. They typically provide tools for designing forms (or importing them from a GUI-Builder), designing sequential or conditional routes, and scripting languages to specify the business logic. The routes and workflow definitions are sometimes stored in SQL databases. Templates are provided to help jump start the creation of a workflow application.

■ ***Integration with e-mail, MOM, or RPC.*** The new workflow packages use loosely coupled forms of communication, such as e-mail or MOM message queues, to inform humans or programs that their intervention is required. Action Technologies, for example, defines a set of message formats that can be conveyed using all the popular mail transports. These formats are used to convey, capture, or initiate workflow commands and actions. Action also supports the transmission of workflow commands using DDE, Named Pipes, RPCs, and peer-to-peer protocols.

■ ***Provide facilities for tracking work-in-progress.*** Most of the packages allow you to query the status of work-in-progress and what stage of the workflow it's in. Some of the better packages help you identify inefficiencies in the routes and bottlenecks.

■ ***Provide users with tools to complete an action.*** In addition to notifying users that an action is required, some of the better tools provide users with help panels that tell them how to complete an action and sometimes even the tools to perform the requested action. The user may also be able to obtain information about where the task fits in the overall process.

■ ***Provide APIs that let developers customize workflow services.*** Of course, no standard APIs for workflow exist, so this feature is very vendor-specific.

The heart of a workflow system is the server that receives requests and events from the various client workstations and interprets them according to a user-defined workflow. The client agents are programmed to execute the repetitive parts of a user-defined script. The workflow server acts as a clearinghouse that determines what needs to be done next based on the global state of the system (and the rules). It usually maintains a database that dynamically tracks the work-in-progress and contains instructions (and rules) for what needs to be done at a given instance of a workflow process.

Workflow Models

*T*he three R's of workflow are: Routes, Rules, and Roles.

> — *Ronni T. Marshak, Editor,*
> *Workgroup Computing Report*
> *(May, 1993)*

The workflow software must create electronic renditions of real-world collaborative activity. The "real world," however, covers a wide spectrum of activities from tax return processing to co-authoring a paper. These activities differ radically in their structure, number of users, flow of control, and process predictability. Almost any workflow can be represented using raw code; however, the trick is to minimize custom development using shrink-wrapped workflow models. The workflow packages must be able to visually define who does "what, when, and to what"; parallel routes; logic for dynamically determining routes at run time; and the exceptions to any rules. It must deal with Ronni Marshak's three R's: routes, rules, and roles.

- **Routes** define the paths along which the object moves. They also include definitions of the objects—documents, forms, events, electronic containers and parts, messages, and so on—that are to be routed.

- **Rules** define what information is routed and to whom. Rules define both the conditions the workflow must meet to traverse to the next step and how to handle exceptions: "If the loan is over $100,000, send it to the supervisor or else send it to the next hop."

- **Roles** define job functions independently of the people who do it. For example, the "supervisor" role can be handled by users "Mary" and "Jeri." Any one of these people can do the job; just put the job on the next available supervisor's queue.

Groupware packages must provide the three R's for automating well-defined applications—*process-oriented workflow*—as well as the more ad hoc spontaneous type of applications—*ad hoc workflow.* Here's the differences between the two models:

- ***Process-oriented workflows*** are used to automate business systems that have definable, repetitive, and well understood policies and procedures. For example, a mortgage loan is an understood business process that goes through a pre-scribed set of procedures. Loans are processed in the same way every day. The routing of the work is automatic and requires very little user involvement. It's like taking a train. This type of workflow is a natural candidate for TP Monitor initiated sagas or long-lived transactions.

- **Ad hoc workflow** deals with short-lived and unstructured work processes. They can involve task forces of people working on a common problem. Consider, a short-duration project with a deadline. The workflow is used to assign roles, track and route work-in-progress, monitor deadlines, and track who got what and when. It's an excellent tool for tracking work among people who are physically dispersed. This type of workflow is like driving a car. The navigation is driver-centric, but you need road signs and a map to figure out where you're going. The driver also needs to know the set of options available at every turn. Ad hoc workflow is used for incremental automation—leaving anything the system can't handle to humans. It takes full advantage of desktop power to help humans navigate through the country roads.

Workflow Routes

Modern workflow packages support the same type of topologies that are common in human communications (see Figure 19-5). Typically, these packages let you specify a route that defines the set operations a unit-of-work traverses. They also let you define rules that specify acceptance conditions for moving from one operation to the next. You can create sequential routes, parallel routes (alternate paths), routes with feedback loops (for example, rework), circular routes, wheel-spoked routes, and fully interconnected routes. The first four routes are used in process-oriented workflows, while the last two are used in more ad hoc workflows.

Workflow Splits and Joins

Workflow objects can go off on different routes and then merge back into a single route at a "rendezvous" point. In addition, a workflow object can be split into multiple parts and merged back into a single part as it moves down the workflow river (see Figure 19-6). This is done using splits and joins, as explained in the following examples:

- **And-Splits** are used to explode an object into many parts. For example, a set of chips on a wafer are tracked as a group until the chips are split with each going their own way.

- **Or-Splits** are used to peel off a few parts from a group. For example, a few chips may be split off the wafer for random testing; they rejoin the group later using an Or-Join.

- **Or-Joins** allow certain members to rejoin the group. For example, in a manufacturing line, a defective part can go to a rework operation and it can then rejoin the group when it's fixed using an Or-Join.

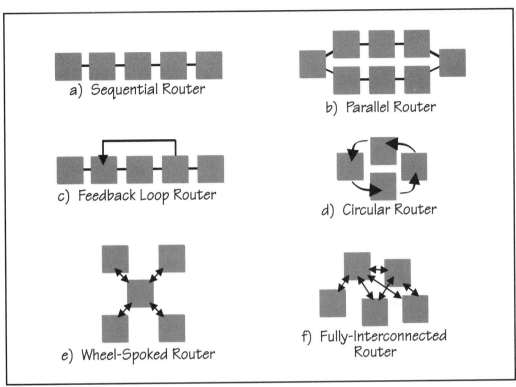

Figure 19-5. Workflows Come in All Patterns.

■ *And-Joins* are rendezvous points that are used to group together objects so that they move in a route as a group. For example, an And-Join can be used to package many units into a container that can be shipped as a unit.

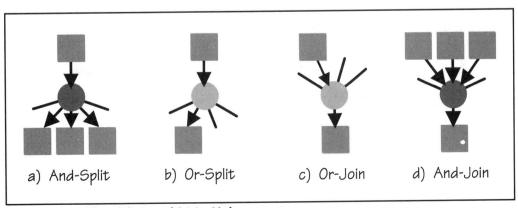

Figure 19-6. Workflow: Splitting and Joining Work.

FYI

The Action Workflow Model

Briefing

Action Technologies Workflow Model—an innovative Windows and OS/2 work-flow product—is based on research by Terry Winograd and Fernando Flores on how people communicate to make an action happen. Action identifies for each unit of work in a workflow the *performer* who is doing the actual work for a *customer* (meaning the person for whom the work is being done). Each step in the workflow involves a negotiation loop between a customer and a performer (see Figure 19-7). At the end of each step the conditions must be fulfilled to have a satisfied customer.

According to the Action Technologies methodology, every action in a workflow consists of four phases in which customers and performers coordinate with each other (see Figure 19-8):

1. *Preparation* is when the customer prepares to ask for something—often, for example, by filling out a form or preparing an e-mail.

2. *Negotiation* is when the customer and performer agree on the work to be done and on the conditions of satisfaction—exactly what must be done to complete this job to the satisfaction of the customer.

3. *Performance* is the phase in which the actual job is done. At the end the performer reports to the customer that the work requested has completed.

4. *Acceptance* of a job or task is not considered complete until the customer signs off and expresses satisfaction to the performer.

At any phase there may be additional actions, such as clarifications, further negotiations, and changes of commitments by the participants. The Action Technologies approach does more than just coordinate between tasks: It helps specify the client/server contract and does it all very recursively. The entire application is a client/server task that gets broken down recursively into sub-tasks as defined by the workflow. The application is a series of "who is getting what done for whom" steps and the conditions of satisfaction. Action provides a set of visual tools to help capture the negotiation semantics and automatically generates the scripts from them. ❑

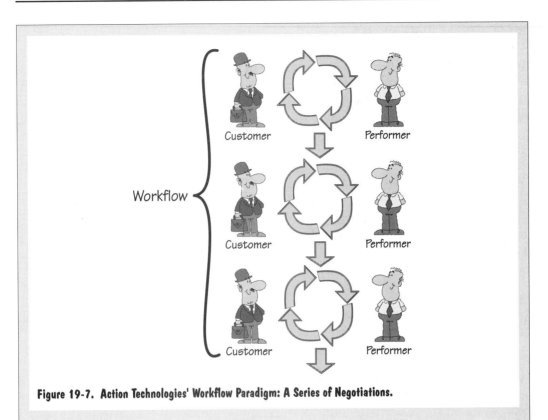

Figure 19-7. Action Technologies' Workflow Paradigm: A Series of Negotiations.

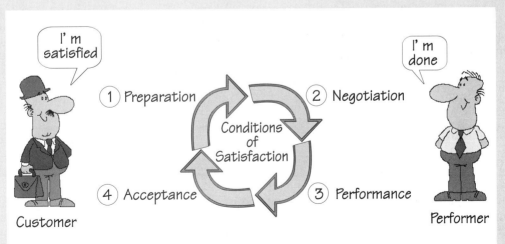

Figure 19-8. Action Technologies' Workflow: The Negotiation Details.

Workflow: The Bottom Line

Workflow helps bring the information to the people who can act on it. It coordinates existing software and tracks the processes to make sure the work gets done by the right people. Workflow by itself cannot do too much; but with other software—such as e-mail, databases, and desktop productivity tools—it can create some dynamite combinations.

The Electronic Mail Component

For many organizations, all the groupware they need may be an e-mail package that's closely tied to group calendaring and scheduling features. This is the philosophy behind *WordPerfect Office*, which has more than one million copies in use. Of course, groupware allows you to do much more with electronic mail; it uses it to extend the client/server reach. Why is e-mail so important to groupware? Because it matches the way people work. E-mail can be used to send something to others without making a real-time connection; the recipients don't have to respond to senders until they're ready to do so. In addition, it's one of the easiest ways for electronic processes to communicate with humans. And it's ubiquitous.

According to IDC, there were 50 million electronic mailboxes in 1992—over half of them on PC LANs. IDC foresees that the number of LAN e-mail users will grow tenfold by 1997. Mail-enabled groupware applications can take advantage of this very extensive mail infrastructure to send and receive information and communicate directly with users—electronic mail is one of the most hassle-free forms of distributed interactions. E-mail front-ends are not the only way to send messages. The new mail APIs, such as VIM and MAPI, are designed to let any application work with the mail messaging infrastructure. Most electronic mailboxes will soon be interconnected through mail backbones and gateways.

The Electronic Mail Infrastructure

Most LAN-based e-mail systems are very good at handling mail within workgroups and departments. However, these networks are still poor at providing intergalactic mail capabilities. Fortunately, most of the infrastructure components required to create ubiquitous mail backbones are coming into place. It's important to note the distinction between the mail application—the front-end—and the mail infrastructure—the back-end. Ideally, the front-end and back-end should communicate along client/server lines—this is what Lotus Notes does today (see Figure 19-9). Unfortunately, most LAN-based e-mail packages bundle the front-end and the back-end in the same process and use a file server on the LAN for the mail store. This is the approach used by Lotus cc:Mail, the most popular e-mail product in the industry.

Most PC LAN e-mail products follow the cc:Mail file server approach, but that's changing. For example, Lotus is redesigning cc:Mail along client/server lines. Both cc:Mail and Notes will eventually share the same back-end mail server.

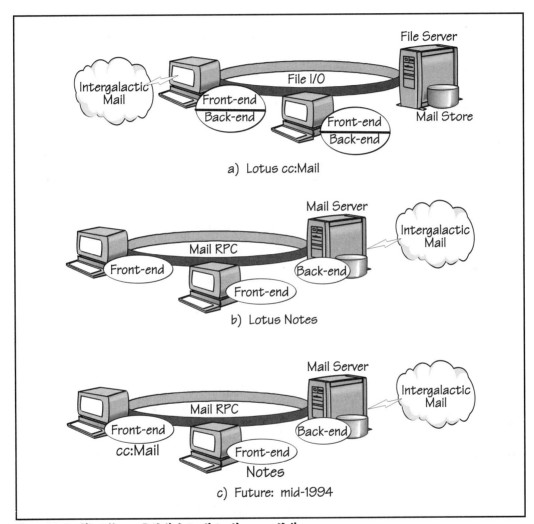

Figure 19-9. Client/Server E-Mail: Lotus Notes Versus cc:Mail.

However, it takes more than cc:Mail or Notes to create an intergalactic mail infrastructure. How do you connect cc:Mail or Notes to other mail networks? There are two ways to do that:

■ *Gateways*—you'll need one gateway for each different e-mail system you need to access. But this could quickly turn into a management nightmare. Gateways also limit some functions like the capability to search for an address. They're also poor at providing synchronized directory management services, efficient message routing, global system management, and so on.

■ *Mail backbone*—you'll need one gateway to the backbone, period. But the question is: Which backbone? The contenders are the X.400 international standard, Novell's Message Handling Service (MHS), and the Internet's Simple Message Transport Protocol (SMTP) mail service. The pendulum seems to be swinging in X.400's favor—it is much simpler and less expensive than it once was (see the following Details box). Of course, MHS, SMTP, and X.400 back-bones will most likely be interconnected via gateways. So all the backbones may win.

The separation of mail functions along client/server lines will facilitate the creation of front-end clients that are totally independent of the back-end mail engines. We'll now look at the mail API standards that will help bring this about.

X.400 Mail Backbones

Details

The X.400 mail protocol is finally hitting the critical mass as the common mail backbone for the industry. It has been adopted by all the major public service providers across the world. Most e-mail vendors—including Lotus, Microsoft, HP, IBM, and SoftSwitch—are coming out with X.400 products. Several large vendors—such as IBM, Tandem, and DEC—use X.400 as a way to link their messaging systems. An X.400 version of cc:Mail should be available by the time you read this book—it will give X.400 a friendly look on all platforms. X.400 provides the following features:

■ *Support for BLOB exchanges.* X.400 defines a way to exchange images, fax, and other binary attachments to messages.

■ *Electronic Data Interchange (EDI) support*. EDI defines the contents and structures of messages that are used in electronic business exhanges (for example, invoices, billing forms, and so on). X.400 consolidates both e-mail and EDI on the same backbones. It maintains audit trails of EDI exchanges as required by the X.435 EDI standard.

■ *Support for distributed directories*. The X.500 standard, developed as part of the X.400 1988 specification, defines how a single system image is provided using directories that are distributed over multiple nodes.

- **Security.** X.400 adheres to the X.509 security standard that specifies the mechanisms for password identification, digital signatures, encryption, and audit trails.

- **Mail API.** The X.400 Common Mail Calls (CMC) API combines subsets of MAPI and VIM, and it has been adopted as a "compromise" API by both parties. We'll have more to say about that in the mail API section.

Clearly X.400 offers a secure, standards based approach to creating electronic mail backbones.

The New E-Mail APIs: VIM, MAPI, and CMC

A new hot area in our industry is *mail-enabled applications*. The primary purpose of these applications is not mail, but they still need to access mail services. Most groupware products fall into that category. E-mail becomes just another form of client/server middleware. *Electronic Data Interchange (EDI)* is becoming an important source of mail-enabled business transactions (see Details box). Personal agents will be making extensive use of EDI to pay your bills and do your electronic shopping. And e-mail by itself supports the exchange of faxes, files, BLOBs, documents, and workflow events at an application-to-application level—it's a powerful form of middleware that may already be in place in an organization (in that case, it's free and ready to be exploited). One of the main advantages of using e-mail over lower level APIs—like NetBIOS or RPC—is the store-and-forward capability that's built into the mail system.

An application becomes mail enabled by using e-mail APIs that allow programs to directly access mail transport services, mail directories, and message stores (see Figure 19-10). These used to be the *private domain* of mail vendors. The newly-exposed APIs are making it easy for developers to mail-enable their applications without becoming e-mail experts. What kind of functions can we expect from an open e-mail API that can work across multiple mail transports?

The following is a composite of functions provided by the three leading contenders for the "common" mail API:

- **Simple messaging services.** These are functions for addressing, sending, and receiving a mail message—including files and enclosures—an optional user interface is provided for logon, addressing the mail, and text entry.

- **Message store manipulation.** This includes opening and reading messages delivered to a message store, saving messages, deleting messages, navigating through the contents of the store, searching for messages, and moving messages across containers. The message store can be external to the mail package. For example, a message store could be an SQL database, a Lotus Notes document database, or an Object Database. The same APIs should work across all stores. Message stores contain a wealth of information that is of interest to groupware applications. We expect to see a lot of exciting developments in this area.

- ■ **Address book and directory services.** An address book is a collection of individual or group—i.e., distribution lists—recipients. Address books can be personal (i.e., cached on the local system) or part of a global directory. The API should let you read and write directory information as well as navigate through hierarchies of address books. You should be able to add/remove groups or members from address books and search through them.

- ■ **Mail object manipulation.** The APIs should let you access the subcomponents of a mail object. For example, a message may consist of heading fields and various data items.

- ■ **Authentication and security services.** This includes APIs that let an application log on to the mail system and authenticate its users.

- ■ **Service provider interface.** This interface allows service providers to supply their own back-end services to the front-end mail APIs. For example, a Lotus Notes mail server is accessed through the proprietary Lotus RPC. We've already encountered the concept of the service provider interface in the SQL CLI section in Part 4 (both IDAPI and ODBC support one). The service provider interface creates an open environment for the providers of mail services; it doesn't do much for the developers of mail-enabled applications.

The separation of the mail front-end from the back-end allows a single API set to work with multiple mail back-ends. In addition, different vendors can offer their own specialized plug-in services (for example, message stores). So what is the common API set that gives us access to all this mail server power?

Surprise! The e-mail industry has more than one common, open API set. Remember, we *always* get to choose from more than one standard. In the case of e-mail, we started with five standards. However, Novell and Apple may be gravitating toward VIM, so that leaves us with three key ones: VIM, MAPI, and CMC. Let's find out what these standards can do for us and who is behind them.

- ■ **Vendor Independent Messaging (VIM)** is an interface that is jointly backed by Lotus, Apple, IBM, Borland, MCI, Oracle, WordPerfect, and Novell. VIM was designed from the ground up as a cross-platform interface. Apple will provide a version of VIM for Macintosh; Novell will support VIM on MHS; and Lotus provides it on all the cc:Mail and Notes client platforms. VIM consists of 55 API calls—10 of which are optional—that support simple mail, message store, and

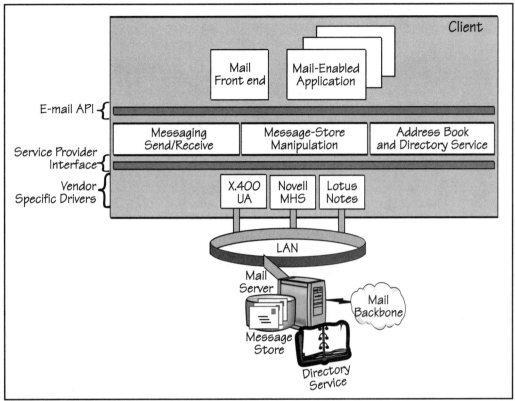

Figure 19-10. A Generic API for E-Mail.

address book services. VIM also provides a *Simple Mail Interface (SMI)* that consists of two calls: SMISendMail and SMISendDocuments. The main strength of VIM is its cross-platform support and the vendors who are behind it. Its main weakness is that it does not provide a Service Provider Interface (SPI).

■ *Messaging API (MAPI)* is Microsoft's WOSA offering for e-mail. MAPI is a Windows first client API—it's a Windows DLL—that works primarily with Microsoft Mail back-ends. MAPI is also getting endorsements from mail server vendors including DEC, HP, Banyan, CompuServe, and SoftSwitch. The MAPI front-end APIs are written to the Windows *Mail Spooler*. Mail server providers can redirect the Mail Spooler calls to their back-end services using the MAPI SPI. Simple MAPI consists of 12 API calls that provide simple mail, message store, and address book services. *Extended MAPI*—a future technology that will be included in Chicago—will support 100 API calls that allow applications to handle large numbers of messages, filter through mail, manage message stores, and access complex addressing information. Extended MAPI exposes the SPI to the application. There are three types of SPIs: Transport, Address

Book, and Message Store. MAPI's strength is in its Windows packaging; its weakness is that it is specific to Windows.

■ ***Common Mail Calls (CMC)*** is the X.400 API Association (XAPIA) interface. It was published in June 1993 as part of a negotiated truce in the mail API wars—both the VIM and MAPI camp endorse it. Microsoft provides a free DLL library for CMC, and Lotus will do the same for VIM developers (it will also be included in cc:Mail and Notes). CMC consists of 10 API calls—a subset of the VIM and MAPI calls (see Figure 19-11). It does not include the Extended VIM or Extended MAPI functionality. CMC only does simple mail.

The first round of the mail API wars is over: Everyone won. Round two of the mail API wars is just starting. On the VIM front, work is continuing on advanced e-mail functions; Lotus, IBM, Action, and Plexus are working on Workflow VIM APIs and a VIM-aligned consortium is working on VIC (see the next section). Meanwhile, on the MAPI front, Microsoft is working on Extended MAPI (see the next Soapbox).

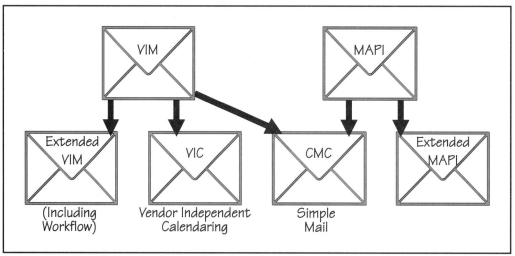

Figure 19-11. CMC: The Grand Unification of Simple MAPI and Simple VIM.

Scheduling and Calendaring

Scheduling is a native groupware technology. There's extensive innovation behind the electronic scheduling of meetings, sharing calendars and "to do" lists, and all that good stuff. Scheduling was designed from the ground up on a solid client/server foundation. The client front-ends make excellent use of GUI facilities; the servers use background tasks, shared data, and triggers to manage and schedule group events. Now, imagine what could happen if we combine this scheduling and

Thank You for CMC

Soapbox

CMC is a very positive development in our industry. It's an example of how user power can stop the mindless proliferation of standards. Apparently the mail API debate irked enough users that it forced vendors to agree to work together through the revived X.400 API Association (XAPIA). XAPIA was originally formed to create an API to X.400 services. The result of this revival was the CMC standard—a poor man's e-mail API. CMC can only do simple tasks like reading or sending messages or looking up an address. Unlike VIM and MAPI, it doesn't support fancy mail tasks like enclosures and interfacing to message stores. But we are still very thankful for CMC—a "baby step" in the right direction.

CMC frees developers from having to write separate versions of their programs for MAPI and VIM. However, the mail API wars are not over yet. In fact, they're just starting. Groupware, calendaring, data collection, and personal agent applications still need the advanced mail functions that MAPI and VIM are defining: interfaces to message stores, message filters, calendaring, scheduling, and advanced directory services. These are the "crown jewels" of e-mail—it's literally where all the big e-mail client/server money is going to be made. Unfortunately, these functions are not part of CMC. And they will be much harder to unify than simple mail. The good news is that some key participants are talking about merging VIM with CMC to provide CMC with the needed functionality. So we may have more to be thankful for. ❑

calendaring technology with workflow managers, e-mail, and multimedia document stores. This could result in some dynamite combinations of groupware. A workflow manager would be able to automatically add a meeting to the calendars of all the participants, schedule a meeting room, and send them reminder notices. Or, a workflow manager could consult group calendars to discover who is on vacation and route (or re-route) work accordingly.

So, how do we get to the services provided by the scheduling and calendaring servers? Using APIs and client/server exchanges, of course. But which APIs? This is where the *Vendor-Independent Calendaring (VIC)* API effort comes into the picture. The VIC effort, spearheaded by IBM and Lotus, allows VIM-compliant programs—such as Lotus Organizer 1.1, WordPerfect Office 4.0, and IBM's Time and Place/2—to seamlessly exchange scheduling and calendar data. Of course, VIC is not the only game in town; Microsoft is developing similar group scheduling and calendaring capabilities for Chicago's Extended MAPI. In addition, XAPIA launched an effort to define a standard for LAN-based calendar and schedule exchanges. However, XAPIA is moving in the direction of a "common file format" as an interim solution until APIs are defined. The good news is that the standards competition is heating up, and we may end up with some sort of "open" calendar and scheduling service API on client/server LANs.

Conferencing

Conferencing, or "electronic meetings," is another native groupware technology. Millions of PC users are now discovering the wonders of conferencing through electronic bulletin boards on CompuServe, Prodigy, and Internet. We can divide client/server conferencing technology into two types: realtime and anytime.

Realtime Conferencing

Realtime conferences allow groups to interactively collaborate on a joint project using instantly refreshed document replicas, electronic whiteboards, different-colored cursors with the initials of each participant, and a designated chairperson that controls access to the shared document. Participants can speak on their microphones and see each other in video windows on their computer screens. Eventually—when we get the cheap bandwidth—we will be able to augment these conferences with movie clips. Conferencing packages, like IBM's Person to Person/2 and FutureLabs TalkShow, are selling for as little as $250 per seat, making this technology affordable for the first time.

Anytime Conferencing

Anytime conferences allow people to participate in group discussions when and where they want. You can join the discussion, add your own two cents, and leave at anytime. And because you can jump into an ongoing discussion at anytime, you can see the entire discussion in context. This flexible environment helps articulate spontaneous groups around a topic of interest—customer support, operating system advocacy, shared problems, and project tracking. The medium is open and democratic. Everyone gets the opportunity to express themselves—ideas are never lost.

Using replicas, the system makes all the contributions available to all participants in close to realtime. The contributions then become part of the group memory—they are stored for posterity in the document databases that manage this wealth of shared information. As these conferences flourish and multiply, tools are provided for viewing and navigating through the mazes of information they contain. Lotus

Notes is the premier technology for the creation of these electronic discussion groups. Its enormous popularity is an indication of the mass acceptance of the asynchronous electronic meeting place paradigm.

Conferences provide one more technology that helps articulate the "group" in groupware. Electronic meeting environments provide an almost bottomless set of opportunities for client/server technology. We're just seeing the tip of the iceberg.

Groupware: Is It Hype?

Soapbox

Groupware lets us move from personal applications to interpersonal applications. In so doing, it's creating new client/server markets and new types of applications.

— Jeri Edwards (February, 1994)

Like every new client/server technology, groupware is getting its share of high-decibel marketing hype. What makes it worse is that any multiuser piece of software can be called "groupware." All client/server software deals with group communications in some form or another. Even though we carefully defined the constituent technologies in groupware, there is still a tremendous amount of fuzziness associated with the term. You can't find two people—even from Lotus—that can give you a common definition of Lotus Notes; yet Notes is selling like hot cakes. So it must be fulfilling some need somewhere.

We believe that any new technology will be fuzzy at first. The trick is to sort out reality from marketing hype, and then understand what we can do with the technology. In the case of groupware, the opportunity is in creating client/server applications—unlike any we've ever seen—using multimedia document databases, e-mail, workflow, conferencing, calendaring, and scheduling technology. The groupware industry is creating the common interfaces between these disparate pieces. All we need to do is learn how to use them and perhaps even integrate them with database warehouses, TP Monitors, and the distributed object technology that we will be covering in Part 7. ❑

GROUPWARE: BRINGING IT ALL TOGETHER

This chapter dealt with many of the emerging technologies that form a new genre of client/server software called "groupware." What's new is the synergy gained by bringing the pieces together on client/server networks. Groupware supports the asynchronous distribution of information to groups. It's a flexible technology that can adapt to the way people do business in both structured and ad hoc settings. The e-mail foundation helps bring humans into the loop. The information that is collected and distributed can be highly unstructured and rich with meaning. Workflow allows the creation of highly intelligent "routing clouds" that deliver information to the points where it can be processed. It also creates what Forrester calls "value-added rivers" as information moves from one point to the next along an intelligent route.

Chapter 20

Lotus Notes

Notes enables rich forms of human communications by exploiting the true potential of client/server technology; it helps create more than just reborn, downsized versions of traditional apps.

> — *John Landry,*
> *Lotus Senior VP and Chief Technologist*
> *(September, 1993)*

Lotus Notes—now in its third release—is the premier client/server groupware product in the industry. Even though Notes has been in the field for over three years and has sold over 500,000 seats, it still remains a mystery to the vast majority of PC users. It's even a mystery to its competitors. Some call it a "cute bulletin board," others label it as "glorified e-mail," and some SQL purists pooh-pooh it as—Heaven forbid—an "unstructured database." In reality, Notes is a multifaceted, client/server groupware product. And as we know from the last chapter, it is hard to define groupware in 25 words or less. The secret of a good groupware package is that it creates a whole that is *much* more than the sum of the parts. Notes does this very well.

So What Is Lotus Notes?

The combination of the maturing of Notes Release 3 and the competition's inability to understand the Notes phenomenon virtually assures Notes' domination of the client/server workgroup applications for the foreseeable future...Notes is still breakthrough technology and is still without real competition.

— **David S. Marshak, Seybold Group**
(March, 1993)

Lotus Notes allows groups of users to interact and share information that can be of a highly unstructured nature. It provides a client/server application development and run-time environment that provides the following functions (see Figure 20-1):

■ *A document database server* stores and manages multiuser client access to semi-structured data—including text, images, audio, and video.

■ *An e-mail server* manages multiuser client access to mail.

■ *A backbone server/server infrastructure* supports both mail routing and database replication. The replication mechanism synchronizes copies of the same database, which can reside on multiple server (or client) machines. Notes comes with a mail backbone infrastructure; X.400 is available as an optional component.

■ *A GUI client environment* presents views of the document databases and provides an electronic mail front-end. Users can navigate through the databases and their document contents. Views are stored queries that act as filters for the information in the databases. The e-mail front-end is just a specialized view of a mail database. Notes can attach GUI forms (private or public) to the various databases that are used for data entry.

■ *Distributed services* include electronic signatures, security and access control lists, database administration services, system management, and an X.500 based global namespace.

■ *Application development tools* include a GUI forms generator, tools and templates for creating databases, a primitive scripting language consisting of *formulas*, and an open API set—including the Notes API, VIM, and DataLens (SQL access). ODBC support is planned for a mid-1994 release.

All Notes communications—client/server and server/server—are done using a proprietary RPC. Notes supports client/server drivers for NetBEUI, TPC/IP, IPX/SPX, and AppleTalk stacks. Optional APPC and X.25 drivers are available for server to server communications.

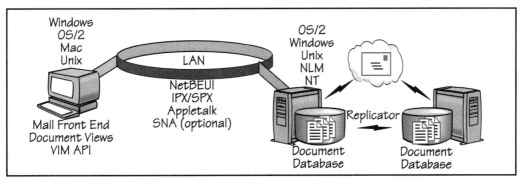

Figure 20-1. The Components of Lotus Notes.

The Multimedia Document Database

Ray Ozzie—founder of Iris Associates, the company that developed the original Notes under contract to Lotus—describes the foundation of the Notes architecture as a "database engine for semi-structured and unstructured information." Ozzie's model of a database is more akin to computer conferencing than Online Transaction Processing (OLTP). The Notes database was designed as a vehicle for gathering and disseminating all types of information; it was not meant to be a "database of record" that reflects the real-time state of the business. In this respect, Notes is more like an Information Warehouse except that the data tends to be highly eclectic. Another way of putting it is that Ray Ozzie was more interested in adding and capturing real-time information than providing synchronized access to shared data for updates. You'll get a better feel for this after we explain the Lotus Notes replication model.

The primary commodity in a Notes system is a semi-structured, multimedia *document* that can contain a variety of data types—including voice, BLOBs, video, and multifont text (see Figure 20-2). A Notes system organizes, stores, replicates, and provides shared access to documents. Related collections of Notes documents are stored in a *database*, which can then be indexed and retrieved by any of the documents' properties, or by the actual contents of the documents. Notes supports full-text indexing and searching. A Notes *document* consists of a set of fields, also known as *properties*; each has a name, type, and value. For example, a Notes document can be tagged with properties such as *client*, *region*, and *subject*. The regions can contain any number of BLOB-like *attachments* (or embedded files). Embedded files are managed and organized as part of a Notes document.

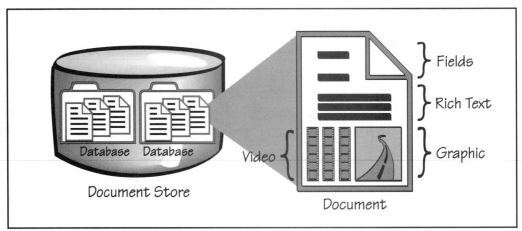

Figure 20-2. The Notes Document Store Hierarchy.

Notes Release 3 supports databases that can be up to 1 GByte in size (up from 300 MBytes in Release 2.1). More importantly, Release 3 removes any limitations on the number of documents in a database (the limit was around 20,000 documents in Release 2.1). Notes stores an entire database in a single file. A Notes application typically consists of many databases that are organized by topic. Again, the Notes concept of a database is more akin to conferencing (data is organized by topic) rather than relational DBMSs (all data is organized in a single database consisting of multiple tables).

Notes Database Replication

Like information warehouses, Notes allows databases to be replicated across servers (and clients). Unlike the warehouses we covered in Part 4, Notes has no notion of a master database—it uses replicas. The *replicator* is responsible for bidirectionally adding, deleting, or updating documents among all *replicas* of the database. Notes uses replication as a means to disseminate (or broadcast) information across geographically distributed locations.

The Notes replicator supports both full and partial replication and has a tunable level of consistency based on the desired frequency of replication. Notes time-stamps all new and edited (or updated) documents that are known to have replicas. Unattended servers can dial each other up, compare notes, and swap changes at times configured by an administrator. You can also store replicas on client workstations and initiate swaps from there.

Notes Release 3 introduced *background replication*, which allows Notes laptop clients to continue working in Notes while replication is taking place in the background. Laptop users will find replication to be very helpful for on-the-road activity. You copy a Notes database, work on it, and then swap changes with the server when you can make a connection (see Figure 20-3). *Selective replication* limits the sections in documents that get replicated. You can choose not to replicate binary attachments to save on local disk space. You can also limit the size of each document to be replicated (for example, the first 200 characters). Or you can choose to only replicate unread messages from your boss.

This loosely synchronized style of information update is adequate for most conferencing applications, but it is a far cry from the synchronous two-phase commit updates used in OLTP applications. So how are concurrent updates handled? Prior to Notes Release 3, if two users simultaneously updated a server-based document, the first save was accepted and the next save was notified that it was overwriting someone else's changes. The decision of whether or not to overwrite the data was left to the user (not a very comforting thought if you were the first user). Notes Release 3 introduced a versioning capability that lets an edited document become a response to the original document, or the last updated version can become the main document with all previous versions displayed as responses.

Versioning does not guarantee that the last version is the most accurate, and it cannot merge changes into a single copy of the data. So even Release 3 of Notes is not a suitable technology for OLTP database applications or applications that require high concurrency controls involving immediate updates. However, versioning eliminates the loss of data through concurrent updates or through replication. It's quite useful for its intended use: document-centric groupware applications—an area that OLTP doesn't even touch.

How to Build a Notes Application

A new Notes *database* is typically created by using one of the Lotus-provided templates and customizing it. A database is simply a new file; it can be given an identifying icon, a title, help panels, and a *policy document* that explains what it's all about. *Forms* are used to enter information or view information in a database. To create a form, you can start with one of the pre-existing forms and modify it using the GUI editor. Forms provide data entry fields, text fields, and graphic areas where pictures or other sources of multimedia data can be pasted (or attached). Lotus provides a scripting language—it's like 1-2-3 spreadsheet formulas—that allows you to associate commands with specific events and actions. The forms you create are associated with the database. You can designate them as either *public*, which means they're available to all client applications that have access to the database; or you can make them *private*, which means only the creator can use them.

Figure 20-3. Replicated Databases Can Be Used on the Road.

Views are stored queries that display the contents of a database or of a particular document. They're used for navigation and for the filtering of information—examples are display documents less than one month old "by region" or "by salesperson." The view will display the list of documents in a tabular or outline fashion. Any database has one or more views that the designer creates for easy access to information. Users also can create *private* views to provide a listing or access criteria that the database designer didn't anticipate.

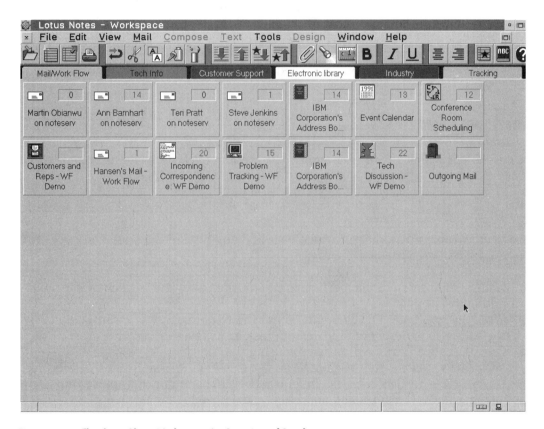

Figure 20-4. The Notes Client Workspace: An Organizer of Databases.

On the client side, a user has a *workspace*—a notebook-like visual that organizes databases by topics (see Figure 20-4). A notebook consists of six color-coded workpages; each has a folder-like tab that identifies a category into which you want to organize your databases. Each workpage can contain from zero to hundreds of databases. Each database is represented by an icon and a title. You must associate a new database to a workpage. You then double-click on it to open it and work with its views. Release 3 lets you open multiple databases and gives each its own window. However, you still can't join documents from different databases into a single view.

But you can create hypertext links from any document in any database to any other database.

The process of creating a new Notes client/server application and tailoring forms and views can take less than an hour. It's that simple. For the more adventurous, the Notes scripting language—or *formula macro language*—provides about 200 functions to control almost everything from field input validation to database queries and document routing. A prompt command can be associated with any event to display a dialog box that prompts users to enter data or to select an entry from a list-box. Release 3 provides *periodic macros* that can be used to launch macros at a specific time interval or as a result of a particular action or condition—for example, when a document is deleted. This is the Notes equivalent of a trigger.

The Lotus Notes API

Notes also provides a C programming API, which developers can use to store and retrieve Notes documents; it also gives you broad access to many of the features of the Notes user interface. The API allows you to:

- Create or delete databases.
- Read, write, and modify any document and any field in the document.
- Create and use database views.
- Control database access with access control lists.
- Gather and report server performance statistics and register new workstations and servers.
- Write custom tasks that you can add to the Notes server software and specify the schedule under which the custom task executes.
- Create, read, and run Notes macros using the API.
- Perform full-text searches using the new search-engine (see the next Details box).
- Issue calls to restrict what documents get exchanged during replication.
- Obtain the list of names and address books in use locally or on a server.
- Issue mail gateway calls.

In addition, Notes supports an e-mail client API based on VIM—an open industry "standard." You'll need to purchase the separate Lotus VIM Developer's Toolkit ($395). But the Notes VIM run-time libraries are part of the product. You cannot use the APIs to modify or remove features of Notes including the "Notes Desktop."

Notes and SQL Databases

An external database API based on DataLens drivers is available free of charge. It lets Notes users access data stored in external databases using Notes' keywords and

329

Chapter 20. Lotus Notes

lookup capabilities. The foreign data can be displayed in Notes fields. However, still missing is a way for programs to access the Notes database using an open SQL CLI. This may change when Lotus provides its relational database interface using the ODBC CLI (mid-1994). The ODBC drivers will allow Notes programmers to write SQL queries that can be translated into Notes queries. And, it will provide the capability to bring Notes data into a relational database. In other words, it will provide bi-directional Notes/SQL capability (see Figure 20-5).

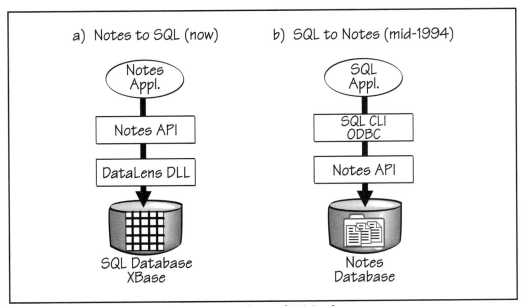

Figure 20-5. Bidirectional Data Exchanges Between Notes and SQL Databases.

The Notes Text-Search Engine

Details

Lotus Notes Release 3 adds some very sophisticated text search and retrieval capabilities. The good news is that text can now be searched across more than one database. The bad news is that the search engine user interface is still not very intuitive. Before you perform a search, you must first create a content index on all the databases that you're going to target. This process consumes time and eats up disk space. The content index can now be created in a background process that incrementally indexes the words found in a database's documents. Once you've indexed the databases, you can specify your query using the following search criteria:

- The target databases for the search

- Boolean search operators (AND, OR, NOT)

- Wild-card operators and pattern searches

- Text strings that are within the same sentence or in relative proximity to each other

- Text searches that are limited to a specific field

- Text searches that are limited to a specific document

- Searches on numeric and date fields using the operators ($>$, $<$, $<>$, $>=$, and $<=$)

- Sort results by date or relevance—you can also set the maximum number of matches to be returned

Queries that are submitted using the expanded Query Bar can be saved by title, run periodically, and associated with scripting actions. Developers can also access the search engine using APIs. ❑

Notes E-Mail

We want to enhance Notes as the place to live on the network.

— *Jim Manzi, Lotus CEO (October, 1993)*

From a client workstation's perspective, e-mail is just another Notes database that contains a collection of mail documents. The procedures to read incoming mail, sort through mail, or create a mail document are the same ones used to create and read documents in any Notes database. You simply use forms and views that are tailored to your mail documents. Of course, one of the differences is that the mail documents you create will be sent to somebody else's mailbox. Notes provides visual indicators to let you know that you have incoming mail. You then open the database and read it. Ray Ozzie's design seems to be very consistent.

The Notes e-mail server is open. If you don't like the Notes mail front-end, you can use the VIM API to create your own. Or you can simply use VIM to mail-enable your applications using the Notes server as a back-end. By mid-1994, cc:Mail clients will be able to use the Notes mail server. So what kind of services does a Notes Mail server provide? It provides mail backbone functions with the following features:

- **Routing optimization.** The techniques include outbound message prioritization and dynamic adaptive route selection based on link costs.

- **Separate router threads.** All server-to-server communications are handled by separate transfer threads. Threads allow multiple concurrent transfers to occur on different backbone routes. In addition, threads prevent large mail messages from delaying other server tasks.

- **Delivery failure notification.** Senders can be notified when delivery isn't possible (including the reasons).

- **X.500 namespace support.** Notes Release 3 supports the full X.500-compliant hierarchical naming as its native means of identifying *users* within the system. This makes it straightforward for Notes directories to interoperate at the naming level with other X.500-compliant systems. It avoids naming conflict headaches.

- **Mail gateways and directory services.** Notes provides e-mail gateways to the most popular e-mail networks, including X.400, SMTP, cc:Mail, MHS, PROFS, VinesMail, FAX, VAXmail, and SoftSwitch (see Figure 20-6).

- **Electronic signatures.** Notes uses the RSA public key cryptography for all aspects of Notes security, including encryption. (In Part 3, we explained that RSA was good for electronic signatures but very slow when it came to general encryption.) If you sign a message, it takes Notes a few seconds longer to send it because it must generate an RSA electronic signature. If it takes a few seconds just to encrypt a name, how long does it take to encrypt a medium-sized document?

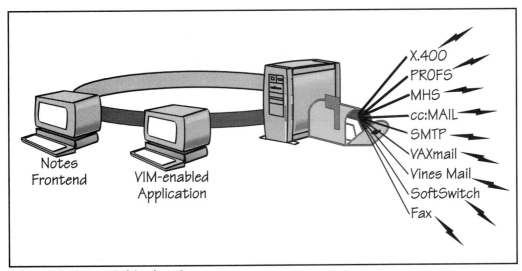

Figure 20-6. Notes E-Mail Reach via Gateways.

■ *VIM open client support.* Notes Release 3 supports VIM calls, which means that Notes users can select their mail clients independently from the server. Of course, the mail clients must be VIM-compliant.

As we explained in the last chapter, the Notes mail engine will serve both Notes and cc:Mail front-ends in mid-1994. Notes provides a true client/server e-mail architecture. The clients and servers communicate via RPC. VIM provides the call level interface on the client side.

How Revolutionary Is Notes?

Soapbox

Notes is a very exciting product that makes you want to jump in and create a client/server application just for the fun of it. Notes databases have the tendency of proliferating like rabbits. Once you get the hang of them, they're contagious. With Release 3, Notes starts to address the client/server needs of mobile users and intergalactic enterprises. You can carry your Notes databases in a laptop or have them replicated to the far corners of the universe. Lotus is also doing more to open up the Notes environment at the API level so that ISVs and IS programmers can jump in and provide add-ins. So in many ways, Lotus Notes may be a "killer app" that does for client/server what Lotus 1-2-3 did for PCs and DOS.

We like Notes and highly recommend it for certain classes of applications. But it's important to understand what it can and cannot do. Notes is a very good fit for applications that collect multimedia information, perform very few updates, and need to be integrated with e-mail. But Notes is not very good at handling applications that deal with structured data, are query intensive, and require multiuser updates with high-levels of integrity. Notes does not do very well with transactions and does not even know how to spell ACID. These types of applications are best handled by TP Monitors, Information Warehouses, transactional MOMs, and SQL and Object databases. ❑

Part 7
Client/Server With
Distributed Objects

An Introduction to Part 7

So did you all enjoy that night on the town? Oh, you want to play elephant and blind men again? We can't afford it—you Martians party too hard. But, we have a great new adventure ahead of us, and it's going to be fun. We're going to explore the uncharted territory of distributed objects. No, we're not talking about *Unidentified Flying Objects (UFOs)*—that's Martian stuff. Sorry, that was rude: Of course you Martians are not objects and, yes, you have identities. What we're dealing with here are computer objects. Do they fly? Yes, some do over wireless networks. And, we know of roaming objects that live on networks and their brokers who organize communities of objects. Yes, it's another new frontier and there may be a pot of gold there, too. Are you all packed and ready for another adventure?

Part 7 is about distributed objects. The word *distributed* is important because it means we're dealing with objects that participate in client/server relationships with other objects. More plumbing? Yes, but this is supposed to be the "mother of all plumbing." Objects can do everything we've covered in this book, and, supposedly, *they do it better*:

- **Objects** themselves are an amazing combination of data and function with magical properties like polymorphism, inheritance, and encapsulation. This magic works wonders in distributed environments.

- **Object brokers** provide the ultimate distributed system. They allow objects to dynamically discover each other and interact across machines and operating systems.

- **Object services** allow us to create, manage, name, move, copy, store, and restore objects.

- **Object TP Monitors** may emerge as the most powerful and flexible transaction managers yet. Objects and transactions are a dynamite combination.

- **Object groupware** may change the way we interact. The new groupware will be built using roaming objects, intelligent event managers, and object replication services.

- **Object databases** provide the ultimate management system for BLOBs, documents, and almost any type of information—especially new information types.

- **Object linking** technology allows us to create highly flexible webs among programs that don't know about each other. The webs emanate out of ordinary looking desktop documents.

- **Object frameworks** promise to revolutionize the way we build our distributed systems. They provide flexible, customizable, prefabricated software subsystems.

Objects may provide the ultimate infrastructure for building client/server systems. We say "may" because success depends on more than just great technology. What products are available? Are the major players lined up behind the technology? Are the key standards in place?

We think you Martians will love this distributed object stuff. It has all the elements of a new gold rush. But first we must clearly understand what makes this 25-year old technology finally ready for prime time. The answer is CORBA. You'll have to read the ORB chapter to discover what's behind CORBA magic. Complementing CORBA are distributed object services, compound document technology (including OLE and OpenDoc), object databases, and object frameworks. We devote a chapter to each one of those topics. We conclude the part with a product review to give us a "reality check" on the technology. So we have an exciting (but long) journey ahead of us. Pack lots of trail mix and energy bars—you'll need it all. And yes. it's new frontier country. So bring along all your exploration gear and let's hope we don't lose any of you in those uncharted and potentially treacherous mountain passes and ravines.

Chapter 21

Object Request Brokers

---

*A*n object is a living, breathing blob of intelligence that knows how to act in a given situation.

— *Steve Jobs*
(March, 1994)

By now, anybody associated with computers knows that objects are wonderful—we simply can't live without them. SmallTalk can be used to create GUI front-ends, C++ is the only way to write code, and the literature is full of articles on the wonders of encapsulation, multiple inheritance, and polymorphism. But what can these things do on a client/server network? Where do objects fit in a world dominated by SQL databases, TP Monitors, and Lotus Notes? What happens when we stray away from the cozy single-address space of a program and try to get objects to talk across a network? What happens to inheritance in a world of federated operating systems separated by networks? In a nutshell, we need to understand how object technology can be *extended* to deal with the complex issues that are inherent in creating robust, single-image, client/server systems.

The purpose of the next few chapters is to describe exactly what objects can do for client/server systems. The key word is *systems*—or how objects work together across machine and network boundaries to create client/server solutions. We're not going to rehash the marvels of Object-Oriented Programming (OOP), SmallTalk, and C++ because we assume you've heard about them all before. We're moving on to the next step: objects in client/server systems. We strongly believe that this is the area where objects will realize their greatest potential; in the process, they will become the new "mainstream computing model." We also believe that client/server technology needs objects to fulfill its promise of plug-and-play computing across networks and dissimilar operating systems. Finally, we believe that without a strong distributed object foundation the management of client/server systems is a lost cause (more on that in Part 8). In this chapter, we go over *Object Request Brokers*—or "ORBs," as the natives call them. The ORB is the mechanism that allows objects to communicate with each other across a network. We will look at the OMG's CORBA specification for ORBs and put the whole thing in a familiar client/server perspective. As you'll see, some key distributed object pieces are still lacking. So we will also look at what's brewing in the upcoming OMG specifications.

WHAT DISTRIBUTED OBJECTS PROMISE

> *Data will be encapsulated in objects that will in some cases be able to roam to where they are most needed.*

> — *Peter Wayner, Byte Magazine*
> *(January, 1994)*

Object technology radically alters the way software systems are developed. The promise is compelling: We will be able to put together complex client/server information systems by simply assembling and extending reusable software components. Any of the objects may be modified or changed without affecting the rest of the components in the system or how they interact. The components may be shipped as collections of class libraries preassembled in *frameworks*, where all the pieces are known to work together to perform a specific task. Frameworks are working subsystems that revolutionize the way we create client/server systems. They promise to provide the ultimate in mix-and-match capabilities.

Snapping Together Distributed Objects

> *Object technology has the ability to revolutionize client/server computing because it makes software easier and faster to develop for programmers, easier to use for users, and easier to manage for system administrators.*

> — *Ronald Weissman, Director, NeXT*
> *(April, 1994)*

For objects to be successful, they must reside in open client/server environments and learn how to "plug-and-play" across networks and operating systems. In theory, object technology is well-suited for creating client/server systems because the data and business logic are encapsulated within objects, allowing them to be located anywhere within a distributed system. The *granularity* of distribution is greatly improved. Objects can easily mask the platform-specific elements and make the pieces appear to interoperate seamlessly.

Object-oriented client/server applications can afford to be much more flexible than traditional vertical applications—frameworks allow end users to mix-and-match components without making the distributed application *less* robust. Objects have the inherent potential to become intelligent, self-managing entities; this allows us to manage very complex systems by broadcasting instructions and alarms. In summary, distributed objects allow granular components of software to plug-and-play, interoperate across networks, run on different platforms, coexist with legacy applications through object wrappers, roam on networks (a la General Magic), and manage themselves and the resources they control (Figure 21-1 shows some of these benefits). What more could we want?

Are Objects Ready for Prime Time?

Enabling easier client/server application development is one of the factors that might fuel explosive growth in the object marketplace during the rest of this decade.

> — **Ronald Weissman, Director, NeXT**
> **(April, 1994)**

A recent IDC study of 800 corporations indicates that 12% of those surveyed are using object technology, while 44% are exploring object technology benefits—and 73% of those moving to objects are using them to build client/server solutions. The object marketplace is estimated by Datapro to be growing at 67% annually; it is expected to become a $4 billion market by 1997. Why is there this sudden interest in a technology that's been around for 25 years? One answer is that the stars may be aligning and the pieces are finally coming together. The more likely catalyst was the formation of the *Object Management Group (OMG)* in April 1989. This non-profit, international consortium, which now has over 300 members, is dedicated to establishing standards for distributed objects. The best way to understand client/server object technology is to look at the OMG's distributed object management standards.

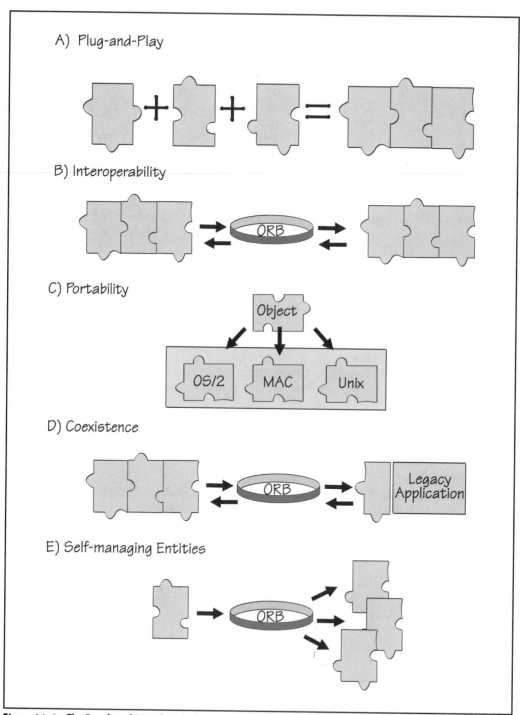

Figure 21-1. The Benefits of Distributed Objects.

The World's Shortest Tutorial on Objects

Briefing

If you want to shrink something, you must first allow it to expand. If you want to take something, you must first allow it to be given. This is called the subtle perception of the way things are.

— Lao Tzu

An *object* is a piece of code that owns things called *attributes* and provides services through *methods*. Typically, the methods operate on private data—also called instance data—that the object owns. A collection of like objects make up a *class*. A class also acts as a template for describing the behavior of sets of like objects. Technically speaking, objects are run-time *instances* of a class. This all sounds pretty straightforward, so why all the fuss about objects? First, they provide a better programming model for representing the world. We can create intelligent software objects that mirror the things around us. Second, objects have three magical properties that make them incredibly useful: encapsulation, inheritance, and polymorphism. In our book, **Client/Server Programming with OS/2 2.1**, we call them "the three pillars of object-oriented programming." They allow us to create reusable objects without distributing the source code. They form the essence what Lao-Tzu calls "the subtle perception of the way things are."

Encapsulation

Encapsulation means "don't tell me how you do it; just do it." The object does that by managing its own resources and limiting the visibility of what others should know. An object publishes a public interface that defines how other objects or applications can interact with it (see Figure 21-2). An object also has a *private* component that implements the methods. The object's implementation is encapsulated—that is, hidden from the public view. Instance data can be declared private—usually, the default—or public. Private instance data can only be accessed by methods of the class. Public instance data, on the other hand, is part of the published external interface. The public methods and instance data are the permanent interface between the object and the outside world. Old methods must continue to be supported when an object changes. The public interface is a *binding contract* between the class providers and their clients.

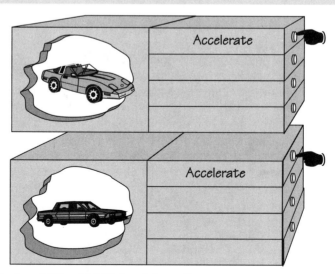

Figure 21-2. The First Pillar of OO Wisdom: Class Encapsulation.

Polymorphism

A *true living object can be replaced.*

> — *Christine Comaford,*
> *PC Week Columnist (March, 1994)*

Polymorphism is a high-browed way of saying that the same method can do different things, depending on the class that implements it. Looking at Figure 21-3, you can see polymorphism in action (hit the "accelerator" on a Corvette and on a Volvo, and then compare notes). Objects in different classes receive the same message yet react in different ways. Polymorphism is also the mechanism that allows subclasses (see next paragraph) to override an inherited method—and "do their own thing"—without affecting the ancestor's methods.

Figure 21-3. The Second Pillar of OO Wisdom: Polymorphism.

Inheritance

Inheritance is the mechanism that allows you to create new child classes, also known as *subclasses*, from existing parent classes. Child classes inherit their parent's methods and data structures. You can add new methods to a child's class or *override*—that is, modify—inherited methods to define new class behaviors. The parent's method is not affected by this modification. Figure 21-4 shows a typical class family tree—start with a generic "car" class and derive from it Volvos or Maseratis.

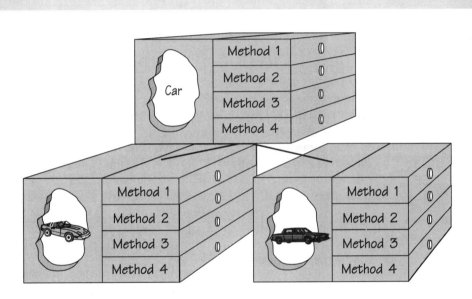

Figure 21-4. The Third Pillar of OO Wisdom: Inheritance and Subclassing.

Frameworks and Class Libraries

The three pillars of OO provide the foundation for creating, assembling, and reusing objects. The first generation of OO relied on *class libraries* to package objects for reusability. A more promising approach is the use of *object frameworks*. These are preassembled class libraries that are packaged to provide specific functions. Frameworks will make it easier to assemble objects; they raise the level of abstraction. We cover frameworks in more detail in Chapter 25, "Object Frameworks: A Closer Look." ❑

OMG'S OBJECT MANAGEMENT ARCHITECTURE

If objects are to be assembled, they must be compatible with one another. This is rarely a problem when writing a single program because all the objects are written in the same language, run on the same machine, and use the same operating system. But building entire information systems out of objects is quite a different matter. Objects have to interact with each other even if they are written in different languages and run on different hardware and software platforms.

— **David. A Taylor** [1]

Clearly, we need standards for objects to interoperate in heterogeneous client/server environments. Fortunately, this time around the industry anticipated this need and the Object Management Group (OMG) was founded specifically to create distributed object standards *before* any major products were introduced—a truly amazing phenomenon in our industry. As a result, over 300 vendors (and corporate associate members) are working on CORBA-compliant software products. The noticeable exception is Microsoft. But even that may change soon—OMG is in the process of creating a compound document architecture standard that may include both OLE and OpenDoc. We expect the remote object links in the compound documents to be managed via CORBA-compliant ORBs (OpenDoc supports this feature, and DEC may provide the same support for OLE). But we're getting ahead of our story.

In the fall of 1990, OMG first published the **Object Management Architecture Guide (OMA Guide)**; it was revised in September 1992. Figure 21-5 displays the four main components of the architecture:

■ ***The Object Request Broker*** is the mechanism that lets objects transparently make requests to—and receive responses from—other objects located locally or remotely. The client is not aware of the mechanisms used to communicate with, activate, or store the server objects. The ORB serves as the *foundation* for building distributed object applications. In the words of OMG, "the ORB component will guarantee portability and interoperability of objects over a network of heterogeneous systems." The current specification includes a generic *Interface Definition Language (IDL)* that is used to define the interfaces to objects that communicate via the ORB. However, we'll have to wait for ORB 2.0 (late 1994) to get a solid interoperability standard (it's work in progress). The ORB component is also commonly referred to as *CORBA*—which stands for *Common Object Request Broker Architecture*. Like the rest of the industry, we'll use both names interchangeably.

---

[1] Source: David A. Taylor, **Object-Oriented Information Systems** (Wiley, 1992). This book provides an excellent introduction to object technology.

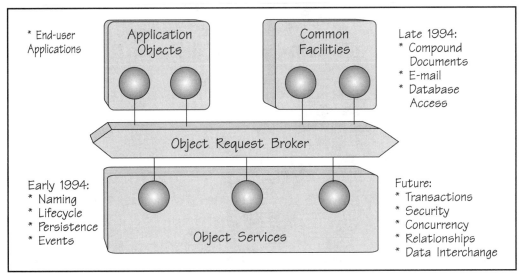

Figure 21-5. The Object Management Architecture Components.

■ **Object Services** are collections of services with object interfaces that provide basic functions for using and implementing objects. You can think of object services as augmenting and complementing the functionality of the ORB. The object services that are close to becoming standards include object naming, event notification, persistence, and object lifecycle management. A bit further on the horizon are object services for transaction management, security, concurrency control, relationships, data interchange, change management, trading, licensing, query, and properties.

■ **Common Facilities** are collections of end-user oriented services. Examples include e-mail, compound documents, database access, services that specifically support the construction of word processors, and network management applications. The dividing line between Common Facilities and Object Services is imprecise. Object Services *must* be implemented on every ORB, while Common Facilities are optional. Most of the OMG activity is currently in the object services area. But in December 1993, the OMG created a Common Facilities Task Force to look at compound documents and object-sharing facilities at the desktop level.

■ **Application Objects** are objects specific to end-user applications. These objects must be defined using the Interface Definition Language if they are to participate in ORB-mediated exchanges. An application is typically built from a large number of basic object classes; some of these may be provided by the OMG's Common Services.

Are ORBs the Mother of All Middleware?

Briefing

Orb—A jeweled globe surmounted by a cross that is part of a sovereign's regalia and that symbolizes monarchical power and justice.

— American Heritage Dictionary

Orb—Putting down some pavement on the dirt road called distributed computing.

— Chris Stone, President of OMG

The ORB becomes the "mother of all middleware" by providing granular levels of interoperability between objects in heterogeneous distributed environments. OMG hopes to achieve this ambitious goal by following two steps: 1) It will turn everything into nails, and 2) It will give everyone a hammer.

■ The "nail" is the CORBA *Interface Definition Language (IDL)*. The IDL allows object providers to specify in a standard definition language the interface and structure of the objects they provide. An IDL-defined *contract* binds the providers of distributed object services to their clients. For one object to request something of another object, it must know the target object's interface. The CORBA *IDL Repository* contains the definitions of all these interfaces.

■ The "hammer" includes the set of distributed services OMG providers will supply. These services will determine which objects are on the network, which methods they provide, and which *object interface adapters* are supported. The location of the object should be transparent to the client and object implementation. It should not matter whether the object is in the same process or across the world.

Does this all sound familiar? It should. We're describing the "object wave" of client/server computing; this time it's between cooperating objects as opposed to cooperating processes. The goal of this new wave is to create multivendor, multiOS, multilanguage "legoware" using objects. Vendors such as Sun, HP, IBM, and NCR are all using CORBA as their standard IDL-defined interface into the object highway. The IDL is the *contract* that brings it all together. We'll spend the next few sections digging into the details of how this all comes together. ❑

THE OBJECT REQUEST BROKER

ORBs facilitate coarse-grained class reuse by providing a layer beneath the application but above the programming language, operating system, and hardware fray. In this middle ground, reuse grows and object technology blossoms.

> — **John Gidman, Fidelity Investments**
> **(April, 1994)**

The ORB is the middleware that establishes the client/server relationships between objects. Using an ORB, a client object can transparently invoke a method on a server object, which can be on the same machine or across a network. The ORB intercepts the call and is responsible for finding an object that can implement the request, pass it the parameters, invoke its method, and return the results (see Figure 21-6). The client does not have to be aware of where the object is located, its programming language, its operating system, or any other system aspects that are not part of an object's interface.

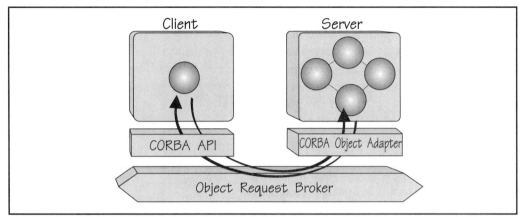

Figure 21-6. The Client/Server Request Using the ORB.

The Structure of a CORBA ORB

Figure 21-7 shows the client and server components of an ORB. Even though there are many boxes, it's not as complicated as it appears to be. This section provides the big picture of what these components do. We then go into more details in the sections that follow. The key is to understand that CORBA, like SQL, provides *both* static and dynamic interfaces to its services. This happened because the OMG received two strong submissions to its ORB Request For Proposal (RFP): one from HyperDesk and DEC that was based on a dynamic API, and one from Sun and HP that was based on static APIs. The OMG told the two groups to come back with a single RFP that combined both features. The result was CORBA. The "Common" in CORBA stands for this two-API proposal, which makes a lot of sense because it gives us both static and dynamic APIs.

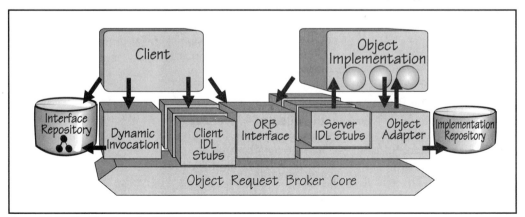

Figure 21-7. The Structure of a CORBA ORB.

Let's first go over the ORB components on the client side:

- *The client IDL stubs* provide the static interfaces to object services. These precompiled stubs define how clients invoke corresponding services on the servers. The services are defined using the Interface Definition Language (IDL), and both client and server stubs are generated by the IDL compiler.

- *The Dynamic Invocation APIs* let you discover the method to be invoked at run time. CORBA defines standard APIs for obtaining the service definitions, generating the parameters, issuing the remote call, and getting back the results.

- *The Interface Repository APIs* allow you to obtain descriptions of all the registered classes, the methods they support, and the parameters they require. CORBA calls these descriptions *method signatures*. The Interface Repository is a run-time database that contains a machine-readable version of the IDL-defined interfaces. The APIs let your programs access this information.

- *The ORB Interface* consists of a few APIs to local services that may be of interest to an application (the calls are not part of the client/server invocation mechanism). The next Details box describes some of the ORB APIs.

The client and server components communicate using the *ORB Core*, which is implementation-specific (i.e., not defined by CORBA). The idea is that CORBA provides the interfaces above the ORB Core that mask the differences between vendor implementations. Vendors may use any transport they want for the networked ORB traffic and for the basic representation of objects in their system. Sun's DOE uses the ONC RPC over TCP/IP, HP's DOMF uses DCE RPC, HyperDesk's DOMS supports Netwise's RPC over TCP/IP, and IBM's DSOM supports sockets over TCP/IP, NetBIOS, or IPX/SPX (IBM is also working with HP on a DCE-based ORB). The result is that the different vendors' ORBs don't interoperate. The ORB 2.0 committee is leaning towards a gateway solution for ORB interoperability—the proverbial compromise. Vendors are also resorting to bilateral technology exchanges to make their ORB Cores interoperate (for example, the IBM/HP common DCE-based ORB Core).

CORBA-defined components appear on the server side between the ORB Core and the object implementations. Here's a quick explanation of what the pieces do:

- *The server IDL stubs* (also known as skeletons) provide the static interfaces to each service exported by the server. These stubs, like the ones on the client, are created using the Interface Definition Language compiler. The server cannot tell the difference between incoming static or dynamic invocations. They're both invoked through server stubs.

FYI

ORB versus RPC

Briefing

Brokers of all types—stock brokers as well as object brokers—exact a price for their services.

— Bill Andreas,
Chief-Architect, HyperDesk

So how are ORB method invocations different from RPCs? The mechanisms are very similar, but there are some important differences. With an RPC, you call a specific function (the data is separate). In contrast, with an ORB, you're calling a method within a *specific* object. Different object classes may respond to the same method invocation differently through the magic of polymorphism. Because each object manages its own private instance data, the method is implemented on that *specific* instance data (see Figure 21-8).

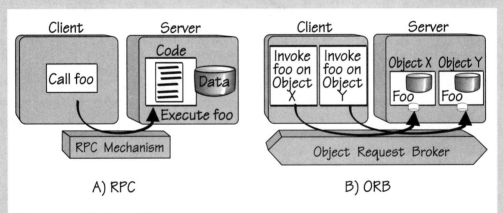

Figure 21-8. ORBs Versus RPC.

ORB method invocations have "scalpel-like" precision—the call gets to a *specific* object that controls *specific* data, and then implements the function in its own *class-specific* way. In contrast, RPC calls have no specificity—all the functions with the same name get implemented the same way. No differentiated service here. Of course, the ORB is usually built on top of an RPC service, so you end up paying a performance penalty for this "refined" level of service. It's worth every penny if you're taking advantage of new levels of distributed granularity provided by objects. Otherwise, you just bought yourself another layer of middleware—with all the costs and headaches that come with it. ❑

■ *The object adapter* interfaces with the ORB's core communication services and accepts requests for service on behalf of the server's objects. It provides the run-time environment for instantiating server objects, passing requests to them, and assigning them object IDs—CORBA calls them *object references.* The Object Adapter also registers the classes it supports and their run-time instances (i.e., objects) with the *implementation repository.* CORBA specifies that each ORB must support a standard adapter called the *Basic Object Adapter.* Servers may support more than one object adapter.

■ *The Implementation Repository* provides run-time directory information about the classes a server supports, the objects that are instantiated, and their IDs. It also serves as a common place to store additional information associated with the implementation of ORBs. Examples include trace information, audit trails, security, and other administrative data.

■ *The ORB Interface* consists of a few APIs to local services that may be of interest to an application (the calls are not part of the client/server invocation mechanism).

This concludes our panoramic overview of the ORB components and their interfaces. If you're confused, keep reading—the next level of detail may help clarify things.

CORBA Client/Server Requests

Figure 21-9 shows the two types of client/server invocations that are supported by a CORBA ORB: static and dynamic. In both cases, the client performs a request by having access to an *object reference* (i.e., object ID) and invoking the method that performs the service (see the following Details box). The dynamic and static interfaces for performing the service satisfy the same request semantics. The receiver of the message cannot tell how the request was invoked. In both cases, the ORB locates a server object adapter, transmits the parameters, and transfers control to the object implementation through the server IDL stub (or skeleton).

Clients see the object interfaces through the perspective of a language mapping— or *binding*—that brings the ORB right up to the programmer's level. Client programs should be able to work without any source changes (on *any* ORB that supports the language binding) with *any* object instance that implements the interface. The implementation of the object, its object adapter, and the ORB used to access it is totally transparent to both static and dynamic clients.

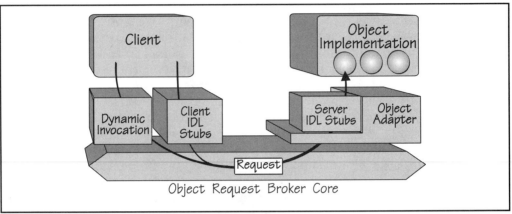

Figure 21-9. The ORB-Based Static and Dynamic Invocation Services.

What's an Object Reference?

Details

An object reference provides the information needed to uniquely specify an object within a distributed ORB system—it's a unique name or identifier. The implementation of object references is not defined by the CORBA specification, which means it is implementation specific. Two CORBA-compliant ORBs may have different representations for object references. So how is client/server program portability maintained in such an environment? By using language bindings to insulate the programs from the actual representation of the object references (see Figure 21-10).

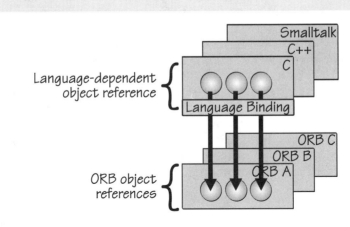

Figure 21-10. Language-independent Object References.

All ORBs must provide the same language binding to an object reference (usually referred to as an *Object*) for a particular programming language. This means that the language provides the portability and allows you to reference objects that run on different ORBs from within your programs. What happens if your program is accessing object references on two different ORBs? According to CORBA, your programs should still work fine; it is up to the vendors to resolve any object reference conflicts that may be encountered by the client code.

How do the client programs obtain object references? They usually receive them from directories or invocations on other objects to which they have references. An object reference can be converted to a string-name that can be stored in files. The string-name can be preserved or communicated by different means and then turned back into an object reference by the ORB that produced the string. CORBA defines two functions—*object-to-string* and *string-to-object*—to help store, communicate, and retrieve object references. Client programs can use these two functions to obtain a string-name and convert it to an object reference and vice versa. We also expect the OMG to get into the business of allocating "well-known object references." Somebody's got to do it. ❏

The CORBA Process: From IDL to Interface Stubs

Figure 21-11 shows the steps you go through to create your server classes, provide interface stubs for them, store their definitions in the Interface Repository, instantiate the objects at run time, and record their presence with the Implementation Repository. Let's go through these steps one-by-one and see what's involved:

1. *Define your object classes using Interface Definition Language (IDL).* The IDL is the means by which objects tell their potential clients what operations are available and how they should be invoked. The IDL definition language defines the types of objects, their attributes, the methods they export, and the method parameters. The CORBA IDL is a subset of ANSI C++ with additional constructs to support distribution. The IDL is purely a declarative language. It uses the C++ syntax for constant, type, and operation definitions, and it does not include any control structures or variables.

2. *Run the IDL file through a language precompiler.* A typical CORBA-compliant precompiler processes the IDL files and produces C language *skeletons* for the implementation server classes. By the time you read this, the OMG may have also published specifications for C++ language bindings.

3. *Add the implementation code to the skeletons.* You must supply the code that implements the methods in the skeletons. In other words, you must create your server classes.

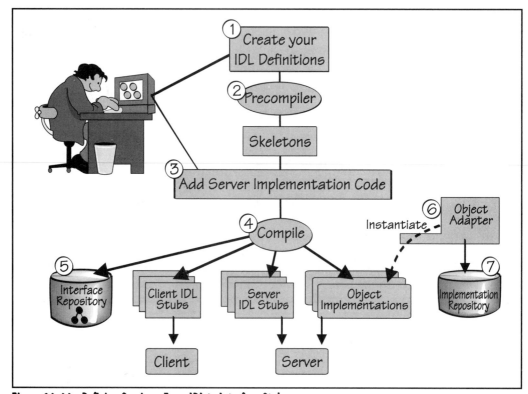

Figure 21-11. Defining Services: From IDL to Interface Stubs.

4. ***Compile the code.*** A CORBA-compliant compiler is typically capable of generating at least four types of output files: 1) *import files* that describe the objects to an Interface Repository; 2) *client stubs* for the IDL-defined methods—these stubs are invoked by a client program that needs to statically access IDL-defined services via the ORB; 3) *server stubs* that call the methods on the server—they're also called *up-call interfaces*; and 4) the code that implements the server classes. The automatic generation of stubs frees developers from having to write them and frees applications from dependencies on a particular ORB implementation.

5. ***Bind the class definitions to the Interface Repository.*** Typically, a utility is provided to bind—or, if you prefer, compile—the IDL information in a persistent store that can be accessed by programs at run time.

6. ***Instantiate the objects on the server.*** At startup time, a server *Object Adapter* may instantiate server objects that service remote client method invocations. These run-time objects are instances of the server application classes. CORBA specifies different Object Adapter strategies that are used to create and manage the run-time objects (more on that in later sections).

7. ***Register the run-time objects with the Implementation Repository.*** The Object Adapter records in the *Implementation Repository* the object reference and type of any object it instantiates on the server. The Implementation Repository also knows which object classes are supported on a particular server. The ORB uses this information to locate active objects or to request the activation of objects on a particular server.

The seven steps we just outlined are typical of most CORBA implementations. CORBA, of course, allows deviations. For example, it is not a requirement for IDL source code to be available, as long as the interface information is available in stub form or in an Interface Repository. It is not necessary for the server objects to be implemented as classes as long as they're encapsulated by IDL stubs. The separation of the interface from the implementation makes it possible to incorporate existing (legacy) systems within an ORB environment.

How Methods Are Dynamically Invoked

CORBA's *Dynamic Invocation* APIs allow a client program to dynamically build and invoke requests on objects. The client specifies the object to be invoked, the method to be performed, and the set of parameters through a call or sequence of calls. The client code typically obtains this information from an *Interface Repository* or a similar run-time source. The dynamic invocation provides maximum flexibility by allowing new object types to be added to the distributed system at run time. Visual tools will use this API to create interfaces through point-and-click interactions with a user.

To invoke a dynamic method on an object, the client must perform the following steps (see Figure 21-12):

1. ***Obtain the method description from the Interface Repository.*** CORBA specifies about ten calls for locating and describing objects within the repository. After an object is located, a *describe* call is issued to obtain its full IDL definition.

2. ***Create the argument list.*** CORBA specifies a self-defining data structure for passing parameters, which it calls the *NamedValue list*. The list is created using the *create_list* operation and as many *add_arg* calls as it takes to add each argument to the list.

3. ***Create the request.*** The request must specify the object reference, the name of the method, and the argument list. The request is created using the CORBA *create_request* call.

4. ***Invoke the request.*** The request may be invoked in one of three ways: 1) the *invoke* call sends the request and obtains the results; 2) the *send* call returns

control to the program, which must then issue a *get_response* or *get_next_response* call; and 3) the *send* call can be defined to be "oneway"; in this case, no response is needed.

As you can see, it takes effort to dynamically invoke a method. You're trading off complexity and performance for added flexibility.

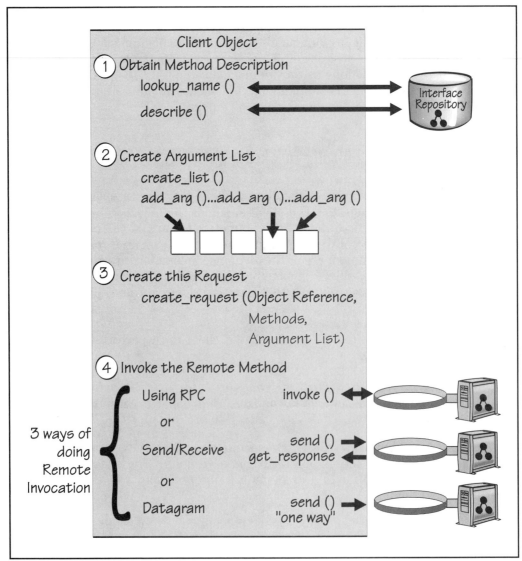

Figure 21-12. The CORBA Dynamic Invocation Interface.

Static Versus Dynamic Method Invocations

The static interface is directly generated in the form of stubs by the IDL precompiler. It is perfect for programs that know at compile time the particulars of the operations they will need to invoke. The static stub interface is bound at compile time and provides the following advantages over the dynamic method invocation:

- *It is easier to program*—you call the remote method by simply invoking it by name and passing it the parameters. It's a very natural form of programming.

- *It provides more robust type checking*—the checking is enforced by the compiler at build time.

- *It performs well*—a single API call is issued to the stub, which takes it from there.

- *It is self-documenting*—you can tell what's going on by reading the code.

In contrast, the dynamic method invocation provides a more flexible environment. It allows you to add new classes to the system without requiring changes in the client code. It's very useful for tools that discover what services are provided at run time. You can write some very generic code with dynamic APIs. However, most applications don't require this level of flexibility and are better off with static stub implementations.

CORBA Servers

A *primary CORBA goal was to permit a wide variety of implementations. The specification does not rule out any of the different approaches to an ORB.*

> — *Geoff Lewis, Chairperson of OMG*
> *Object Services (May, 1993)*

CORBA *represents the least common denominator. It treaded on nobody's product.*

> — *Anonymous vendor* [2]

What does an object implementation need from an ORB on the server side? It needs a server infrastructure that registers the application's classes, instantiates new

---

[2] Source: Robert E. Shelton, "OMG's CORBA 2.0," **Distributed Computing Monitor** (May, 1993).

objects, gives them unique IDs, advertises their existence, invokes their methods when clients request it, and manages concurrent requests for their services. If we want to get more sophisticated, we could add transaction management, load balancing, and fine-grained security to the list. In other words, we need a program that takes raw class libraries and transforms them into a multiuser server environment. We're talking about the equivalent of a TP Monitor for objects. So who does this type of work? The answer is the *Object Adapter.*

What's an Object Adapter?

The Object Adapter is the primary mechanism for an object implementation to access ORB services (see Figure 21-13). It provides a total environment for running the server application. Here are some of the services provided by the Object Adapter:

1. ***Registers server classes with the Implementation Repository.*** You can think of the Implementation Repository as a persistent store that is managed by the Object Adapter. Object Implementation classes are registered and stored in the Implementation Repository.

2. ***Instantiates new objects at run time***. The Object Adapter is responsible for creating object instances from the implementation classes. The number of instances created is a function of the incoming client traffic loads. The Adapter is responsible for balancing the supply of objects with the incoming client demands.

3. ***Generates and manages object references***. The Object Adapter assigns references (unique IDs) to the new objects it creates. It's responsible for mapping between the implementation-specific and ORB-specific representations of object references.

4. ***Broadcasts the presence of the object servers.*** The Object Adapter may broadcast the services it provides on the ORB—or it may respond to directory type queries from the ORB core. It is in charge of letting the outside world know of the services it manages. Eventually, we expect to see some tight levels of integration with global directory services such as X.500.

5. ***Handles incoming client calls.*** The Object Adapter interacts with the top layer—typically, an RPC—of the ORB core communication stack, peels off the request, and hands it to the interface stub. The stub is responsible for interpreting the incoming parameters and presenting them in a form that's acceptable to the object's method invocation.

6. ***Routes the up-call to the appropriate method.*** The Object Adapter is implicitly involved in the invocation of the methods described in the stubs (or the skeleton). For example, the Object Adapter may be involved in activating the implementation. And it can authenticate the incoming requests.

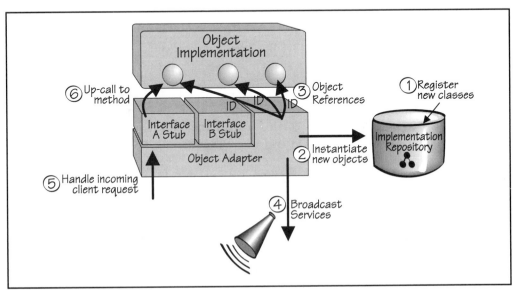

Figure 21-13. The Structure of a Typical Object Adapter.

An Object Adapter defines how an object is activated. This can be done through the creation of a new process, through the creation of a new thread within an existing process, or through the reuse of an existing thread or process.

BOA and Other Object Adapters

A server could support a variety of object adapters to satisfy different types of requests. For example, an Object Database (ODBMS) may want to implicitly register all the fine-grained objects it contains without issuing individual calls to the Object Adapter. In such a case, it doesn't make sense for an Object Adapter to maintain a per-object state. The ODBMS may want to provide a special-purpose Object Adapter that interfaces with the ORB core, and at the same time meets its special requirements. However, OMG prefers not to see a proliferation of Object Adapter types. To avoid this proliferation, CORBA specifies a *Basic Object Adapter (BOA)* that "can be used for most ORB objects with conventional implementations."

CORBA requires that a BOA adapter be available in every ORB. Object implementations that use it should be able to run on any ORB that supports the required language bindings. CORBA requires that the following functions be provided in a BOA implementation:

■ An Implementation Repository that allows the installation and registration of applications. It also contains information describing the application.

■ Mechanisms for generating and interpreting object references; activating and deactivating object implementations; and invoking methods and passing them their parameters.

■ A mechanism for authenticating the client making the call. BOA does not enforce any specific style of security. It guarantees that for every object or method invocation, it will identify the client (or principal) on whose behalf the request is performed. What to do with this information is left to the implementation.

■ Activation and deactivation of implementation objects.

■ Method invocations through stubs.

BOA supports traditional and object-oriented applications. It does not specify how methods are packaged or located—this could be done through DLLs or a system call at startup that identifies the location of the methods. To get the widest application coverage, CORBA defines four activation policies that specify the rules a given implementation follows for activating objects. Think of them as scheduling policies. The four policies are: *shared server, unshared server, server-per-method*, and *persistent server*.

BOA Shared Server

In a *shared server* activation policy, multiple objects may reside in the same program (i.e., process). The server is activated by BOA the first time a request is performed on any object implemented by that server (see Figure 21-14). When the server has initialized itself, it notifies BOA that it is prepared to handle requests by calling *impl_is_ready*. All subsequent requests are then delivered to this server process; BOA will not activate another server process for that implementation. The server handles one request at a time and notifies BOA via a *deactivate_obj* call when it finishes processing a request. When the process itself is ready to terminate, it notifies BOA by issuing a *deactivate_impl* call.

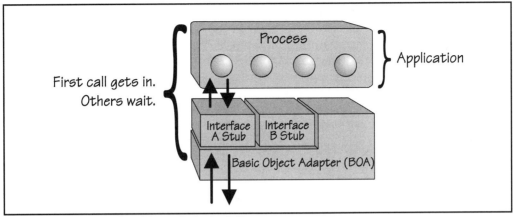

Figure 21-14. The BOA Shared Server Activation Policy.

BOA Unshared Server

In an *unshared server* activation policy, each object resides in a different server process. A new server is activated the first time a request is performed on the object (see Figure 21-15). When the object has initialized itself, it notifies BOA that it is prepared to handle requests by calling *obj_is_ready*. A new server is started whenever a request is made for an object that is not yet active, even if a server for another object with the same implementation is active. A server object remains active and will receive requests until it calls *deactivate_obj*.

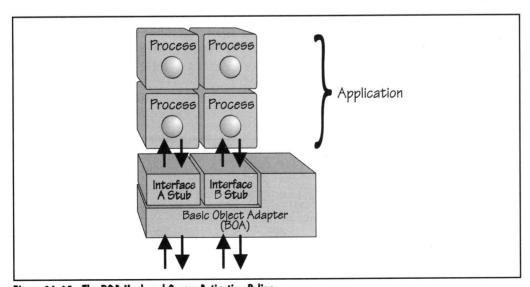

Figure 21-15. The BOA Unshared Server Activation Policy.

BOA Server-per-Method

In a *server-per-method* activation policy, a new server is always started each time a request is made. The server runs only for the duration of the particular method (see Figure 21-16). Several server processes for the same object—or even the same method of the same object—may be concurrently active. A new server is started for each request, so it's not necessary for the implementation to notify BOA when an object is ready or deactivated. BOA activates a new process for each request, whether or not another request for that operation or object is active at the same time.

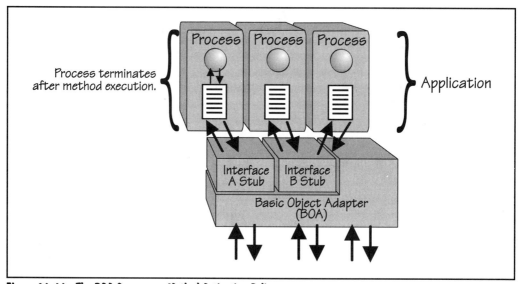

Figure 21-16. The BOA Server-per-Method Activation Policy.

BOA Persistent Server

In a *persistent server* activation policy, servers are activated by means outside BOA (see Figure 21-17). BOA may start the server application, which then notifies BOA that it's ready to accept work by means of an *impl_is_ready* call. BOA treats all subsequent requests as shared server calls; it sends activations for individual objects and method calls to a single process. If no implementation is ready when a request arrives, an error is returned for that request.

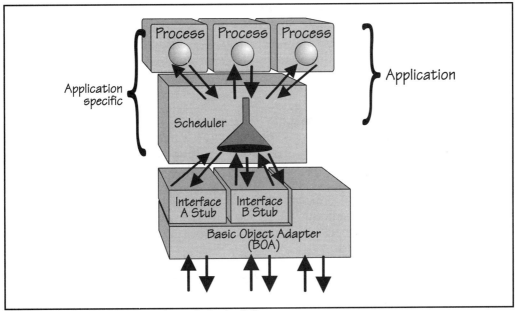

Figure 21-17. The BOA Persistent Server Activation Policy.

The CORBA Interface Repository

The Interface Repository is an online database of object definitions. These definitions may be captured directly from an IDL-compiler or through APIs—CORBA doesn't care how the information gets there. The CORBA specification, however, details how the information is organized and retrieved from the repository. It does that in a *very creative* fashion by specifying a set of classes whose instances represent the information that's in the repository. The class hierarchy mirrors the IDL specification. The result is a highly flexible object database that keeps track of collections of objects organized along the same lines as the IDL. Of course, all the objects in the repository are compiled versions of the information that's in an IDL source file.

Why is an Interface Repository needed anyway? Because an ORB needs to understand the definition of the objects it is working with. One way to get these definitions is by incorporating the information into the stub routines we introduced earlier. The other way to get this information is through a dynamically accessible Interface Repository. What does an ORB do with the information in the repository? It can use the object definitions to do the following:

■ **Provide type-checking of request signatures**. The parameter types are checked regardless of whether the request is issued using dynamic APIs or through a stub. Signatures define the parameters of a method and their type.

■ **Assist in the creation of inter-ORB gateways**. The information in the repository can be used to translate requests that go across heterogeneous ORBs.

■ **Provide information to dynamic clients and tools**. Clients use the interface repository to create on-the-fly method invocations. Tools—such as class browsers, application generators, and compilers—can use the information to obtain inheritance structures and class definitions at run time.

Interface Repositories can be maintained locally or managed as departmental or enterprise resources; they serve as valuable sources of information on class structures. An ORB may have access to multiple Interface Repositories.

Is CORBA Ready for Prime Time?

Soapbox

Interoperability is the customer organizations' single most requested upgrade to CORBA.

— Richard Soley,
VP of Technology, OMG (May, 1993)

Transactions are the primary concern of our customers, seconded by interoperability, after they get the basic distributed object transparency the ORB provides.

— Cliff Reeves,
Director of Objects, IBM (May, 1993)

The best way to answer the question is to look at what's missing from CORBA, when the missing pieces can be expected, and what, if any, are the showstoppers in the technology. Richard Soley and Cliff Reeves started a list of what's missing in CORBA; now let's complete it:

Interoperability standards for ORBs. CORBA took an "anything goes" approach to creating ORBs. Now they have the problem of how to get these ORBs to communicate with each other. CORBA must deal with the typical NOS level communication stuff—including authentication, object FAPs, directory services, federated naming, and stacks—and it must deal with object naming and representation issues across the different vendor implementations. OMG would have been much better off building on top of DCE or some existing NOS platform.

■ *What happened to ACID motherhood?* In Part 5, we established that it would be insane to build client/server systems without transaction protection. The anemic BOAs are nowhere close to providing the functionality of a TP Monitor: process management, load balancing, transaction protection, high availability, etc. They're obviously not ready for mission-critical prime time.

■ *Where's MOM?* MOM is extremely important in heterogeneous environments. We absolutely need object messaging queues on both the client and the server.

■ *BLOBs.* The current CORBA standard has almost nothing to say about BLOBs and multimedia objects.

■ *Broadcast.* The current CORBA standard does not support broadcast or multicast, which are needed in groupware applications, for systems management and for the creation of ORB-mediated object bazaars.

■ *Shared object concurrency control, locking, versioning, and replicas.* CORBA needs to address these issues to be on par with other client/server architectures.

■ *Persistent object support.* How is the object state saved and restored between machine shutdowns? The Implementation Repository is a first step, but it is nowhere close to providing a persistent store for objects.

■ *Object interchange standard.* In the future, objects will be able to roam across machines. General Magic does some of that today. We need standards that specify object interchanges.

■ *Certification suites.* What does it mean to be CORBA-compliant? What are the levels of compliance? Who's going to provide the seal of approval?

■ *Support for fine-grained objects.* How does CORBA deal with millions of small objects? Who manages the object references? How are these references stored persistently?

That's a pretty nasty list of deficiencies in the current CORBA 1.1 specification. So what's OMG doing about it? This may come as a surprise, but they're really on top of the majority of these issues. Most of the action is outside the ORB; it has shifted to the Object Services—including naming, event services, lifecycle management, concurrent access, persistent stores, object replication, and transactions. We'll be covering Object Services in the next chapter. The ORB is limited to providing the basic distributed infrastructure. The ORB 2.0 committee is addressing the interoperability question (through gateways). OMG is subcontracting X/Open for a set of CORBA-certification test suites. In addition, it is working on a more complete definition of the Implementation Repository, and it is looking at broadcast and MOM (but we don't expect them until ORB 3.0).

Are there any showstoppers? As far as consortia go, OMG is very proactive and has an excellent technical staff. But it's still a vendor-dominated consortium—it costs $50k per year to be a full-voting member—and vendors have their own agendas of what standards should cover and, more importantly, not cover. For example, vendors prefer to provide interoperability through gateways to preserve their current product investments. For the same reason, vendors don't want any changes to the ORB or APIs; the major architectural changes go into the Object Services.

In the long run, these are all minor issues. Are there any real technical showstoppers? From our vantage point, there appears to be solutions to all the issues we raised, with one exception: Can ORBs handle fine-grained objects? We don't have enough experience at this time with ORBs to answer this question. The current BOA is certainly not capable of dealing with millions of fine-grained objects. For example, how do you handle a database of one million bank accounts where each account is an object? The ODBMS people have working solutions, but they did that by bypassing BOA and even the ORB itself. We will return to this issue after we cover ODBMSs.

So are ORBs ready for prime time? They're getting there. You can use the current generation of ORBs in homogeneous environments to develop a better understanding of distributed object technology and encapsulate some of your key legacy applications with object wrappers. The current ORBs will help you create and manage a consistent set of distributed interfaces to all your important networked applications, tools, utilities, and medium-grained objects. The ORB becomes the "great integrator." Object-oriented production applications with fine-grained distributed objects will come *later*. These are the applications that will ultimately revolutionize the way we do client/server computing. ❏

Chapter 22

Distributed Object Services

OMG envisions a day where users of software start up applications as they start up their cars, with no more concern about the underlying structure of the objects they manipulate than the driver has about the molecular construction of gasoline.

— *Object Management Architecture Guide* (September, 1992)

An ORB by itself doesn't have all it takes for objects to interoperate at the *application* level. The ORB is like a telephone exchange—it provides the basic mechanism for brokering object requests. All other services are provided by objects with IDL interfaces that reside on top of the ORB. The IDL and ORB provide the function of a "software bus"; the services and end-user object applications plug into this bus. We've finally reached a point where we don't have to introduce more layers of infrastructure—you simply plug your objects into the ORB and play them.

As we explained in the last chapter, OMG is working hard on defining object services. Its *Object Management Architecture* separates services into two categories: the system-oriented *Object Services* that each ORB must provide, and optional *Common Facilities* that are more end-user oriented. Vendors are expected to package both types of services in *system frameworks*. A budding object component "cottage industry" is expected to provide application object classes (or even frameworks) that plug directly into CORBA-compliant ORBs. All these services take advantage of the inherent self-describing nature of objects and the uniform interfaces they provide.

This chapter provides a brief introduction to the OMG Object Services (the white area in Figure 22-1). We first cover the Object Services that became OMG standards in late 1993 and early 1994—including Lifecycle, Naming, Persistence, and Event Notification. These services provide very basic functions that are needed by all distributed object applications (and services). We also speculate on what's coming beyond that.

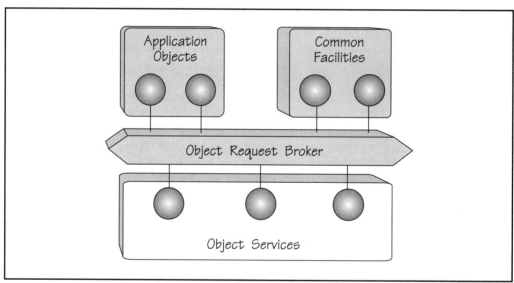

Figure 22-1. The Object Services and Common Facilities.

DISTRIBUTED OBJECT SERVICES

In CORBA-compliant ORB environments, distributed object services are classes of IDL-defined objects that provide useful middleware functions for all objects. These are functions that each application would have to recreate if they didn't already exist. More specifically, these functions help manage, distribute, store, exchange, find, copy, protect, and version objects on a network. Some of the services—for example, directory and protection—may already be provided by NOSs. If that's the case, they may simply be encapsulated with IDL-defined wrappers and used "as is." In other words, OMG is not trying to reinvent *all* the client/server middleware;

however, it wants all the relevant existing services to be "objectified" so that they can be accessed via ORBs. This is classical "hammer and nails" OMG stuff.

WHICH DISTRIBUTED OBJECT SERVICES?

Table 22-1 provides a list of object services OMG is currently working on (or considering). The "objects" in the table refer to code that responds to an IDL-defined interface. In addition to the object services described in the table, the OMG *Object Services Architecture* identifies a need for *system-related* object services including archive, backup/restore, startup, installation, operational controls, replication, threads, and time. These services may end up in a future ORB specification. Some of these services are also being addressed by NOS and distributed system management standards.

Table 22-1. The OMG Object Services.

Service	Function
Object Lifecycle	Provides functions for managing object creation, deletion, copying, and equivalence.
Object Persistence	Makes an object instance live (or persist) beyond the lifetime of the process that created it or the client applications that access it.
Object Events	Sends event notifications to interested objects.
Object Naming	Supports the mapping of meaningful names to objects.
Object Security	Provides access control list protection on objects and interfaces.
Object Relationships	Supports associations between two or more objects and defines containment relationships.
Object Transactions	Extends ACID properties to objects.
Object Concurrency Control	Mediates the concurrent access to one or more objects by one or more objects.
Object Externalization	Deals with the issues of external and internal object representations.
Object Data Interchange	Supports the exchange of some or all of an object's state information between two objects.
Object Licensing	Provides hooks for enforcing license management on object classes (for example, how many objects of a given class can be instantiated).
Object Trading	Matches available services to the services needed by a client.

Table 22-1. The OMG Object Services. (Continued)

Service	Function
Object Query	Supports operations on sets and collections of object attributes. The queries return sets and collections. The service also supports the indexing of objects.
Object Change Management	Manages the consistent evolution of objects, including versioning and configuration management.
Object Properties	Provides dynamic named attributes associated with an object.

The Event, Lifecycle, and Naming Services became OMG standards in September 1993. The object services bring together some of the best distributed technology in the industry. For the first time, a common IDL language is used to define services that can incrementally be added to CORBA-compliant ORBs. A wide coalition of vendors are using this common language and infrastructure to build the next generation of distributed services. Vendors use the IDL to define the interfaces and protocols they can all live with; they can then compete with implementations.

THE OBJECT EVENT SERVICE

The *Object Event Service* allows objects to dynamically register or unregister their interest in specific events. An *event* is an occurrence within an object specified to be of interest to one or more objects. A *notification* is a message sent to the interested parties informing them that a specific event occurred. Normally, the object generating the event doesn't have to know who the interested parties are. This is all handled by the Event Service, which creates a loosely-coupled communication channel between objects that don't know much about each other. Events are more loosely-coupled than RPC but less loosely-coupled than MOM.

The event service defines two roles for objects: suppliers and consumers. The *suppliers* produce events and the *consumers* process them via event-handlers. Events are communicated between suppliers and consumers using standard CORBA requests. In addition, there are two models for communicating event data: push and pull. In the *push model* the supplier of events takes the initiative and initiates the transfer of event data to consumers. In the *pull model*, the consumer takes the initiative and requests event data from a supplier. An *event channel* is an intervening object that is both a supplier and consumer of events. It allows multiple suppliers to communicate with multiple consumers asynchronously and without knowing about each other. An event channel is a standard CORBA object that sits on the ORB and decouples the communications between suppliers and consumers.

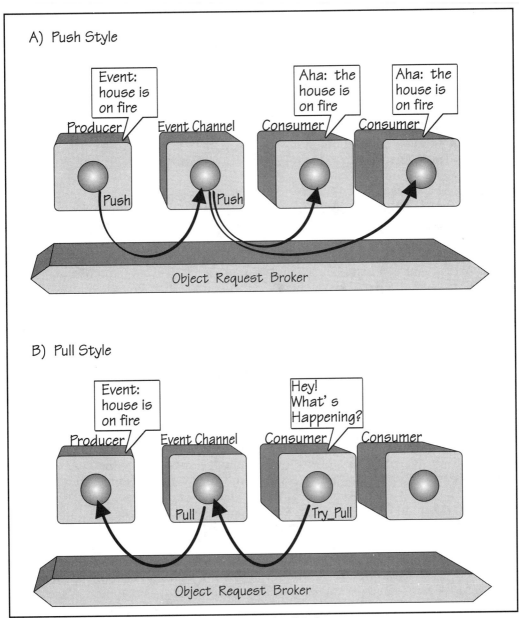

Figure 22-2. The OMG Event Notification Service: Push and Pull Styles.

The event channel supports both the "push and pull" event notification models (see Figure 22-2):

- With the ***push model***, the supplier issues a *push* method invocation on the event channel object; the event channel, in turn, pushes the event data to the consumer objects. A consumer can stop receiving events by invoking a *disconnect* method on the event channel. The consumer invokes an *add_push_consumer* method on the event channel to register its interest in some event type.

■   With the ***pull model***, the consumer issues a *pull* method invocation on the event channel object; the event channel, in turn, pulls the event data from the supplier. Using the *try_pull* method, the consumer can periodically poll for events. A supplier can stop accepting requests for supplying events by invoking a *disconnect* method on the event channel. The supplier issues an *add_push_supplier* method on the event channel to register its object reference and offer its services.

An event channel can communicate with a supplier using one style of communication, and it can communicate with a consumer using a different style of communication.

The generic event channel object does not understand the contents of the data it's passing. It leaves it up to the producers and consumers to agree on common event semantics. However, the Event Services also support a *Typed Event* model that allows applications to describe the contents of events using the IDL. The parameters passed must be input only; no information is returned. Typed events support both the pull and push model. Using the IDL, you can define special event types—for example, document or system management events. Consumers can then subscribe to a particular event type; typing becomes a powerful means of filtering event information. You can track the exact events you're interested in (it's a rifle instead of a shotgun).

The event interface supports multiple levels of service (for example, different levels of reliability). A persistent store of events may be supplied by the event channel object as part of its service (for example, some key events may be stored for up to a week or whatever). The event channels are *well-known objects*. They can serve as anchor points to help objects discover each other at run time. The consumers and suppliers of events use the standard CORBA IDL interfaces—no extensions are required.

In summary, the Event Service introduces a minimalist form of MOM communications into CORBA. It is minimalist because it doesn't support message priorities, filters, rich message typing, transaction protection, reception confirmation, time-to-live stamps, or sophisticated queue management. The channel objects make it easier to develop groupware applications and to help objects discover each other. Event typing allows you to zoom-in on the events of interest. The fan-in and fan-out capabilities of event channel objects can serve as a broadcast or multicast system, which can help create online object bazaars. The Event Service is extremely useful; it provides a foundation for creating a new genre of distributed object applications.

THE OBJECT NAMING SERVICE

The Object Naming Service is the principal mechanism for objects on ORB-based systems to locate other objects. *Names* are humanly recognizable values that identify an object. The naming service maps these human names to object references. A name-to-object association is called a *name binding*. A *naming context* is a namespace in which the object is unique. To *resolve a name* means to find the object associated with the name in a given context. To *bind a name* is to create a name-to-object association for a particular context. In other words, we're creating federated naming services for objects. It should be "deja vu" for readers of this book (if not, see Part 3). The Object Naming Service was originated by 15 companies that go under the name of JOSS, which stands for Joint Object Services Submission. It became an OMG standard in September 1993.

The Object Naming Service does not try to reinvent the wheel. It was designed to be built on top of existing name and directory services such as the DCE CDS, ISO X.500, or Sun NIS+. The service supports naming hierarchies that allow clients to navigate through different naming context trees in search of the object they're looking for. Objects can register their characteristics with the Naming Service to help clients locate them through searches on attributes.

Figure 22-3 shows the two classes—**NamingContext** and **BindingIterator**—that implement the Naming Service and the methods (or interfaces) they export. The binding methods add and destroy names and contexts within a naming hierarchy. After they're named, objects can be found using the *resolve* method. The *list*

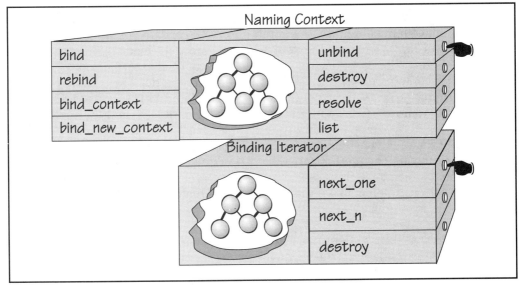

Figure 22-3. The OMG Object Naming Service.

method allows a client to iterate through a returned set of names; the iteration is done using *next_one* and *next_n*; and *destroy* frees the iteration after it is complete.

In summary, the Object Naming Service is provided by instances of two object classes that export methods for managing namespaces and querying and navigating through them. These objects live on the ORB and can be implemented by encapsulating existing procedural naming services with CORBA wrappers. The OMG simply defines the interfaces to these services, not the implementation.

THE OBJECT LIFECYCLE SERVICE

The Object Lifecycle Service provides operations for creating, copying, moving, and deleting objects. All the operations must handle associations between groups of related objects. This includes containment and reference relationships, as well as the enforcement of referential integrity constraints between objects. The lifecycle services provide an important element of the infrastructure required to support *nomadic* objects.

Let's walk through an example of how the lifecycle operations are implemented on an object that has explicit associations with other objects. Figure 22-4 shows a document object that contains one or more page objects, which in turn contain multimedia and text objects. The document is stored in a folder object and *references* a catalog object that contains an entry for it. The Lifecycle Service maintains a graph of all these associations.

A "deep move" causes the document to be moved along with all its dependent objects (the pages and their contents); the reference in the catalog is updated; and the document gets removed from the source folder and gets inserted into the target folder (see Figure 22-5). Likewise, when the document is externalized to a file, all the objects it contains go with it. When the document is deleted, its page objects and the graphic objects they contain are also deleted. The references to the document are removed from both the catalog and the folder (see Figure 22-6).

Clients have a simple view of Lifecycle operations. In the example in Figure 22-4, the clients simply invoke methods to move, copy, delete, externalize, and internalize the document object; all the associated objects are handled transparently. The lifecycle service implementation must be able to handle simple containment and reference relationships.

To create a new object, a client must find a *factory object* (meaning an object that knows how to instantiate an object of that class), issue a create request, and get back an object reference. A client can also create an object by cloning an existing object using a template. The factory objects must allocate resources, obtain object

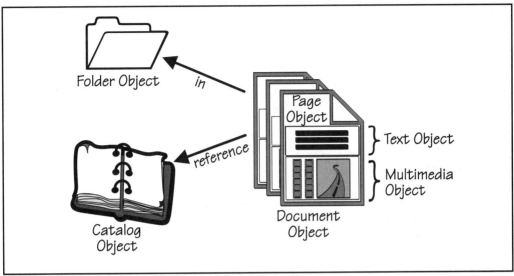

Figure 22-4. Object Lifecycle Services Must Handle Associated Objects.

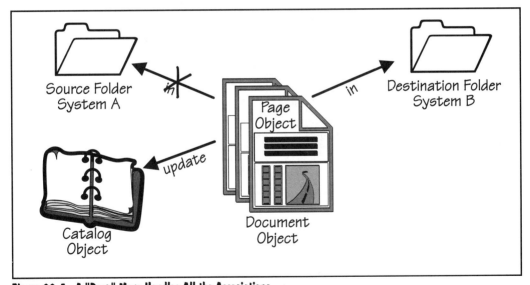

Figure 22-5. A "Deep" Move Handles All the Associations.

references, and register the new objects with the Object Adapter and Implementation Repository. When an object is copied across machines, the factory object on the target node is involved.

Figure 22-7 shows the three class interfaces defined by the OMG specification for providing Lifecycle services. The **LifeCycleObject** defines the copy, move, and

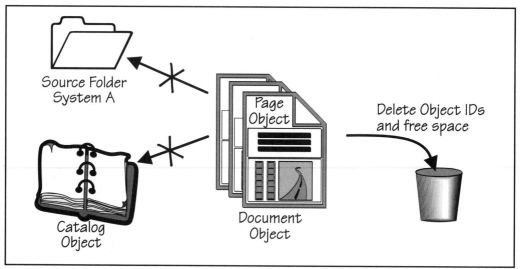

Figure 22-6. Delete Removes Objects and Dependents and Manages References.

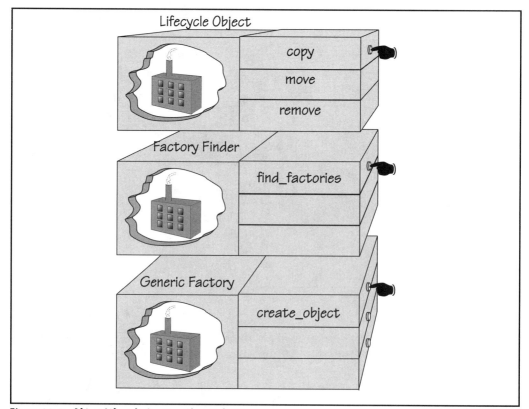

Figure 22-7. Object Lifecycle Services Class Definitions.

remove operations; it provides the client's primary view of lifecycle operations on target objects. The *copy* operation makes a copy of the object and returns an object reference; the *move* operation allows the object to roam to any location within the scope of the factory finder; and the *remove* operation deletes the object. The **FactoryFinder** defines an interface for finding factories. Because every object requires different resource information for its creation, it's impossible to define a single factory interface for all objects. The **GenericFactory** simply defines a general *create_object* operation.

THE OBJECT PERSISTENCE SERVICE

The Object Persistence Service allows objects to "persist" beyond the application that creates the object or the clients that use it. The lifetime of an object could be relatively short or indefinite. The service allows the state of an object to be saved in a persistent store and restored when it's needed (see Figure 22-8). The state of the object can be cached in local memory; data access speeds in this case are comparable to a native programming language. The caching is done transparently.

The Object Persistence Service is the result of the merging of the IBM and SunSoft submissions to the OMG (see the next Soapbox). The result is a specification that can accommodate a variety of storage services including SQL, Object Databases, document filing systems (like Bento), and others. The Persistence Service defines the interface to data as a collection of objects using IDL-defined interfaces. The implementations of the interface can be lightweight file systems or heavyweight full-featured SQL or Object Database systems. The idea was to create an open implementation that meets the different persistent storage requirements of objects—it encompasses the needs of large-grained objects (such as documents) as well as fined-grained objects (such as SQL table rows).

The Object Persistence Service can accommodate different levels of client involvement. At one extreme, the service can be made transparent to client applications. At the other extreme, client applications can use storage-specific protocols that surface all the details of the underlying persistence storage mechanism. Again, the idea is to accommodate different object needs: Some objects need a fine-grain level of control over their persistent store, and for others ignorance is pure bliss. The object has the choice of how much persistent data management it wants to delegate to the service.

Figure 22-9 shows the components of the Object Persistence Service. Let's quickly review what they each do starting from the top down:

■ **Persistent Objects (POs)** are objects whose state is persistently stored. Objects can be made persistent by inheriting (through the IDL) the **Persistent Object** class behavior. The service also provides a "back door" to persistence

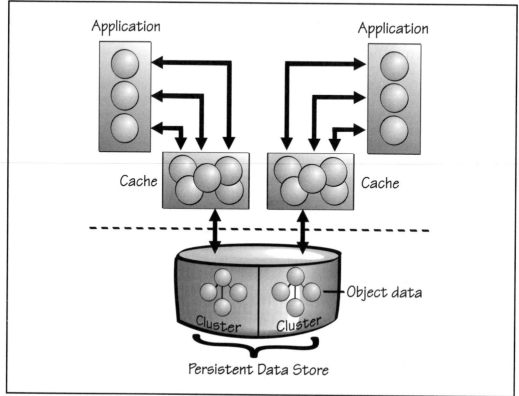

Figure 22-8. An Example of a Persistent Object Store.

using *persistent factories* instead of the IDL (i.e., all objects created through these factories are persistent). Every persistent object has a *Persistent Identifier (PID)* that describes the location within a datastore of that object using a string identifier.

■ ***Persistent Object Manager (POM)*** is an implementation-independent interface for persistence operations. It insulates the POs from a particular Persistent Data Service. The POM can route the calls to the appropriate Persistent Data Service by looking at information that's encoded in the PID. A Persistent Storage Service has a single POM that typically sits between the objects and the Persistent Data Services.

■ ***Persistent Data Services (PDSs)*** are interfaces to the particular datastore implementations. The PDSs perform the actual work of moving data between an object and a datastore. The PDSs export a set of uniform IDL-specified interfaces and an implementation-dependent *protocol*. The protocol provides a mechanism for getting data in and out of an object. The Persistent Object Service currently specifies three protocols: *Direct Attribute (DA)*, *Object*

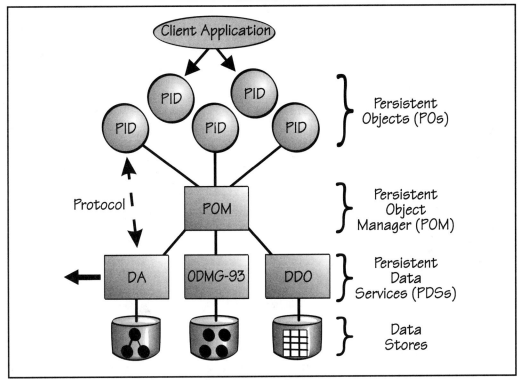

Figure 22-9. The Components of the OMG Object Persistence Service.

Database Management Group (ODMG-93), and *Dynamic Data Object (DDO)*.

- **DataStores** are the implementations that store an object's persistent data independently of the address space containing the object.

In a nutshell, the Persistent Storage Service provides different levels of abstraction that hide different storage implementations (see Figure 22-10). For most applications, the persistent mechanism will be totally transparent. If you need more data intimacy, the POM provides a generic interface that allows different PDSs to plug-and-play transparently. The PDSs provide three generic interfaces coupled with implementation-specific protocols—that's where the rubber meets the road:

- The **Direct Access (DA) PSM** protocol is the basis of the original JOSS proposal; it provides direct access to persistent data using an IDL-like *Data Definition Language*.

- The **ODMG-93** protocol provides direct access from C++ using an ODMG-specific DDL. We cover ODMG in the Object Database chapter.

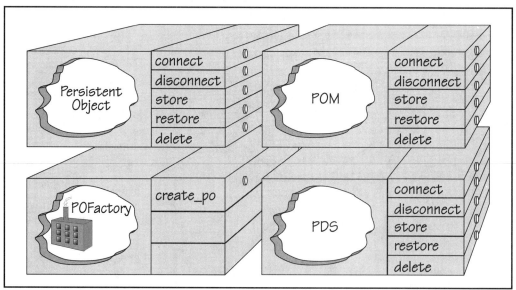

Figure 22-10. Object Persistence Service: The Main Interface Classes.

■ The ***Dynamic Data Object (DDO)*** protocol is a datastore-neutral representation of an object's persistent data; it defines a structure that contains all the data for an object.

How Standards Are Really Created

Soapbox

*T*hose IBM guys gave us a hard time.

> — **Unnamed friend,**
> **JOSS (January, 1994)**

*Y*ou're lucky we were persistent (no pun intended). We've done the world a service by standing up for the idea that objects can be stored in any form of persistent storage.

> — **Roger Sessions,**
> **IBM (January, 1994)**

The combination of the JOSS and IBM proposal for Object Persistence Services is more than just the merging of two proposals—it really combines the best of two worlds. The original JOSS proposal was centered around providing a transparent persistent store for C++ objects. The emphasis was on data objects—not CORBA objects. It was very much in line with the strategy of the Object Database vendors. The JOSS proposal even abandoned the IDL in favor of direct APIs to the objectstore. The idea was to maximize the persistent store performance of fine-grained C++ objects.

The IBM proposal (the work of Roger Sessions and Dan Chang) was a more traditional CORBA object approach that used the IDL to encapsulate the Persistent Object Services. It decoupled the client from the service and allowed different persistent stores to plug-and-play behind the interface. This means that the service could be used to encapsulate any persistent store—including SQL databases, Bento-like containers, file systems, or Object Databases. It's the standard OMG encapsulation stuff (hammer and nails).

The merger of the two proposals—an effort that lasted over six months—gave us the best of all worlds. This includes CORBA persistent objects with IDL interfaces, a wide choice of objectstore implementations, and fine-grained object performance. These are the components that we covered in this section.

But since we're on a Soapbox, let's give Roger and Dan a hand. They were really the underdogs, who as Spike Lee would put it, "did the right thing." JOSS had the formidable endorsement of 17 vendors. The IBM people couldn't even agree among themselves; they came in with two separate proposals—one from Roger (from IBM, Austin) and one from Dan (from IBM, San Jose). Even after Roger and Dan joined forces, everybody (even at IBM) felt their cause was totally hopeless. But they persevered (Roger can be tenacious). Eventually, about half the JOSS contingent, in a tumultuous meeting in Paris, felt there was enough technical merit (and benefits) in the Roger/Dan proposal to warrant a merger. As a result, we have another great OMG standard. ❏

Chapter 23

Compound Documents: OLE 2 and OpenDoc

By 1997 enterprise business documents will become the primary paradigm for capturing corporate information, challenging the dominance of record-oriented data. Compound document technology will become the overall framework for managing various non-record oriented information.

— Meta Group (February, 1994)

The OMG's *Common Facilities* will provide standards for objects that are closer to the end user. However, there's been very little activity from the OMG in this area—they were waiting for the first wave of Object Services to finalize so that they could build on top of that foundation. But, this is all changing. OMG fearlessly accepted the mission of standardizing *Compound Object Architectures*. As a result, the Common Facilities standardization effort may find itself in the midst of the *OpenDoc versus OLE 2.0* mini war. For most users, their first interaction with objects will be through these compound documents. So it is important to understand how this technology and the distributed CORBA infrastructure come together. In this chapter, we explain the compound document approach for objects. We then go over OLE 2 and OpenDoc (the two de facto standards for compound object documents), and finally, we see if it all fits with CORBA. It's like building a railway starting at the two ends of a continent—eventually, you want the rails to seamlessly come together at some intersection point.

WHAT'S A COMPOUND DOCUMENT?

Compound documents are documents composed of many different kinds of content, all of which share a single file. Several editors can work on a document at the same time.

— Kurt Piersol, OpenDoc Architect,
Apple Computers (March, 1994)

A compound document is a *container* for data that comes from a variety of sources, including other applications. The container provides the appropriate hooks to activate the foreign applications (or objects) that are associated with the separate data elements. It does that by directly *embedding* the foreign data within a document or by maintaining pointers—or *links*—in the document to the external data sources. In either case, the document is still editable by various applications; each sees its data in native format.

End users work with a single document in a single-viewing window. Multiple tools—such as editors, forms, database query dialogs, and paint programs—magically take over the document window when needed—that is, when their portion of the data needs to be worked on. For example, if you're working on a document within WordPerfect and double-click on a spreadsheet object, the WordPerfect menus magically become those of Excel—the editor becomes a spreadsheet right in the same window frame. Users can create compound documents with data of different formats, and then focus on the data rather than on the applications responsible for it. The compound document preserves the identity and behavior of the information it contains. Think of it as an object-oriented document-centric user interface.

Compound document technology facilitates this type of integration by defining a set of interfaces and run-time facilities through which applications can exchange data and invoke each other's services. They also provide protocols for sharing the viewing window and for navigating within the shared file container. A file becomes more than a stream of bytes; it must be divided into units of ownership and navigation that all the applications can understand. A simple file is transformed into a container system. Microsoft calls it "creating a file system within each file."

In summary, compound document technology provides the protocols that let the application managing a document communicate with the applications owning objects within the document. The protocols must also let these applications effectively share resources such as a document or a window on the screen. The trick is to make these protocols general enough to allow independently developed applications, with no prior knowledge of each other, to discover each other's existence and collaborate at run time. In the words of OpenDoc architect Kurt Piersol, "The whole point of a compound document is to be able to mix the types of content, and to create the boundaries that sort out where one kind of content ends and another begins. This must all be done without the parts losing either their identities or boundaries."

OLE 2.0 AND COM

OLE 2 is the first step in the evolution of Windows from the function call-based OS we have today to an object-oriented operating system in the future.

— *Kraig Brockshmidt,*
Author, Inside OLE 2,
(Microsoft Press, 1993)

In 1990, Microsoft introduced *Object Linking and Embedding (OLE)* technology as its basic strategy for integrating multiple applications and multimedia data types within a compound document framework. OLE 1 was a clumsy and slow protocol built on top of DDE. When an application was launched from within a compound document, it was given its own window and the data it needed was copied into its address space. There was no way for the application to directly access the document. OLE 2.0, introduced in 1993, fixed many of these shortcomings with a new object-encapsulation technology called the *Component Object Model (COM)*. COM is the foundation of "Window Objects"; it is a single-machine version of the technology that will be used in Cairo.

OLE 2.0 has over 350 COM-based API calls organized into 42 *interface classes*. Some of these calls introduce new functions; some simply mask the Windows API surface with a COM encapsulation layer—for example, the clipboard and file systems can now be manipulated as classes through COM. OLE is a complex product that provides a variety of functions that don't easily fit into a simple classification scheme. Now that we've put ourselves out on a limb, we offer Figure 23-1 as our best shot for what constitutes OLE 2.0 (it seems we enjoy living dangerously).

Let's go over the constituent OLE 2.0 pieces and see how they relate:

■ The *Compound Object Model (COM)* specifies interfaces between *component objects* within a single application or between applications. COM, like CORBA, separates the interface from the implementation. Like CORBA, it provides APIs for dynamically discovering the interfaces an object exports and how to load

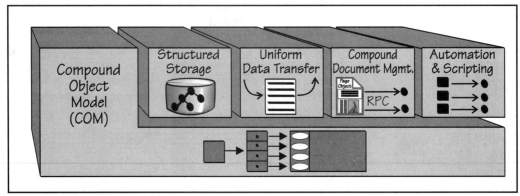

Figure 23-1. The Components of OLE 2.

and invoke them. Like CORBA, COM requires that all shared code be declared using object interfaces (Microsoft even provides its own proprietary Interface Definition Language). Unlike CORBA, COM only provides *local* RPC facilities and does not support remote method invocations or distributed objects (i.e., it does not provide an ORB). COM provides an object factory, but its class model is very limited in the sense that it does not support inheritance or polymorphism. COM is mostly an encapsulation mechanism (see Figure 23-2). Clients use pointers to an array of function pointers known as a *virtual table (VTBL)*. The functions that are pointed to by the VBTL are the object's implementation methods. Each OLE object has one or more VBTLs that define the contract between the object implementation and its clients. COM provides the foundation on which the rest of OLE is built.

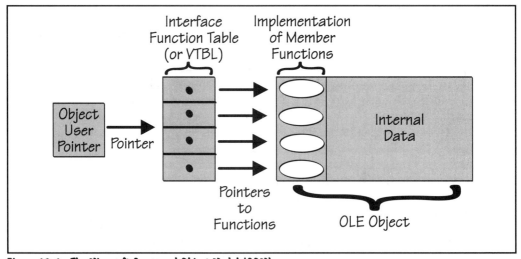

Figure 23-2. The Microsoft Compound Object Model (COM).

- The **Structured Storage System** provides a file system within a file (also known as DocFiles). It breaks the file into *storages*—that is, directories—and *streams*—that is, raw files or BLOBs. This internal directory system can be used to organize the contents of a document. OLE allows objects to control their own storage in the compound document. The directories describe the streams; the hierarchical structure makes it easy for OLE objects to navigate within the document. The Structured Storage System is packaged as 7 COM interface classes.

- The **Uniform Data Transfer Model** allows users to transfer data uniformly with drag and drop, copy and paste, or through API calls. The data can be represented in a variety of formats. OLE associates two types of data with a compound document: *presentation data* and *native data*. The presentation data is needed to display the object, while the native data is needed for editing. The Uniform Data Transfer is packaged as 6 COM interface classes (including drag and drop).

- The **Compound Document Management** is implemented as a document within a *container application* that seamlessly integrates data of different formats, such as bitmaps or sound clips. Each piece of integrated data, referred to as a *compound document object*, is created and maintained by its *object application*. (Warning: The term object used in this context is misleading. We're not dealing with OO objects or even COM objects.) Document objects can either be linked or embedded in the document. Embedded objects can be edited or activated *in place*. OLE 2 allows object applications to be invoked via local RPCs across address spaces or via DLLs in the same address space. The container applications manage storage and the window for displaying the document. The Compound Document Management function is packaged as 16 COM interface classes (including drag and drop).

- The **OLE Automation and Scripting** component allows applications to expose their COM interfaces for other applications and scripting languages to use in building custom solutions. An object can expose a set of commands and functions through its interfaces. Each command can take any number of parameters. OLE 2 provides a way for these objects to describe their interfaces. This function is particularly useful for creating system macros from within tools or scripting languages.

In summary, OLE 2 is much more than a compound document architecture. It includes a foundation for defining object interfaces independent of the implementation; it also introduces a primitive form of method invocation and object encapsulation. As Microsoft begins to lay the foundation for its object architecture, it will rely on OLE as the technology that can do everything OMG can (see next Soapbox).

OPENDOC

> *OpenDoc allows developers to move their existing applications to the compound document world and provides interoperability across Macintosh, OS/2, DOS, Windows, Taligent, and UNIX.*
>
> — *David Nagel, Senior VP,*
> *AppleSoft (September, 1993)*

OpenDoc is a set of APIs and software for doing compound documents. It is similar in scope and function to OLE 2, but it comes from Apple rather then Microsoft. Apple developed the technology, and has gathered partners to form a consortium for the care and feeding of this technology across multiple platforms. In September 1993, Apple—along with IBM, Novell, Oracle, Taligent, SunSoft, WordPerfect, and Xerox—announced the *Components Integration Laboratories (CI Labs)*. The purpose of CI Labs is to establish, promote, and certify OpenDoc and related compound document technologies. CI Labs technology will eventually integrate multimedia, three-dimensional models, text, graphics and other types of information in any application.

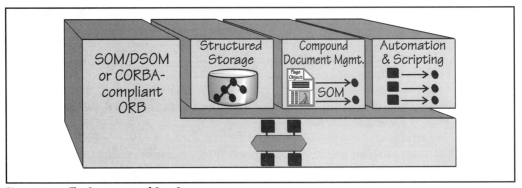

Figure 23-3. The Components of OpenDoc.

The initial CI Labs technology includes Apple's OpenDoc software for Windows, OS/2, Macintosh, and UNIX; Apple's Bento technology for the storage and interchange of multimedia information; Apple's Open Scripting Architecture (OSA) for the coexistence of multiple scripting systems; and IBM's System Object Model (SOM) architecture, a platform and language-independent run-time mechanism for dynamic object linking. We offer Figure 23-3 as our best shot for what constitutes OpenDoc's answer to OLE 2. (This is another one of those fearless attempts.) Let's go over the constituent pieces and see how they relate:

■ **SOM and DSOM** provide local and remote interoperability for OpenDoc objects. SOM is a language-independent, CORBA-compliant protocol for objects that communicate in a single address space or across address spaces on the same machine. DSOM allows SOM objects to communicate across networks—it's a CORBA-compliant ORB. SOM and DSOM support both static and dynamic method invocations. Static invocations using IDL stubs are for objects that know about each other at compile time; dynamic invocations are for objects that know nothing about each other at compile time and end up discovering each other's services at run time. DSOM will eventually support the Object Services introduced in Chapter 22. SOM and DSOM allow OpenDoc objects to communicate using powerful industry-standard protocols across address spaces in a single machine or across machines on a network. SOM/DSOM also support multiple inheritance on object classes. We cover SOM/DSOM in the product chapters.

■ **Bento Object Containers** provide a system of structured files; each file contains many streams. Each container may contain a number of document objects; each object can contain one or more draft objects. Bento—named after Japanese plates with compartments for different foods—defines a container format that can be used in files, network streams, clipboards, etc. Bento also defines an API that reads and writes the container format very efficiently. The Bento API is implemented in a library that currently runs on Macintosh, Windows, OS/2, and several Unix systems. A Bento container allows applications to store and retrieve collections of objects (both streams and piece-based). The container format is platform-neutral and can store data, regardless of its content. In a Bento document, each object has a persistent ID that moves with it from system to system. Bento also supports references between objects in different files (documents). If there are several drafts of a document, Bento only stores the incremental changes. All this makes Bento a good protocol for the interchange of compound documents, or groups of objects, between different platforms and applications.

■ **OpenDoc Compound Document Management** provides a container in which *parts* can be inserted. Parts are the fundamental building block of OpenDoc. Every part contains data—for example, spreadsheet parts contain spreadsheet cells with formulas, and video parts contain video clips. Every document has a top-level part in which all other parts are embedded. A part can contain other parts. *Part handlers* are the independent programs that manipulate and display a part type. Part handlers are divided into two types: editors and viewers. *Part editors* display a part's contents and provide a user interface for modifying that content. *Part viewers* allow a user to display and print a part's content but not edit it. *Frames* are areas of the display that represent a part. They also represent the part in the negotiations for space during the layout of a document. Bento gives each part its own data stream in persistent store. References can be made from one stream to another, enabling parts to be integrated into a single document. The parts call each other using SOM/DSOM.

■ *Open Scripting Architecture (OSA)* is modeled on the Mac's AppleScript. It defines about 14 polymorphic commands that tell a part what to do. For example, "next" can mean the next cell or the next word, depending on the type of part that receives the command. Each part is scriptable, allowing users to customize their applications with user-specific tasks. This is called *content-centered* scripting. A part handler must be prepared to provide at run time the list of objects it contains and the operations it supports. In addition, OpenDoc can deliver event messages from the scripting system to the part handlers. Scripting provides a medium for coordinating the work of parts in documents, and allows users and parts to work together to perform tasks. OpenDoc supports recordable macros that allow an application to record a user's actions and then save them to a user's preferred scripting language for later use.

CI Labs plans to make source code available to the industry for these technologies, and its sponsors plan to support the technologies across multiple platforms. Initial target platforms include Microsoft Windows, Macintosh, and OS/2, with plans to support UNIX systems. The CI Labs Consortium plans to make OpenDoc compatible with OLE. This means that an OpenDoc container would see an OLE object as an OpenDoc part, and vice versa. The translation layers are being developed by Wordperfect with help from Borland, Apple, and Lotus. The OpenDoc products will start becoming widely available in late-1994.

COMPARING OPENDOC AND OLE

Microsoft views the OMG's CORBA as the chief obstacle to OLE 2.0's success. And so, during most of 1993, Microsoft sought to demolish CORBA.

— **John R. Rymer, Editor,**
Distributed Computing Monitor
(January, 1994)

Table 23-1 provides a comparison of OpenDoc and OLE 2, based on the best information we have today. Clearly, OLE has the advantage of being here today. OpenDoc has the advantage of being vendor-independent and richer in function. OpenDoc, at least on paper, has a stronger object model: All objects are CORBA-based. Eventually, the two technologies may interoperate, meaning that users may be spared the pain of having to go through another standards war. However, developers will have to choose between a Microsoft standard and a multiplatform, multivendor standard.

Table 23-1. A Preliminary Comparison of OLE 2 and OpenDoc.

Feature	OLE 2	OpenDoc
Availability	Now.	Late 1994.
Ease of programming	Low.	Low.
Support for inheritance	No.	Yes.
Support for recordable macros with script generators	No.	Yes.
Platforms	Windows and Mac.	Windows, OS/2, Mac, and Unix.
Networking	Late 1994 using DEC's CORBA ObjectBroker.	Built-in using SOM/DSOM or other CORBA-compliant ORBs.
Source code licensing	Controlled by Microsoft.	Available to anyone via CI Labs consortium.
Content shape support	Non-overlapped rectangles only.	Overlapped rectangles, circular objects, and other irregular shapes—text can wrap around a variety of shapes.
Storage subsystem	Hierarchical structure within a DOS FAT file. CAIRO will provide true object store in 1995.	Bento containers—here today.

COM Versus CORBA

Soapbox

Microsoft's labeling of COM as an object model has drawn jeers from some corners of the industry. To many, the definition of object oriented includes support for inheritance. The object-purists have a point: Some developers value inheritance as a way to speed development of code. However, COM is aimed at construction of interfaces, not objects.

— John R. Rymer (January, 1994)

Underlying OLE and OpenDoc are two competing object models: Microsoft's COM and OMG's CORBA via SOM/DSOM. They're both trying to provide an infrastructure for objects to communicate. Currently, COM only operates within a single machine, while CORBA defines an elaborate architecture for ORBs and distributed Object Services. CORBA supports inheritance; COM doesn't. COM takes the unique position that inheritance is dangerous, citing the "fragile baseclass problem." COM's solution is to encapsulate a group of procedures with an array of pointers. For the rest of the industry, inheritance forms the basis of OO and frameworks; without it, you have simple encapsulation without object reuse. Inheritance allows an object to reuse code without duplication and without code redundancy. Paradoxically, Microsoft supports inheritance in its standalone class libraries—for example, its C++ Foundation Class Library.

In a bizarre turn of events, Microsoft and DEC announced (in late 1993) that they are linking OLE and DEC's CORBA-based ObjectBroker to provide distributed OLE 2. Client applications using OLE 2 will be able to access remote ORB-based servers via ObjectBroker V3 (available late 1994 as part of the Cairo Beta). When all this comes together, Microsoft will provide three object models: language-based class libraries for small objects; COM for larger objects; and indirectly ObjectBroker for CORBA. Which do you choose? And how do they play together?

The beauty of the OpenDoc/CORBA marriage is that the same object model is used for all objects—whether they're local or remote, fine-grained, or large-grained. It scales very gracefully from local to distributed objects. The COM versus CORBA debate transcends OLE and OpenDoc. Even though COM is currently single machine based, Microsoft plans to carry COM (and most of OLE 2.0) *in toto* to Cairo. OLE and COM on Cairo will provide the basis for Microsoft's future distributed computing environment. Chicago will participate as a client. The OLE 2.0 *Local RPC (LRPC)* will become a true RPC in Cairo and Chicago; it will allow OLE calls to be transparently routed over the network. We still don't know how these distributed OLE objects will be stored, located, secured, replicated, and managed; Microsoft has not revealed its plans for an ORB. We may get a better idea of what's "in plan" after the first beta of Cairo ships. What is clear, is that Microsoft is putting some form of distributed objects in its next generation of Windows products and it will be document-centric. It also looks like our industry is heading for a great distributed object showdown: COM versus CORBA. DEC will provide the proverbial gateway. ❑

Chapter 24

Object Database Management Systems

Object Database Management Systems (ODBMSs) provide a client/server architecture that is significantly different from Relational Database Management Systems (RDBMSs). ODBMSs take a revolutionary approach to shared data that's totally centered on the management of persistent objects. We encountered some of this technology in the OMG Object Services. Today, the ODBMS vendors claim they can provide efficient client/server access to fine-grained objects. The major ODBMS vendors recently released their *ODMG-93* standard; it is intended to become the SQL of the ODBMS world. Of course, with a common standard, the market for ODBMSs may take off like its SQL-based RDBMS counterpart. Many people in our industry—including Oracle's CEO Larry Ellison—believe that object databases may ultimately become the successors of RDBMSs.

So, will ODBMSs replace RDBMSs in the same way relational vendors replaced their hierarchical predecessors ten years ago? This is one of the questions we'll try and answer in this chapter (in a Soapbox, of course). But just to give you a preliminary idea, the Cowen Market Research firm believes the market for ODBMSs will grow to $430 Million by 1997 from $32 Million in 1992. In contrast, the RDBMS market is expected to grow to $6.8 Billion in 1997 from $2.7 Billion in 1992.[1] The numbers show that ODBMSs will grow very fast; however, their market size is dwarfed by RDBMSs. ODBMSs will grow in areas like multimedia, object repositories, and groupware—the next wave of client/server technology. The RDBMS vendors won't sit still either. All the major relational vendors have declared that they will incorporate support for objects as it's being defined in the SQL3 standard. According to Larry Ellison, Oracle8 will be fully object-based.

In this chapter, we first look at what an ODBMS is and what it does well. We look at it through the composite technology that's provided by five small but very dynamic ODBMS vendors (together, they own over 90% of the object database market). Then we go over the ODMG-93 standard that was created by these five vendors—incidentally, they all pledged to make their products ODMG-compliant in 1994. We'll look at how ODMG-93 compares with OMG's Object Services and SQL3. As part of living dangerously, we end the chapter with a Soapbox on RDBMSs versus ODBMSs.

WHAT'S AN ODBMS?

We define an ODBMS to be a DBMS that integrates database capabilities with object-oriented programming language capabilities. An ODBMS makes database objects appear as programming language objects, in one or more existing programming languages.

> — *Rick Cattel, Chairman ODMG-93,*
> *(Morgan Kaufman, 1993)*

---

[1] Source: **Cowen Research Report**, "Object Development Strategies" (September 15, 1993).

An ODBMS provides a persistent store for objects in a multiuser client/server environment. The ODBMS handles concurrent access to objects, provides locks and transaction protection, protects the objectstore from all types of threats, and takes care of traditional tasks such as backup and restore. What makes ODBMSs different from their relational counterparts is that they store objects rather than tables. Objects are referenced through *Persistent Identifiers (PIDs)*, which uniquely identify objects, and are used to create referential and containment relationships between them. Objects also enforce encapsulation and support inheritance. The ODBMS combines object properties with traditional DBMS functions such as locking, protection, transactions, querying, versioning, concurrency, and persistence.

Instead of using a separate language like SQL to define, retrieve, and manipulate data, ODBMSs use class definitions and traditional OO language (usually C++ and SmallTalk) constructs to define and access data. The ODBMS is simply a multiuser, persistent extension of in-memory language data structures (see Figure 24-1). In other words, the client is the C++ program; the server is the ODBMS—there are no visible intermediaries like RPCs or SQL. The ODBMS integrates database capabilities directly into the language.

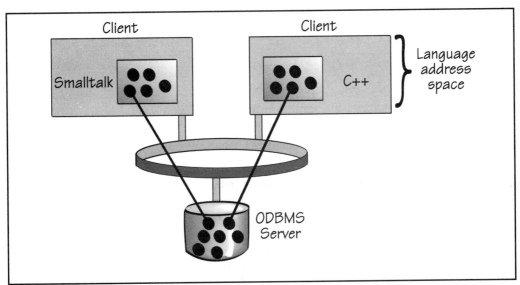

Figure 24-1. ODBMS: An Extension to OO Language Data Structures.

Of course, not everything is transparent to the language. By necessity, the ODBMS introduces extensions to the OO language such as container classes and operations that help you navigate through the containers. The ODMG-93 specification includes a full-blown *Object Manipulation Language (OML)* that supports queries and transactions. In an attempt to make the data-definition language neutral, ODMG-93 specifies a generic *Object Definition Language (ODL)*. As a result, the ODBMS, like SQL, requires a precompiler to process the object definitions, language extensions, and queries. The output of the compiler, like SQL plans, must also be linked to the ODBMS run time. So we've come a full circle.

WHAT'S AN ODBMS GOOD FOR?

Object databases have evolved more rapidly than any other database approach in history.

— *Dick Loveland,*
Director, Digital Consulting
(January, 1994)

For a long time, ODBMSs were an area of great interest to academicians and OO researchers. The earliest commercial ODBMSs made their appearance in 1986 with the introduction of Servio and Ontos. The three firms that currently lead the industry today—Object Design (ODI), Versant, and Objectivity—all entered the market in 1990. The ODBMS vendors first targeted applications that dealt with complex data structures and long-lived transactions—including computer-aided design, CASE, and intelligent offices. With the emergence of multimedia, group-ware, and distributed objects, the esoteric features of ODBMSs are now becoming mainstream client/server requirements. ODBMS technology fills the gap in the areas where relational databases are at their weakest—compound data, versioning, long-lived transactions, nested transactions, persistent object stores, inheritance, and user-defined data types.

Here's a list of the features that were pioneered by the ODBMS vendors (see Figure 24-2):

- **Freedom to create new types of information**. ODBMSs give you the freedom to create and store any data type using standard object descriptions. The data type is part of the object class definition. You can easily store arbitrarily complex data structures in an ODBMS (like container hierarchies). In contrast, traditional databases offer a limited number of hard-wired data types; complex structures must be converted into artificially "flattened" table representations.

- **Fast access**. ODBMSs keep track of objects through their unique IDs. A search can move directly from object to object without the need for tedious search-and-compare operations using foreign keys and other associative techniques.

- **Flexible views of composite structures**. ODBMSs allow individual objects to participate in a multiplicity of containment relationships, creating multiple

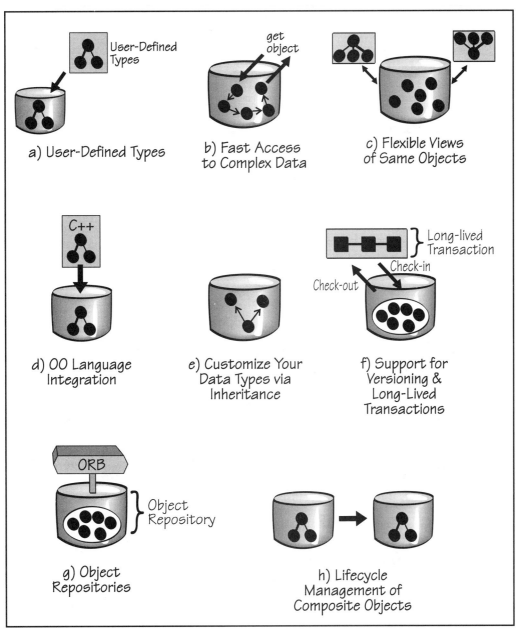

Figure 24-2. The Eight Wonders of ODBMS.

views of the same objects. Objects can maintain pointers to other objects in a very recursive manner; there's no limit to the different container relationships that can be assembled. A container typically maintains references to object IDs as opposed to the objects themselves—it's a form of *linking* as opposed to *embedding*.

- ■ **Tight integration with object-oriented languages.** ODBMSs present themselves as persistent extensions of the OO language's in-memory data structures. This allows them to minimize the impedance mismatch between programs and data while maintaining the strong encapsulation features that are inherent in OO languages. OO programmers should find an ODBMS to be a natural extension of their paradigm. ODBMSs provide the fastest and most direct access to objects they store; they also do a good job of preserving the characteristics of these objects. In contrast, RDBMSs require multiple transformations to represent the complex in-memory data structures of an OO language in tabular form. Relational systems can store objects, but they must first break them down into components and flatten them into structures that can fit in tables. SQL people, of course, may think that chasing corporate data via in-memory C++ pointers is a travesty. (We'll resume this discussion in the Soapbox.)

- ■ **Support for customizable information structures using multiple inheritance.** The ODBMS data types are defined using object classes. This means that any class can be subclassed to create custom structures that meet exceptional data needs. In addition, the ODBMS allows you to mix desirable characteristics from different classes and combine them using multiple inheritance. So the ODBMS extends the concept of object reuse through inheritance to the database.

- ■ **Support for versioning, nesting, and long-lived transactions.** Many commercial ODBMSs (including ObjectStore, Ontos, and Objectivity) support nested transactions and versioning for long-duration transactions. Objects can be grouped in configurations and managed as one transaction. ODBMSs are most popular in engineering design applications that require the management of complex documents. A typical Computer Aided Design (CAD) system also depends on version control to track the progressively more enhanced versions of an engineering design. Because of their long involvement with CAD, ODBMSs have perfected the art of versioning and long-lived transactions. ODBMSs have introduced the concept of *configurations*—meaning a collection of objects that are managed as a locking and versioning unit. CAD users typically *check out* a configuration of objects from the ODBMS, work on it, and *check in* their configuration as a new version.

- ■ **Repositories for distributed objects.** ODBMSs provide natural multiuser repositories for run-time objects. We believe the ODBMS vendors have a huge lead in providing solutions for concurrent access to large numbers (in the millions) of fine-grained objects with ACID protection. Eventually ODBMSs will provide true stores for *roaming objects* (a la General Magic's Telescript product); they serve as object servers for roaming objects—think of them as object Hiltons.

■ ***Support for life-cycle management of composite objects.*** ODBMSs have also perfected the art of managing composite objects as a unit. For example, a composite object can be assembled, disassembled, copied, stored, restored, moved, and destroyed. The ODBMS automatically maintains the relationships between the parts and treats the aggregate as a single component. This is also a result of their long involvement with CAD.

In summary, ODBMS vendors have had the luxury of being able to create pure object databases without being encumbered by debt to history. As a result, they were able to provide some missing pieces of technology needed to create the new generation of multimedia intensive databases with flexible data types. An ODBMS has the advantage over a relational database of knowing the overall structure of a complex object (like a document, for example) and sometimes its behavior (i.e., methods) as well; it can refer to any constituent object by its ID. In contrast, RDBMS vendors are attempting to provide object technology (with SQL3) by using a hybrid approach that decomposes the data from the object and then stores it in tables. This is an area where relational databases are at a disadvantage, but we'll defer that discussion to the Soapbox, too.

ODBMS CLIENT/SERVER IMPLEMENTATIONS

Most ODBMSs store the data part of an object but not the behavior [methods]...An object without behavior is just a complex data structure. It is not an object.

— Dr. Raymond Vorwerk,
Object Magazine (January, 1994)

There are several architectural alternatives to implementing ODBMSs on client/server networks. The effects of the architecture show up in various ways, even though the underlying programming model is the same. Mary Loomis, VP of Technology at Versant, defines two basic approaches for splitting the application between ODBMS clients and servers:

■ The ***object server*** balances the load between the client and the server. The client and server communicate by moving objects from the server's persistent store to the client's memory (see Figure 24-3). Clients request objects by specifying their Persistent IDs. The client component manages the object in the local memory; the server provides a multiuser ODBMS with transaction protection and locking. The unit of locking is an object. Methods can be executed on either the client or the server, depending on the location of the object. The processing of queries is done on the server.

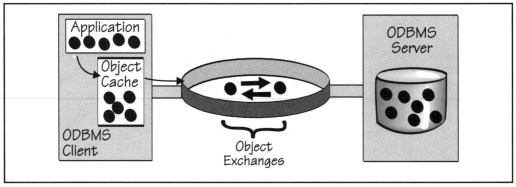

Figure 24-3. ODBMS Object Server Architecture.

■ The ***page server*** is a fat client approach that treats the ODBMS as a shared multiuser virtual memory store. The server pulls pages off the disk and moves them to the client's memory cache (see Figure 24-4). There are no persistent object IDs. All the intelligence and the object model is on the client. The page server locks pages, not objects. The methods are executed on the client where the object's logic resides. Queries are processed on the client, requiring the movement of candidate objects to the client's address space before applying selection criteria.

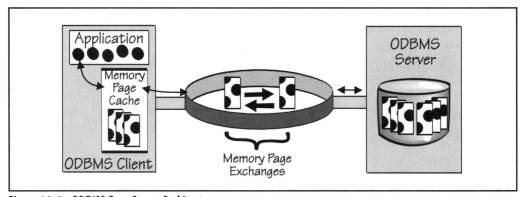

Figure 24-4. ODBMS Page Server Architecture.

We believe the object server is the better implementation. It allows objects to be moved to where they're needed. The access can be made transparent to the application (but it's done via RPCs). In contrast, a page server application needs to be aware of the distribution of objects across database systems. References within a single database are traversed as C++ pointers. However, references across databases require the use of remote functions or RPCs. This means that objects cannot be moved around to improve performance without changes to the application's code.

ODMG-93: THE NEW LINGUA FRANCA FOR ODBMS

The ODMG-93 standard, published in September 1993, is the ODBMS answer to SQL. The standard is the result of work done by the *Object Database Management Group (ODMG)*—a consortium that includes all the major ODBMS vendors. The ODMG is a working subgroup of the OMG and intends to submit its standard to both ISO and ANSI. In theory, the adoption of ODMG-93 should allow applications to work with ODBMSs from any of the major vendors. Today, most of the ODMG vendors are shipping systems that are compliant with large subsets of the specification. But the ODMG members have committed to bring their systems into *full* compliance within 18 months of the publication of the standards document.

ODMG-93 and CORBA

ODMG-93 is an extension of the OMG Object Persistence Service that defines how to implement the components of an efficient *Persistent Data Service (PDS)* for fine-grained objects. The standard uses the OMG object model as its basis. If you haven't done so, please review Chapter 22, "Distributed Object Services," for an explanation of where an ODBMS fits in the OMG Persistent Object Service architecture. The ODBMS's role in an ORB environment is to provide concurrent access to persistent stores capable of handling millions of fine-grained objects. To do that, the OMG refers to a special PDS protocol called ODMG-93. This protocol supplements the IDL-defined RPC invocations with direct API calls to the objectstore for faster access to data.

The ODBMS vendors are also actively promoting within the ORB 2 committee a *Library Object Adapter (LOA)* that provides direct API access via the ORB to specialized high-speed APIs. ODMG-93 states that the ODBMS vendors would like CORBA to standardize on a specialized version of LOA called the *Object Database Adapter (ODA)*. Figure 24-5, adapted from ODMG-93, shows the differences among BOA, LOA, and ODA—yes, more TLAs (three-letter acronyms) you can use to impress the folks back home.

The ODA should provide the ability to register subspaces of object identifiers with the ORB instead of all the millions of objects that are stored in the ODBMS. From the client's point of view, the objects in the registered subspace appear just as any other ORB-accessible objects. The ODA should allow for the use of direct access—as in the LOA—to improve the performance of ORB/ODBMS applications. To

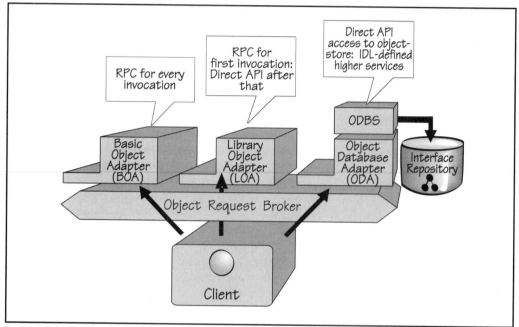

Figure 24-5. ODMG-93: ODBMS as Object Manager on an OMG ORB.

summarize, the ODBMS vendors are pushing CORBA to be more flexible when it comes to dealing with applications that manage millions of fine-grained objects. The new Object Persistence Service specification indicates that OMG got the message. But it remains to be seen if OMG will extend this new permissiveness to the ORB itself.

The ODMG-93 Components

The ODMG-93 standard consists of three major components (see Figure 24-6):

■ *Object Definition Language (ODL)*—ODMG-93 uses the OMG IDL as its data definition language. ODL is a "clean" superset of IDL in the sense that it defines elements that are not in IDL such as new collection classes and referential relationships. The ODL provides a programming language-independent way of describing metadata. The ODL is processed through a precompiler, which generates stubs that get linked to the ODBMS and the client language (C++ or SmallTalk). ODL provides interface and data definition portability across languages and ODBMS vendor platforms.

■ *Object Query Language (OQL)*—ODMG-93 defines a SQL-like declarative language for querying and updating database objects. It supports the most

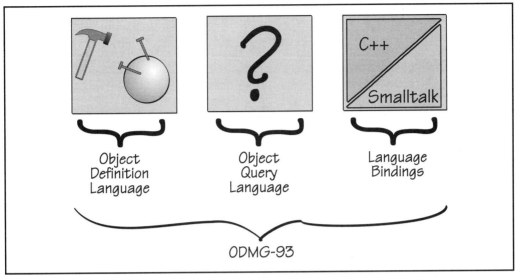

| Object Definition Language | Object Query Language | Language Bindings |

ODMG-93

Figure 24-6. ODMG-93 Components.

commonly used SQL SELECT structures including joins; it does not support SQL INSERT, UPDATE, or DELETE (it uses C++ or SmallTalk extensions for that). ODMG-93 purposely did not use the SQL3 semantics for objects because of "limitations in its data model and because of its historical baggage." However, they hope that OQL and SQL3 can converge at a future date. It's a nice thought, but highly doubtful. OQL provides high-level primitives to query different collections of objects—including *sets*, which means unordered collections with no duplicates; *bags*, which means unordered collections with duplicates; and *lists*, which are ordered collections. OQL also supports structures in queries—a very powerful construct.

■ *C++ and SmallTalk language bindings*—ODMG-93 defines how to write portable C++ or SmallTalk code that manipulates persistent objects. The standard defines C++ *Object Manipulation Language (OML)* extensions. The C++ OML includes language extensions for OQL, iterations for navigating through containers, and transaction support. The ODMG-93 people do not believe exclusively in a "universal" Data Manipulation Language (a la SQL). Instead, they propose "a unified object model for sharing data across programming languages, as well as a common query language." According to ODI's Tom Atwood, "The OML should respect the syntax of the base language into which it is being inserted, so that programmers feel they are writing in a single integrated programming language that supports persistence." In theory, it should be possible to read and write the same ODBMS from both SmallTalk and C++, as long as the programmer stays within the common subset of supported data types.

Figure 24-7 shows the steps involved in using an ODMG-compliant ODBMS. The process is very similar to the CORBA IDL, except that the stub bindings are for an ODBMS and the OO Language application that manipulates persistent objects.

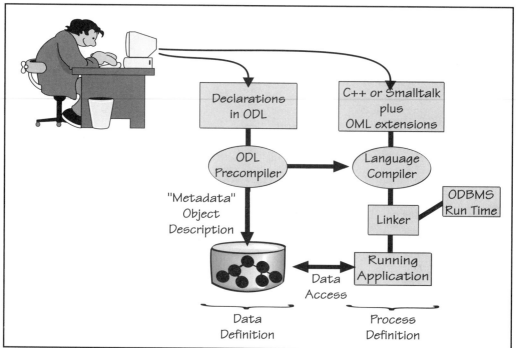

Figure 24-7. The ODMG-93 Process.

So, What's Wrong With ODBMSs?

*P*ure ODBMSs are mere pretenders to the DBMS throne.

— *Michael Stonebraker (February, 1994)*

Stonebraker notes that pure ODBMSs still lack functionality in the areas of complex search, query optimizers, and server scalability. Furthermore, many ODBMSs run their products in the same address space as user programs. This means that there is no protection barrier between a client application and the ODBMS. In addition, ODBMSs have a minuscule market penetration when compared to relational DBMSs. The debate continues in the following Soapbox.

The Future of Database: Object or Relational?

Soapbox

Object Mania has taken over the industry. Proponents of object orientation are heralding object databases and ODBMSs as a cure for the purported weakness of relational technology. Poppycock...Applying object orientation directly and indiscriminately at the database level reintroduces problems that took the relational approach two decades to get rid of.

> — Fabian Pascal, Author of
> *Understanding Relational Databases*
> (Wiley, 1994)

Among users, few doubts remain that ODBMS will ultimately be the successor to RDBMS...In the imagery of the poet William Blake, the young god of revolution Orc has begun to age into the icy tyrant Urizen—keeper of the law and standards.

> — Thomas Atwood, Chairman,
> Object Design (October, 1993)

We can have our cake and eat it, too! The point is to marry the two technologies instead of throwing mud at each other...It would be a great shame to walk away from the experience gained from more than 20 years of solid relational research and development.

> — Chris Date (June, 1993)

Date and Pascal both acknowledge that current SQL database implementations have weaknesses; however, they both feel the relational model per se can handle the problems that ODBMSs solve. The power of ODBMS can be approximated in the relational world using nested relations, domains (or user-defined encapsulated data types) and a more powerful set-oriented language than SQL. These features can do the job without chasing after object pointers or manipulating low-level, language-specific, record structures. We don't have to mitigate the associative powers of relational theory. Developers won't have to resort to manual methods to maximize and reoptimize application performance—setting the clock back. Date believes that a domain and an object type are the same; the solution is for relational vendors to extend their systems to include "proper domain support."

The ODBMS people feel that there's more to this than just extending the relational model. In fact, they've rejected the SQL3 extensions (due in 1995) as being insufficient. ODBMS diehards believe that they're creating better plumbing for a world where information systems will be *totally* object-based. Relational databases are an impedance mismatch in a plumbing consisting of ORBs, object services, OOUI front-ends, powerful OO languages, and OO frameworks. A pure ODBMS is exactly what's needed. Why keep extending a legacy foundation like SQL with BLOBs, stored procedures, and user-defined types? They prefer to stick to objects all the way and sometimes borrow a few things from SQL (such as queries). They're also recreating the multiuser robust foundation that includes locking, transactions, recovery, and tools.

What about all those great SQL tools with their pretty GUI front-ends, query pickers, and fancy reports? No problem. The ODBMS people will recreate this whole foundation and do it much better using objects. If you have any doubts, a look at the Servio toolset should give you an idea of how objects can seamlessly integrate everything from the client OOUI to the ODBMS. Of course, Servio is currently a proprietary and expensive tool. However, we may not be too far from the day when CORBA Interface Repositories replace database catalogs; method invocations replace stored procedures; transactional BOAs replace TP Monitors; and ODBMSs replace RDBMSs. It could be a total paradigmatic shift.

RDBMS vendors may someday pay heed to the criticisms they've been receiving over the years from the likes of Chris Date, Fabian Pascal, and E.F. Codd, and do something about domains. Will it be too late? It all depends on the state of the distributed object infrastructure. If information systems shift to ORBs and CORBA, if C++ replaces Cobol and C, if OOUIs replace GUIs, and if OO frameworks become the craze, then ODBMSs will be kings. There's no way "legacy" RDBMSs will be able to compete effectively with ODBMSs on a distributed object turf—the impedance mismatch is just too big.

Of course, we're talking about David and Goliath here. SQL databases are the current kings of the hill. They have the big development budgets and wide commercial acceptance that ranges from MIS shops to the low end of the client/server market. Will the king of the hill be deposed because of a few BLOBs, inheritance, and ORBs? We hate to admit it, but we don't really know. Larry Ellison's Oracle8 may simply gobble up objects and multimedia as we know them today and create a new de facto standard. But it's highly unlikely, given the incredible amount of intellectual energy that seems to be gravitating in the direction of distributed objects and CORBA. Can Ellison co-opt that technology? It remains to be seen. But as Esther Dyson puts it, "Using tables to store objects is like driving your car home and then disassembling it to put it in the garage. It can be assembled again in the morning, but one eventually asks whether this is the most efficient way to park a car." ❑

Chapter 25

Object Frameworks: A Closer Look

---

*T*he clearer the view of our dreams, the greater our cohesion.

— *Carlos Castaneda,*
The Art of Dreaming

The real payoff of CORBA technology will be provided by the object frameworks that are starting to come our way. The migration from procedural system APIs to object frameworks will eventually revolutionize the way client/server applications are developed, deployed, and managed on *all* operating system platforms. Think of these frameworks as the "software backbones" of client/server. Distributed objects, like all client/server software, will greatly benefit from the use of frameworks. In this chapter, we explain what a framework is and what problems it solves. We compare frameworks with traditional API sets and object-oriented class libraries. We conclude with some examples on how frameworks will be used in client/server environments, using examples from IBM and Taligent.

YOUR GUIDE TO OBJECT FRAMEWORKS

In this section, we define object frameworks, explain what they do, and what benefits they provide. You'll discover that frameworks are a packaging technology for object classes. They're ideally suited to work with ORBs. Object frameworks are the next level of object abstraction.

What Are Object Frameworks?

In their 1991 paper, "Reusing Object-Oriented Designs," Ralph Johnson of the University of Illinois and Vincent Russo of Purdue offer this widely accepted definition of frameworks:

> "An abstract class is a design for a single object. A framework is the design of a set of objects that collaborate to carry out a set of responsibilities. Thus frameworks are larger scale designs than abstract classes. Frameworks are a way to reuse...high-level design."

Still confused? Let's try an explanation from Taligent's 1993 White Paper:

> "Frameworks are not simply collections of classes. Rather, frameworks come with rich functionality and strong *wired in* interconnections between object classes that provide an infrastructure for the developer."

The "wired-in" interconnections among the classes are meant to provide the right level of abstraction to the consumer of the framework. Think of a framework as a fully debugged software subsystem, that you can customize to create your own applications. It's like buying a hardware board instead of individual chips (see Figure 25-1). But unlike a hardware board, the "software board" can be extended and further customized to fit your needs.

How Do Frameworks Work?

So how do you customize a framework? You tell it which key events you want to personalize and provide the code that handles those events. The framework will then call your code when that event occurs; your code doesn't call the framework. Your programs don't have to worry about structure, flow of execution, and calls to system-level API libraries; the framework does it all for you. All your code does is wait to be called by the framework (see Figure 25-2).

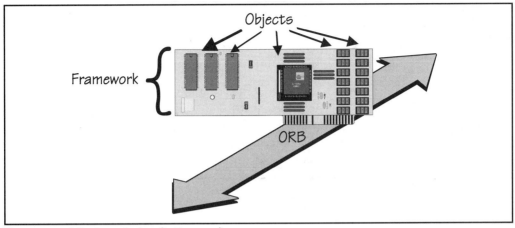

Figure 25-1. A Hardware Analogy for Frameworks.

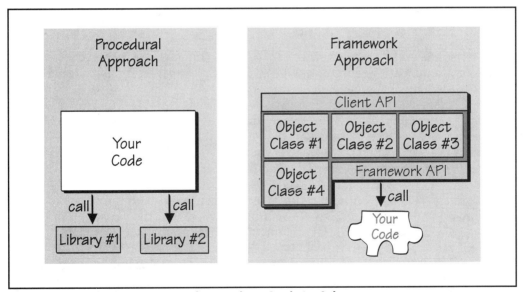

Figure 25-2. Procedural Versus Framework Approaches to Developing Code.

Frameworks, unlike traditional operating systems, are very malleable. If you don't like a particular part of the subsystem, just change it. You can also customize a framework by replacing some of its classes with your own. This is done using traditional object-oriented approaches such as multiple inheritance and method overrides. Of course, frameworks can also play tricks and change their underlying structure to take advantage of new hardware (or software) in a manner that's totally transparent to your software.

Frameworks and Subclassing

Details

How does the framework call your code? Technically, what you do is subclass *certain* framework classes and override specific methods. Overridden methods will be called by the framework when an instance of that subclass is invoked at run time. Your method executes and returns control to the framework. ❑

What else can frameworks do? They integrate well with other frameworks. Going back to the hardware analogy, hardware boards can be plugged into a motherboard (a board with a system bus) to interoperate with other hardware boards and create a system. For example, a system could consist of a motherboard with a microprocessor, a LAN Adapter card, a memory card, and a printer card. Frameworks do the same for software.

But where's the software motherboard? How do frameworks (in separate address spaces) communicate with one another? The framework "software motherboard" consists of two mechanisms:

■ *The framework service interface* provides a set of APIs that are simple abstractions of the services provided by each framework. We show in Figure 25-3 that interface as a layer on top of the frameworks. A CORBA-compliant framework would use IDL-specified interfaces.

■ *An inter-framework object request broker* is used to pass the requests across address spaces. Figure 25-3 shows the software bus (the broker) that carries the traffic across frameworks. A CORBA environment would use regular ORBs.

But aren't we going back to APIs and procedural calls? No, because most of the code you write runs within individual frameworks (the little puzzle pieces in the figure). These little puzzle pieces of code are invoked directly by the framework. The APIs are used to invoke services on other frameworks where you may also have some code (another little puzzle piece).

Key Benefits of Object Frameworks

You may have already surmised that frameworks provide a very powerful approach for creating complex systems. Here's a list of the advantages frameworks provide:

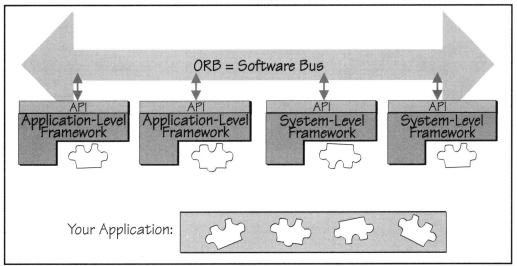

Figure 25-3. An Application in the Era of Frameworks.

- **A prefabricated infrastructure.** Frameworks reduce coding, debugging, and testing by providing working subsystems. This is code that you don't have to write yourself.

- **Architectural guidance.** Frameworks are wired and ready to go. All you need to know is where the hooks are and tap into them to extend the system's behavior. You don't have to wade through thick manuals that describe APIs. And if you're an object-oriented programmer, you won't have to spend half your time shopping for classes, providing the interconnections between classes, discovering which methods are available, and then trying to figure out which ones need to be called and in which order. Frameworks hide all this complexity by providing a higher level of abstraction.

- **Less monolithic applications.** Frameworks encourage you to write small pieces of applications that plug into their appropriate frameworks. When you need a function in another framework, you simply call that piece of the application that runs there (or the framework itself). Instead of writing one monolithic application, you write little pieces of custom code that run in different frameworks.

- **A foundation for a software components industry.** Well-designed frameworks allow third-party software companies to provide parts or entire components that can be assembled or modified by end users or system integrators. Frameworks will create the "critical mass" for software part catalogs. We will see the software equivalents of hardware motherboards, cards, chips, printers, and modems.

■ **Reduced maintenance.** Frameworks provide the bulk of the code that goes into applications—so your maintenance costs should be substantially reduced. Because of inheritance, when a framework bug is fixed or a new feature is added, the benefits are immediately available to derived classes.

The overall benefit of frameworks is that they enable a very high level of code and design reuse in the development of complex systems. Their main weakness is that they're not here. APIs appear first and frameworks will come after. It would be nice if vendors delivered both at the same time. But we're getting ahead of our story.

Frameworks, APIs, or Class Libraries?

The line of code that costs the least is the line of code you don't write.

— *Steve Jobs, 1993*

Yes, you've heard it before. Structured programming, then OO-class libraries, were supposed to save the world from programming drudgery. None were a panacea. Why are frameworks any different? Table 25-1 provides a quick summary of the features that distinguish frameworks from procedural API programming and object-oriented class libraries.

Table 25-1. Comparing Frameworks, OO-Class Libraries, and Procedural APIs.

Feature	Frameworks	OO Class Libraries	Procedural APIs
Application model	Frameworks are the application. The frameworks handle all the control flow.	You must create the control flow of the application and the glue that ties the different class libraries together.	You must create the control flow of the application and the logic that invokes the APIs. The system knows nothing about your code.
Application structure	Multiple cooperative frameworks.	Single monolithic application consisting of class libraries.	Single monolithic application linked to API libraries.
How are services obtained?	The frameworks are the service.	By inheriting function from the class libraries.	By calling API libraries.
How is the system customized?	The frameworks call your code. You can subclass parts of frameworks.	By subclassing or creating new classes.	By writing new code and calling additional APIs.

Table 25-1. Comparing Frameworks, OO-Class Libraries, and Procedural APIs. (Continued)

Feature	Frameworks	OO Class Libraries	Procedural APIs
Granularity of control	Medium. You can only subclass parts of frameworks.	High. You can subclass any class.	High. You can write everything from scratch.
Abstraction of services	High. Hides complexity. Automates standard features. You program by exception.	Low. Hides APIs but creates its own layer of complexity—you must determine which methods are available to call and in which order.	Very low. You need to deal with raw APIs and determine the order in which to call them.
How much code do you write?	Very little	A Medium amount.	A lot
Maintenace costs	Low	Medium	High
Reduced Complexity	Yes. You write small pieces of code within multiple frameworks. Frameworks call you only when necessary. Frameworks provide architectural guidance.	No. You must shop for classes and develop the program. You must integrate the different class libraries.	No. You must develop the entire program and understand how the APIs work together.
Client/Server support	High. Using inter-framework communications.	Low. You must use the native OS's inter-process communications.	Low. You must use the native OS's inter-process communications.
Time to develop an application	Low	Medium. Depends on class reuse.	High
Component reuse	Very high	High. The classes gets reused.	Medium. Some functions get reused.
Is the model familiar?	No	Somewhat	Yes

Procedural Frameworks: Look Ma, No Objects

Not all frameworks are object-based. Many of the middleware services—including transports, NOSs, and transactions—are provided using *procedural frameworks*. Why do we need procedural frameworks? Because the bulk of existing system code was written without the faintest notion of objects. DCE, for example, consists of more than two million lines of procedural "legacy" code. It will take some time to rewrite DCE into a "true" object framework. In other cases, object standards are still being defined. For example, the OMG is working on a specification for transaction services that will be built around some type of object framework. In the interim, we have *procedural* TP Monitor frameworks.

Procedural frameworks are very useful. They encapsulate heterogeneous services with CORBA-defined interfaces. Figure 25-4 shows an example of a SOM encapsulated procedural framework. Each framework provides configuration and installation support for its services. In addition, frameworks register their services with a CORBA-compliant Interface Repository that lets applications discover which services are available and how to invoke them at run time. The OS only has to load the framework itself and handle version control.

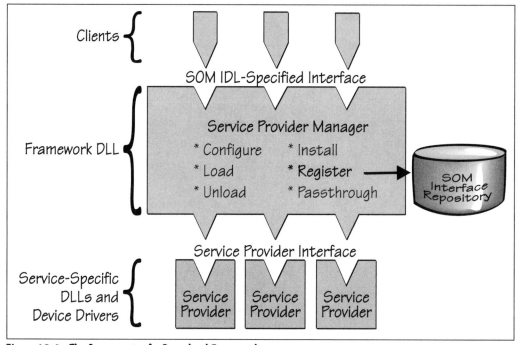

Figure 25-4. The Components of a Procedural Frameworks.

Procedural frameworks are very useful as object-wrappers. They allow us to transition to objects gradually from the existing base of legacy system software. The object wrappers make the legacy code appear object-like to the object-oriented programs, tools, and frameworks. So what do procedural frameworks lack? Their two major limitations are: 1) they don't allow you to modify the service itself using subclassing (for example, you won't be able to modify DCE); and 2) they are still API-based.

IBM/TALIGENT: FRAMEWORKS EVERYWHERE

We will deliver everything we do in frameworks.

— *Cliff Reeves, IBM Director of Objects*

So what's the state of commercial frameworks? We'll answer that question by looking at the IBM and Taligent plans for creating "seas of objects" where frameworks play a central role. If IBM and Taligent succeed, almost every piece of system software they deliver will be wrapped into some kind of framework. The IBM plan calls for layering a series of object frameworks in the place of each of the procedural APIs that make up OS/2 and AIX. Larry Louckes, the IBM Fellow and chief OS/2 and AIX strategist, estimates that the application frameworks alone consist of 1.2 million lines of code. When the frameworks all come into place, developers will have a platform on which they can more easily create applications. Frameworks will also give users an environment where all applications are seamlessly integrated. They will be plugged into SOM, which provides a language-neutral repository for exchanging services between applications created using different tools. DSOM goes even further—it allows applications created on different platforms to interoperate.

So how do we classify these frameworks? Figure 25-5 shows a recent IBM/Taligent classification that breaks frameworks into two general categories: Desktop and System. The Desktop frameworks (also called Application Frameworks) deal with the business logic of an application and provide the tools to build the visual components. The System frameworks cover everything else—including device control, file and print systems, every aspect of intergalactic client/server middleware, and distributed objects. We break down the system frameworks into two categories: Middleware (IBM calls it NOS) and OS. Did that help? Probably not, so let's continue to peel the framework layers until we get to some more familiar ground.

The Names May Change

Warning

These classifications may change with time. Don't get hung up on the names. What's important is to get a feel for what these frameworks can do. We need to keep peeling the layers until we get to something recognizable. ❏

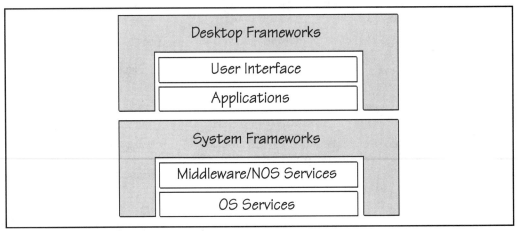

Figure 25-5. Desktop and System Frameworks.

The Desktop Frameworks

Figure 25-6 shows a combination of IBM and Taligent desktop frameworks that promise to change the way visual applications are developed. Cliff Reeves, the director of objects at IBM, predicts a ten-fold increase in programmer productivity with the new desktop programming model. Desktop frameworks cover compound documents, multimedia, mail, groupware, international text, graphics (2D and 3D), OOUI/GUI builders, and decision support systems. Some of the frameworks will allow end users to wire together some applications, but most of the frameworks are productivity tools for programmers.

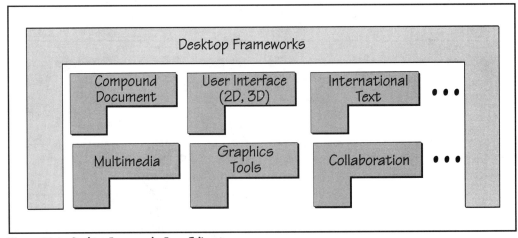

Figure 25-6. Desktop Frameworks From Taligent.

The Middleware Frameworks

Figure 25-7 shows some of the middleware frameworks.[1] This is a very comprehensive set of frameworks that cover all aspects of client/server middleware. As shown in Figure 25-7, IBM intends to provide frameworks that handle the middleware for transaction processing (TX), telephony (CMI), transport-independent calls (Sockets), e-mail (VIM), directory services (DCE, XDS/NSI), database access (IDAPI/ODBC), licensing (NetLS), authentication (DCE/GSS, OMG), System Management (XMP/DMI, SNMP, and DME objects), Print (COSE), Access Control Lists (DCE), etc. Sorry for the new acronyms—remember, we're dealing with client/server middleware! The new acronyms are from the system management area; they will be explained in Part 8.

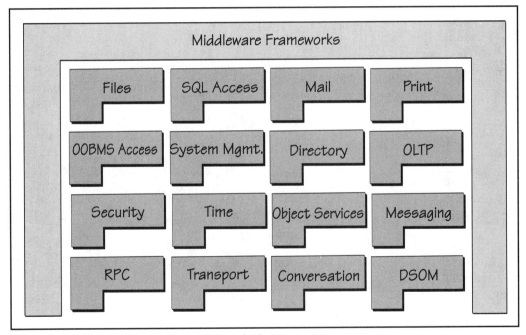

Figure 25-7. Middleware Frameworks From IBM and Taligent.

Most of the middleware frameworks are created by putting SOM-based object-wrappers around existing system software. IBM calls these wrappers *procedural frameworks*. Some of the middleware functions—like object services and mail—will be provided by true object frameworks that support subclassing. Frameworks,

---

[1] IBM provided the first detailed descriptions of its frameworks in September 1993 at the *OS/2 Technical Interchange* in Orlando, Florida. The information on the middleware frameworks is based on a presentation given by John Wilson, a senior architect with OS/2's LAN Systems.

both procedural or object-based, make it easier to create client/server applications. They promise to mask the complexity of the middleware. And some of the frameworks make it unnecessary to learn hundreds of APIs.

The OS Frameworks

With its frameworks, Taligent is creating an object-based operating environment from the bottom up. *Everything is an object* built on top of foundation classes that interface with the IBM Microkernel (see following Briefing box).

What Is Taligent Up To?

Briefing

In Taligent, we are dealing with a system optimized for a very large number of small objects...We don't move a few big objects. We move a lot of very little things around.

— Joe Guglielmi,
Taligent CEO, 1993

Taligent, a joint venture by IBM, Apple, and HP, is creating an environment that is built from the ground up with object-oriented technology. The Taligent environment runs as a set of foundation classes on top of the IBM Microkernel. Everything in the system is an object. The Taligent personality will provide an OOUI with a deep object foundation behind it.

Frameworks are central to the Taligent operating environment. Taligent is in the process of creating frameworks that span the entire system—from application frameworks that assist in developing the user interface to lower level frameworks that provide basic system level software such as communications, printing, and file systems support. Taligent will also provide a set of development tools that are intimately connected to the framework approach of software design.

One advantage of applying frameworks at the lower levels is that they allow the system to be extended to add new kinds of hardware devices. In traditional operating systems, developers who need to support new types of hardware devices have to write entire device drivers for each new device. However, with frameworks, developers only supply the characteristics and behaviors specific to each new device.

Taligent will first make its frameworks available on the OS/2, AIX, System 7, and Workplace OS platforms. The Workplace OS with the Taligent personality will provide frameworks that permeate objects into virtually every component of the system.

What Object Request Broker (ORB) will Taligent use for interframework communications? Taligent has committed to support both IBM's DSOM and HP's DOMF. Hopefully, these two ORBs will interoperate. Within the Taligent system we speculate that they may use the IBM Microkernel as their ORB. The quote from Joe at the top of this Briefing may give you some clue why this may be the case. They need a lot of bandwidth to handle thousands of minute objects like semaphores or the high-speed requirements of interactive 3-D graphic devices. Taligent is stretching object technology to its outer limits. ❑

What Do Frameworks Do for Client/Server?

Integrating client/server technology from 2500 competitors is as much fun as having a root canal.

— *Jim Cannavino, 1993*

Today's client/server industry provides a bag of "piece parts" that must be painfully assembled by skilled system integrators. The thousands of choices quickly become nightmares. How do you integrate and manage multivendor software across networks and disparate operating systems? How much glue code is required? How much of that complex and tricky code gets reinvented with each system integration contract?

Frameworks improve our ability to deal with the complexity of client/server systems. They help coordinate middleware elements that run on distributed heterogeneous platforms. The frameworks create a client/server infrastructure of communicating system objects. Each system object is defined using an ORB's interface definition language. Each service registers itself at run time with an interface repository. The entire system is self-describing. And the best part is that the components have been certified to work together. The integrator simply provides the "last snippets" of code that customize the system at a very fine-grained level.

Eventually all client/server applications will live within frameworks. All the communications between applications will be handled by the frameworks themselves. Visual programming tools will allow us to create and manage client/server applications by wiring together prefabricated software building blocks. This is how hardware is built today; frameworks will extend these techniques to complex system software. In summary, frameworks will provide the software backbone of the client/server infrastructure. They will help pull the multivendor puzzle pieces together.

Conclusion

Personal computing changed the way people worked. Object computing will change the way the world works. It is the wave of the future and it is here today."

— *Philippe Kahn, 1993*

In summary, a continuum of object frameworks—from the very simple to the very powerful—is coming our way. We hope to have made the case with the examples from IBM and Taligent. The IBM frameworks aim at solving an immediate problem: how to create intergalactic client/server solutions across heterogeneous systems. Taligent is trying to solve a less-immediate problem: how to effectively use objects "from the bottom up." IBM and Taligent will create layers of objects and class libraries on top of procedural operating systems. Everything about objects should be "open" and extendable by third parties. Object frameworks are an essential component of the client/server infrastructure. These frameworks will help us realize the vision: *ubiquitous client/server computing*. The smart money will start moving to distributed objects now.

Chapter 26

DSOM and SOMobjects

SOM is the cornerstone of an emerging multiplatform, comprehensive, distributed object computing environment that IBM plans to roll out during the next several years...IBM's reward for its efforts is a large lead over its major competitors in delivering a state-of-the-art distributed object computing technology.

— *John R. Rymer (March, 1993)*

There is a field of dreams approach to this technology—if we build it will they come?

— *Cliff Reeves, IBM Director of Objects (January, 1994)*

This chapter is a very brief description of the **Distributed System Object Model (DSOM)** and some of the frameworks and tools that are part of the **SOMobjects Toolkit**. We hope this example will give you a more tangible feeling of how distributed object management products work. With the release of the DSOM ORB and SOMobjects, SOM is moving into object "prime time." The new DSOM extends SOM communications across address spaces and machines. In fact, it is emerging as one of the industry's premier implementation of the OMG's CORBA specification for an Object Request Broker (ORB). With the release of the C++ class bindings, SOM could set in motion a whole new objectware industry—object providers can now sell language independent object components. SOM and DSOM run on OS/2 and AIX now, and they are being ported to many platforms—including Windows, System 7, OS/400, MVS, and others.

WHAT'S THE SOMOBJECTS TOOLKIT?

SOMobjects are professional programming tools and object services for the System Object Model (SOM) and Distributed System Object Model (DSOM) technologies. This is the toolkit for creating objects for that famous Object Request Broker (ORB) and CORBA specification (see Figure 26-1). Here's what you get with this toolkit:

- The **SOM/IDL Compiler** provides language neutrality using OMG's Interface Definition Language (IDL). IDL is how objects tell potential clients what operations are available, and how they should be invoked. SOM provides language bindings for C and C++ (with bindings for Smalltalk in the works) that let programmers in those languages use SOM objects and create new SOM object classes. SOM provides emitter utilities that let you create bindings for additional languages.

- The **DSOM ORB Services** let objects communicate across processes in a single workstation or across multiple machines on a TCP/IP or NetBIOS LAN. DSOM is a CORBA-compliant ORB; it also includes a fully CORBA-compliant Interface Repository.

- The **Replication Framework** lets you create copies of objects and synchronize changes made by multiple clients. Updates are automatically propagated to all the object copies. This is great for creating groupware-like applications.

- The **Persistence Framework** lets you save and restore SOM objects to and from a repository that can be a file system, database, or object database.

- The **Framework of Collection Classes** lets you create compound objects (that is, objects that point to other objects) and navigate through the elements. SOM provides the following object container types: lists, sets, queues, and dictionaries. You can inherit from and use these SOM classes in your applications.

- The **Event Management Framework** lets you organize application-level events into groups and process all events in a single event-processing loop.

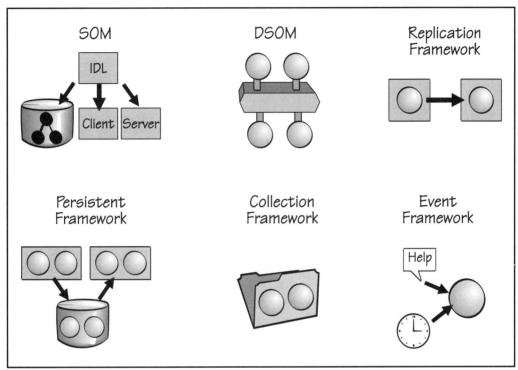

Figure 26-1. The SOMobjects Components.

THE SYSTEM OBJECT MODEL (SOM)

SOM provides the industry's first implementation of a CORBA-compliant, language-neutral environment for defining, manipulating, and releasing class libraries. SOM objects are language-neutral in the sense that they can be implemented in one programming language and used by applications or objects written in another programming language (see Figure 26-2). SOM makes it possible for objects and classes to be shared and ported across OO languages. It does not compete with C++, Smalltalk, C, or any programming language; it complements them. SOM provides a solution to this very real and pressing problem: *How do you develop class libraries that have properties similar to our current procedure libraries?*

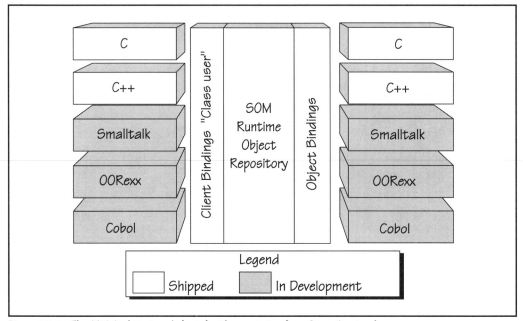

Figure 26-2. The SOM Architecture (adapted with permission from Roger Sessions).

What Problems Does SOM Solve?

Today, SOM allows a developer to define classes and methods using C or C++. This means that C or C++ programmers should be able to use SOM quickly to develop object-oriented programs without having to learn a new language syntax. SOM, however, is specifically designed to work with both procedural and object-oriented languages. Why do I need SOM when I have C++? Because C++ is becoming the language of choice for programmers wanting to build system class libraries. However, C++ without the SOM run time is not usable for building binary class libraries because:

■ The binaries of one C++ compiler are not acceptable to another.

■ An application that binds to a C++ DLL will need to be recompiled if the DLL is replaced with a new release, unless the developers make almost no changes to their implementation.

■ The use of the libraries from any other language (even C) would be almost impossible.

When either C or C++ is combined with SOM, these problems are removed. SOM makes object technology binary (just like DLLs for procedural languages). It's the first commercial technology that makes it possible to package objects as sharable "dynamic binary modules." SOM does that by packaging "neutral" object classes in standard binary library formats—DLLs for Windows and OS/2, and shared libraries for Unix. This makes it possible to ship objects as ordinary DLLs—a technique that's very popular with other forms of shrink-wrapped commercial software. Table 26-1 compares the packaging features of procedural libraries (DLLs), traditional class libraries, and SOM class libraries.

Table 26-1. Comparing Packaging Features for Code Libraries.

Packaging Feature	Procedural DLLs	Ordinary Class Libraries	SOM Class Libraries
Language neutral libraries	Yes	No	Yes
Can ship libraries as binaries	Yes	No (frequently requires shipping the source code)	Yes
Sharable libraries	Yes	Almost never	Yes
Supports inheritance	No	Yes	Yes
Clients must be recompiled when implementation changes	No	Yes	No

The table makes it clear why we haven't achieved *object* code reuse. SOM fixes this problem. For example, in Figure 26-3 SOM lets you change the implementation of the car class without having to recompile the clients. In addition, multiple clients written in different languages can share the same class. SOM classes can be distributed as DLLs or Unix shared libraries. SOM also provides hooks for exchanging class libraries with other object-oriented languages. SOM's language neutrality makes it possible for a Smalltalk object written in SOM to inherit attributes from a C or C++ object. This also means that objects written in different languages can communicate using SOM's common object interface.

SOM class libraries are designed to be part of the operating system (OS/2 and AIX today). The promise of SOM is to make *OO technology part of the operating system, not part of a programming language.* SOM allows the integration between operating-system objects and user-supplied objects to be as efficient as possible without requiring users to recompile their programs when the next version of the operating system ships.

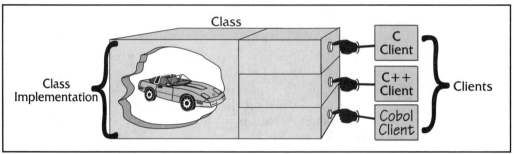

Figure 26-3. SOM Provides Language-Neutral, Sharable, Class Packaging.

THE DISTRIBUTED SOM (DSOM) ORB

Distributed SOM (DSOM) is the CORBA-compliant ORB element that allows SOM objects to talk to other SOM objects across address spaces on the same machine or across networks. SOM insulates clients from the object implementation; DSOM adds to that object location insulation. As we go to press, DSOM is the most comprehensive implementation of OMG's CORBA standard for ORBs. It currently allows Windows, OS/2, and AIX objects to interoperate. Eventually, DSOM will interoperate with other ORBs via gateways.

DSOM is simply distributed SOM. It uses the standard SOM IDL compiler, SOM APIs, language bindings, and dynamic object model. *Workstation DSOM* supports client/server object interactions among processes on the same machine (see Figure 26-4). It uses existing interprocess communication facilities (IPCs). *Workgroup DSOM* supports client/server object exchanges across networks of Windows, OS/2, and AIX machines. It uses socket-based TCP/IP, IPX/SPX, and NetBIOS stacks, and it can be customized to other stacks. DSOM programs run unchanged in both environments; they use the same language bindings and stubs. DSOM is packaged as a client and server DLL addition to SOM.

DSOM is a CORBA-compliant ORB. Like all good ORBs, it makes its living by providing interobject client/server communications (see Figure 26-5). This includes creating, destroying, identifying, locating, and invoking methods on remote objects. It also includes managing object references. The default Basic Object Adapter that ships with DSOM—it's called *SOM Object Adapter (SOMOA)*—only supports the CORBA *shared server activation policy.* SOMOA's multithreaded implementation supports multiple objects within the same server process.

DSOM supports both the CORBA Interface and Implementation Repositories. The Interface Repository describes the behavior of objects; the Implementation Repository deals with their location and packaging. DSOM provides a very open architecture that let you subclass and modify the classes that provide the proxy client,

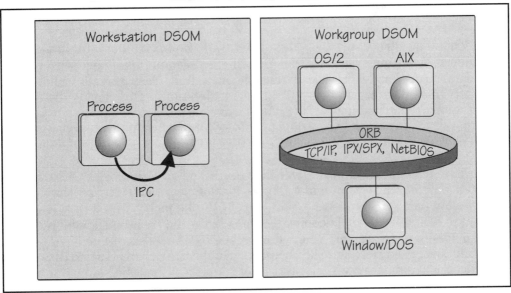

Figure 26-4. DSOM: Workstation Versus Workgroup.

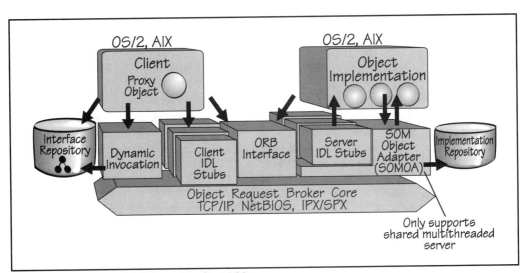

Figure 26-5. DSOM Is a CORBA 1.1 Compliant ORB.

server, and socket functions. As a result, you can tailor the key pieces of the ORB implementation to suit your needs. Of course, it takes some serious programming to do that.

SOM/DSOM FUTURES

ORB technology, object services, and object frameworks are the infrastructure of postmodern operating systems—they provide flexible and highly adaptive plumbing. The object model is also extensible in a first class way; its underlying client/server model scales very well in every direction. This means distributed objects make great middleware. SOM started out as a technology to package operating system services. According to IBM's Cliff Reeves, future versions of SOM will be packaged with OS/2 2.2 (October, 1994). Perhaps AIX will do the same.

The next release of SOMobjects will include the new CORBA Object Services—Persistence, Lifecycle, Event, and Naming. It's not clear that all these services will be in the operating system. We expect the ORB to be incorporated first. In other words, the SOMobjects kit becomes the vehicle for the early introduction of new SOM technology. However, when the technology matures, it ends up in the operating system—where it really belongs. Taligent Frameworks are also being introduced in a similar way. The first set of frameworks will be shipped in toolkit form until it gets integrated into the operating system proper.

In 1994 we expect to see *Enterprise DSOM*—a version of DSOM that integrates with the DCE NOS. The following are target schedules for SOM/DSOM platform shipments in 1994: Windows (April), Macintosh System 7 (July), OS/400 and MVS (late 1994), and COSE (end of 1994). In addition, we expect to see shipments of SOM visual tools and an Interface Repository class browser. We also expect to see more "Direct to SOM" compiler support—for example, the MetaWare C++ compiler can produce SOM objects and IDL descriptions. SOM will also be supported in interpreter languages like OO REXX and Basic. Finally, IBM is expected to ship a large number of procedural frameworks with SOM class wrappers for almost every type of middleware described in this book, including system management. In summary, SOM and DSOM are living proof that object technology is finally moving into the commercial mainstream. They're being used to create distributed system middleware and operating system substrates.

Part 8

Distributed System Management

Before DSM

After DSM

An Introduction to Part 8

You Martians have so far been getting the scenic tour of client/server computing. You've seen all the cool stuff—objects, groupware, database, and NOSs. But there's also a seamy side to client/server—the nasty little secrets that are normally kept out of the grand tour circuit. So what are these nasty little secrets? In a nutshell, the first generation client/server applications were "systems from Hell" when it came to keeping them up and running. These client/server projects were either single-vendor based or kept very small until we could figure out the kinks. Many of the early "Kamikazes" who attempted to build large scale open systems often fell prey to the technology; some never returned to talk about it. We call this nasty secret "Client/Server burnout."

So what is the cause of client/server burnout? The root cause is that we all got the scenic tour and fell in love with the promise of client/server. However, no one ever told us that we were *totally* on our own after we unwrapped the glossy packages from the different vendors. There was no single number to call when something went wrong. Yes, the different vendors gave us some rudimentary tools to manage their products, but these tools did nothing to help us manage the *sum of the products*. When something went wrong it was always "the other vendor's fault."

We were left in the great "no vendor's land" of client/server, trying to make our systems work or face loosing our jobs. Many of us burned the midnight oil trying to learn how to read the bits and bytes that flew over the network using Sniffers and other protocol analyzers. These early tools were real lifesavers—without them, we would have been totally blind. However, this is not the answer. We can't expect every client/server installation to have its resident TCP/IP, SQL, and object guru.

OK, you want us to get to the point—enough of this early "pioneer" talk. But we have news for you: We're *still* in the pioneer days of client/server. The *Distributed System Management (DSM)* technology—the topic of Part 8—*may* be the cure to client/server burnout. We say "may" because DSM products are just coming out of the labs; most are still untested in the battlefield. In addition, the success of a DSM platform depends on how easy it is for third-party tools to "snap into" it. And that won't happen overnight. So the good news is that there is a cure: DSM platforms. The bad news is that DSM platforms are in their infancy; you may have to pack a Sniffer back to Mars and be prepared to look at some bits and bytes.

Part 8 starts out by going over DSM platforms and what they can do for you today. Next, we spend time going over DSM standards and middleware. DSMs can only succeed by creating an open-platform based on standards. Standards allow management applications to "plug and play" into the DSM and access their agents anywhere in the intergalactic client/server universe. As usual, there are many standards from which you can choose. We will review the Internet, OSI, and CORBA-based standards for system management; they're also called the neoclassical and postmodern standards. So welcome to the seamy side of client/server. We hope that this won't be a Conrad-like journey into the "Heart of Darkness."

Chapter 27

Client/Server Distributed System Management

Now that my applications have moved off the mainframe, how am I going to manage this mess?

— *Anonymous MIS Manager*

The mere existence of a problem is no proof of the existence of a solution.

— *Yiddish proverb.*

Client/Server has applied a giant chainsaw to centralized systems, slicing them into small pieces and scattering them all over the network. Then along came "open systems," which sliced up the software even further, so that each piece comes from a different vendor. How do we manage the pieces? Management and support issues are the Achilles' heel of client/server computing. Even though the benefits of client/server systems are real—lower hardware and software costs, more flexible systems, easier to use front-ends—we're discovering that administration and support is far more costly than for centralized systems. Client/server computing disperses applications across multiple systems on a network and creates daunting problems for all types of administrators concerned with keeping these systems running. The gap is widening between what users expect and what the support organization can deliver. It obviously doesn't make economic sense to ship a database and network administrator with every new client/server application that we deploy. So the rapidly escalating support burden of client/server systems must be brought under control, or the entire edifice may crumble.

Are we in a no-win situation like the one described by the Yiddish proverb? Is there a solution to the problem of distributed system management in multivendor client/server environments? Until *very* recently, client/server management tools and products were totally inadequate for dealing with the complexities of distributed environments—they were always far less developed than their mainframe counterparts. You had to be a total masochist (or suicidal) to deploy a client/server solution in intergalactic environments. Departmental-sized solutions had slightly better success rates because somebody local was willing to put in the long hours of "volunteer" work. The first generation of client/server systems were mostly a "labor of love" by people who were willing to put in long hours to gain control over their local computing environment.

Fortunately, the situation may be turning around. Some very creative solutions to systems management are starting to come on the market. Most of them use client/server technology to help manage client/server systems. It's very recursive in that sense. Vendors of all sizes have finally come to the realization that no single system management product (or suite) can solve all the world's problems. The new trend is for vendors to create products that plug-and-play in one of the "open" distributed system management platforms—including LAN NetView, OpenView, SunNet Manager, NetView/6000, Tivoli, and the NetWare Management System (NMS).

These open management platforms can exchange management information with almost anything that lives on the network—including low-level devices, system software, and user applications—using standard protocols such as SNMP and CMIP. The distinction between the network management and system management disciplines is quickly fading. Object-oriented user interfaces are providing single views of the managed environment; management information databases are providing common views of the managed data. Finally, management platforms can interoperate in all sorts of flexible arrangements, ranging from peer-to-peer to complex manager-of-manager relationships. This chapter looks at the distributed management problem: Why the chaos? What needs to be managed? Next we explain the popular management/agent paradigm for solving the world's problems. Then we take a quick look at the services that management platforms and applications provide. We briefly introduce some open management platforms such as HP's OpenView, LAN NetView, and Tivoli.

NEW WORLD DISORDER

In many large companies the network control center room seems as complex as the bridge deck of the starship Enterprise. Many systems are linked into the control center, but few are integrated...As a result, operations staff must be rocket scientists to integrate fault, performance, configuration, and other information gleaned from multiple management systems.

— Gartner Group (March, 1993)

System management is, of course, much more complex in distributed environments—especially heterogeneous ones. Unlike past generations of computers, client/server systems consist of three logically integrated but physically dispersed types of components: computer nodes, networks, and applications. The health of the system is dependent on the individual health of its component parts, as well as their interrelationships. All the problems associated with managing a typical computer system exist, and they are exacerbated by a substantial set of problems unique to the network itself.

Ironically, the multivendor diversity that's inherent in client/server solutions is also the primary obstacle to effective and affordable system management. You save money by buying components "a la carte," but you must turn around and spend what you just saved (and often more), making these components "whole" again. The great variety of vendors, networks, software packages, and system configurations

make each client/server system different from the last one. And, until quite recently, vendors' management tools were customized for their own set of products and were generally targeted at the workgroup or departmental level.

As a result, client/server control centers in large organizations *do* look like the bridge deck of the starship *Enterprise*. So who takes care of the correlation between the different management platforms? The operators, of course. They must learn a different set of commands for each user interface and product. And they must continuously correlate information—such as fault, configuration, and performance—from the different management consoles. Because each system has its own separate management database, it's not unusual for the same information to be re-keyed multiple times. A single error may cause hundreds of different messages to flash on all the different consoles at the same time. In many cases, functions may overlap leading to more confusion. The first generation client/server systems were much too complex to manage—even in limited configurations with only a few vendors involved.

DEALING WITH CHAOS AND LEARNING TO LOVE IT

> Sometimes the most vexing questions have simple answers: Distributed applications need distributed management.
>
> — James Herman,
> VP, Northeast Consulting Resources, Inc.

By 1990, the industry began to realize that multiplying incomplete tools by multiple vendors created an unmanageable mess that threatened to derail the entire client/server movement. Something had to be done fast; the industry met that challenge and introduced many innovations very quickly. In the last four years, *three* generations of management architectures were introduced in rapid succession: *Manager of Managers, Distributed System Management (DSM)*, and *Open DSM platforms* (see Figure 27-1). We cover these architectures in the rest of this section.

Manager of Managers

IBM's NetView was one of the first attempts to solve the problems of distributed system management at the enterprise level. NetView introduced the concept of *manager of managers*, which made it possible for a "mainframe in the sky" to oversee an entire enterprise. The idea was to create a single system image using a three-level hierarchy of management elements: low-level *Entry Points* that collect management information and send it upward; middle-manager *Service Points* that

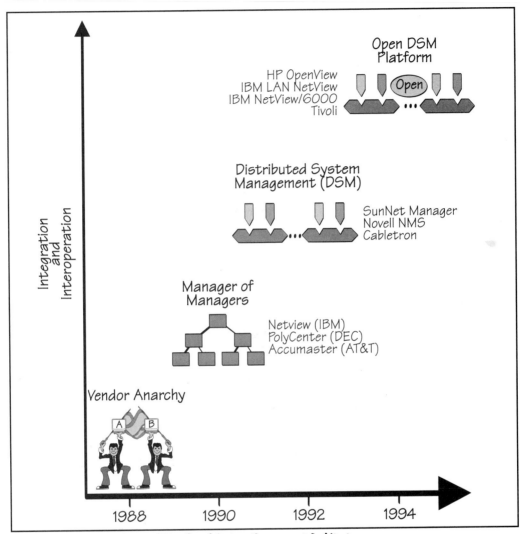

Figure 27-1. Four Generations of Distributed System Management Architectures.

act on some of the information and send the rest upward; and *Focal Points* at the top that maintain a central database of management information and present a unified view of all the distributed resources. NetView/PC—the first *Service Point* product introduced by IBM—also served as a gateway that could convert management information from non-SNA devices into a format the mainframe Focal Points could understand: using the SNA Network Management Vector Transport (NMVT).

It didn't take long for DEC and AT&T to introduce their own manager of managers: *PolyCenter Framework* and *Accumaster Integrator*. Each product was based on a proprietary distributed management architecture. So the race was on between IBM, DEC, and AT&T to see who would be the first to manage the entire universe. It quickly became apparent that no one vendor—not even IBM, DEC, or AT&T—could possibly anticipate all the customer needs and requirements for a manager-of-managers product. There was just too much diversity for any one vendor to absorb—it was a huge and costly undertaking. IBM, DEC, and AT&T must have come to that same conclusion because they're now among the strongest proponents of open management platforms.[1]

Distributed System Management Platforms

The next step in the evolution of management systems was the *Distributed System Management (DSM)* platform approach pioneered by Sun Microsystem's *SunNet Manager*, Cabletron's *Spectrum*, and Novell's *NetWare Manager System (NMS)*. These systems introduced two innovations:

- *The use of client/server technology in system management.* Instead of a hierarchy of managers, these systems split up management applications along client/server lines. A GUI-based client workstation can work with any management server using RPCs to obtain management information. The servers collect their information from agents all over the network. The client workstation can provide a single view of the LAN by visually integrating management information that resides on multiple servers. The back-end data can be managed by peer-to-peer or manager-of-managers arrangements among servers—the architecture is very flexible.

- *The use of "toaster" platforms.* The new DSM systems pioneered the concept of the "toaster" model that allows management applications to plug into the platform and play. They accomplished that by creating a "barebones" management infrastructure consisting of published APIs, a starter kit of system management middleware, a system management workstation with integrated graphical utilities, and a management database on the server. The infrastructure was designed to entice third-party management application providers to write to the platforms. The success of a platform is measured by the number of applications that it supports, the type of services these applications provide, and how well they integrate with other applications.

---

[1] Source: **Management Platforms for Networked Systems**, Gartner Group (March 31, 1993).

The combination of client/server and toaster platforms caused a massive migration by third-party management application developers to the DSM platforms. The flexible client/server architecture provided scalability from entry level LANs to enterprise systems.

Open DSM Platforms

The most recent step in the evolution of distributed management systems is *open DSM platforms*. Simply put, this is a DSM platform model that uses industry standards for its main interfaces. So where do these industry standards come from? The usual places, of course. Here's the list of standard bodies and consortia that *together* provide all the pieces needed to create a working distributed management platform: X/Open for management APIs; UI-Atlas and OSF-DME for conceptual frameworks and object technology; OMG for ORBs and object services; OSI and the *Internet Engineering Task Force (IETF)* for specialized middleware; and the *Desktop Management Task Force* DMI standard for managing the desktop and PC-attached devices.

MANAGER TO AGENTS: WHAT'S GOING ON OUT THERE?

Mirror Worlds are software models of some chunk of reality, some piece of the real world going on outside your window. Oceans of information pour endlessly into the model (through a vast maze of software pipes and hoses): so much information that the model can mimic the reality's every move, moment-by-moment.

— David Gelernter, Author, Mirror Worlds
(Oxford, 1992)

In his fascinating book, **Mirror Worlds**, David Gelernter defines five key ingredients that make up a mirror world: A deep picture that is also a live picture, agents, history, experience, and the basic idea that knits these all together. We found the "mirror world paradigm" to be very applicable to distributed system management. To make sense out of a chaotic distributed environment, we need to be able to grasp the whole and then move selectively into the parts. This is done by creating a mirror world of the client/server environment. Even though Gelernter does not mention it in his book, today's open management platforms provide the most advanced mirror world implementations.

So what does an open management platform do? It manages mulivendor devices and applications on the network, runs management applications, interoperates with other managing stations, provides an integrated user interface of the managed components, and stores management data. How does it do it? By running an elaborate network of agents—it's like the CIA. The agents reside on the different managed entities on the network and report on their status. The management station can "parachute" its software agents anywhere on the network to look after its interests and gather the data it needs. The agents are also capable of executing commands on its behalf.

The agents help the manager create a "mirror world" of the client/server universe to be managed. Each agent monitors one piece of the universe. Potentially, there may be thousands of agents parachuted throughout the network. They all run simultaneously, never stopping to take a break, always on the lookout for what may go wrong, and always gathering data that may be of use to some manager. The manager software sifts through the massive amounts of real-time information it collects looking for the nuggets—the trends and patterns as they emerge. It must make sure the operator isn't overwhelmed with data. To do that, it must create a data model of the "chunk of reality" it manages. "Data refineries" must convert the data into useful information. A managing workstation should include either a relational or object database for managing and organizing the information that's collected and to remember past occurrences.

A mirror world isn't a mere information service—it's a *place*. You can stroll around inside the mirror world. To allow you to do that, the managing station uses iconic images to create visual computer representations of "what's going on out there." Multiple views allow you to zoom in, pan around, and roam through the network. You can read the screen like a dashboard when you need to see the status of a system

at a glance, or you can wade through massive amounts of information organized in many views when you need to do some serious detective work. At every level the display is live; it changes to reflect the changing conditions of the system as you watch. The way things are presented is a very important aspect of system management. Ideally, you should be able to see and control every aspect of a managed system from a single managing workstation. System management has the visual look and feel of an electronic arcade game, but in the background it deals with real agents that collectively control every aspect of a distributed system.

A management platform also provides the middleware needed for communicating with all types of agents. This ranges from simple agents that manage hardware devices (such as routers) to complex agents that chase after objects that roam on networks. The simple agents may be reached using a simple protocol like SNMP; the complex agents may be invoked via an ORB. In between, we have traditional agents for client/server applications that communicate using RPCs and MOM. In summary, distributed system management uses client/server technology to manage client/server systems. It's all very recursive. Mirror worlds are examples of how client/server technology will be used in the years to come. We can get a jump start by understanding the workings of the system management mirror world.

THE COMPONENTS OF AN OPEN DSM PLATFORM

Figure 27-2 shows the main components of an open management platform. It's a composite of the OSI, OSF-DME, UI-Atlas DM, and IBM SystemView conceptual models of distributed management. More importantly, the figure is also a good composite model of commercial open management platforms such as HP's Open-View, IBM's LAN NetView on OS/2 and NetView/6000 on AIX, and Tivoli. Because of the common standards, the main commercial platforms are starting to converge at the implementation level. For example, HP's OpenView is the basis for the OSF-DME implementation of network management technology. LAN NetView and NetView/6000 contain large amounts of code that IBM licensed from HP's Open-View. Tivoli provides object technology that's used in both the OSF DME and UI-Atlas. The irony is that LAN NetView and NetView/6000 have much more in common with HP's OpenView than their mainframe namesake, NetView. A more appropriate name would have been "OpenView for OS/2" and "OpenView for AIX/6000."

Let's quickly introduce the management components of an open management platform before getting into the details. We start at the top of Figure 27-2 and work our way downward:

■ The *OOUI User Interface* provides visual representations of managed objects. The managing workstation should be able to automatically discover the topology of agents on a network and display them in a top view. Background maps can

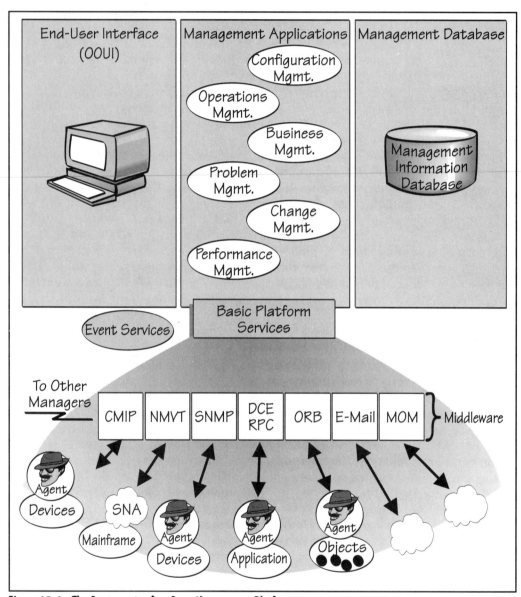

Figure 27-2. The Components of an Open Management Platform.

be used to indicate the geographic locations of agents. Clicking on an icon representing a managed object displays a view of its current status and options for observing and controlling its state. You should be able to visually define event/action combinations. Query dialogs are provided to view information in the management database. Tree views can be used to traverse information that's stored on any remote agent.

■ The ***Management Applications*** are typically provided by third parties on top of the management platform's underlying facilities—including the user interface, the management database, the topological discovery services, and the facilities for communicating with remote agents and other managing applications. The management applications fall into the following categories: problem management, change management, configuration management, performance management, operations management, and business management.

■ The ***Management Information Database*** is a database of information collected from the agents under the managing workstation's control. It can be implemented using an RDBMS or ODBMS. The database engine may provide active backgound daemons that monitor the historical data for trends and unusual developments. Triggers can be used to proactively launch corrective actions. It's important to note that a portion of the real-time management data is maintained by the agents themselves and stored in the local nodes they manage—the MIBs. So in a sense, we're dealing with a distributed database of hierarchical information. The data is spread on MIBs throughout the network. The managing workstation maintains aggregate snapshots of this distributed data. However, the data in the central database is not as up-to-date as the data kept in the remote MIBs (the point of capture).

■ The ***Basic Platform Services*** provide high-level APIs that allow a managing application to communicate with agents, other managing applications, other managing platforms, and the event management service. These APIs conform to open industry standards.

■ The ***Middleware Stacks*** provide the elaborate communication infrastructure needed by a management workstation and its applications to talk to distributed agents, other management workstations, and operators via e-mail. A good management platform should support all the industry standards for agent to managing station communications—including SNMP, CMIP, DCE, and CORBA. It should also support legacy management protocols such as SNA NMVT alert packets. E-mail and MOM services are needed for sending asynchronous alerts and notifications. Finally, either SNMP2, CMIP, RPC, or CORBA may be used for communications between management stations.

In summary, the management platform isolates the managing applications from the distributed environment and provides the common OOUI, database, and event services needed to create a single-system image of client/server management. The managing applications themselves are written by third parties. The more standard the APIs supported by a platform, the easier it is for third parties to port their applications. Of course, the real management work is done by these management applications—the platforms just provide the necessary plumbing and the install base.

MANAGEMENT APPLICATIONS: COPING WITH DIVERSITY AND COMPLEXITY

With standardized APIs and what we believe will be the convergence to a small number of management platforms, an entirely new market is being created. A major opportunity now exists for the development of best-of-breed management applications.

— *Gartner Group (March, 1993)*

Management applications do the real work in distributed system management. They help us answer the following questions: How is my client/server system doing? What is out there and where? Who is doing what to whom? How do I install new software? What went wrong? How do I fix it? Is everything being backed up? Can my system survive an 8.0 earthquake? In this section, we take a quick look at the categories of system management software that help us answer these questions.

How Is My Client/Server System Doing?

Collecting real-time information from various system components in a client/server environment and pinpointing the causes of performance problems can be a real headache for system and database administrators. The management software must be able to collect extensive data, in real time, from different sources in a client/server environment. It must then act on that data or present it in graphical or numerical form for further analysis. You should be able to correlate the performance data with information collected from configuration management tools and proactively identify system bottlenecks.

Performance monitoring tools gather statistical data on resource utilization levels of key components in a client/server system, and then generate alarms when some administrator-defined criteria are not met. Some of the tools may even provide scripting facilities for generating repair actions or doing preventive maintenance. The tools monitor utilization levels on typical resources—including networks, CPUs, disks, memory, file space, processes, server transactions, e-mail, modems, routers, and so on. The better systems use histograms and standard deviations to monitor the response time of servers. Performance monitoring tools maintain a database on the historical performance of the system so that trends can be discovered. You should be able to obtain graphical displays of usage data on any computer, network, or database resource. The tool should be able to automatically collect relevant data over a period of time so that resource utilization during peak hours can be analyzed before making hardware or software capital expenditure decisions.

Unfortunately, very few generic tools can be used to automate the corrective actions in the areas of performance tuning. In this case, what's needed are tools that automate load balancing in response to varying loads. Some of that is done by specialized system components such as TP Monitors and routers.

What Is Out There and Where?

Inventory management tools, also known as "asset managers," keep track of what programs run on which machines, what levels of software they run, and the like. They also keep track of hardware inventory and maintain a database of inventory information. Most tools can automatically notify you when they detect changes to the hardware and software on the LAN. Some of the more "authoritarian" tools may do more than just report changes; they may automatically revoke and restore files to the parameters that an administrator sets—for example, login files.

In theory, an automated inventory manager should be able to automatically determine all the software, workstations, peripherals, routers, and servers directly attached to the LAN. Unfortunately, most tools require you to key in some data; there is no way to automatically gather information such as the serial number of devices. In addition, it is hard to track all the software that's used on the LAN because no single comprehensive list of software exists. Vendors typically rely on a list from the Software Publisher Association (SPA). This list is updated twice a year and contains only the software from vendors that have paid to have their applications included. Some tools can isolate unknown software by checking the file size and version number, and then making educated guesses as to what the application is.

Configuration management tools can set software parameters and fine-tune complex systems such as relational databases or operating systems. Fortunately, generic software management tools are becoming less scarce. However, hardware configuration tools are still what most people think about in terms of configuration control—they've been around longer. These tools can set device thresholds and tuning parameters. They can also collect configuration information from any managed system via its MIB. You should be to track changes in the configuration of the client/server environment over time and use that information to perform crucial maintenance and tuning work such as identifying and balancing the load around bottlenecks. For example, a database management tool should be able to monitor database resource utilization, database space fragmentation, application deadlocks, application throughput, computer resources, dead processes, and resource "hogs."

The client/server computing environment is always in flux as new clients and applications log on and off the network. *Topology management tools* keep track of how the network is interconnected, what nodes are out there, and how to best reach them. They make it easy for an administrator to continuously monitor the changes in the client/server environment. The administrator can graphically display crucial information, such as which client is using which server, which database resource resides on which server, and which applications are available on each server.

Who Is Doing What to Whom?

Security tools monitor access to resources and manage who can access what. These tools provide a friendly interface that help you maintain user and group account information as well as access lists and the like. The NOS provides the middleware that does the actual authentication and access protection. The management tool provides the user interface and the environment to manage passwords, run virus scans, and track intruders. The idea is to provide an integrated view of client/server system management. So it makes sense to have the NOS services (such as security and directories) managed through the open system management platform.

How Do I Install New Software?

The number of programs on each individual machine has risen dramatically over the last few years. Administrators have had a hard time managing this explosion; it's one of their top five headaches. *Software distribution and installation tools* let you download, update, track, and deinstall software packages on any networked machine. These packages can include anything from new operating system releases to end-user applications. Most of these tools can track the version number and status of the software. The better tools can perform unattended pushes from the code server to a particular client machine. *Software license management* tools can meter and enforce the use of licensed software. They typically support a wide range of licensing policies. This is an area where proper standards are important.

Users can subscribe to a particular software package and have it automatically delivered and installed on their machine. Of course, this delivery must be coordinated with the license metering application. A typical installation tool is divided into three components: clients or recipients of a delivery, the software package to be distributed, and the delivery schedule. You should be able to create distribution lists of recipients making it easier to send software updates to a group of users. The delivery can be scheduled for a particular date and time. Clients can also perform installations on their own time—the *pull method*.

You should be able to define software distribution packages and subscription lists using a GUI (or preferably an OOUI). The "management by subscription" approach is used to automatically push the packages to all the subscribers. An OOUI allows a subscription list to be created by simply dragging and dropping individual host icons on a software package. The package typically consists of two component types: the files and directories that make up the software to be distributed, and the name of a program to be executed after the software is copied on each subscriber machine. Adding a new subscriber to a distribution list is just a matter of dragging a new icon and dropping it on the package.

Still missing is a "software vending machine" concept that lets clients browse from a wide selection of applications available on the server and try out an application before they buy. If they want to buy, the system should generate a purchase order, inform the licensing tool that it's OK to use this application, and update the inventory tool.

What Went Wrong? How Do I Fix It?

The number one headache of any administrator is, of course, how to deal with faults. The distributed nature of client/server systems—different transports, OSs, and databases—add several degrees of complexity. Failures can be caused by any single component or from mysterious combinations of conditions. *Fault management and help desk tools* receive alarms, identify the failure, and launch corrective actions. The best tools can combine network, systems, and application-level management views. They help break down walls between database, network, and system management functions, making it easier to correlate failure symptoms. The tool should maintain error logs and issue *trouble tickets* to the people who need to know about the problem.

If an alarm occurs, a tool should be able to perform any combination of the following: send a notification, send an e-mail message, call a beeper, invoke a user-supplied program, update a log file, flash an icon, and pop up an alarm window. The better management systems provide scripting facilities that make it easy to automate the known corrective actions. Some tools provide mechanisms for associating events with actions (event handlers). It's a typical event-driven system—for each failure event, there is an event-handler action script. The event-handler script language should be able to call on other managing applications (for example, the configuration control tool) to perform some corrective action or to gather information on what went wrong. It's also important to provide sophisticated filters for events to narrow down the conditions that require intervention.

Most tools do a good job gathering real-time data on device and connection status, but fall short on tasks like trend analysis, trouble ticketing, and reporting on network elements. The management software should continuously monitor the system for potential problems and be able to automatically launch preventive or corrective actions to resolve problems before they occur. Instead of relying on problem *autopsy* and after-the-fact repair actions, potential problems should be avoided without requiring human interaction. This makes managing client/server systems less tedious and less susceptible to human error.

Can My System Survive an 8.0 Earthquake?

It's not just for disaster recovery anymore. Network backup is becoming part of a storage-management strategy that removes the weak link: you.

— *Michael Peterson, PC Magazine*
(September, 1993)

Data on the network is continually growing, leaving the administrator with another big headache: How can you manage this growth within the allocated budget, while keeping the data safe from disasters? Disaster recovery includes everything from scheduling daily backups to maintaining hot-standby sites. *Disaster backup, archive, and recovery tools* can initiate the backup or restore action where the source and destination of the operation can be located anywhere on the network. These tools provide a user interface for scheduling the operations in unattended mode. The backup can be performed on any type of media. The better tools provide *hierarchical storage management* for multiple levels of storage—including memory caches, file servers, and an archive medium such as an optical juke box or tape drives. The tool should allow you to monitor where all the data resides and let you set policies like backup times. The best tools have the ability to learn from access patterns; they have some understanding of how information is related.

Chapter 28

Distributed System Management Standards

As we move to this new distributed client/server relationship, the question is: Are we going to have to put an administrator in each location? At $100,000 a year or so for each person, that gets expensive.

— *Gary Falksen, DBA with XES Inc.*

This chapter introduces about a dozen distributed management standards and a gaggle of new acronyms. We cover the traditional manager/agent standards—including SNMP, SNMP2, RMON, XMP, and XOM. We cover a standard for tiny desktop agents—the DMTF's DMI. And we cover two CORBA-based system management standards—the OSF's DME and UI's Atlas-DM. Of course, there is a Soapbox that gives you *our* opinion of system management in client/server environments. What would life be without Soapboxes?

Two "standard" management protocols have been defined: the Internet's SNMP and OSI's CMIP. Both are manager/agent protocols. Each of these protocols is capable of describing management information. The two protocols have much in common (including a confusing similarity in terminology), but they differ in a number of important ways. SNMP's approach is simple and straightforward, while CMIP's is both more powerful and more complex. The SNMP2 protocol introduced in 1993 fixes many of the "simple" SNMP's shortcomings, but it cannot be called simple any more—the specification is now over 400 pages. To isolate developers from the underlying management protocols, X/Open defines the *X/Open Management Protocol (XMP) API* that works on top of either SNMP or CMIP. The other contending standard is based on the use of distributed objects (of the CORBA variety) for system management.

THE INTERNET MANAGEMENT PROTOCOLS

The impact of adding network management to managed nodes must be minimal, reflecting a lowest common denominator.

> — **Marshall T. Rose, Chairman of the SNMP Working Group**

In 1988, the *Internet Engineering Task Force (IETF)* decided it needed an immediate stopgap solution to system management. The *Simple Network Management Protocol (SNMP)* was created to fill that need. IETF originally planned to pursue a two-track approach: SNMP in the short term, and the OSI *Common Management Information Protocol (CMIP)* in the long term. The OSI CMIP was far too complex for the needs of most devices; SNMP was simple and easy to implement. To help the transition, it was originally intended that the SNMP *Management Information Base (MIB)* and *Structure of Managed Information (SMI)* be subsets of the OSI systems management. Eventually, that requirement was dropped, and each protocol went its own way; but they still retain a lot of common terminology. SNMP is the dominant network management protocol today. However, SNMP has a lot of deficiencies—it cannot meet modern system management needs. SNMP2, introduced by the IETF in 1993, is intended to remove some of these deficiencies. In the meantime, many large corporations, telephone companies, and governments are committed to the OSI approach.

Defining Management Information: SMI and MIB-II

The Internet and OSI have introduced their own versions of a Data Definition Language for system management; in the process, they've also introduced a lot of strange and confusing terminology. To put it simply, the OSI and Internet people have created a language for defining the structure of the data that's kept on the managed devices. Their language defines a hierarchical (tree-based) database and names the components within the tree. The managing workstation uses this information to request data via a protocol such as SNMP or CMIP. The two protocols use the same type of architecture and terminology; however, CMIP is much richer and more complex than SNMP. CMIP uses richer data structures, more object-oriented data definition techniques, and a more sophisticated protocol for exchanging the data.

Both SNMP and CMIP use object-oriented techniques to describe the information to be managed; each resource to be managed is called a *managed object*. The managed objects can represent anything that needs to be managed—an entire host, a program, or just a variable maintaining a counter of received TCP packets. A *Management Information Base (MIB)* defines a structured collection of managed objects. The *Structure of Management Information (SMI)* defines the model, notations, and naming conventions used to specify managed objects within a particular protocol (such as CMIP or SNMP). If you view the MIB as a database, then the SMI provides the schema.

SMI identifies the data types and the representation of resources within a MIB as well as the structure of a particular MIB. The ISO *Abstract Syntax Notation One (ASN.1)* is a formal language used to define MIBs for both SNMP and OSI management systems. ASN.1 describes the data independently of the SMI encoding technique used. The Internet's RFC 1155 defines a simple SMI to be used with SNMP MIBs; it only supports a subset of simple data types consisting of scalars and two-dimension arrays of scalars. (In contrast, OSI supports complex data structures and inheritance relationships for data.) An *object identifier* consists of a left-to-right sequence of integers known as subidentifiers. The sequence defines the location of the object within a MIB tree.

RFC 1123 defines MIB-II, which is a superset of MIB-I (RFC 1156). MIB-II adds additional groups of managed objects. Figure 28-1 shows the structure of managed objects that are defined in MIB-II. Objects are defined by their hierarchical location in the tree—for example the IP object group is 1.3.6.1.2.1.4. New objects are always added "down and to the right." The ten object groups defined by the Internet are essential for either fault or configuration management. All devices that claim to be Internet managed nodes must implement the MIB; however, not all functions need to be present on all nodes. The *group* provides a convenient way to organize management objects according to the functions they provide. All objects within a group must be supported to be MIB-II compliant. For example, an implementation must include all objects within the IP group if it implements the IP protocol. The *experimental* node is used to introduce and debug new Internet-defined object categories before they become official MIB objects. The Internet believes that ideas must be proved in a working environment before they are considered for standardization.

The ten MIB-II object groups are not particularly thrilling. They contain several hundred low-level objects that perform TCP/IP based network management functions (from the transport layer down). The interesting system management stuff is left to the private MIB extensions.

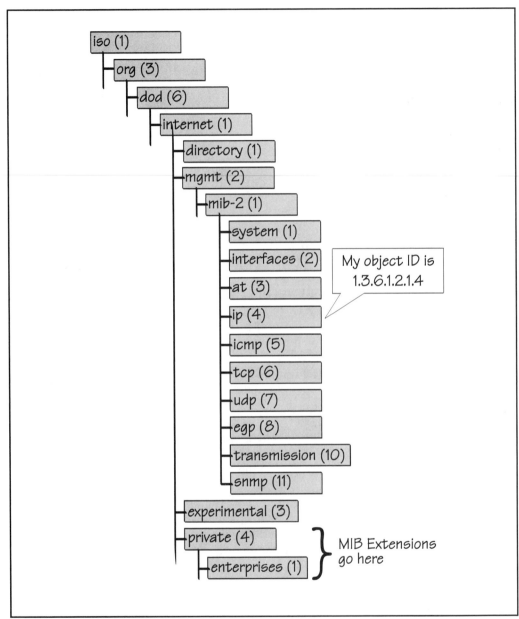

Figure 28-1. The MIB-II Object Groups.

New management objects are typically defined as MIB extensions in the *private* subtree; they allow vendors to create extensions that make their products visible to a managing station. The *enterprises* group is used to allocate *enterprise object IDs* to each vendor that registers for one. Vendors must describe their MIB extensions using formal descriptions—as defined in RFC 1155 or RFC 1212— inside a text file. Enough information must be provided to allow a managing station to load and compile the vendor-specific MIB definition and add it to the library of managed object descriptions. The managing station can only access information it knows how to ask for. The private MIB extensions are the heart of SNMP and OSI system management, but they're also the areas of greatest confusion. Users must make sure that the management platforms they select can handle the private MIB extensions for their systems. Different managing systems are known to produce different results when managing the same MIB data; it's scary stuff.

MIB Tools

Most management platforms provide tools that make MIBs friendly. A MIB is, in essence, a form of hierarchical database that's distributed across managed stations. Like any database, it requires tools that make it accessible. Here are the typical tools that make it easier to work with MIBs:

■ A *MIB compiler* takes a file in RFC 1155 format and converts it to a format that can be used by the management station. The compiler is also used to update an existing MIB and add new vendor-specific definitions.

■ A *MIB browser* displays the MIB tree in a graphical manner; it allows you to search for objects by groups or attributes. You can refresh instance data from any managed node. The browser should allow you to create aliases for MIB objects (i.e., give them names that you find meaningful). The browser is really nothing but a specialized query tool for MIB databases. Some vendors allow you to overlay the MIB information on maps or on pictures of the objects you're interested in.

■ A *MIB report writer* allows you to graphically create reports of the managed data. These reports may be augmented with business graphs, maps, and other forms of visual presentation.

MIB tools are typically integrated with other visual management tools. For example, an agent discovery tool can display the location of the agents on the network and the MIB query tool can be used to browse through the data they contain.

The Internet's SNMP

The *Simple Network Management Protocol (SNMP)* is the most widely implemented protocol for network management today—it is supported by a constantly growing number of network devices. SNMP, as defined in RFC 1157, is designed to do exactly what its name suggests—it performs relatively simple management of the components in a network. It is used to alter and inspect MIB variables. SNMP is an asynchronous request/response protocol that supports four operations (see Figure 28-2):

■ **GET** is a request issued by a managing station to read the value of a managed object. The get operation is atomic; either all the values are retrieved or none are. SNMP only supports the retrieval of leaf objects in the MIB.

■ **GET-NEXT** is a request made by a managing station to traverse a MIB tree; it reads the value of the "next" managed object in the MIB.

■ **SET** is a request issued by a managing station to modify the value of a managed object. This operation is often not supported because SNMP provides no effective security or ways to control who is allowed to perform SETs. The last thing you need are intruders causing havoc on the network using unprotected SNMP SETs.

■ **TRAP** is a notification from a managed system to a managing station that some unusual event occurred. SNMP traps are very limited; they report one of seven events: cold start, warm start, link down, link up, authentication failure, external gateway neighbor loss, and enterprise specific trap. The traps use unacknowledged datagrams.

SNMP exchanges use TCP/IP's *User Datagram Protocol (UDP)*—this is a very simple, unacknowledged, connectionless protocol. It is also possible to support SNMP over the ISO stack using the connectionless transport system. Most SNMP agents are implemented as TSRs or Daemon background tasks.

SNMP's Limitations

So what are the limitations of SNMP? The list is long; it's a classical tradeoff between simplicity and the complex requirements of modern management systems. Here's a quick of summary of SNMP's more blatant shortcomings:

■ ***SNMP is not secure.*** The protocol provides a very trivial form of authentication; it is child's play for an intruder to break into the system. Most network managers do not allow the use of the SET command. This can be very limiting.

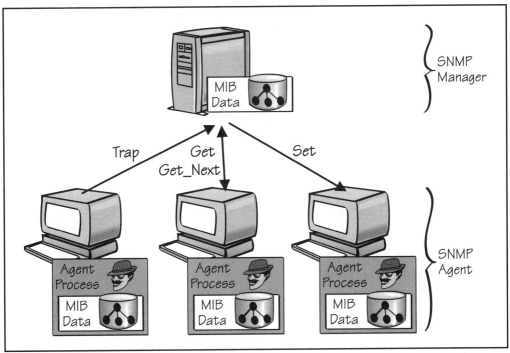

Figure 28-2. SNMP Manager/Agent Exchanges.

- ***SNMP is inefficient.*** The protocol is not suited for retrieving bulk data; you must send one packet for each packet of information you want returned. SNMP relies on polling, which can swamp a network with traffic. Because the event traps cannot be extended, they cannot be used to create an event-driven environment. The server calls the agent and not the other way round. Polling limits the number of variables that can be monitored by a managing station, which translates into more cost.

- ***SNMP lacks important functions.*** The protocol cannot be used to create new instances of MIB variables; it cannot execute management commands; and it does not support manager to manager communications.

- ***SNMP is unreliable.*** The protocol builds on the UDP, which is an unacknowledged datagram mechanism. The traps are unacknowledged, and the agent cannot be sure they reach the managing station. The SNMP designers believe that a datagram may have a better chance of reaching its destination under catastrophic conditions (that may be a bit far fetched).

In summary, SNMP is excellent at its intended task—simple network management. However, it is too limited to handle the more complex functions of systems management.

Stretching SNMP's Limits: The RMON MIB-II Extensions

The *Remote Network-Monitoring (RMON)* standard defined in RFC 1271 is a very significant extension of MIB-II that stretches SNMP to its limits. The moving forces behind RMON were the network monitor vendors; they needed extensions to SNMP that would allow their equipment to participate in the management of networks. A *network monitor*—for example, Network General's *Sniffer*—is a "promiscuous" device that sits on the network and can capture and view any packet, regardless of who sends it to whom. Clearly, these sniffer-like devices collect a tremendous amount of information that can be very useful to an SNMP managing station. Monitors are the ultimate "secret agent." They're tapped into the network and can see anything that moves on it. So the question is: How does a managing station obtain this massive information using SNMP? The answer is through the RMON MIB-II extensions.

What makes RMON so interesting is that it is the most intelligent entity ever defined by the Internet; it breaks the mold of the simplistic, simple-minded, and brain-dead managed device. A monitor must have enough intelligence to filter and act on the information it collects without directly involving the managing station for every action or swamping the network with massive amounts of bulk data transfers. Through *preemptive monitoring*, the sniffer continuously runs diagnostics on the network traffic, notifies the managing station when a failure is detected, and provides useful information about the event. This activist style is a far cry from the typical SNMP philosophy that views each managed node as a set of remote MIB-defined variables.

RMON defines the conventions, using MIB-II extensions on standard SNMP, for telling a remote monitor what data to collect. Remember that SNMP does not support imperative commands and it cannot create new instances of objects. So, RMON does it all via conventions that allow a MIB variable to represent a command and other variables to represent the parameters to the command; it's all very clumsy, but it shows what can be done in desperation. RMON defines a number of new MIB-II objects that represent commands. The monitor executes the command when the managing station writes to these objects using the SNMP SET command. The RMON specification defines how rows are to be added, deleted, or modified in a MIB setting. The bulk of RMON defines nine MIB-II object group extensions that are used to store data and statistics gathered by a monitor (see Figure 28-3).

Each of the nine RMON groups provide a set of control variables that allow a managing workstation to remotely control the operation of a monitor agent. These variables can be seen as state tables that tell the monitor what to collect and how to handle the events it generates. In a more modern setting, all of this could have been done using RPCs, MOM, or ORB invocations. RMON is a weird data-centric protocol that uses MIB variables to pass instructions, parameters, and control information between a managing station and an agent. It's a "kludge."

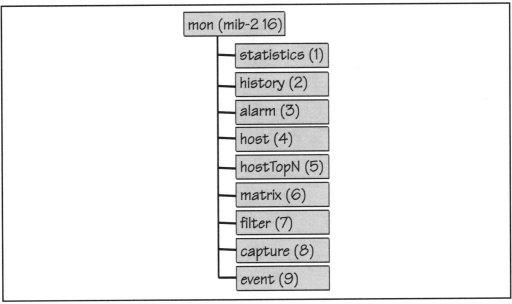

Figure 28-3. The RMON MIB-II Group Extensions.

SNMP2: What's New?

SNMP Version 2 (SNMP2) is the creation of Jeffrey Case, Keith McCloghrie, Marshal Rose, and Steven Waldbusser—the designers of the original SNMP and related Internet management standards. SNMP2, adopted as an Internet standard in March 1993, is designed to fix some of the more blatant problems in the original SNMP. The new specification consists of 12 RFC documents that total over 416 pages. SNMP2 improvements over SNMP include a new security protocol, optional encryption, manager-to-manager communications, bulk data transfer, new SMI data types, new MIB objects, and the ability to add or delete table rows (a la RMON).

SNMP2 Operations

An SNMP2 node can now be both a managing and a managed object. This makes it possible to create manager-of-managers arrangements, and it allows SNMP2 to share management information with its fellow managers. A new *Manager-to-Manager (M2M)* MIB is provided to support this topology. SNMP2 is a "proper extension of SNMP."

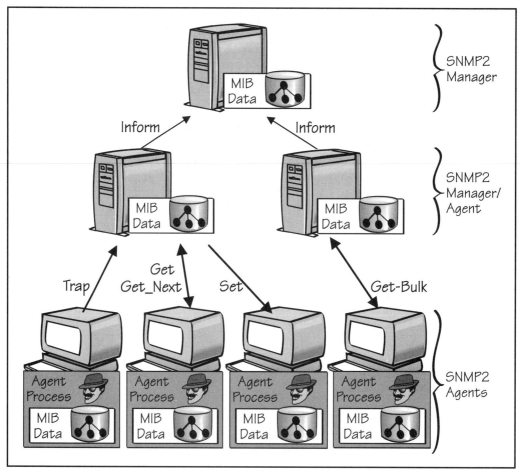

Figure 28-4. SNMP2: Manager/Agent and Manager/Manager Exchanges.

Here's the list of the old and new operations SNMP2 supports (see Figure 28-4):

■ **GET** is identical to SNMP. The only difference is in the way responses are returned. SNMP2 removes the atomic constraint, meaning that it will return whatever values can be returned—partial results are allowed. In contrast, SNMP either returns all the required variables or it posts an error.

■ **GET-NEXT** is identical to SNMP except that the atomic requirement is relaxed.

■ **GET-BULK** is a new command issued by a managing station. It is similar to GET-NEXT. However, instead of just returning the next variable, the agent can return as many successor variables in the MIB tree as will fit in a message.

- **SET** is identical to SNMP. It is a two-phased operation. The first phase checks that all the variables in the list can be updated; the second phase performs the update. Like SNMP, it's an all-or-nothing proposition.

- **TRAP** performs a role similar to SNMP, but it uses a different packet format (the SNMP trap header only recognizes a TCP/IP address type; SNMP2 is more general). And, like SNMP, the trap is unacknowledged.

- **INFORM** is a new command that's sent by an SNMP2 manager to another manager. It is used to exchange management information. The messages can be sent to all the manager nodes specified in the M2M MIB or to a particular manager. The M2M MIB allows a superior manager node to define the subordinate events it's interested in.

Like SNMP, SNMP2 is connectionless; it uses a datagram service. The specification includes mappings to UDP, IPX, AppleTalk, and the OSI connectionless service.

THE OSI MANAGEMENT FRAMEWORK

Many of SNMP's deficiencies are addressed by OSI network management. Some, however, see this as a case of the cure being worse than the disease, given the complexity and the size of OSI network management.

> — *William Stallings, Author,*
> *SNMP, SNMPv2, and CMIP*
> *(Addison Wesley, 1993)*

OSI distributed system management is defined by over 30 standards. Are you ready for a new dose of acronyms? In the OSI worldview, network management is divided into five application-level components called *System Management Functional Areas (SMFAs)*. These include fault management, accounting management, configuration management, performance management, and security management (see Figure 28-5). SMFAs rely on the services of 13 OSI-defined *System Management Functions (SMFs)*, which can be used by one or more SMFAs. The SMFs rely on the *Common Management Information Services Element (CMISE)*. CMISE is a combination of the protocols defined by the *Common Management Information Services (CMIS)* and the *Common Management Information Protocol (CMIP)*. CMIP, like SNMP, performs the actual exchanges between a managing station and an agent on the managed system. And like SNMP, it relies on a MIB to understand the capabilities of the managed agents and the data they store. OSI, of course, has its own CMI that defines information using ASN.1 notation; the basic unit of information is an object.

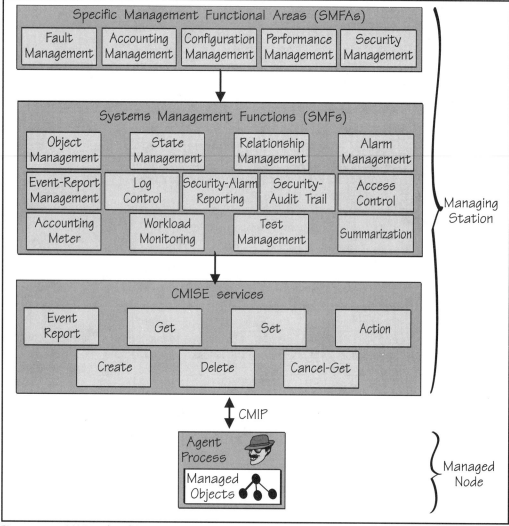

Figure 28-5. OSI Distributed System Management Overview.

What's an OSI Object—and What Can It Do?

While SNMP was intended to be simple, immediately useful, and quickly deployed, the groups developing OSI management took a different approach. The goal of OSI management is to provide a comprehensive solution to the broad problems of network (and, to some extent, systems) management. Because of its ambitious goals, OSI provides a comprehensive framework for defining *managed objects* borrowing heavily from object-oriented technology. The OSI notation used for describing managed objects is much richer than that used by SNMP. CMIP relies on a series of *templates* for defining managed objects and their attributes. You can specify the following characteristics for each managed object:

- **Attributes** are variables that represent the data elements in a managed object. Each attribute represents a property of the resource the object represents.

- **Operations** are the actions that can be performed on the attributes of an object or on the object itself. The actions that can be performed on the object's attributes include *get, replace, set, add,* and *remove members.* The actions that can be performed on the object itself include *create, delete,* and *action.* OSI does not provide the semantics for defining the behavior of an object (i.e., method implementations or inheritance).

- **Notifications** are events that are emitted by a managed object. For example, when some internal occurrence that affects the state of the object is detected. ISO defines a number of notification types, including the format of the data carried in a CMIP *event-report* and an object ID that uniquely identifies the source. Notification types include various alarms and violations, attribute value changes, object creation and deletion, and object state changes.

- **Inheritance** is a managed object class that inherits all the characteristics of its parent class. ISO defines a number of object classes that can be used as parent classes for the purposes of inheritance, including an *alarm record, log, system, security alarm reports,* and an *event forwarding discriminator.*

The notation for defining objects is defined in *ISO 10165*, a document entitled **Guidelines for the Definition of Managed Objects (GDMO)**. The notation is commonly referred to as GDMO templates; it is substantially more powerful (and complex) than the simple language for defining SNMP objects. As we explained, ISO objects have a rudimentary level of object-oriented characteristics; in contrast, SNMP MIB objects are just glorified variables in a hierarchical tree. The GDMO is closer in intent to the CORBA IDL. However, CORBA provides much more advanced and complete object semantics.

Surprisingly, no widely agreed upon ISO MIB has yet been defined; we do not have the equivalent of the Internet MIB-II. The good news is that a number of groups are working on such MIBs—including ISO itself, the *National Institute of Standards and Technology (NIST)*, the *European Workshop on Open Systems (EWOS)*, and the *Network Management Forum* (a consortium of vendors interested in developing vendor-neutral network management solutions). It remains to be seen when these groups will have completed a set of object definitions that don't conflict.

OSI Management Protocols: CMIP, CMOT, and CMOL

CMIP is really an abbreviation for the (overly) Complex Management Information Protocol.

> — Marshall T. Rose, author,
> The Simple Book
> (Prentice Hall, 1991)

CMIP is the OSI protocol for manager-to-agent and manager-to-manager communications. In sharp contrast to SNMP, *CMIP* is a connection-oriented protocol that runs on top of a complete seven-layer OSI stack. *CMIP over TCP/IP (or CMOT)* provides a skinnier version of CMIP for TCP/IP networks. *CMIP over LLC (or CMOL)* is the skinniest CMIP yet; it was designed by IBM and 3Com to run directly on top of the IEEE 802.2 logical link layer. CMIP is much richer in functionality than its SNMP counterpart. The CMIP protocol provides the following services:

■ **Get** requests data from the agent's management information base. The request may be for a single managed object or a set of managed objects. For each managed object value, one or more of its attributes can be requested.

■ **Event-Report** is a notification sent by an agent to a managing system indicating that some event has occurred. The service can optionally request a confirmation. Five parameters are passed with the notification event to specify the class of object and instance where the event originated, the type of event, the time it was generated, and any user information about the event.

■ **Action** is a request that directs a managed object to perform some particular action. The action is implemented by a procedure that's specified as part of the managed object. The *action-information* parameter, if present, can be used to pass input parameters and other information.

■ **Create** is a request made by a managing system to create a new instance of a managed object class.

■ **Delete** is a request made by a managing system to delete an instance of a managed object class.

All the CMIP services may be optionally performed with confirmation. To specify the context for the management objects of interest, CMIP employs two constructs: *scoping* and *filtering*. Scoping marks a node within the information tree where the search tree starts; filtering is a boolean search expression applied to the attributes of the scoped objects.

TINY AGENTS: THE DESKTOP MANAGEMENT INTERFACE (DMI)

Intel's winning strategy is to get a management agent on every X86. We opened up that technology to the world and created the DMTF.

— **Ed Ekstrom, Intel Corp.**

Not a single vendor adapter should be sold without a MIF...MIF everything in sight. MIFing now means users will be a lot less miffed later.

— **Jamie Lewis, PC Week (February 14, 1994)**

At the other end of the spectrum, an industry consortium called the *Desktop Management Task Force (DMTF)* is creating a lightweight agent to manage all components on a PC—including hardware, OSs, applications, storage, and peripherals. The DMTF consortium includes DEC, HP, IBM, Intel, Microsoft, Novell, Sunconnect, and Synoptics. DMTF is developing a set of agent APIs called the *Desktop Management Interface (DMI)* that will allow different vendors' desktop management applications to share common memory space on a PC. About 70 other companies, including Apple Computers, are working with the DMTF on DMI specifications. In October 1993, DMTF released version 1.0 of the *DMI Service Layer* for DOS, Windows, and OS/2 at its first developer's conference. Over 35 vendors demonstrated beta implementations of the technology. Both IBM and Microsoft announced they would build the DMI into future releases of their OSs by the end of 1994. DMI, however, is a protocol-independent multiplatform interface.

The DMI agent will be able to communicate with any type of *management system*, including those based on SNMP and CMIP, without implementing SNMP or CMIP. IBM has already demonstrated CMIP/CMOL support for DMI. The idea is that SNMP or CMIP are simply impractical when it comes to managing a DOS or Windows PC. They require anywhere from 40 KBytes to a MByte of memory—that may be unacceptable on DOS PCs. So DMTF is trying to create an agent that's skinnier and simpler than even SNMP. Using a concept called "slushware," the DMI agent can load and unload different pieces of code on demand, never taking up more than 6 KBytes. The DMI agent is packaged as a terminate-stay-resident (TSR) program for DOS and as a DLL for Windows and OS/2; it only consumes RAM when activated. The agent loads on demand the code needed to manage a device. After it is loaded, the DMI software agent unobtrusively collects information while other applications are running.

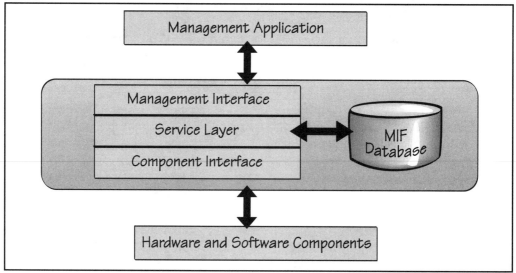

Figure 28-6. The DMTF Architecture.

The DMTF architecture (see Figure 28-6) consists of four components:

■ The **Component Interface** allows vendors of PC components such as memory boards, CD-ROMS, LAN adapters, and modems to register their devices and interfaces with DMI.

■ The **Service Layer** provides generic agent services. This device-independent layer interfaces to the local MIF database to deal with device-specific issues.

■ The **Management Interface File (MIF)** contains descriptions of the managed devices; it's similar in function to a MIB. The MIF is interpreted by the Service Layer, which uses the information to determine what actions to take on a managed device. The idea is that each of the 10,000 or so PC components will have a MIF provided by the component vendor. The vendor supplies the MIF and DMI handles the management.

■ The **Management Interface** provides a platform-independent API to the DMI services. The DMI agent can be externally accessed via SNMP, CMIP, or local applications; it provides the protocol to get to the MIFs.

DMI solves a real problem: It makes it practical to manage the 10,000 PC add-ins. One of the reasons management hasn't proliferated down to PC components through SNMP is *cost*. To be SNMP-compliant, add-in vendors had to create a private MIB, work out the interfaces to SNMP agents, and negotiate with vendors of management platforms to have their MIBs interpreted. In addition, most PCs running DOS and Windows don't have enough RAM to support multiple SNMP agents or their protocol stacks. To compensate, proprietary agents were sometimes placed in adapter cards—for example, Ethernet cards from 3Com or Cabletron. With DMI, component vendors only have to "MIF" their device; DMI does the rest. DMTF is also working with the Internet task force to add a *Host Resource* MIB group that manages objects on the PC.

X/OPEN MANAGEMENT STANDARDS

Wherever there are APIs, there's an X/Open standard lurking. So of course there are some X/Open standards for distributed system management calls. The idea is to provide a set of standard management APIs that isolate applications from the underlying management protocols (such as SNMP or CMIP). It's a very strange business we're in—we need standards to isolate us from other standards. X/Open defines two API sets: *XMP* and *XOM* (see Figure 28-7).

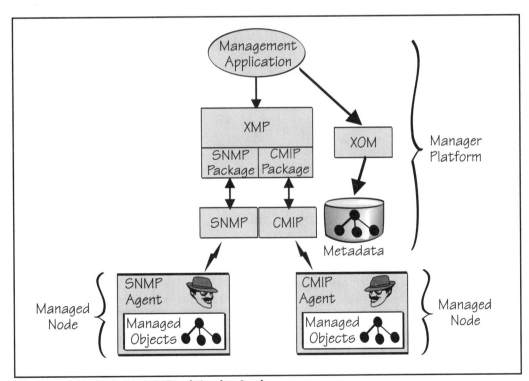

Figure 28-7. X/Open's XOM, XMP, and Metadata Database.

The X/Open XMP API

The *X/Open Management API (XMP)* is derived from an earlier interface called the *Consolidated Management API (CM-API)* from Bull and HP. The XMP API is used for standards-based, process-to-process communications between a managing system and a managed system. XMP defines a set of C API calls that allow access to both SNMP and CMIP. The interface semantics are more like CMIP than SNMP. Because of the differences in the representation of managed data, XMP does not make SNMP or CMIP totally transparent to the application. But as a compromise solution, XMP provides different XOM-based "packages" for use with the different protocols (XOM is explained in the next section). One package is defined for standard SNMP operations, and one is defined for standard CMIP operations.

The X/Open XOM API

XMP relies on another X/Open-defined API called *X/Open Object Manager (XOM)*. The XOM API is used to manipulate the data structures associated with managed objects. The XMP data structures are prepared using XOM API calls. The current version of XOM provides a way to deal with complex ASN.1-defined types in C. Both SNMP and CMIP use ASN.1. XOM is general enough to be used by protocols that are not even related to system management. For example, DCE uses XOM in its Global Directory Services.

To support the more complex CMIP object hierarchies, X/Open includes a *Package Development Kit (PDK)*. The primary component of the PDK is a *metadata compiler*, capable of reading GDMO definitions and producing a package (which is actually a set of C data types). These C structures can then be used with XMP and XOM. The metadata compiler populates a local database with information derived from GDMO definitions. The information about CMIP managed object classes includes their superior and subordinate object classes, the attributes of the class, and whether a given object class supports create and delete requests. The metadata database can be accessed using normal XMP calls. This process is similar in nature to the CORBA IDL compiler and Interface Repository. But the CORBA architecture is generally much more consistent; and it provides more advanced functions.

THE OSF DME STANDARD

In July 1990, the OSF issued a request for technology for a *Distributed Management Environment (DME)*, which was to provide a total solution for system and network management in heterogenous multivendor environments. Anyone, OSF member or not, could respond. 25 organizations submitted technologies. In September 1991, OSF announced the winners, which included HP's OpenView,

Tivoli's WizDOM, IBM's Data Engine, Groupe Bull's CMIP and SNMP drivers, and a few others. In May 1992, OSF published a very comprehensive architecture that combined a traditional network management framework with a postmodern CORBA-based object framework. As we go to press, it appears that OSF is scaling down its DME effort. Instead of using the Tivoli ORB, OSF now specifies management interfaces to any CORBA-compliant ORB. It also appears that OSF is putting most of its efforts in the management of DCE and interfacing DCE to ORBs (see following Soapbox). As a result, open platform vendors are acquiring parts of the DME technology directly from its originators and incorporating them into their products. For example, IBM licensed parts of OpenView from HP, which got incorporated into NetView/6000 and LAN NetView.

Regardless of what happens to DME (again, see the following Soapbox), its architecture remains of great interest. It provides a comprehensive framework for understanding distributed system management in its classical and postmodern approaches. The DME architecture uniquely reconciles these two approaches by using object wrappers and a CORBA-compliant IDL and ORB. This section provides a brief overview of DME's two design points:

- The *Network Management Option (NMO)* takes a classical manager/agent approach to system management.

- The *Object Management Framework (OMF)* provides a "postmodern" object-oriented solution based on CORBA.

In addition, DME includes a *Distributed Services* component that provides an infrastructure for services in a distributed environment. It also includes a user interface component.

The DME Network Management Option (NMO)

DME's *Network Management Option (NMO)* provides a traditional management platform for applications that wish to access SNMP and/or CMIP. DME augments the traditional X/Open components with an *Instrumentation Request Broker (IRB)*; see Figure 28-8. The IRB provides additional services on top of SNMP or CMIP. These services include the use of the DCE directory services to locate agents on the network, configurable retries, and a gateway service to the future DME CORBA-based management environment. Via the IRB, objects will be able to access SNMP and CMIP managed resources.

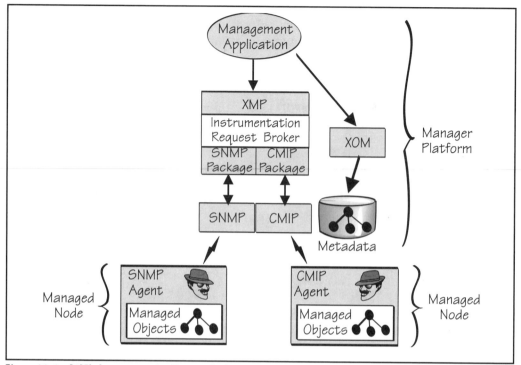

Figure 28-8. DME's Instrumentation Request Broker.

The DME Object Management Framework

DME's *Object Management Framework (OMF)* takes a radically new approach towards unifying network and system management; it builds on CORBA and the OMG services. The DME OMF is composed of multiple objects that cooperate and share information. The new framework goes beyond the traditional manager/object relationship. Instead, an object may at any time take either of two roles: a client requesting a service or a service provider. The DME *I4DL*—an upwardly compatible CORBA IDL with some extensions for event management and installation instructions—is used to describe the interfaces, attributes, and inheritance relationships of any management object. The communication between objects takes place over any standard CORBA ORB that uses DCE for its core communications (see Figure 28-9). DME calls this DCE-based ORB the *Management Request Broker (MRB)*.

How does the postmodern object-oriented DME incorporate devices that are managed using traditional protocols such as SNMP and CMIP? The answer is through special DME encapsulators called adapter objects (not to be confused with the CORBA object adapters used on servers). The I4DL is used to encapsulate legacy

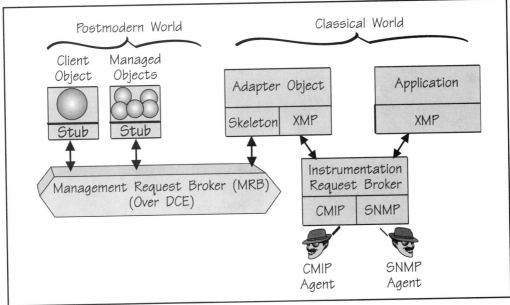

Figure 28-9. The DME Object Management Framework.

protocols and bring them to the object world. The adapter object looks like any other IDL-defined object. An application object can invoke operations on the adapter just like it does on any object using the typical remote invocations. Proxy methods invoked on the adapter call XMP to perform SNMP or CMIP functions. The adapter may define a set of operations that emulate the corresponding CMIP or SNMP calls, or it could augment them in some useful ways. For example, a CMIP adapter object might aggregate several CMIP operations on some managed object into one, providing a higher level of abstraction to the legacy object.

In summary, DME's OMF uses objects to encapsulate the implementation of any management resource. A managed object can only be accessed through an IDL-defined set of interfaces. The combined network and system management is modeled as the communication and interaction between objects that represent the resources of the system and objects that represent the user interface and managing applications. DME primarily deals with communication between management objects. Object adapters are used to encapsulate standard management protocols—such as SNMP, CMIP, and DCE. The DME Management Request Broker (with the help of the DCE directory services) provides a uniform naming space for all its objects (legacy or postmodern) and knows how to find them and invoke their services. DME may extend its security services to cover SNMP and other vulnerable spots in the system. So welcome to the postmodern world of system management with distributed objects.

Is DME Dead?

Soapbox

The ultimate goal of DME is unchanged: To provide a platform for integrated system and network management. Much of its work is aimed at providing better integration with DCE, but the scope of DME remains broader than simply managing DCE.

— Michael Goulde
Distributed Computing Monitor
(January, 1994)

After the demise of UI, the trade press has been ripe with speculation about the long term viability of OSF (the other Unix consortium). The press started reading the tea leaves when the Tivoli-based ORB technology was dropped from the DME plans. Is DME really dead? To paraphrase Mark Twain, "The rumors of DME's death have been greatly exaggerated." It appears that DME is alive and well and has simply been redirected. This is in line with the recent restructuring of OSF to focus on architecture, subcontracting, and the distribution of standards-based infrastructure software. They no longer have a complete software development organization.

The "redirected DME" has adopted a secular approach to the management ORB—any CORBA-compliant ORB will do. The original *Management Request Broker (MRB)* was based on Tivoli, which was not CORBA-compliant. When OSF members decided to move to a CORBA-compliant management ORB, they made the decision that OSF should leave the ORB business to OMG. Any CORBA-compliant ORB now qualifies as an MRB. DME was restructured (late 1993) to define management services on top of the MRB. The OSF was also chartered to provide lower-level interfaces between any CORBA-compliant ORB and DCE. (For example, DCE needs to provide a dynamic invocation API to support CORBA).

According to the new plan, OSF will release (in late 1994) management services that run on any CORBA 1.1 compliant ORB. These services will include discovery agents, maps, collections, and topology displays. OSF will also define a set of management APIs to these services. The OSF is submitting its APIs for the future enhanced DCE to the OMG as part of the CORBA 2.0 RFT. OSF would like DCE to become the future basis for interoperability between ORBs. In addition, OSF is working with OMG on the management services. In a separate move, Tivoli is submitting its management APIs to X/Open; OSF may also end up adopting these APIs. (Source: **Distributed Computer Monitor**, January 1994). ❑

UI-ATLAS DISTRIBUTED MANAGEMENT FRAMEWORK

Unix International (UI) was the industry's other Unix consortium; its 270 members defined the requirements for the evolution of distributed software for Unix within an architecture framework called *Atlas*. In July 1991, UI published its *Atlas-Distributed Management (Atlas-DM)* requirements—distributed objects were the key unifying concept. USL elected to implement the first release of Atlas using existing Tivoli technology. The second release, which was due in 1994, was to be CORBA-based. The UI requirements, in the pre-Novell acquisition days, were implemented by USL (or whomever USL contracted out for the job). We're using the past tense because UI was dissolved on December 31, 1993. We still cover Atlas-DM in this section because it's an important architecture that may still end up being implemented in some Unix variants.

Architecturally, UI went even further than OSF's DME in its support of objects—the first release of Atlas didn't even bother with SNMP and CMIP. Atlas-DM, like the postmodern DME, defines management applications as collections of objects that interact with each other and with objects that represent the managed resources. The UI *Management ORB (MORB)* provides transparent access to managed objects across the network (see Figure 28-10). The objects represent generic resources in the distributed environment—including hosts, users, LANs, DBMSs, applications, disks, files, and OSs. A single dynamic API call—the Tivoli *objcall*— is used to invoke methods on objects (all parameters are passed as ASCII character strings). Object references can be passed at run time. In addition, Tivoli allows the dynamic discovery of objects and the operations they support. The second release

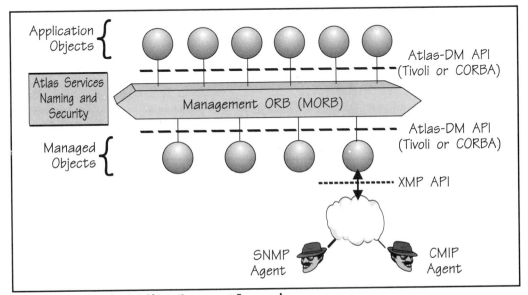

Figure 28-10. The Atlas-DM Object Management Framework.

of Atlas-DM would have used CORBA IDL stubs, dynamic method invocations, and a CORBA-compliant ORB. It was going to implement the X/Open XMP API for interfacing to SNMP and CMIP.

COMPARING CMIP, SNMP, SNMP2, AND CORBA

Table 28-1 compares the features of SNMP, SNMP2, CMIP, and CORBA. SNMP and SNMP2 place a minimum amount of event-emitting logic in the agents so as to keep the managed nodes simple; the smarts are in the managing station. As a result, the traps are infrequently used and the managing station must poll the agents to find out what's happening. In contrast, CMIP and CORBA are event-driven, which means the agents are smarter; the managing station doesn't have to poll as much. As a result, a CMIP managing station can handle a much larger number of managed objects. In general, CMIP or CORBA are better suited for the management of large, complex, multivendor networks than SNMP. Of course, SNMP's simplicity allows it to be deployed on more devices, which, in turn, makes it easier to manage large networks. The designers of SNMP understood these trade-offs very well. They opted for the least common denominator approach and were willing to live with the consequences. SNMP2 makes the same architectural trade-offs as SNMP. It looks like the Internet designers still feel that their original assumptions are valid. But looking at the comparison table, we're not so sure SNMP is still the way to go (see the following Soapbox).

Table 28-1. Comparing SNMP, SNMP2, CMIP, and CORBA Objects.

Feature	SNMP	SNMP2	CMIP	CORBA Objects
Installed base	Huge	Small	Small	Very small
Managed objects per managing station	Small	Small	Large	Large
Management model	Manager and agents	Manager and agents	Manager and agents	Communicating objects
View of managed objects	Simple variables organized in MIB trees	Simple variables organized in MIB trees	Objects with inheritance defined in MIBs	Objects with IDL defined interfaces, attributes, and multiple inheritance
Manager/agent interactions	Polling. Infrequent traps	Polling. Infrequent traps	Event driven	Event driven
Explicit manager to agent command invocations	No	No	Yes	Yes

Table 28-1. Comparing SNMP, SNMP2, CMIP, and CORBA Objects. (Continued)

Feature	SNMP	SNMP2	CMIP	CORBA Objects
Security	No	Yes	Yes	Yes
Manager-to-manager exchanges	No	Yes	Yes	Yes
Bulk transfers	No	Yes	Yes	Yes
Create/delete managed objects	No	No (but can add table rows)	Yes	Yes
Communication model	Datagram	Datagram	Session-based	ORB
Standards Body	Internet	Internet	ISO	OMG
Approximate Memory requirements (in KBytes)	40-200	200-500	300-1000	300-2000

SNMP, CMIP, or Objects

Soapbox

A *network-management system is limited by the capabilities of the network-management protocol and by the objects used to represent the environment to be managed.*

— *William Stallings, Author,*
SNMP, SNMPv2, and CMIP
(Addison Wesley, 1993)

We believe CORBA provides a modern and natural protocol for representing managed entities, defining their services, specifying instance data, and invoking methods via an ORB. The CORBA Interface and Implementation Repositories can be used to discover and dynamically invoke methods on these managed objects at run time. The managed objects can directly call the managing station when they have something significant to report (in contrast, SNMP relies mostly on polling). The CORBA Event Manager service is ideal for distributing asynchronous system management events. And the CORBA object services are providing a ton of useful functions that would have to be reinvented by SNMP or

CMIP (lifecycle, naming, transactions, persistence, etc.). Using CORBA, Distributed System Management becomes just another service on the ORB. Objects can manage themselves. Management applications provide views on collections of self-managing objects.

Unfortunately, many of today's managed devices don't have the memory or processing power to support a full ORB; these devices can only support the "simple" version of SNMP or, better yet, DMI. However, hardware is getting cheaper while the cost of administering systems isn't. In addition, "simple" SNMP is too limiting for the requirements of total systems management—it needs to be replaced. This means that in the next few years we'll be experiencing a large migration to more sophisticated agent software.

The three contenders for replacing SNMP are SNMP2, CMIP, and CORBA. All three require more memory and smarter processors than SNMP. So the question is: Which one do you choose? In our opinion it should be CORBA. SNMP2 and CMIP are both antiques and incredibly clumsy to program. MIBs are an anachronism in the age of IDL and object persistent stores. SNMP2 does not allow you to register operations on managed objects; CMIP does it in a very clumsy fashion. We feel the "simple" SNMP was a wonderful, basic protocol that solved many real problems in the age of scarcity and simple network management. But now that we're moving to total systems management, the sooner the world moves away from SNMP, SNMP2, and CMIP and replaces them with CORBA, the better off system management will be. ❑

Part 9
Bringing It All
Together

An Introduction to Part 9

Are you Martians still with us? All that talk of problem management and disaster recovery didn't faze you? We're reaching the end of our journey. We realize this tour was really long, but client/server is a broad topic. You probably want us to net it all out for you: Which technology do I pick? How do I get an application out in record time? What help can I expect? It turns out these are the one million dollar questions of client/server.

Which technology do I pick? This is like predicting the future. Anybody can predict it, but the trick is getting it right. We'll give you our two cents worth on where we think this technology is going. You Martians now know how to surf, so we'll throw in a wave theory of client/server. The idea is to look at technology cycles and figure out which wave to ride. If you read this book, you won't be too surprised by the answers.

How do I get an application out in record time? This takes us into the subject of tools. Here on earth, we've had tools since the dawn of our civilization to help us with our work. The job of toolmakers is to look at all the raw technologies and create the tools that ordinary mortals can use to get a job done. With tools, we can develop client/server applications quickly. The better tools can even help us deploy and manage our client/server applications. Toolmakers are constantly trying to keep up with the types of information presented in this book; they use it to decide the raw technology on which to build their tools. Picking a tool is not easy. It locks you into a client/server paradigm. And we know that there's more than one way to do client/server; in fact, there are hundreds of ways to do it. So we'll answer the question by throwing at you a few models on how to pick a tool. Then you'll have to decide which tool is best for your job.

What help can I expect? You'll need a good tool, a working methodology, and lots of good luck. You'll mostly be on your own—but that's when the real fun starts. This book provides a Survival Guide; it's just one more aid that will help you filter the signal from the noise in this overhyped field. Of course, you can always get the advice of consultants and attend seminars. But good advice doesn't come cheap. This final part gives you an overview of tools and methodologies. Are you Martians ready for your return trip home? Time does fly when you're having fun.

Chapter 29

Client/Server Tools and Application Development

Sitting quietly, doing nothing, Spring comes, and the grass grows by itself.

— A Zen poem

This is the chapter that's going to bring it all together. We'll bring out our infamous crystal ball and speculate on where client/server technology is heading. We may even jump on a Soapbox and give you a fearless forecast of which technology wave looks most promising. The million dollar question is: Which magic tool can take the pain out of client/server application development and deployment? And a related question is: Does client/server require a new approach to application development? All these questions are very dear to your authors' hearts. For the last five years, two of your authors were building client/server application development and visual programming tools; the third author, Jeri, manages client/server tool development, among other things. Our elusive goal has always been to create the perfect tool for developing, deploying, and maintaining client/server applications *quickly*. However, we learned the hard way that you have to make some serious compromises. There is no such thing as a "one size fits all" client/server tool. And there is no magic tool (including ours), so the next best thing we can do is leave you with a model for how to evaluate them. We'll even throw in our two cents on client/server development methodologies.

THE WAVES OF CLIENT/SERVER TECHNOLOGY

Figure 29-1 offers our fearless "wave forecast" of where client/server technology is heading. The first wave of client/server was brought about by NOSs. The NOSs make it easier for applications to share files, printers, and other networked devices; they perform their magic by extending the reach of the operating system. We could call the first wave of client/server the "NetWare wave." We're well into the second wave of client/server—the wave of database-centric applications. The predominant technology in the second wave is the "SQL database server." However, we're also experiencing two other major technology ripples caused by groupware and TP Monitors. The third wave of client/server is the distributed object wave. We devoted almost 100 pages of the book to this technology, which we feel is almost ready for prime time. Objects encompass all the technologies of the first and second wave and add considerable new value. They have the unique potential to distribute intelligence among clients and servers to where it's needed most.

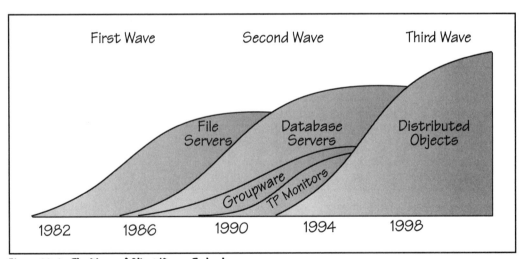

Figure 29-1. The Waves of Client/Server Technology.

Which Wave Should I Ride?

We shouldn't have to get on a Soapbox to state the obvious: Distributed objects are the future of client/server technology. Objects encompass all aspects of distributed computing including OOUIs, compound documents, transactions, groupware, database, and system management. So the million dollar question is: Should you invest in interim technologies, or should you just catch the object wave? It's a trade-off between using proven technologies and the ones that are at the "bleeding edge." We constantly face this same dilemma as client/server tool providers: Should we build our tools around proven SQL databases and TP Monitors, or should we go to ORBs and ODBMSs? We're really at a painful technological juncture. Mixing paradigms typically gives you the worst of both worlds. However, in some cases, if you know what you're doing you can also get the best of both worlds. We recommend that you get your feet wet now. There's enough raw technology for you do that. Unfortunately, you can't depend on open distributed object development tools—they're nowhere in sight. (Yes, we know about Forte, but its ORB is proprietary.)

The Client/Server Scalability Issue

In addition to technology waves, we must factor the issue of scalability into the choice of a client/server platform. It is much easier to deploy client/server in small enterprises and departments. Over 80% of the existing client/server installations are single server and have less than 50 clients. The small installations are typically easier to deploy and manage. Almost all of the existing client/server tools address that market. These tools can successfully be used to create client/server applications for decision support, e-mail, and groupware. They provide excellent facilities for building GUI front-ends and are adept at working with shrink-wrapped middleware and server packages (mostly SQL DBMSs and Lotus Notes). However, even at the low end, we don't have adequate tools for creating mission critical solutions. By this we mean applications you can depend on to run your everyday business operations. These type of applications, especially at the low end, must support transactions, built-in system management, and high-availability. It is also sad to report that with over 200 hundred front-end tools on the market, not a single one can create a decent OOUI interface (they all do GUIs).

Intergalactic client/server is much more complex. It requires the sophisticated middleware described in this book—including DCE, MOM, distributed transactions, and ORBs. It requires proven tools that can take advantage of this middleware. Intergalactic client/server is by definition multiserver. So the tools should be able to deploy applications on multiple servers, manage transactions that are distributed across them, perform some form of load balancing, deploy the software to the clients and servers, and manage the multiserver environment. To be open, these tools are expected to do all this on multivendor operating systems, multivendor resource managers, and multiple GUI front-ends.

In short, MIS people are demanding the level of cohesiveness and scalability they have grown accustomed to on single vendor mainframe platforms, but now they want it for an open client/server world. Of course, we're nowhere close to meeting these expectations. As we explained in this Survival Guide, much of the technology and standards that are needed to make this happen are finally coming together; it will be another few years before the tools can catch up. Perhaps massive downsizing is a bit premature. It can be done, but using raw third-generation languages and some rudimentary tools that help build the front-end clients. It won't be a picnic. However, some tool vendors seem to understand the requirements and perhaps in a few years we'll have the luxury of being able to create intergalactic client/server applications by pointing and clicking (or better yet, dragging and dropping).

The Secret Shame of Client/Server

Soapbox

There's another scam in progress. People are stampeding toward client/server because they're being told it's easy, and that's just not true. No matter what application development tools you choose, it's extremely difficult to design a high performance client/server application. It's worse than black art.

> — Patricia Seybold, "The Secret Shame of Client/Server Development," ComputerWorld (August, 1993)

The real secret is that there are two client/server paradigms: PC LAN client/server and intergalactic client/server. Some call it "Small Client/Server" and "Large Client/Server." Let's face it, client/server started as a PC LAN phenomenon and has done quite well there. It doesn't take a rocket scientist to deploy a NetWare server or write a Lotus Notes application. Tools like Gupta's Quest allow a novice to create a front-end to a SQL database in a matter of hours. And how difficult is it to write a client application using VisPro/REXX, Digitalk Parts, or Visual Basic? In general, the PC world has been babystepping into client/server from the bottom up, and most of us have been quite happy with the pace of progress.

The current technology frontier for PC LAN development tools is in the following two areas:

■ **Stored procedures.** How do you visually create stored procedures on the server and associate their parameters with the visual elements on the client side?

■ **Preloaded client/server.** How do you package, deploy, and manage turnkey client/server applications? And, how do you bundle the system components—including middleware and an SQL database—with the turnkey application?

If client/server is to succeed in the PC market, it must be sold through regular PC software marketing channels. So we need to find ways to easily create shrink-wrapped client/server applications that match the rest of the PC software packages in terms of price, ease of use, and installation. We think these problems are solvable. So there is really no "secret shame of client/server" in the PC LAN side of the house—things are on track and moving at a fast pace.

The secret shame may be in the intergalactic side of the house. Perhaps all the relentless client/server hype has led some to believe that they could junk all the mainframes that couldn't fit on a desktop and instantly recreate their 100,000 terminal-based airline reservation systems using Visual Basic. Of course, we can't do that right now.

But you can see from the extensive technology we covered in this book that a solid foundation for intergalactic client/server is coming together. The important standards are behind us. The DCE and MOM infrastructures are almost ready for prime time, SQL servers are in their second generation, open TP Monitors are now a reality, and open platforms for distributed system management are here today. A little bit further out on the horizon are CORBA-based distributed objects and the services that surround them. And, we're finally getting ready for object frameworks that promise to revolutionize the way client/server applications are written and deployed. So there is not much to be ashamed of. The one exception, of course, is intergalactic client/server development tools—as we said earlier, don't expect to see any soon.

We believe that client/server for PC LANs is ready for business today. You would be at a disadvantage not to make immediate use of the technology PC LANs provide. The tools are not stellar, but they're adequate (we can always do better when it comes to tools). We also believe that you should start laying out some of that intergalactic client/server foundation we've talked about in this Survival Guide. You can do that by introducing some pilot projects that can help you stay on top of the technology as it evolves.

Pssst...Here's the Real Secret to Client/Server Success

But since we're on the topic of "secrets," we'll offer you an opinion that may sound like heresy. (Hopefully, it's too late for a refund now.) With our deep apologies to the open movement, we believe that the *real secret* to client/server success today is to apply the KISS (Keep It Simple Stupid) principle. Pick a single client/server platform, limit the number of vendors, limit mix-and-matching, keep the project simple, use a single server, and get the system up and running fast. Don't think in terms of posterity. Instead, think in terms of *disposable* client/server solutions.

> If it takes six weeks to develop and deploy an application that runs on PCs, then it won't hurt you to dispose of it when something better comes along (the PCs can be salvaged). Of course, you should also stay on top of all that "strategic" intergalactic client/server stuff. However, only deploy it when it's as easy and simple as the "disposable" client/server technology. The rule is: If it's easy, then it's ready for prime time. The corollary is: If it's that easy, then it's disposable. So you're constantly introducing new technology by rapidly creating and deploying "disposable" client/server applications. ❑

CLIENT/SERVER APPLICATION DESIGN

Mainframe application designers and programmers have had it easy. In the past, user interfaces were simple constructs driven by simple terminals. The primary focus was on the database and transaction code, leaving the human to simply respond, like an extension of the application. But with client/server applications, the tables have turned. The ultimate goal of client/server solutions is to provide mission-critical applications that have the ease-of-use and responsiveness of stand-alone PCs. In this section, we present a methodology for designing OLTP-based client/server applications.

Client/Server is primarily a relationship between programs running on separate machines. As such, it requires an infrastructure to do things standalone PCs never had to worry about. For example, robust interprocess communications over LANs must be included in the design. Graphical interfaces using GUIs and OOUIs must be exploited to make applications look and feel more like real-world objects instead of programming processes. User interfaces are becoming complex, responsive, ad hoc environments that put the emphasis on the human task. OOUI clients bring humans into the distributed loop, which inevitably adds a host of complications. Humans make lots of errors, do unexpected things, and typically require lots of information from diverse sources. The more advanced OOUIs will introduce a new breed of *superclients* that turn the client workstation into multimedia "workplaces" where many parallel dialogs are conducted with a variety of servers.

OOUIs also give the user much more freedom than GUIs or terminal-based systems. Users are free to organize their visual objects (and desktop) in any way they please. They are not tied to the rigid logic of task-oriented applications. OOUIs have no main panels and navigation screens. They make it hard to tell where one application starts and another ends (or what an application object is versus a system object). There are just visual objects everywhere. This begs two important questions: Does client/server require a new approach to system development? Where design used to predominantly start at the database, which comes first now: the client or the server?

What Makes Client/Server Different?

Traditional (terminal-based) system design started with the data. The screens were developed primarily to drive the process of filling in the database, so they were designed after the transactions and tables were defined. Client/Server OLTP applications, on the other hand, require a far more complex design approach:

- The interface is more flexible than terminals, and the user is allowed more latitude.

- The object-based, front-end designs place a lot more intelligence on the client side of the application.

- The messages between the client and the server are custom-built and application-specific.

- The design must be optimized to take advantage of the parallelism inherent in the distributed application.

This leads us to a design approach unique to client/server applications: You must start your design with both the client and the server. So, you have two starting points in a client/server application: the GUI/OUUI and the data (unless the data for a business process is already in place). The GUI/OOUI and data designs come together at the transaction level. The transaction maps the screen to the database, and vice versa. Does this seem complex? Don't worry: It's not nearly as ominous as it sounds.

Rapid Prototyping Is Essential

One way to avoid a "chicken and egg" situation from developing—like the one in Figure 29-2—is to use a rapid prototyping methodology. Rapid prototyping allows you to develop your system incrementally. You start with the client and work your way iteratively towards the server. You always move in small steps, constantly refining the design as you go along. Make sure to involve your end user during all the stages of the interface design. In this form of delta development, the system is incrementally refined until you develop a working prototype that is mature enough to be placed into production. This approach may place a larger burden on the programmer than the traditional approaches, which rely on up-front analysis and design. And, with rapid-prototyping, you also run the risk that a cost-cutting management decision may place a non-optimized "working" prototype prematurely into production. At the other extreme, you may encounter another risk: the perpetual prototyping syndrome.

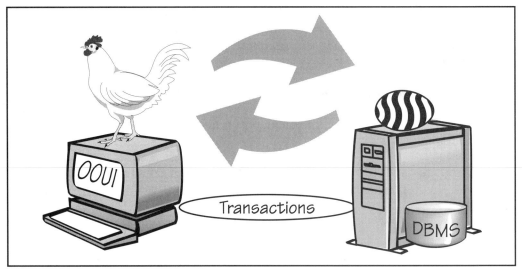

Figure 29-2. The Client/Server Chicken and Egg.

These risks are easily outweighed by the benefits that "rapid prototyping" provides in developing an OOUI client/server system. In client/server environments, it is difficult to determine beforehand how the system is supposed to work (the OOUI design, the network performance, and multiuser loading). It has been our experience that user specifications cannot anticipate all the needs of the users. They cannot adequately account for the potential OOUI technology offers. If you ask the users for guidance, the chances are that they'll give you the wrong answers based on existing solutions (manual or terminal-based solutions). Instead, you should show them what the technology can do for them and what new visual dimensions OOUIs offer; then work with them on developing the application.

Invariably, OOUIs can capture more of the business process than either GUIs or terminal-based front-ends. A rapid prototype will help in the discovery of the application objects (or business objects). Users will find it easier to discuss visual business objects, and the visual prototype will help develop the design specifications.

Build a prototype; try it out. The trick is to be able to build the application many times. It is easier to talk about something that can be demonstrated live and used. Moreover, it is important that the prototype be developed in an environment where the issues of client/server performance, network overheads, system management, and transaction server design can be tested live. Client/Server systems require a lot of monitoring, fine-tuning, and administration. It is better for you to get acquainted with these issues early in the game.

From Prototype to Working System

The OOUI objects permeate the entire application and determine its shape. An application can be seen as a collection of visual business objects. The design of the application starts from the objects (and views) the user sees on the screen, and then works its way towards the server and the database structure. Prototypes are used to identify, with your customer's participation, the user model: What business objects are needed, and what do they do? Prototyping is an iterative activity with many false starts. Here is how the typical prototype evolves:

1. ***Understand the business process***. It is a prerequisite that you understand what the application is all about at the business level. So gather the requirements and study the tasks: What does the customer really want?

2. ***Define your business objects***. What the user sees in an OLTP application are objects containing views that react to user input and actions. The objects are manipulated according to the requirements of the business process. You should create user objects that correspond to real-life entities; for example, a seat on an airplane. What are the main object types in the application? What other objects do they contain? What are the attributes of the objects? What functions do they have? How do they behave? What are the relationships between objects? What are the "composed of" relationships (is-part-of)? What are the dependency and collaboration relationships (is-analogous-to, is-kind-of, depends-upon)?

3. ***Work on the detailed object views***. What context menu actions apply to each object? What views are required? Are business forms views required? Can the views be grouped in Notebook pages? What widgets controls—including input/output fields, list boxes, pushbuttons, menus, sliders, value-sets, and so on—will appear in the views? What level of help is needed? What data validation at the field level is required? What level of triggers are required (on error, on message, etc.)? How are external procedures and RPCs invoked?

4. ***Develop dry run scenarios***. You can create your screen objects and animate the application (OOUI tools should provide this capability). Use the scenarios to validate the object model of the user interface. The scenarios should also help you identify the major event-driven interactions.

5. ***Walk through a system scenario***. Such a scenario should follow a transaction from its source through its execution. Identify the protocols that link the different elements. Blow up this scenario in areas that require more detail. Run an application scenario for each business object. Identify redundant behaviors. Which objects can be reused?

6. ***Identify transaction sources***. A client/server system can be thought of as a client-driven event system. The server is, in a sense, passively waiting on

requests from clients. The client, in turn, is driven by the user who is at the "controls" within the confines of the business process. The drag and drop of visual objects is typically the source of transactions. Information required upon opening a container or view may also be the source of a transaction. Object/action intersections almost always lead to the generation of a transaction. There is also a high probability that events such as data entry, menu selections, pushing a button, and action dialogs will generate transactions. The visual client interface will eventually be "brought to life" by writing the transactions that are triggered by the user interaction. OO purists can think of transactions as methods that manipulate persistent data.[1]

7. ***Define your database tables***. You are now in a position to take a first stab at defining the database objects that correspond to the visual business objects you just created. Iterate on this step until you get it right. Many trade-offs are involved. The object/action orientation of the client design can help transform the visual objects into an entity-relationship model for database objects. The actions translate into transactions on database entities. A database entity, in turn, consists of a structure of relationships and constraints between database tables. Publish the resulting CREATE TABLE statements, and then use them to document the data types and the relationships between tables (such as referential integrity constraints).

8. ***Publish the client/server messages***. Messages are the methods by which the clients execute transactions on servers. Define the major transactions and the request/reply messages associated with them, including any required file transfers. The messages provide the only coupling between the clients and the server. The publication of the messages advertises to the world what a server does. It is a *binding contract* between the server and its clients. A message typically has a command field and a data field, which contains the command parameters. In our scheme of things, we divide transactions (or commands) into two broad categories based on the type of responses they produce:

    ◆ ***Request/reply transactions*** are transactions that generate short replies. These transactions are usually updates, inserts, deletes, or single-row queries against database objects.

    ◆ ***Bulk response transactions*** are transactions that generate one or more result files. Think of a result file as a BLOB, which may result from a multirow SELECT or from the request for a metafile or bitmap.

---

[1] In strict OO terms, a raw transaction server is a single object that encapsulates the entire database (as its private instance data). A back-end application could be written as a set of objects that export methods (the transactions). You will eventually hit a design point where SQL's shared data tables and OO's encapsulation discipline don't mix very well.

Another way to create a binding client/server contract is by using an *Interface Definition Language (IDL)*. The IDL defines the functions exported by the server. It provides a higher-level of abstraction than messages. For example, you could use the DCE RPC IDL or better yet CORBA, whose *Interface Repository* offers a way to discover services dynamically.

9. ***Develop your code one object at a time***. Write the SQL code for each transaction. Do that one object at a time. There are typically many transactions per business object. Validate the user interface and the performance of the system with your customer.

10. ***Move from prototype to working system***. A working system is the sum of all the business objects it contains. You are developing your system incrementally, so you will have a full working system when you've coded your last business object.

We're not done yet. After a suitable prototype is developed, you can involve the user with writing the reports and the decision support forms, and then try them out against the prototype. This may lead to some changes in the design of the system. In the final production system, it may be wise to provide a separate server for decision support. The decision support server can then be fed replicated snapshots of the production data at predetermined intervals (remember all that Information Warehouse stuff we covered in Part 4).

Walking On Two Feet

Client/Server technology offers developers the potential to create revolutionary new visual applications. Creating these kind of applications requires the seamless integration of OOUI technology, operating systems, network architectures, and DBMSs. To succeed, we will need new approaches to systems development that emphasize rapid prototyping and the end-user involvement. Doing that will allow us to exploit the synergy between database objects and OOUI objects. We will also be in a better position to understand, early in a project, the opportunities (for example, parallelism) and pitfalls (for example, performance and error recovery) introduced by splitting an application across a network.

This prototype-based approach to design eliminates the need for lengthy specifications. More importantly, this approach allows the customer to participate in the specification of the product and its stepwise refinement. The approach also lends itself well to the design of distributed applications, because you can refine and fine-tune the distribution of function as you learn more about your system's real-life behavior.

So, the successful OLTP design starts in parallel with both the client and the server. The two starting points are the OOUI objects and the data objects. The "glue" that ties them together are the transactions using network RPCs or ORBs. Start with the client and move towards the server, or vice versa. In either case, move in small steps and iterate. The visual prototype brings the design to life early. So, which comes first: the client or the server? They both come first!

CLIENT/SERVER APPLICATION DEVELOPMENT TOOLS

Development tools are the hot issue in client/server today. We predict that the U.S. market will grow from 35,000 development seats shipped in 1992 to almost 700,000 seats shipped in 1996.

> — *Forrester Research,*
> *"Client/Server Power Tools Future,"*
> *(April, 1993)*

Development tools are the linchpin in client/server. Tools encapsulate the client/server technology described in this book and make it easier for users to write applications. The best tools are highly visual. Most of today's client/server tools are used to create departmental decision support systems. Over the next four years, Forrester believes that "improvements in client/server infrastructure, vendor viability, and the tools themselves will set the stage for the power tools to blast out of departmental bunkers." So how do we classify those client/server tools? Which is the right tool for the right job? Like everything else in client/server, it seems everyone has an opinion on tools. In this section, we present two tool classification schemes: Forrester's and ours.

The Forrester Model of Client/Server Tools

Forrester Research breaks down client/server tools into five categories:

■ **Purebred client/server.** These are GUI-centric client/server tools that were designed from the ground up for client/server development. Examples include SQL Windows, Visual Basic, Enfin, PowerBuilder, HockWare, VisualAge, and Digitalk Parts.

■ **Born-again 4GLs.** These tools grew out of the high-end minicomputer market. Examples include Cognos, Progress, FOCUS, Dynasty, Uniface, and Oracle's SQL*Forms.

- **Desktop wannabes**. These tools started out as standalone database development tools, but their new GUI releases reposition them as power tools. Examples include Paradox and dBASE from Borland, and FoxPro and Access from Microsoft.

- **CASE retreads**. These tools grew out of the mainframe market. They provide data modeling, code generation, lifecycle tracking of projects, and multiuser repositories. The leading tools are KnowledgeWare's Application Development Workbench, TI's Information Engineering Facility (IEF), and Andersen Consulting's Foundation for Cooperative Processing.

- **Facelifters**. These tools let you strap a GUI on a terminal-based legacy application. The code for the legacy server remains unchanged. The leading tools in this category are Easel and Mozart.

We found the Forrester classification to be quite useful but somewhat limiting. Instead, we propose the alternative classification that is covered in the next section.

The Latest and Greatest Model of Client/Server Tools

Tool evaluation is fun. There are literally hundreds of products. How do you make a decision? One possibility is to stay in tool evaluation mode until you're told that the decision is due tomorrow, then just pick one!

— Anonymous MIS Developer,
HPTP Proceedings (September, 1993)

Yes, client/server tool evaluation can be a lot of fun. You're probably being bombarded with tons of glossy advertisements for tools that all promise to deliver instant and hassle free client/server solutions. At trade shows, you've probably watched those slick demonstrations that seem to create entire client/server applications with a few mouse clicks. But with over 200 tools on the market, which do you pick for evaluation? These days, we could probably safely assume that you don't have an infinite budget for tools or the time to evaluate all 200 of them. So you could start pruning tools by platform, but most seem to run on all the popular platforms. Or you could prune them by price, but you could end up getting what you paid for. Or you could prune them by brand name and miss out on the most avant-garde tools with the latest and greatest features.

To help you with your evaluation, we propose a simple model that breaks the tool market around four axes (see Figure 29-3):

- **Roots.** What's the tool's ancestry? At one end of the axis are tools that originated on mainframes; they tend to have a CASE-centric focus. At the other end of the axis are tools that originated on PC LANs; they tend to have a GUI-centric focus. Somewhere in between are the supermini 4GL tools. The approach (or paradigm) a tool uses for application development is intimately tied to its roots.

- **Distributed Technology.** What's the client/server technology? What applications does the tool create? The axis moves from fat clients with thin servers that specialize in decision support to thin clients with fat servers that do OLTP. In the middle are Groupware and Distributed Objects that split the logic more evenly.

- **Scope.** How much of the client/server function does the tool provide? The axis ranges from tools that specialize in the client, the server, or the middleware to tools that provide all three. Some tools may even go as far as bundling a run time that includes system management, resource managers, and single point of installation.

- **Scalability.** How well does the tool scale for enterprise solutions? The axis moves from single-server tools to multiserver intergalactic tools. The middleware that the tool targets becomes an important factor in the more intergalactic tools.

You'll need all four axes to understand where a tool fits in the scheme of things and what it can do for you. We will briefly go over these four axes and tell you what to consider. Because your authors are in the tool business, we will refrain from naming tools and making any endorsements. We don't want this section ending up as one big Soapbox for our products.

Roots: What's the Tool's Ancestry?

Tools have been around ever since we started writing applications for computers. Over the years, some great tools have emerged around the leading methodologies of the time. When it comes to tools there are "different strokes for different folks." From the dawn of history, people like to work with the tools they are familiar with and that help them get the job done quickly. When it comes to client/server tools, you have choices that span many architectural eras—including COBOL Workbenches, CASE tools, 4GLs, SmallTalk, and object-oriented client/server purebreds. The purebred client/server tools that originated on PC LANs tend to provide event-driven visual programming environments, and they encourage rapid prototyping on PCs. The CASE, 4GL, and Workbenches reflect their mainframe ancestry's emphasis on group development, up-front design and analysis, and structured methodologies (see Figure 29-4).

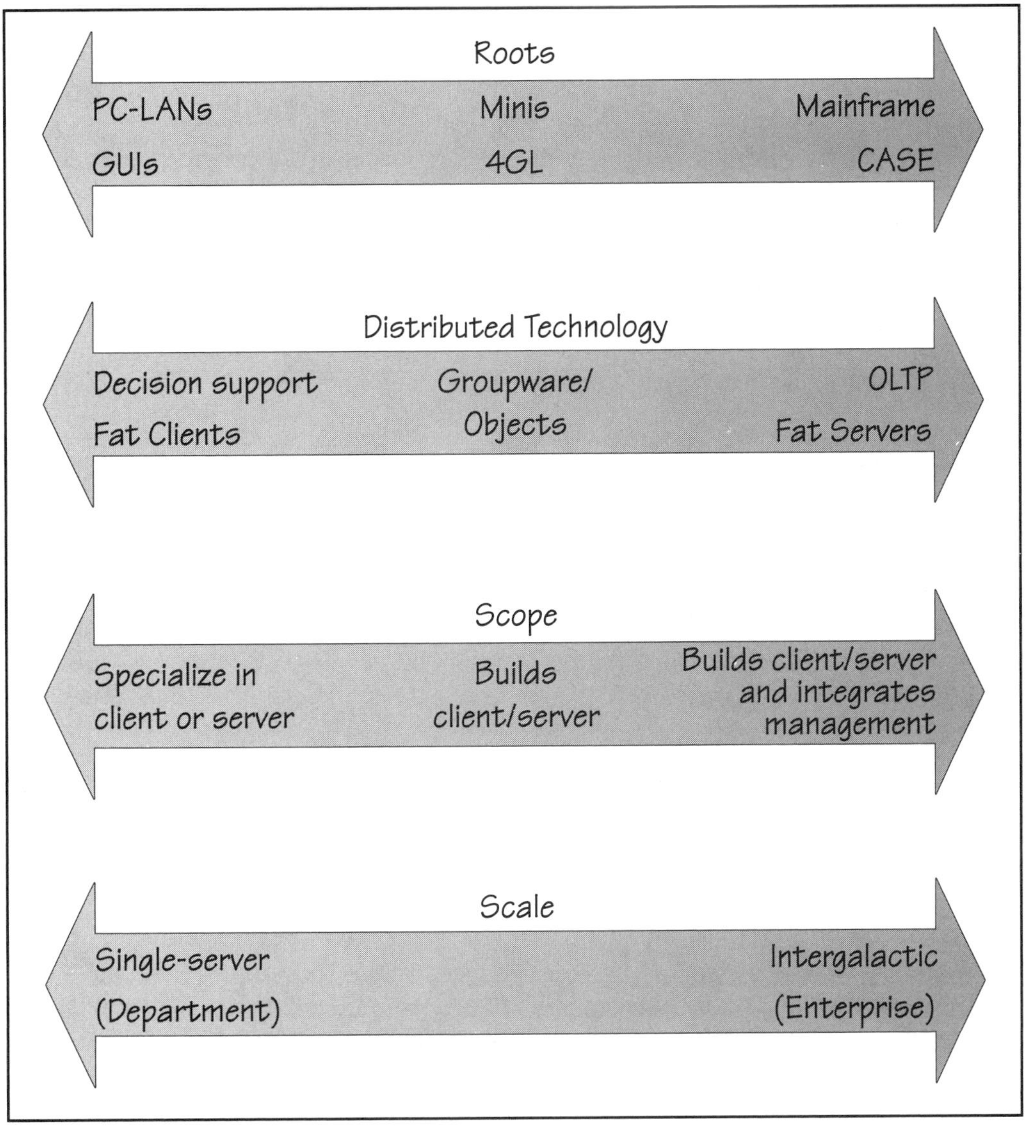

Roots

| PC-LANs | Minis | Mainframe |
| GUIs | 4GL | CASE |

Distributed Technology

| Decision support | Groupware/ | OLTP |
| Fat Clients | Objects | Fat Servers |

Scope

| Specialize in | Builds | Builds client/server |
| client or server | client/server | and integrates management |

Scale

| Single-server | | Intergalactic |
| (Department) | | (Enterprise) |

Figure 29-3. The Four Axes of Client Server Tools.

Figure 29-4. Check Your Client/Server Tools's Ancestry.

So what's a 4GL? It stands for a *Fourth Generation Language*. A 4GL is typically a vendor proprietary scripting language that's less procedural than a 3GL (like C or C++). It is also frequently tied to a database. Some 4GLs are associated with a forms generation package. Almost all 4GLs are interpreted; the best are compiled to some intermediate level. In the PC world, Basic, REXX, Apple Script, and the Lotus Script language play an equivalent role to 4GLs. The 4GLs offer increased programmer productivity at the expense of application performance; the intermediate code must be re-interpreted for each function (the performance is about five times slower than a 3GL).

The ancestry of a tool tends to determine how it uses the 4GL. Tools with a mainframe ancestry use the 4GL as the main program. The 4GL calls the visual forms and controls the interaction with the user; it maintains control at all times. In contrast, tools with a PC ancestry call 4GL code snippets when GUI events occur; the GUI is in control at all times.

We recommend the use of 4GLs for rapid prototyping and to write the event handlers for the client side of an application. But remember: They're slow; you'll need a 486 type machine on the client side. At some point, parts of the 4GL code should be converted to a 3GL on the server to improve performance.

Another point to consider is that tools with a mainframe ancestry encourage you to do a lot of design up-front. They provide Entity-Relationship diagrams and all types of methodologies for doing analysis and for documenting the design. These tools are also heavy into version control and team development; they tend to make use of repositories for tracking shared objects. The better tools can directly generate 4GL code from the top-down design. In contrast, tools with a PC ancestry encourage you to build the application visually using GUI painters. The design tends to be client-centric. The code is broken down into small event handlers that are associated with GUI events; the application is the GUI. The code is just an appendage of the GUI objects. Rapid prototyping is essential.

Distributed Technology: Is it SQL, OLTP, Groupware, or Objects?

Tools can be classified according to the underlying client/server technology and the applications they create. Until recently, almost all PC-based client/server tools were used to create decision-support applications and Executive Information Systems (the Danny De Vito tools). Some of the newer tools provide facilities for creating OLTP-Lite applications via stored procedures; a very small number of tools can even be used to create OLTP-Heavy applications using TP Monitors (the number is less than six). Groupware tools mostly center around Lotus Notes. But some non-Groupware tools provide mail-enabling facilities. Finally, a few vendor proprietary tools are available for creating applications that work with ODBMSs (the number is less than three). ORB-based tools are currently non-existent (there's a lot of chartware in this area).

So what's a Decision Support tool? Decision Support Systems (DSSs) are built using dynamic SQL on database servers. The client side of the application is typically built using a screen-layout visual editor; non-programmers can build GUI front-ends and reports by painting, pointing, and clicking. These tools are data-base-aware; they let you combine graphical objects like radio buttons, check boxes, menus, and scrollbars to create sophisticated display panels that integrate directly with the database. Most of these GUI tools have built-in capabilities to automatically generate forms that can be used to add, update, and delete database records. They provide the ability to create multitable queries (joins) and display the results in record-per-form format or multiple-record columnar forms with pick lists. The tools make use of the database catalogs to map table columns to fields on a screen. SQL statements can be built "on-the-fly" and associated with a particular push button or menu item. Point-and-click query builders take the work out of formulating the question. The tools provide visual facilities for creating base tables and defining relations between tables. All this is done with "canned" event handlers provided by the tool vendor.

Most decision-support tools allow you to create links with other applications on the desktop using the clipboard, DDE, OLE, or drag-and-drop. Cut-and-paste through the clipboard is used to transfer information into other applications under user control. DDE is used to automatically update documents and spreadsheets with the results of a query. It lets you automate scripts such as "Place the output of this query into this spreadsheet; then run it through a graphics package, print the report, and send the results to a distribution list through electronic mail."

So what's an OLTP tool? As stored procedures became popular, some tools branched out into the server generation side; they allow you to create stored procedures and associate them with client events (via RPC pickers). The tricky part is generating efficient code on the server—most tools are lacking in this area. Another tricky area is how to associate the RPC parameters with the visual fields—most tools are also lacking in this area. Most tools are poor at managing the stored procedures on the server side; they leave that to the database engine or TP Monitor. In summary, OLTP tools (Lite or Heavy) are still in their infancy.

So what's a groupware tool? We covered groupware tools in the Lotus Notes chapter in Part 6. We expect that most ordinary GUI tools will soon provide canned dialogs for creating mail messages and reading mail as well as invoking mail APIs. Mail-enabling will become a checklist item for most tools.

So what's a distributed object tool? We covered object frameworks in Part 7. The object tools should allow you to wire together those frameworks using visual elements. Object chartware promises ten times (or more) improvements in productivity; it all remains to be seen. We still don't know how to create the server side of a distributed object application. The CORBA-IDL and Interface Repository will play a major role in tying the client and server sides of the equation; they will do for objects what the database catalog does for decision support tools.

Scope: Does it Do Clients, Servers, or Both?

Tools can be broken down by how much of the client/server function they provide. They range from tools that specialize in the client, the server, or the middleware to tools that provide all three (see Figure 29-5). Some tools may even go as far as bundling a run time that includes system management, resource managers, and a single point of installation. This may sound like heresy, but the more bundling the tool provides the less integration you have to do. Integration is a major headache in client/server systems.

The question is: Do you want to spend your time developing applications or integrating the base client/server and middleware components? Many tools, especially on the low-end, will have to provide a totally bundled package that takes care of installation, system management, and configures the required middleware and resource managers. The more creative tools may even provide a run time component that integrates a TP Monitor like facility. The TP Monitor should provide crossovers in case of failures. It also must provide ACID protection, dynamic load balancing, and some system management. This is called *preloaded client/server*. We do not know of any tool with these capabilities (Bachman/CSI's Ellipse came closest). With the current state of the technology, we're lucky just to find a tool that can generate both the client and server sides of an application and take care of some middleware; most tools only do the client side of the application.

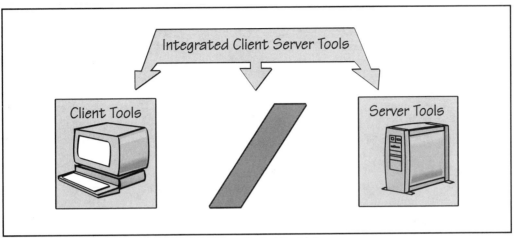

Figure 29-5. How Much Client/Server Coverage Does the Tool Provide?

Scalability: Can it Create Enterprise-Wide Applications?

Enterprise client/server tools are the current vogue (but only in literature). We haven't seen too many of them lately (Dynasty and Forte are on the right track). The industry seems to have an idea of what functions such tools should provide. Briefly, enterprise tools must do the following:

■ ***Provide flexible application topologies***. The tool should provide lego-like facilities that let you split the application (at many different points) between the client, the server and, more importantly, across servers.

■ ***Provide portable applications***. The tool should spit out code for Windows, OS/2, Macintosh, and Unix front-ends and all the known server platforms. You should be able, at run time, to transparently deploy the right version of code to the appropriate machine.

■ ***Version control***. The tool should track the versions of code running on the clients and servers and make sure they're consistent.

■ ***Load balancing and cross-over facilities***. The tool should keep track of client/server performance and dynamically reroute traffic across applications as required by workloads and failure conditions.

■ ***Create compiled code on the server***. The tool should be able to automatically compile the 4GL code on the server to obtain maximum performance.

- *Work with a variety of resource managers*. The tool should adapt itself to the resource managers that exist on various servers on the network; its interaction with resource managers should be negotiable at run time.

- *Work with a variety of middleware*. The tool should adapt its client/server communications to the existing middleware. For example, it should know when an ORB is present and how to exploit it. It should also figure out when MOM is better than RPC. At a minimum, the tool should adjust time-outs based on whether the traffic is moving over a LAN or WAN.

- *Team development and a group repository*. The tool should allow groups of programmers to work on a common project; it should provide check-in/check-out facilities for tracking forms, widgets, controls, fields, business objects, DLLs, and so on.

We could keep that list going. But what are the odds of getting all these facilities in our current lifetimes? We know that the demand for such tools exists in the high-end of the market. Much of the technology for creating such tools exists. But it's still a very big project. However, we know of at least three well-funded tool efforts that are headed in that direction. We believe that the best way to get this type of intergalactic distribution is through ORBs and distributed object technology.

Which Tool Should You Use?

We can't answer this question. However, you can—now that you have two models to guide you. Start with the type of application you want to build. Is it decision support? Is it OLTP? What do you really want? Next, decide on which methodology you feel more comfortable with: Is it top-down design or visual prototyping? Finally, decide on the scope of your application and its scalability requirements. Is it intergalactic? Or is it single server? These simple questions will help you narrow down your decision on tools to at most two or three (unless you picked decision support). Now you can play the evaluation game until the decision is due, then "just pick one." Can you create client/server applications without tools using raw 3GLs? Yes, but the size of our book, **Client/Server Programming with OS/2 2.1** (1100 pages), should give you an idea of the magnitude of effort required. (Sorry, but we couldn't resist another shameless advertisement.)

IT'S TIME TO SAY GOOD-BYE

Yes, the journey was a long, tumultuous one. We hope you enjoyed the guided tour as much as we enjoyed playing guides. To our friends from Mars, we hope you have a safe trip home—it was a pleasure having you here. We hope you'll find that client/server gold somewhere. Don't forget to tell your friends in Mars about our guided tour. We also have an expanded version of this Survival Guide for those of you who can afford the time to read an additional 400 pages. It's called **Client/Server Survival Guide with OS/2** (VNR, 1994). The extra pages give us the luxury of describing 100 OS/2 client/server products, many in depth. These descriptions bring to life the concepts described in this book.

We're scratching our heads trying to come up with some words of wisdom to leave you with at the end of this long tour. But we don't have much to add that wasn't already said. We just want to say that this was our attempt to make some sense out of this traumatic shift our industry is going through. It's a very painful shift for many of us; for others, it's the start of a new dawn in computing with the sky being the limit. OK, enough of that fluffy stuff. We'll say good-bye with a *parting* Soapbox on where things are going.

Can We Survive the Client/Server Revolution?

Soapbox

Yes, but to do that we need 100,000 new applications. How did we come up with that number? Client/server technology makes it possible to redeploy most of our computer applications on commodity hardware where the profit margins are razor thin. If we keep recomputerizing the same application base, using PC LANs instead of mainframes, most of us will end up without jobs. This is because we're going after a downsized pie where the profits are dramatically lower. If our profits are lower, we cut down on the research that helps us create those new technologies. And our customers won't get new applications or technology. Everybody ends up losing. It's called the "cannibalizing effect."

Instead, we need to take advantage of client/server technology to extend the boundaries of computerization. In other words, we need to move on to new frontiers like the information highway. But can we create thousands of new client/server applications *quickly* to populate these new frontiers? To do that effectively, we need a technology base, standards, and tools. The 500 pages in this Survival Guide make the case that the technology base, standards, and even some products are here today. However, still missing are a set of adequate tools that can help us mine the new frontier. It's not enough to create the application; it must also be effectively packaged, deployed, and managed.

So who's going to package, deploy, and manage these applications? We can't expect everyone to read this entire book just to become client/server literate (don't get us wrong—we would love the sales). Instead, we need to simplify the packaging and distribution of our client/server products. Of all the technologies discussed in this book, distributed objects (with frameworks) offer the best hope for creating—in record time—new client/server applications that can go where no other applications have gone before. So we're excited about the long-term prospects. However, in the short term, we're in for some rough times. You may have noticed that no tool yet exists for creating CORBA-compliant client/server applications. We're just starting to see some commercial ORBs.

So we'll be in the doldrums until we can figure out how to unleash the true power of this technology. This is sad—but true. The good news is that after we get over that rough hump, those of us that are still around will be headed straight for a new gold rush. As the Chinese proverb puts it, "We're condemned to live in interesting times." ❑

Trademarks

3Com Corp—3Com

Allen Systems Group, Inc.—IMPACT

Allerion, Inc.—Allerion

American Telephone and Telegraph—AT&T

Anderson Consulting—Foundation for Cooperative Processing

Apple Computer, Inc.—Apple; AppleTalk; Macintosh; System 7

Banyan Systems, Inc.—Banyan; Banyan Vines; Vines SMP; VinesMail

BRG Systems, Inc.—Analyze for OS/2; BEST/1-Visualizer for OS/2; Performance Assurance

Borland International, Inc.—Application FrameWorks; dBase; FoxPro; Paradox

Channel Computing—Forest & Trees

Client/Server Technologies (Microcom)—LANlord

Club Med Sales, Inc.—Club Med

Compaq Computer Corp.—Compaq SystemPro

Computer Associates, Inc.—CA-UNICENTER

Cooperative Solutions—Ellipse

DataTrade, Inc.—DataTrade

Digital Equipment Corp.—Data Distributor; DECnet; Digital; OpenVMS; VMS; VAX; VAXMail

Easel Corp.—Easel; Enfin

Evolutionary Technologies—Extract Toolsuite

Gpf, Inc.—GPF

Gradient Technologies, Inc.—Gradient Technologies; iFOR/LS

Gupta Technologies, Inc.—Express Windows; Gupta; Quest; SQLBase; SQLWindows

Hewlett-Packard Corp.—DOMF; Hewlett-Packard; HP; HP-UX; OpenView

High Technology Software, Corp.—HiTechSoft

HockWare, Inc.—VisPro/REXX

HyperDesk—DOMS

Informix, Inc.—Informix; INFORMIX

Ingres Corp.—INGRES

Intel Corp.—Intel; Pentium

International Standards Organization—Remote Data Access

IBM Corp.—Advanced Peer to Peer Communications; Advanced Peer-to-Peer Network; AIX; AnyNet/2; APPC; APPN; CICS; CM/2; Communications Manager; CPI-C; CUA; DAE; Database Manager; DataGuide/2; DataPropagator Relational; DataRefresher; DB2; DB2/2; DB2/6000; DDCS/2; DDCS/6000; DRDA; DSOM; High Performance File System; IBM; IMS; Information Warehouse; LAD/2; LANDP/2; LAN Gateway/2; LAN NetView; LAN NetView Agents; LAN NetView Agents Extended; LAN NetView Agents for DOS; LAN NetView Fix; LAN NetView Manage; LAN NetView Management Utilities; LAN NetView Monitor; LAN NetView Scan; LAN NetView Tie; LAN Network Manager; LAN Requester; LAN Server; LU 6.2; MPTN; Netview; NetView DM/2; NetView/6000; NetView/PC; NetFinity; NTS/2; OS/2; OS/2 Named Pipes; OS/400; PAS/2; Person-to-Person/2; PowerPC; Presentation Manager; PROFS; PS/2; Query Manager; REXX; RS/6000; SAA; SQL/400; SQL/DS; SNA; SOM; System 370; SystemView; VM; VisualAge; VSAM; VTAM; Win-OS/2; WinSNA; Workplace Shell; Workplace OS

Information Builders, Inc.—EDA/Data Drivers; EDA/Extenders; EDA/Link; EDA/SQL; EDA/SQL Server; Focus

International Institute of Electrical Engineers (IEEE)—POSIX

KASEWORKS, Inc.—KASE:VIP; KASE-

WORKS

Knowledgeware, Inc.—Application Development Workbench

Legat Systems, Inc.—Legato Systems; NetWorker

Lotus Development Corp.—cc:Mail; DataLens; dBASE; Lotus; Lotus Document Imaging; Lotus Link; Lotus Notes

Luxcom, Inc.—Universal Premises Network

Massachusetts Institute of Technology—Kerberos; X Window

mdbs, Inc.—mbds; Object/1

Micrcom, Inc.—LANLord; Micrcom

Microsoft Corp.—Access; Compound Object Model (COM); MS DOS; LAN Manager; LAN Manager/X; Mail; Mail Gateways; Microsoft; Object Linking and Embedding; ODBC; OLE; SQL Administrator; Windows; Windows for Workgroups; Windows NT; Windows NT Advanced; XENIX

Micro Focus Inc.—Micro Focus COBOL

Mips, Inc.—Mips

Mozart Systems Corp.—Mozart

Network General Corp.—Sniffer

Neuron Data, Inc.—Open Interface

NeXT, Inc.—NeXTStep

Novell, Inc.—IPX; NetWare; NetWare Loadable Module; NetWare Management System; NetWare for UNIX; Novell; SFT III; SPX; Systems Fault Tolerance III; UnixWare

Object Design, Inc.—Object Design; ObjectStore

Objective Solutions, Inc.—ObjectPM

Object Management Group—CORBA; Object Management Architecture

Open Software Foundation, Inc.—DCE; Motif; OSF; OSF/1

Opening Technologies, Inc.—Opening Technologies; OPENT1

Oracle, Inc.—ORACLE; SQL*NET; Oracle Card; Oracle Forms; Oracle Glue; Oracle Open Gateway; Oracle V6; Oracle*Designer; Oracle7; OracleWare; PL/SQL; SQL*NET

PeerLogic, Inc.—PIPES

Pragma Systems, Inc.—Tower

Progress Corp.—Progress

ProTools, Inc.—Cornerstone Agent; Foundation Manager; ProTools

Red Brick, Inc.—Red Brick

Santa Cruz Operations, Inc.—SCO UNIX

Pragma Systems, Inc.—Tower

Prism Solutions, Inc.—Warehouse Manager

Shany Computers, Ltd.—AlertView

SQL Access Group—OpenSQL

Stratus, Inc.—Stratus

Sun Microsystems Inc.—DOE; RPC; SUN; SPARC

Sunsoft, Inc.—Distributed Object Mangement; Network File System; Network Information System; NFS; OpenLook; Open Network Computing; Solaris; SunNet Manager

Sybase, Inc.—Sybase; Sybase SQL Server; Transact-SQL

Taligent, Inc.—Taligent

Tandem Computers—NonStop SQL; NonStop Guardian; Pathway

Texas Instruments, Inc.—Information Engineering Facility

Tivoli Systems Inc.—Tivoli Management Environment; WizDOM

Transaction Processing Council—TPC-A

Transarc Corp—Andrew File System; Encina

University of California at Berkeley—Berkeley Software Distribution; BSD

UNIX International, Inc.—UI; UI-Atlas

UNIX Systems Laboratories, Inc.—Destiny; OpenLook; Tuxedo; UNIX; UNIX System V

VZCorp, Inc.—VZ Programmer

WATCOM, Inc.—VX REXX

XDB Systems, Inc.—XDB

Xerox Corp.—ethernet; XNS; Xerox Network Systems

XVT Software, Inc.—XVT

X/Open Corp.—X/Open

Index

Numerics

A